UNPRESIDENTED

UNPRESIDENTED

A BIOGRAPHY

of

DONALD TRUMP

MARTHA BROCKENBROUGH

FEIWEL AND FRIENDS
New York

A Feiwel and Friends Book
An imprint of Macmillan Publishing Group, LLC
175 Fifth Avenue, New York, NY 10010

Our books may be purchased in bulk for promotional, educational,
or business use. Please contact your local bookseller or the Macmillan
Corporate and Premium Sales Department at (800) 221-7945 ext. 5442 or
by e-mail at MacmillanSpecialMarkets@macmillan.com.

Library of Congress Cataloging-in-Publication Data is available.

ISBN 978-1-250-30803-0 (hardcover) / ISBN 978-1-250-30804-7 (ebook)

Book design by Raphael Geroni

Trump family photos courtesy of the White House, A. Shaker/VOA, Alamy,
Gage Skidmore, Getty, and Shutterstock.

Feiwel and Friends logo designed by Filomena Tuosto

First edition, 2018

1 3 5 7 9 10 8 6 4 2

fiercereads.com

To SUSAN SAUNDERS,
who started me on this path.

And to the Parkland generation:
You know what to do.

CONTENTS

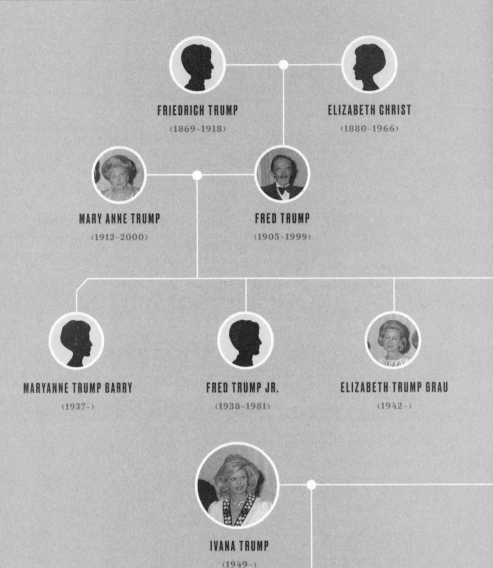

FRIEDRICH TRUMP
(1869–1918)

ELIZABETH CHRIST
(1880–1966)

MARY ANNE TRUMP
(1912–2000)

FRED TRUMP
(1905–1999)

MARYANNE TRUMP BARRY
(1937–)

FRED TRUMP JR.
(1938–1981)

ELIZABETH TRUMP GRAU
(1942–)

IVANA TRUMP
(1949–)

DONALD TRUMP JR.
(1977–)

IVANKA TRUMP
(1981–)

ERIC TRUMP
(1984–)

DONALD TRUMP'S FAMILY TREE

DONALD TRUMP

(1946–)

ROBERT TRUMP

(1948–)

MELANIA KNAUSS TRUMP

(1970–)

MARLA MAPLES

(1963–)

TIFFANY TRUMP

(1993–)

BARRON TRUMP

(2006–)

FOREWORD

HISTORY WASN'T MY FAVORITE SUBJECT IN school, although I definitely loved writing hilarious speech bubbles in the margins of my textbooks.

Eventually, I realized that history isn't about dates and themes. It's about *people*—our beliefs, our actions, the relationships we have with each other, and the choices we make with our lives. History is made of human choices, human beliefs, and human relationships. Nothing fascinates me more.

I've been interested in Donald Trump for years, and in a way, he was with me for the birth of my second child in 2004. It was a long labor, the TV was on in the delivery room, and my daughter arrived with a squall just as Trump said his famous catchphrase: "You're fired."

I liked the show that first season, and I liked Donald Trump, who seemed sensible and down to earth. His common-sense business advice was appealing. It surprised me, given what I'd read of him in celebrity gossip magazines.

Years later, I saw Trump again on TV, this time speculating that President Obama's birthplace was Kenya. Obama was born in Hawaii, not Kenya. This fact was confirmed in 2008, several years before Trump initiated a media campaign questioning the president's birthplace.

This showed me another side of Trump.

Facts are facts, and it does not serve the public interest when a person with influence and power knowingly spreads false information.

How do we know Trump spread lies? The state of Hawaii released Obama's birth certificate in 2008 and another version of it in 2011. News outlets carried images of the birth certificate. Regardless, Trump ignored factual evidence and contributed to a false belief that remains widespread, especially among Republicans.

A birth certificate provided by the government is a credible document. In the democratic United States, we have good reason to trust the public records government agencies keep. This doesn't mean they don't contain mistakes from time to time. Human beings make these records, after all, and humans are invariably prone to error. But human error and intentional distortion of the record are two different things. Some governments around the world *do* intentionally distort the record; the former Soviet Union was a notable example.

In the United States, the Freedom of Information Act gives all citizens—not just journalists and historians—the right to request and obtain records from agencies of the federal government. States have additional laws regulating the public's access to information.

Public records are an important source for historians and journalists, who sometimes describe their work as writing the first draft of history. In writing history's first draft, journalists make routine use of public information as they report on the actions, statements, and decisions of government leaders, employees, and politicians.

The job of journalists is to get the story right. Good journalists independently verify claims with photos, videos, public documents on file in government agencies, and input of verified experts. Good journalists also correct their errors promptly and thoroughly.

Their work is why we know about dangerous products, pending legislation, and sometimes even whether our political leaders are telling us the truth and performing their jobs with integrity.

Every day, the media report facts. Some seem trivial, like the temperature outside. Others are more important: that a brand of lettuce is contaminated with substances that make it dangerous to eat.

In any case, trust in basic facts is a vital part of civil society. Facts become the basis of our decisions, and good decisions are made with verifiable facts.

It can sometimes get complicated. It's possible for something to be true and also unfair. This is where context comes in, and why I have looked at the entirety of Trump's life—and then some—to tell this story. My goal is to be both accurate and fair. This means I take care to get the facts right, show where I got them, and choose elements that faithfully represent the bigger picture.

One instance of a behavior is interesting, but a pattern becomes important. For example: Trump complained that the media lied about the numbers of people who attended his inauguration.

Plenty of photographic evidence proved that Trump and his surrogates got the numbers wrong. It's possible that this was an innocent error on Trump's part.

However, it wasn't the first time in his life that Trump made false claims about crowd size at a public event. He was a grand marshal for a veteran's day parade in 1995. The *New York Times* reported more than half a million people attended. Trump insisted the crowd size was 1.4 million. He also routinely overestimated the crowd sizes at his rallies.

This is where patterns of behavior are useful in understanding and establishing character. Trump likes big crowds, especially when they are there for him. We can even see evidence of this in some of his earliest writing: a poem he wrote in elementary school, which contains this line: *"I like to hear the crowd give cheers, so loud and noisy to my ears."*

When we have patterns and supporting documentation like this, we can feel confident we have an accurate understanding of an aspect of a person's character. We can feel confident it is also fair to include in a biography. In choosing material for this book, a quest for fairness demanded that I look for patterns, rather than the most outrageous or entertaining tidbits (although on occasion they were one and the same).

Sometimes we define fairness as a balance of positive and negative information. It's an understandable impulse.

But this is a bit like saying you can create balance by putting ten elephants on one side of the scale and ten babies on the other. Ten and ten are equal, but they are not necessary equivalent. Fairness demands a writer examine the whole and select representative parts. It demands a writer constantly consider the credibility of sources. It's not easy work.

Another reason it's difficult to write accurately about Trump is that he often speaks inaccurately about himself.

For example, in his ghostwritten book *Trump: The Art of the Deal*, Trump claims his ancestry is Swedish. This is not true. A later book by Gwenda Blair, *The Trumps: Three Generations that Built an Empire*, was written with the Trump family's involvement. It offers verifiable facts about Trump's German heritage. I reviewed some of the same historical records Blair did. And I also watched video of Trump talking about his German ancestry.

This means he is of German descent and he knows it.

Did he know he was German when he told his *Art of the Deal* co-author he was Swedish? That is harder to determine. Only Trump knows why he said he was Swedish. His father could have told him as much, but his father is dead, so we can't be certain without written documentation of the conversation. It's also possible that Trump gave incorrect information about his heritage because he wanted to avoid anti-German bias that was common in America after World War I and World War II.

To research this book, I read newspapers, magazines, and books written by Trump critics and Trump allies. I read works by Trump and his family members. I watched video clips. I listened to audio clips. I scoured legal documents, records of arrests, police and FBI investigations, and Congressional testimony. I read additional books about the FBI and Russian president Vladimir Putin. I paid close attention to things that Trump said himself, particularly on Twitter, because so often what he said there became news.

My goal, as always, was to look for patterns, to find verifiable facts, and to put all of this information into context.

I am indebted in particular to the excellent work being done by the nation's journalists covering Trump, not just during the 2016 presidential campaign, but for decades before that. His performance as a businessman and public figure has been richly documented, and it is a fascinating, compelling, and important American story.

History is forever being made, day by day. My hope is this book gives readers a broad and deep understanding of Donald Trump and his place in the past and present, an understanding that is both fair and accurate.

I write this for young people in particular so that they have a better understanding of the future, which is not just one you inherit.

It's one you get to write . . . with your actions, your votes, and your engagement in the world.

Martha Burn

CHAPTER 1

The NIGHT AMERICA BLED RED

> "Certainly has been an interesting 24 hours!"
>
> —@realDonaldTrump, October 8, 2016

October 7, 2016. Thirty-two days before Election Day.

DONALD TRUMP SAT IN the conference room on the twenty-fifth floor of Trump Tower in New York while his team worked to get him ready for his second presidential debate against Hillary Clinton. Trump didn't like preparing for debates. He hadn't practiced much for his first one and lost steam after the first half hour. To avoid another disaster, his team was taking another run at it. In the midst of this, the deputy campaign manager's phone rang.

Hope Hicks, the campaign spokesperson, was on the line with bad news.

A *Washington Post* reporter had called her with a bombshell. He'd sent her a transcript of crude and troubling comments the Republican presidential candidate had made in 2005. The reporter was planning a story and wanted the campaign's comment.

A group of aides huddled in another room, trying to figure out what to do next. First, they decided, they'd show Trump the transcript. But when he glanced at it, he waved it off. "It doesn't sound like something I would say."

By then, the reporter from the *Post* had sent the campaign the video. Recorded not long after Trump married his third wife, the footage began with a shot of an oversize bus rolling onto a Hollywood production lot. Trump, wearing a live microphone inside the bus, hooted as he caught a glimpse of the actress he was about to meet.

"Yeah, that's her!"

Something rattled; then he said, "I better use some Tic Tacs just in case I start kissing her. You know, I'm automatically attracted to beautiful—I just start kissing them. It's like a magnet. I just kiss. I don't even wait. And when you're a star, they let you do it. You can do anything . . . Grab 'em by the pussy. You can do anything."

Trump headed down the steps of the bus, joking that he'd better not trip like former President Gerald Ford. After a bit of trouble with the door, he emerged and greeted the actress with a hug, a kiss, and a disclaimer: "Melania said this was okay."

Once he saw the video, Trump agreed the remarks were his, which meant his team had to come up with a response for the press. Coverage was sure to be intense.

Trump's daughter Ivanka, on the verge of tears, wanted her dad to apologize. This did not interest Trump. Along with his aides, Trump crafted a response that was equal parts excuse, apology, and attack on his opponent.

> . . . Trump crafted a response that was equal parts excuse, apology, and attack on his opponent.

"This was locker room banter, a private conversation that took place many years ago. Bill Clinton has said far worse to me on the golf course—not even close. I apologize if anyone was offended."

Nonetheless, the story drowned out other major headlines of the day, at least temporarily. And it wasn't as if the breaking news was inconsequential. Two government agencies jointly released a statement saying the US intelligence community was "confident" the Russian government had directed hackers to steal e-mail from American citizens and institutions. An hour later, two thousand potentially damaging e-mails stolen from John Podesta, the chair of Clinton's campaign, appeared online.

Though the e-mails would make headlines in the days to come, there wasn't much coverage of the Kremlin's part in it. For whatever reason, Trump's eleven-year-old hot microphone banter was more interesting to the media than cyber warfare from a foreign government.

Later that night Trump did make the apology Ivanka had urged. He released a video statement on Twitter, bypassing the mainstream media.

"This was locker room banter, a private conversation that took place many years ago. Bill Clinton has said far worse to me on the golf course—not even close. I apologize if anyone was offended."

DONALD TRUMP

October 7, 2016

But damage had been done, and many in Trump's corner worried it was the last straw. It was far from the first.

When he'd launched his campaign at Trump Tower in 2015, he embellished his prepared remarks and suggested Mexico was sending horrible people to the United States: criminals, drug dealers, rapists.

Not long afterward, he argued that a judge who happened to be of Mexican descent would be unfair in the high-profile fraud suit against Trump University, his real-estate education program.

This unusual language shocked even members of his own party. House of Representatives Speaker Paul Ryan called the remarks "the textbook definition of a racist comment . . . It is absolutely unacceptable."

But Trump's base of voters did not seem to mind. And they loved his promise to build a "big, beautiful wall" that Mexico would pay for.

> "I could stand in the middle of Fifth Avenue and shoot somebody and I wouldn't lose voters."

His rallies sometimes turned violent, and although Trump claimed he didn't condone this, he also said his people would investigate paying the legal fees of a man who'd been charged with assault after sucker-punching a protestor. Trump even joked about getting away with murder himself at an Iowa rally: "I could stand in the middle of Fifth Avenue and shoot somebody and I wouldn't lose voters."

Trump tested the loyalty of his voters in other ways. Candidates typically don't insult the parents of soldiers who die in combat, but Trump picked a fight with the parents of a Muslim immigrant killed by a car bomb in Iraq. Trump didn't like what the Gold Star family had said about him at the Democratic National Convention. He also claimed that Hillary Clinton's speech writers had probably written the family's remarks, and he implied the mother had been forced to remain silent because of her religion.

This followed a pattern of hostility toward Muslims he'd displayed on the campaign trail, even promising a potentially unconstitutional ban of Muslim immigrants.

Trump also took a shot at Senator John McCain, a Vietnam war hero blasted from the sky by a Russian missile the size of a telephone pole. McCain had been severely injured in the fall, and his captors imprisoned him for five and a half years, torturing him on many occasions.

Trump, who avoided military service altogether, wasn't impressed: "He's a war hero because he was captured. I like people who weren't captured."

All along, Trump's disregard for political norms astonished observers. But something about the crude remarks about women and the admission that he repeatedly touched them sexually without their consent distressed Republican Party donors and officials. It seemed to corroborate the accusations of at least fifteen women who'd accused Trump of sexual misconduct. What's more, Trump's personal lawyer was in the midst of frantically securing a hush agreement from an adult film star Trump had slept with months after his youngest child was born.

Reince Priebus, the party chairman, suggested Trump had two options after the latest debacle: drop out, or face an epic loss.

That was all Trump needed to hear.

He wasn't going to quit. What's more, he wasn't going to lose.

Donald Trump hated losing more than anything else in the world. His father had raised him to be a tiger, and in his life, Donald Trump had figured out what it took to come out on top, even when defeat looked inevitable. Sometimes, you had to do things other people wouldn't. Sometimes you had to bend or even break the rules. And sometimes, it all came down to how you told the story afterward.

He had a message for Priebus and the rest of the party.

"I'm going to win," he said. "And second, if the Republican Party is going to run away from me then I will take you all down with me. But I'm not going to lose."

> "We must not let #CrookedHillary take her CRIMINAL SCHEME into the Oval Office. #DrainTheSwamp"
>
> —@realDonaldTrump, October 28, 2016

October 28, 2016. Eleven days before Election Day.

FOR MORE THAN A YEAR, THE FBI HAD BEEN probing Hillary Clinton's use of a private e-mail server for government business when she was secretary of state. FBI Director James Comey concluded his work in July, calling the e-mail extremely careless but not criminal. He closed the case, largely ending the extensive media coverage of the subject.

But then FBI agents working on a separate investigation involving the disgraced husband of Clinton's top aide made a discovery: more e-mails.

Comey, torn between disclosure and the risk he'd influence the election, let Congress know he was taking another look.

If anything could upend the race in favor of Donald Trump, this was it. The media eagerly jumped back on board. Clinton's e-mail stories—both the ones about her use of a private server for classified material, and the ones about correspondence leaked from the hack on Democratic Party officials—had been their favorites of the year, dwarfing the amount of airtime and ink they spent covering public policy.

Comey, meanwhile, said nothing of another FBI investigation the bureau had launched days after he ended the one into Clinton's e-mails.

This investigation focused on disturbing contacts Trump and his top advisers had with the Russian government. The silence infuriated Democrats and puzzled some who knew exactly what the FBI had found on Trump, which included the sort of salacious material blackmailers loved.

> "Our American comeback story begins 11/8/16. Together, we will MAKE AMERICA SAFE & GREAT again for everyone!"
>
> —@realDonaldTrump, November 6, 2016

November 6, 2016. Two days before Election Day

Comey announced there was nothing in the new Clinton e-mails, after all. She would not face criminal charges.

But her lead in the polls had withered to 2.5 points, down from the 7.1-point advantage she had before Comey's October surprise.

Even so, analysts at the influential FiveThirtyEight website predicted Trump had only about a one-in-three chance of winning. Most other pollsters gave him even worse odds.

> "I will be watching the election results from Trump Tower in Manhattan with my family and friends. Very exciting!"
>
> —@realDonaldTrump, November 8, 2016

Election Day

ALL MORNING, TRUMP'S TEAM HUDDLED IN THE war room on the fifth floor of Trump Tower. Boxes of fat frosted donuts lined white tables, and workers in black chairs studied computer data and social media while an image of a red, white, and blue Donald Trump looked on, dwarfing the American flag nearby.

When a Fox News reporter stopped by to see how things were going, a campaign spokesman told her he thought they were on the "verge of something historic."

It didn't feel that way to everyone. Trump's endless controversies had filled the Republican National Committee with doubts. Several top staffers were sniffing around TV networks for jobs. Trump himself was figuring out how to parlay his increased fame into a lucrative television network.

Around 5 P.M., Trump's phone rang. It was his daughter and son-in-law, Jared Kushner, calling with bad news. Exit polls, where journalists queried people leaving voting booths, looked grim.

Trump chucked the phone across his bed. "What a waste of time and money."

"What a waste of time and money."

He broke the news to Melania. "Baby, I'll tell you what, we're not gonna win tonight because the polls have come out."

He planned to give a quick concession speech and get back to his "nice, easy life," where he and three of his adult children—Don Jr.,

Ivanka, and Eric—ran his real estate and branding companies, while Melania focused on his youngest son, Barron. (Another adult daughter, Tiffany, had recently graduated from the University of Pennsylvania, her father's alma mater.)

Around 9 P.M., Trump left his bedroom and took an elevator down from his apartment to the campaign's war room to watch coverage on the half dozen seventy-five-inch televisions mounted on the wall.

"Hey, geniuses," he said, laying on the sarcasm, "how's this working for us?"

Better than most had predicted, actually.

As the night wore on and the pizza boxes were emptied, the electoral college maps on the big TVs began "bleeding red," as Trump put it.

Although a lot of attention is given to the popular vote, the electoral college is what matters in US presidential elections. Each state chooses people to be electors, receiving a number equal to the numbers of senators and representatives they have in Congress. That means two for each of the two senators per state, plus additional electors equal to the number of seats in the House of Representatives, which is based on population.

As the hours ticked by, crucial battleground states fell, and the electoral votes stacked up. The world watched, astonished at the biggest upset in modern American politics. By 2:30 A.M., as world leaders were starting their day across the Atlantic, Hillary Clinton had conceded. Even though Clinton had received almost 2.9 million more votes than Donald Trump, he had won the presidency.

While his campaign team and children celebrated, Melania reportedly burst into tears. This wasn't what she wanted. It wasn't what he'd promised her, that she need hang on only until Election Day. There would be no return to their easy life.

Not that he'd planned a gracious loss, anyway. Some of his most ardent supporters had threatened a "bloodbath" if Trump lost. Joe Walsh, a former Congressman, tweeted, "On November 9th, if Trump loses, I'm grabbing my musket. You in?"

Fear drove the violent rhetoric. Were he not elected, Trump warned, immigrants would flood through open borders and cause unending waves of crime, and terrorists, extremists, and radicals would fill schools and infect communities. Trump also claimed a Clinton presidency would not only risk American lives, it would create a Constitutional crisis, land her in a criminal trial, and destroy America.

"When the people who control the political power in our society can rig investigations," he said, "they can wield absolute power over your life, your economy and your country, and benefit big time from it."

This was the America that Trump predicted if he lost: one where the most powerful person in the land would contrive to live above the law, menace citizens, jeopardize businesses, and subvert American values—all while profiting personally.

Despite Trump's dark musings, the nation had "bled red" for him. The upset stunned much of the nation and the world, but it was happening: Donald Trump would be the forty-fifth president of the United States.

232 DEMOCRAT
Electoral Votes

Source: AP

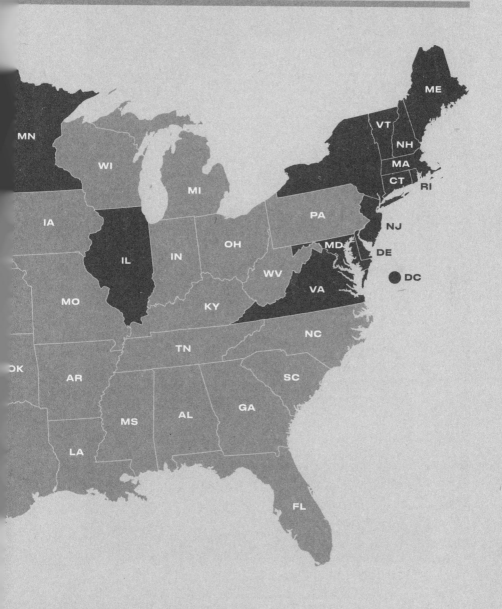

REPUBLICAN **306**
Electoral Votes

2016 ELECTORAL MAP

ABOVE: President-elect Donald Trump walks into the inaugural ceremony. Friday, January 20, 2017. *(Official White House Photo by Shealah Craighead.)*

CHAPTER 2

The ACCIDENTAL AMERICAN

N SOME WAYS, DONALD Trump's presidency hinged on the stubbornness of a prince in Germany, where Trump's grandfather Friedrich was born March 14, 1868.

His village of Kallstadt, a hamlet in Bavaria's wine region, was known as pig-stomach paradise after a signature dish. Kallstadt sat close to the Rhine River, which was used to ferry goods across Europe before railroads and highways existed. Because of its prime location, its fortunes changed along with invading empires: Romans, Christian crusaders, the French, Austrians, and then Bavarians.

The German Empire swallowed the town when Friedrich was two, which meant once again that an old world was giving way. In this new world, every boy owed the army three years of military service. The alternative was jail.

The alternative was jail.

Friedrich was one of six children. Thin and dark-eyed with a large forehead, he was too sickly to help much in the family vineyard, where the work was arduous and endless, sometimes requiring even Friedrich to work late into the night painting grape leaves with copper sulfate to fight off insects.

When he was eight, his father died from emphysema, a lung disease made worse by inhaling pesticides. The illness impoverished the family, and Friedrich's mother, Katherina, who had young children to care for, scraped along by baking bread for the neighborhood. At fourteen, Friedrich went to Frankenthal to learn a trade. He worked seven days a week as a barber's apprentice. Once he'd mastered the work, he returned home. But the town only had a thousand heads—not enough to make a good living. What's more, Friedrich was now sixteen and he would soon owe his country military service, a debt that could kill him.

The service requirement made it difficult for Kallstadt to keep its citizens. German law also ordered that families pass down their land in equal parcels to their children. While this decree sounded equitable, it meant that children of minor landowners were stuck with parcels too small to eke out a living. There were better opportunities elsewhere, including America, where the new Homestead

Act gave 160 acres to people who paid a small filing fee and put in five years' labor on the land.

The town's survival depended on its population, so Kallstadt tried to prevent departures. People bent on escape often pretended they had plans for short excursions. They'd bid their farewells and then retrieve hidden suitcases stuffed with indispensable things.

One dark October night in 1885, after the last pick of the grape harvest, Friedrich left his mother a good-bye note and a bit of money, and then traveled 345 miles north to Bremen, where he embarked on a ten-day journey to New York City aboard the SS *Eider*.

The 430-foot German ocean liner had room for more than 1,200 passengers. People who could afford it occupied small cabins, a privilege that also meant easier passage through immigration once they arrived.

> Friedrich rode steerage with 504 others, crammed like sausages in a tin.

Friedrich rode steerage with 504 others, crammed like sausages in a tin. There were no baths aboard the ship, and not enough food. Passengers cooked what they brought with them on deck when they could. The *Eider* stank so much New Yorkers could smell it coming.

The railroad tycoon Cornelius Vanderbilt, whose fortune would be worth around $212 billion today and who lived in a place so ostentatious an architectural critic called it one of the "thingiest edifices" in the city, complained bitterly about the smell, which could penetrate all the wealth and thinginess in the world.

Friedrich's sister Katherine, who'd left Kallstadt two years earlier, awaited him in New York. First, though, he had to make it through customs. Agents recorded his entry: "Friedr Trumpf, 16, M, none, Germany, Kallstadt."

Kallstadt had more than a thousand years of history. New York City had been colonized and fought over, burned, and rebuilt until it was finally established as part of the United States. It had been under construction ever since. Katherine had arrived the year the New York and Brooklyn Bridge opened, the first-ever built with steel cables arranged like the rays of a sun. Overhead lines in the city carried electricity, telegraphs, and even voices, and an elevated train steamed over the city for a dime a ride (half that during rush hour). All around, the streets and alleys teemed with people, horse-drawn carriages, and carts; some parts of the city were the most densely crowded in the world.

Friedrich lined up work at a barbershop. He lived with Katherine and her husband in a crowded tenement amid other Germans in Manhattan's Lower East Side. It was a slum: cobbled streets thick with horse manure and polluted air, and nowhere near enough outhouses. Poverty and homelessness abounded. While there might have been only a few city blocks between the ostentatiously rich and the struggling poor, the distance felt like another ocean.

Friedrich, Katherine, and Katherine's husband kept on the move, always hoping for something better. Friedrich shaved faces and trimmed hair feverishly, setting aside money and keeping an eye open for opportunity. One came in 1889, when a catastrophic fire leveled twenty-nine blocks of Seattle's business district. Rebuilding sixty wharves and 465 new buildings on top of the bones of the old would be an ordeal: seventy million bricks and ten million dollars.

Friedrich wasn't yet thinking of construction. Rather, he was thinking about all the money in the pockets of construction workers.

By the end of 1891, he'd gone to Seattle, likely by train, about as far from New York City as a man could get. The journey probably took weeks, and Friedrich, now going by Fred, hopped various lines from New York to Philadelphia, on to Chicago and then St. Paul, before the last and longest leg to Seattle. With $600 he'd saved from barbering, he bought a restaurant near the waterfront and changed its name from the Poodle Dog to the Dairy Restaurant, after a popular restaurant back in New York.

Fred lived near the Dairy in an upper-floor room in a two-year-old gambling den called the Pacific House. Saloons and dance halls and sex workers masquerading as seamstresses abounded. Seattle's population was booming in the midst of hurried construction. A man could pile away a heap of money by serving the people at the center of the action.

> A man could pile away a heap of money by serving the people at the center of the action.

In addition to making money, Fred made himself at home in Seattle, and by 1892 he became a naturalized US citizen. He'd also cast his first vote.

Hungry for even more opportunity, risk, and money, on February 10, 1893, he sold the Dairy and shortly thereafter moved east to a town called Monte Cristo, where prospectors hoped to mine a fortune in silver and gold.

Just as working the fields wasn't for Fred, neither was mining. Real estate was another story. For $200, he bought forty acres east of Seattle. And because he didn't have enough money to buy land near the train station to build a hotel, he fudged things.

He bought lumber and built a boarding house and restaurant on land another man already had claimed under mining laws. For a while, it worked. He dodged rent collection efforts from the rightful owner, and even got into politics, winning in a landslide election for justice of the peace in 1896.

> He dodged rent collection efforts from the rightful owner, and even got into politics...

But the mines proved to be more bust than boom, so in 1897 he returned to Seattle, opened another restaurant not far from his first, and made such a killing he was able to pay off his mortgage in a month and have enough money left over to go into business in the Yukon, where a gold rush had begun in 1897.

In July that year, he and two partners spent $15 on a claim in the Klondike region of the Yukon in Canada (which would later become part of the state of Alaska). They sold half of it the next day for $400. They staked another in September. By December, they'd split it and sold both halves for $2,150 total.

By 1898, Fred had enough money to get to the Yukon himself as a restaurateur. His journey there was rough, and he opened a restaurant in a tent beside the trail—even selling meals made from the remains of horses who'd dropped dead from exhaustion.

By May, Fred and a partner arrived in Bennett, British Columbia, where they set up the New Arctic Restaurant and Hotel, which was a two-story affair that served single men extravagant dishes—including fresh fruit, duck, goose, salmon, moose, goat, sheep, rabbit, and a type of grouse called a ptarmigan. They also sold liquor and female companionship; this was why a letter written to the *Yukon Sun* about the place told "respectable women" to sleep elsewhere lest they hear things "repugnant to their feelings."

Before long, Fred set up a new restaurant called the White Horse that cranked out three thousand meals a day. But his business partner was a drinker, and that plus a crackdown on liquor, gambling, and prostitution soured Fred's interest in the business. He sold the business to his partner, and having a newly minted fortune, he returned home to Kallstadt in 1901, where his mother still lived. He was a rich man now and old enough for the danger of compulsory military service to have passed, and he was at last financially ready for a new adventure: marriage.

He knew who he wanted. Miss Elizabeth Christ had been one of his neighbors—just a child when he left, but now a grown woman, blond and curvaceous. Even though his mother thought Elizabeth was low class, Fred proposed to her, promising her father the couple would return to Kallstadt if America wasn't to her liking. When he came back the next year, he wed Elizabeth in August and swept her away to New York City. He briefly resumed the barber trade but was soon back in the hotel and restaurant business.

The young couple lived in a German neighborhood in the Bronx, sharing a language, food, and traditions with their neighbors. Despite that, after a baby girl arrived in April 1904, Elizabeth's homesickness grew so acute that Fred took her back to Kallstadt in June.

He brought a considerable fortune with him: the equivalent of over a half million 2018 dollars. He hoped to reestablish himself as a Bavarian with this impressive pile of cash, but authorities bristled at his return. On Christmas Eve, they announced an investigation into the matter. Their conclusion: His draft-dodging would cost him his German citizenship.

Desperate to stay, Fred wrote to the German monarch:

Most Serene, Most Powerful Prince Regent! Most Gracious Regent and Lord!

I was born in Kallstadt on March 14, 1869. My parents were honest, plain, pious vineyard workers. They strictly held me to everything good—to diligence and piety, to regular attendance in school and church, to absolute obedience toward the high authority.

After my confirmation, in 1882, I apprenticed to become a barber. I emigrated in 1885, in my sixteenth year. In America I carried on my business with diligence, discretion, and prudence. God's blessing was with me, and I became rich. I obtained American citizenship in 1892. In 1902 I met my current wife. Sadly, she could not tolerate the climate in New York, and I went with my dear family back to Kallstadt.

The town was glad to have received a capable and productive citizen. My old mother was happy to see her son, her dear daughter-in-law, and her granddaughter around her; she knows now that I will take care of her in her old age.

But we were confronted all at once, as if by a lightning strike from fair skies, with the news that the High Royal State Ministry had decided that we must leave our residence in the Kingdom of Bavaria. We were paralyzed with fright; our happy family life was tarnished. My wife has been overcome by anxiety, and my lovely child has become sick.

Why should we be deported? This is very, very hard for a family. What will our fellow citizens think if honest subjects are faced with such a decree—not to mention the great material losses it would incur. I would like to become a Bavarian citizen again.

In this urgent situation I have no other recourse than to turn to our adored, noble, wise, and just sovereign lord, our exalted ruler His Royal Highness, highest of all, who has already dried so many tears, who has ruled so beneficially and justly and wisely and softly and is warmly and deeply loved, with the most humble request that the highest of all will himself in mercy deign to allow the applicant to stay in the most gracious Kingdom of Bavaria.

Your most humble and obedient,

Friedrich Trump

His letter failed.

A few months after their return to New York, they had a baby boy and named him Frederick Christ Trump, after his father. By 1907, the Trumps had another baby. As he reestablished himself in America, Fred opened a barbershop in Manhattan, at 60 Wall Street, not far from where his grandson would someday own a skyscraper. The next year, Fred bought real estate in Queens, which, within two years, would become the family home as well as a rental property.

Ever the entrepreneur, he also managed a hotel and acquired land as he could. The family soon moved to a quieter spot than their first home, which was on the trolley line, and the children—there were three—attended school at the nearby Public School 97. There, they spoke English, although they preferred German at home.

> Ever the entrepreneur, he also managed a hotel and acquired land as he could.

World War I started in 1914, making it harder for the Trumps and other German immigrants to feel welcome. The bias against German immigrants was so strong that German names were erased from schools, foods, and maps. Violence erupted, too; people questioned the loyalty of German Americans, tarring and feathering some, and hanging one.

In the midst of this, Fred became ill with Spanish flu while walking down Jamaica Avenue with little Fred, who was twelve. Big Fred died the next day. He was only forty-nine, but he left his family with stocks, cash, and more important, a small real estate empire: their two-story home in Queens, along with five vacant lots.

Elizabeth grieved her husband, but she had three children to raise. They would carry on her husband's legacy. Elizabeth, the daughter, would keep books. John, the diligent student, would be the architect. And young Fred, most like his father, would build, just as soon as he'd graduated from high school.

Not long after his father's death, Fred built a garage for a neighbor. He studied everything relating to building he could think of: carpentry, masonry, electrical work, plumbing, and blueprint reading. Later, he took a construction job that paid $11 a week, kept up the construction classes, and before he was twenty-one, he'd started building houses—paying for the supplies needed to build them by selling a house under construction and using profits to fund the next as he finished the first.

Because Fred was so young, his mother incorporated the business as E. Trump & Son. People loved what Fred Trump built. He included details that made the houses distinct, and he had a salesman's instinct for paying close attention to his customers' desires.

In those early days of his career, he was arrested at a Ku Klux Klan riot. A thousand hooded Ku Klux Klansmen marched through the Jamaica neighborhood of Queens on Memorial Day 1927. They brawled with about one hundred police officers. Fred was detained for "refusing to disperse from a parade when ordered to do so," though he wasn't charged with a crime.

Meanwhile, he kept cranking out houses, while his brother John worked for General Electric and studied architecture in college. The brothers clashed. John saw an aesthetic proposition, and he wanted to get each house perfect before selling. Fred saw a business, which demanded he move quickly and sell houses that weren't yet finished. Fred's drive steamrolled his brother right out of the business. And, free of his brother, he started building bigger and better houses modeled after English manors.

Things were looking up until suddenly they weren't. When Fred was twenty-four, the stock market crashed. With it went the housing market. But, as his father had learned before him, Fred knew people always needed to eat. He opened a grocery store in Queens, but not the old-fashioned kind where a store clerk gathered items. Fred's motto was catchy: "Serve yourself and save!" The concept was a hit, even if his heart wasn't in it.

Five years passed. When a corrupt mortgage-service company crashed, Fred saw an opportunity to get in on the $2 million remaining. He whipped up some F. C. Trump Construction Corporation stationery, made no mention of the fact that he was in the grocery business, and claimed years of experience servicing mortgages. It was true enough, he figured. And it would be good money. Mortgage servicers earn a percentage of the loan in exchange for processing payments and figuring out how much interest, tax, and insurance borrowers owe. They also make money on late fees and foreclosures.

Two other builders were in the running for the business, including another guy from Queens who, like Fred, had more enthusiasm than experience. During negotiations, where they were outmatched by a competitor with more money and better connections, the two outsiders teamed up and concocted a plan. Despite a last-minute bid by a Manhattan-based competitor, Trump and his ally won.

The money he'd make managing mortgage payments meant he could finally build houses again. The timing was right, because he would soon marry a tall, pretty, brown-haired Scottish immigrant he'd met at a party. He fell in love at first sight with Mary Anne

MacLeod, a domestic worker, resolving that night to marry her. He made good on his word in January of 1936. They honeymooned in Atlantic City, New Jersey—but only for a weekend, because he had work to do. The real estate business was catching fire, thanks to interventions by the United States government to alleviate the Great Depression.

During this bleak time, one out of every four workers was unemployed. Many had worked in construction. What's more, 10 percent of homeowners had defaulted on their mortgages. The industry was a mess, but houses and lots could be scooped up on the cheap. The government funded programs to put builders to work, which would ideally boost the economy.

And the government, through the Federal Housing Administration, began to insure private banks that lent money for housing. This meant it was less risky for banks to make the loans. The government also put together a team of people to address things like land planning, effective home design, and real estate appraisal.

Fred Trump now had connections and he worked them, even joining an organization of movers and shakers called the Madison Club. Thanks to the FHA, he could turn his big plans into big loans. His ability to build no longer depended on how much money he had in the bank.

Now he could go after large plots of land. He had his eye on a swath of underdeveloped land in East Flatbush, and his partner researched the owners and bought the plots, sometimes at auctions when their owners had failed to pay taxes. Fred devised plans for 450 houses and got $750,000 in mortgage insurance from the FHA.

This he took to a bank for cash, and then he went to work. He knew every inch of the building process and managed his workers himself. He had an instinct for what his middle-class customers wanted: affordable, solidly built homes with porches and garages.

By August 1936, the Trumps not only had a baby on the way, but Fred and his business partner had also completed the first forty-eight homes in his 450-home community. The *New York Times* covered the milestone celebration, which featured local and national dignitaries.

In 1938, the *Brooklyn Eagle* called him the "Henry Ford of the home-building industry." He loved this and the attention he got by devising novel ways to advertise his wares. He dropped balloons with coupons and offered prizes for babies born in his houses. He fed newspapers tidbits to fill their empty columns. He even had women in bikinis hand out bricks for people to throw at old landmarks he was replacing with new buildings. His Trump homes, as they became known, were a hit.

He built his biggest project yet during World War II for defense workers: a seven-hundred-home behemoth covering fifty-five acres. In the midst of the war, he cleverly worked around shortages as he built more housing for defense workers in Norfolk, Virginia. He discovered he liked to build apartments, because he could keep them and make even more on rent.

By the time World War II ended, Fred was a millionaire.

After the war, with three children born and a fourth on the way, Fred was eager to build houses for all those returning servicemen. Supplies were limited.

Fred's fourth child, Donald John, arrived amid this frustrating time. But new rules at the FHA created new opportunities, and as usual, Fred quickly spotted potential profit. He shifted into building giant apartment complexes, starting with a thirty-two-building development called Shore Haven, which was big enough it needed its own shopping center. The *Brooklyn Eagle* nicknamed it Trump City.

A similar development called Beach Haven came next, and as Fred worked the projects, he also worked the room at political clubs, and even behind the scenes with mobsters. Like his father, he did what it took to make money.

He also knew how to sell things. Fred understood women drove the housing decisions, and he catered to them with roses,

ABOVE: At Coney Island, Fred Trump hands over an ax to begin the demolition of Steeplechase Park, where he plans to build a high-rise development. *(Charles Frattini/NY Daily News Archive via Getty Images)*

lectures on childcare, and children's orchestra concerts, among other things. What's more, he understood the value of media. News coverage burnished his image, and this image kept people wanting to live in his apartments. Trump wasn't just a name. It was a brand.

Things were looking great for him, professionally and socially— until the US government accused him of taking advantage of the same housing program that had made him into a household name. The Section 608 program, which enabled him to build thousands of housing units for veterans, worked like this:

Fred estimated how much his projects would cost and how long they'd take to build. The FHA provided mortgage insurance and calculated future rents based on these estimates. This Fred took to the bank for funding. If Fred finished ahead of time and under budget, the extra money he got through the bank loans was technically his to keep.

Because he determined the budget and the timeline, this wasn't hard to do.

Sure, Fred could have lowered the veterans' rents or returned the overages. But the law didn't require it, and he was a business-man, so he kept these windfalls. A related tax issue arose when such windfalls were counted as capital gains instead of income. Had they been considered income, Fred would have owed significantly more to the IRS.

The *Brooklyn Eagle*, which had reported so many Fred Trump success stories, ran one that said: "Federal Investigators Checking the Housing Loan Scandals Have Accused Fred C. Trump, Jamaica, [Long Island,] Builder of Pocketing $4,047,900 Windfall on the Beach Haven Apartments in Brooklyn."

During a US Senate hearing in July 1954, Trump was criticized for "unethical behavior." Fred called the accusation "very wrong, and it hurts me. The only thing I am happy about is that it is not true."

> **". . . The only thing I am happy about is that it is not true."**

President Eisenhower was so mad about it he called Trump and other developers "sons of bitches."

Fred disputed the charge that he'd pocketed more than $4 million. The money wasn't in his pocket. It was in the bank. What's more, he still owed $16 million on the mortgage.

The pocket logic did not impress New York senator Herbert Lehman. "Well, Mr. Trump, without going into the merits or the justification for your having this so-called windfall of $4 million, isn't it a fact that that $4 million, while not paid out to you in the form of a windfall, is in the treasury of the company and could be paid out, at any time? So it is not so very inaccurate as to the amount of the windfall."

Trump replied, "I first have to take it out before I pocket it, Senator; isn't that right? I am happy we haven't taken it out."

The reply was technically correct, but it also missed the point of the question. Of course that $4 million was Trump's—and his children's. And they were benefiting. Fred had set up a complicated corporate ownership structure, a trust fund that paid tens of thousands every year to his offspring.

In the end, Fred and other builders managed to convince people that the laws were to blame. He'd built homes. He'd created value.

This was free enterprise. Free enterprise that meant the veterans who fought in World War II paid higher rents than they otherwise needed to.

This riled some of his tenants. And it wasn't the only tenant complaint. Some thought he was racist.

The folk singer Woody Guthrie moved into a Trump apartment in December 1950 and came to write an angry song about Trump stirring up hatred "in the bloodpot of human hearts" at one of his developments.

Guthrie wasn't the only one noticing biased rental practices. Fred Trump would eventually be sued by the Justice Department for housing practices that violated the Fair Housing Act of 1968.

But it wouldn't just be Fred in the crosshairs of the federal government. His son Donald, in elementary school when Guthrie wrote his song, would stand accused of racism along with his father.

CHAPTER 3

TRUMP in TROUBLE

BORN ON JUNE 14, 1946, little Donald Trump had golden hair, pink cheeks, and a tiny pucker of a mouth. This "blonde and buttery" boy, as a nursery school teacher described him, started life lucky. He had wealthy parents who were strict but loving, and two older sisters and a brother to pave the way. The family's maid, Emma, made a mean hamburger. Their black chauffeur drove Fred's two Cadillacs, which had been tricked out with vanity license plates that said FT1 and FT2.

But when Donald's younger brother, Robert, was born in 1948, disaster struck. Sometime after Robert's birth, his mother lost her uterus and nearly her life from infections and the surgery that followed. But Fred, the sort of guy who wore a business suit to the beach, didn't go to pieces. Instead, he powered through the crisis and expected his kids to do the same. He sent Donald's big sister Maryanne to school with a promise that he'd let her know if anything bad happened.

Donald was just two when he almost lost his mother, too young to understand what was happening, and too young to remember it. But he wasn't much older than that when he developed a reputation as a menace in school, church, and the neighborhood. He chucked rocks at a neighbor's baby in a playpen. He pulled hair and blew spitballs and smashed baseball bats in rage. He also couldn't admit to being wrong, once insisting the wrestler Antonino Rocca was "Rocky Antonino." And Trump regularly talked back to teachers at school, where he was so often in trouble that his initials, DT, became shorthand for detention.

"He was a little shit," one of his teachers would remember, years later.

"Surly," another said.

As an adult, Trump himself claimed he punched a music teacher in the nose.

Despite Donald's struggles in the classroom, he excelled at recess. In merciless games of dodgeball, he was often the last boy standing. He liked baseball well enough to write a poem about it. His elementary school yearbook published this ditty about his favorite things—winning and the adulation of the crowd:

I like to hear the crowd give cheers, so loud and noisy to my ears. When the score is 5–5, I feel like I could cry. And when they get another run, I feel like I could die. Then the catcher makes an error, not a bit like Yogi Berra. The game is over and we say tomorrow is another day.

Mostly, though, people didn't cheer for little Donald. And despite Fred's attempts to teach him discipline and frugality, Donald didn't seem to be outgrowing his belligerent ways. Fred wasn't certain what to do. He'd been twelve when his father died. He didn't have a map for this.

He didn't have a map for this.

When Donald was thirteen, Fred was fed up. Donald had been caught playing with a switchblade, so Fred sent the boy away to school, hoping the rigor and discipline of New York Military Academy would turn him into a winner.

The New York Military Academy was nothing like Donald's home. Since he was four, he'd lived in Queens with his family in a twenty-three-room Georgian mansion. Built by Fred, the Trump house was a huge, brick structure set seventeen steps off the street, dressed up in white shutters, with a pillared entryway topped with an iridescent crest. Equipped with an intercom and one of the neighborhood's first color TVs, the Trump mansion was the fanciest in the upwardly mobile, nearly all-white neighborhood, which Donald's parents fretted over after an Italian family moved in.

The New York Military Academy, over sixty miles away, was the sort of place parents sometimes sent sons who'd gone off the rails, a place meant to bring them back to their better impulses with discipline and messages like the one emblazoned over the front entrance to the school: "Courageous and gallant men have passed through these portals."

Sporting a military-style uniform and golden buzz cut, Donald marched off to the 120-acre campus in the Hudson Valley. His new life meant he'd live in barracks, share bathrooms with other boys, and eat institutional spaghetti, meatloaf, and fried leftover meat formed into "mystery mountains." He'd face inspections of his bed, shoes, and schoolwork.

The freedom that Donald had enjoyed—to ride his bike through the neighborhood shouting obscenities, to sneak away to Manhattan with a pal—was gone. Now he was under the gaze of a World War II veteran named Theodore "Doby" Dobias, a man who'd watched the Italian dictator Mussolini swing from a rope and wasn't afraid to smack an unruly cadet. If students had lousy grades or stepped out of line, Doby would set them in a boxing ring so they could knock sense into each other.

Initially, Donald didn't impress Doby.

> ## Initially, Donald didn't impress Doby.

"We really didn't care whether he came from Rockefeller Center or whatever," Dobias later told a reporter from the *Washington Post*. "He was just another name."

Another name was exactly what Donald *didn't* want to be. He wanted to be the best. He wanted applause. He wanted to bask in

the spotlight (or in a pinch, an ultraviolet light he set up in his room to make it feel as if he was tanning at the beach).

Even then, "he wanted to be number one," Dobias told the *Post*. "He wanted to be noticed. He wanted to be recognized. And he liked compliments."

Before long, Donald figured out what he needed to do to get the kind of attention that didn't leave marks. First, though, he had to make sure his dad didn't come to campus in one of the

ABOVE: Donald Trump in his New York Military Academy uniform. At NYMA, he won neatness medals and set up a makeshift tanning light in his dorm room. *(New York Military Academy)*

limousines. Fred Trump tried that once, and Donald put a stop to it. He didn't want to stand out that way. He did want to stand out in other ways, though, and his first triumphs were a pair of medals he won for neatness.

A roommate, Ted Levine, called him "Mr. Meticulous." It wasn't meant as a compliment. The two got along like orange juice and toothpaste. Once when Ted didn't make his bed, Donald got so mad at him that he ripped the sheets off the mattress and pitched them on the floor. Ted retaliated by chucking a combat boot at Donald and whacking him with a broomstick. When Donald tried to shove Ted out of their second-story window, a pair of cadets broke up the fight, the sort of thing that wasn't uncommon at the school.

The military academy could be rough. By Donald's senior year, the superintendent was dismissed over epidemic student hazing. Donald steered clear of that, although he lost his post as captain of the A Company after one of the boys he commanded was reported for hazing a freshman. Donald, who'd spent more time holed up in his room than managing his officers, was moved out of the barracks and into the administrative building. He still had a leadership position, but he didn't get to oversee any other boys.

During his time in military school, Donald did more than chase neatness medals and indoor UV rays. He excelled at sports, playing varsity baseball, football, and soccer; he was a junior varsity wrestler, and spent three years in a bowling league. He led a Columbus Day parade, served on three dance committees, and joined the Driver Education Club and the Hobby and Model Club (he'd had a large train set at home). During his senior year, he won a captain's award for baseball as well as a coach's award for the same sport. Academically, he won two awards as a "proficient" cadet and four awards as an "honor" cadet. But there was at least one way he surpassed his fellow students: His classmates voted him the campus Ladies' Man.

Through military school, he looked up to his big brother, Freddy, who was handsome and charismatic and knew how to fly planes. Donald kept Freddy's picture in his dorm room. Freddy would also sometimes take Donald for rides in his Century speedboat during summer breaks. But as much as Donald admired Freddy, his brother was also turning out to be a cautionary tale.

Six years older than Donald, Freddy was expected to take over the family business after his graduation from Lehigh University. (For some reason, elder sister Maryanne wasn't expected to do so, despite being a graduate of the more prestigious Mount Holyoke.) He went to work for his dad to build a huge development on Coney Island called Trump Village. But Freddy didn't live up to his father's expectations. Fred Trump made a point of frugality. He would pick up unused nails at construction sites and reuse them. When Freddy once installed new windows instead of fixing old ones, his dad savaged him. Freddy started drinking heavily. Donald watched and learned. Eventually, Freddy left the company to become a pilot.

Meanwhile, unrest in the world was growing, and boys Donald's age were being drafted into the military and sent into bloody conflict. These times tested the character of many, and when Donald graduated in 1964, his school yearbook, *Shrapnel*, told the boys: "Wherever your interests may lead you in this life, let it never be said that you overlooked the essential nature of integration of moral principles with academic training. The countries represented in this graduating class of 1964 look to you to set and to maintain high standards of ethics, of integrity, and of moral and spiritual values. Even though public disclosure of adult corruption comes before us almost daily, you must not yield to it . . .

"Scholastic achievement and moral principles go together—and . . . these are only the minimum requirements for a real leader of men."

Leadership and integrity weren't abstract questions. The United States' involvement in the Vietnam War—a conflict between North and South Vietnam over communism—was ramping up, and Donald was of draft age.

> He had no desire to fight
> in Vietnam.

He had no desire to fight in Vietnam. There were a few ways to avoid this duty—principally, by becoming a conscientious objector or getting a medical or educational deferment, something boys from wealthy families found easier to do than their poorer counterparts. As long as a student made academic progress, he could stay in school until he was too old to be drafted. This is why a high percentage of men who went to Vietnam were everything Donald wasn't: poor, undereducated, blue collar, or African American (unemployment was a factor and black men were particularly vulnerable to that).

Producing movies sounded much more appealing than jungle combat. Donald considered the University of Southern California.

But he was accepted at Fordham College at Rose Hill, a Catholic university in the Bronx. He spent two years there, playing competitive squash and taking time on weekends to golf and work with his father, but he otherwise wasn't a standout, at least beyond his expensive clothes and red sports car.

Donald could afford these things because of a family trust fund. Starting in 1949, Donald and his siblings each took in $12,000 a year—six figures when adjusted for inflation.

Despite having the cash and accessories of a playboy, Donald didn't drink, smoke, or party—he'd seen what that had done to his older brother. He studied. He dated pretty girls. He worked. And he got his first two student deferments from the military draft.

He had bigger ambitions than Fordham, eventually applying and transferring to the Wharton Business School at the University of Pennsylvania. Freddy knew a guy on the admissions committee, and Penn's Wharton School of Finance and Commerce had a real estate department, which appealed to Donald. He couldn't wait to compete with what he perceived as better class students. Once among them, though, he didn't distinguish himself academically, and one former professor, William T. Kelley, ranked him among his least promising students.

Twice more while at Penn, Donald held off the military draft with student deferments. Two months after he graduated with his BS in economics in 1968, he got a 1-Y medical deferment for bone spurs in his heels, a usually painless condition that is common among athletes who've run and jumped a lot. (They're common among the general population, too; about 38 percent of us have them.)

Because Freddy was working as a pilot, Fred Trump elevated Donald, who'd already been working as his sidekick on trips to Cincinnati, to check up on a 1,200-unit apartment complex called Swifton Village. Fred had snapped up the development in 1964 for $5.6 million because he couldn't resist the deal. The garden apartment complex had fifty-seven two-story buildings on forty-one acres, and it had cost $10 million to build using government funds in the 1950s. Within a decade it had become such a wreck half the units were empty. (The original builder, like Fred Trump, also was accused of pocketing windfalls.)

With Donald on hand to witness, Fred cracked the whip and brought Swifton Village back into order. Fresh paint, appliances, landscaping, security guards: They were going to make it a decent place to live. And sure enough, new tenants started filling up the rehabilitated place. But the Trumps only wanted a certain type of tenant.

In 1969, a year after Trump graduated from Penn, a prospective tenant named Haywood Cash put in an application. Trump's rental agent told Cash he didn't make enough money to live there. Cash—who was black—contacted a civil rights organization with his wife. A representative of the organization, called HOME, used the same income information to rent an apartment, which they then tried to turn over to the Cashes. The Swifton staff erupted, and the general manager called the HOME worker a racist slur before booting her and Cash from the complex.

Had this happened before the Civil Rights Act of 1968, Cash might have been stymied, even though Fred had settled previous discrimination complaints at the Swifton outside of court. The

Cashes wanted justice, and the act gave them grounds to file a lawsuit. Over the objections of Donald, who thought his dad had done nothing wrong, Fred Trump offered the Cashes an apartment. The couple also collected the highest amount of damages possible, $1,000 (around $7,000 in 2018 dollars).

When Cincinnati's real estate fortunes turned a couple years later, the Trumps sold the complex for $6.75 million, a profit for the family and Donald's first seven-figure deal. It was a big deal, to be sure.

But it wasn't Manhattan.

But it wasn't Manhattan. That was the big leagues. That was where Donald wanted to play. And that was where—whatever it took—he intended to win.

CHAPTER 4

MANHATTAN by STORM

**LTHOUGH DONALD DID** not attend USC, which would have put him on a path to making movies, his first attempt to succeed in Manhattan was in the entertainment business.

In 1970, he invested $70,000 into coproducing a Broadway show called *Paris Is Out!*

A *New York Times* critic called it a "bad play" and said that he "pitied it more than [he] disliked it," and the venture flopped, closing after 112 shows.

Donald had real estate to fall back on, and he became president of the Trump Organization after his dad took on the new title of

chairman of the board. But there was no way Donald could dominate Manhattan while still living in Queens with his parents. In 1971,
he moved into his first bachelor pad, an apartment on Third Avenue
and East Seventy-Fifth Street, in the borough's posh Upper East
Side. A studio with a view of a water tank, the apartment wasn't
much. But it was close to Central Park and the rest of the city's
most expensive real estate. When he wasn't working at his dad's
office, Donald prowled the city streets, getting a feel for potential
quarry. If the ring around Central Park was like a Monopoly board,
he was hunting for his Boardwalk.

He wanted something big. Something lucrative. He didn't want
to manage lower- and middle-class apartment buildings his whole
life. What's more, the related government subsidies that had made
his father millions were drying up. Meanwhile, collecting rent was
a job for people who didn't mind getting punched in the face.
That wasn't Donald.

Even though the news media hadn't been kind to his musical, he
still considered the press a potential ally. His father had done all
sorts of clever things to get coverage that boosted both his brand
and his business. Here, Donald also had big dreams. The first part
of making his name would happen on the nightclub scene, where
he could meet potential business partners and beautiful women.

Not far from his little apartment was a members-only hotspot
called Le Club, cofounded by the designer Oleg Cassini and his
brother. Le Club was fancy, a place to give the rich and famous
opportunities to see one another and be seen. Donald pressed the
club president a few times for membership, and when he finally pre-
vailed, the president told him his membership had one condition:

that he not use his dashing looks to steal the wives of other men.

One fateful night in 1973, when he was twenty-seven years old, Donald did meet a special someone at Le Club. Not a woman, but a man named Roy Cohn. Cohn was a tough guy. A thug, even, with weather-worn skin, dark eyes, and a nose that looked like it had encountered many fists in his forty-six years. But he'd always lived fast and hard. When he was thirteen, he wrote a gossip column for the *Bronx Home News*. He graduated from law school before he turned twenty-one, the earliest he could have taken the bar

ABOVE: Donald Trump and his father, Fred: Trump's teacher, role model, and the man he wanted to beat. *(Bill Truran /Alamy Stock Photo)*

examination. As a young lawyer, Cohn helped convict Julius and Ethel Rosenberg of espionage—a crime that sent them to the electric chair. Neither the trial nor Cohn's part in it was squeaky clean. Cohn also worked as the attack dog for US Senator Joseph McCarthy during America's infamous Red Scare.

An attack dog was exactly what Donald needed that October. The United States government had filed a lawsuit against him and his father for alleged racist rental practices in their apartment empire after a black woman tried in July 1972 to rent an apartment in Brooklyn from Trump Management Inc., where Donald held the title of president.

She was told they had no apartments to rent. Later that same day, a white woman came looking for an apartment. The organization had two vacancies.

These women weren't potential tenants; they'd been sent to see if Trump Management was discriminating against people of color—a violation of the Fair Housing Act of 1968.

The United States of America sued Fred C. Trump, Donald Trump, and the company they ran, arguing, "The defendants, through the actions of their agents and employees, have discriminated against persons because of race in the operations of their apartment buildings."

It was a big lawsuit, one of the biggest of its kind, meant to send a message to landlords who wanted to violate the civil rights of Americans.

The *New York Times* carried news of the suit on the front page on October 16, 1973. Beneath a headline that read: "Major Landlord Accused of Antiblack Bias in the City," came this report:

> The Department of Justice, charging
> discrimination against blacks in apartment
> rentals, brought suit in Federal Court in
> Brooklyn yesterday against the Trump Management
> Corporation, a major owner and manager of real
> estate here.
>
> The corporation, which owns and rents more
> than 14,000 apartments in Brooklyn, Queens and
> Staten Island, was accused of violating the
> Fair Housing Act of 1968 in its operation of 39
> buildings. Most are in Coney Island, Brooklyn,
> and in Jamaica Estates and Forest Hills,
> Queens . . .
>
> It also charged that the company had required
> different rental terms and conditions because of
> race and that it had misrepresented to blacks
> that apartments were not available.

This wasn't the sort of media splash Trump wanted to make. He argued back with the reporter, calling the charges "absolutely ridiculous. We never have discriminated, and we never would. There have been a number of local actions against us, and we've won them all. We were charged with discrimination, and we proved in court that we did not discriminate."

This was a distortion of the truth. They'd already paid the Cash family $1,000 and given them an apartment.

In Trump's view, he wasn't a racist. He was a businessman. And he shouldn't have to rent to certain tenants. "The idea of settling drove me crazy," he later wrote. "The fact was that we did rent to blacks in our buildings."

Instead of offering a settlement right away, as Fred had done with the Cashes, Trump unleashed Roy Cohn on the Justice Department. Cohn believed in punching back hard, and always, and that if a man said something aggressively enough and loudly enough, he could make it true.

Trump announced Cohn's hire at a press conference at the Hilton Hotel. He said his company had not only done no wrong, it would be countersuing the US government for $100 million ($558 million in 2018 dollars).

It was an audacious strategy, given what was contained in a file FBI agents were assembling about rental practices in the Trump Organization. The City of New York Commission on Human Rights had found them guilty of discrimination in 1968 after a prospective black tenant was told an apartment was not available, when a white friend of the black man was offered a lease on one a few hours later.

"The Commission finds that the respondents have engaged in an unlawful discriminatory practice," the report said. The organization was ordered to stop discriminating. They had to pay the man one hundred dollars for "humiliation, outrage and mental anguish" caused by the Trump Organization's discrimination. They also had to let a fair housing organization know about openings.

Despite all this, the Trumps persisted in discriminating against tenants with brown skin, which led to the Justice Department suit.

> Despite all this, the Trumps persisted in discriminating against tenants with brown skin.

As part of the suit, FBI agents interviewed Trump Organization employees. One signed affidavit said, among other things, that an employee was told to inform black people that the rent was twice as high as it was. Another said, even as Fred Trump knew discrimination was illegal, he instructed the employee "not to rent to blacks." A couple who worked as rental agents testified in court they'd been instructed to rent to Jews and executives, not black people. Employees said they steered black people and Puerto Ricans into certain apartments, and coded applications "No. 9" (for blacks) or "C" (for "colored"). One Trump employee who'd signed an affidavit said he wanted to keep his name confidential because he was afraid the Trumps would have him "knocked off."

Many tenants and employees, including ten black ones, however, insisted there was no discrimination by the Trumps.

Cohn—whose clients included mobsters—claimed the Trump organization had been victimized by a "Gestapo-like" investigation in which the FBI agents had descended on the Trump office like "storm troopers." He also claimed a Justice Department lawyer, Donna Goldstein, had tried to get witnesses to change their stories.

The judge found no merit to Cohn's claims, and ultimately the Justice Department beat the Trumps. In 1975, the Trumps settled and agreed to make apartments available to people of color who wished to rent from them. They wouldn't admit to any wrongdoing and weren't required to by the settlement. They were required to provide the New York Urban League a list of their vacancies every week for two years, and in buildings where black people represented less than 10 percent of the tenants, the League could present them with qualified rental applicants. The Trumps also were required to buy advertising letting prospective tenants of all races know they were welcome.

Donald hated that part.

Donald hated that part. "This advertising," he said, "while it's, you know—I imagine it's necessary from the government's standpoint, is a very expensive thing for us . . . Each sentence we put in is going to cost us a lot of money over the period we're supposed to do it."

He asked the government if they—meaning United States taxpayers—might pick up the tab for the ads for his business.

During the two-year period of government oversight, the Trumps didn't live up to their settlement. Some of the ads the organization had printed were too small, and worse, "We believe that an underlying pattern of discrimination continues to exist in the Trump Management organization," the government reported as it sought to strengthen and increase the affirmative action required of the organization for past noncompliance. The pattern had persisted; the *New York Times* reported in 1983 the Trumps still had 95 percent white tenants in some of their buildings.

T HROUGHOUT THIS PERIOD, DONALD CONTINUED to get boosts from his father: a million-dollar trust fund, ownership of an apartment complex in New Jersey, and commissions on sales of Fred Trump's shares of a real estate partnership. But Donald kept swinging for huge deals of his own. The same year the federal government sued Trump and his father for racist rental practices, Donald went after his biggest deal yet. In combing Manhattan for property he could use to build something spectacular, he came across huge tracts of land owned by the Penn Central Transportation Company, which had gone bankrupt in 1970. The beleaguered railroad company had two sites Donald wanted: one running from Fifty-Ninth to Seventy-Second Streets along the Hudson River, one on West Thirty-Fourth Street. Both were huge, ninety-three and forty-four acres, respectively. One was the biggest developable parcel in all of Manhattan.

There was just one problem: Except for the newspaper headlines about the civil rights suit, Trump was an unknown quantity in Manhattan. He was young and didn't have huge sums of money at his command. Without this, he couldn't buy the land outright. He'd have to cash in on his charm instead.

> . . . Trump was an unknown quantity in Manhattan.

His target here was Victor Palmieri, the lawyer charged with handling the Penn Central real estate assets. Trump negotiated with Palmieri's team for an option to develop the land—basically, first dibs. With endorsement from a Palmieri associate, Ned Eichler, Trump got his way.

But that was just a start. He'd also need tax breaks, changes to city zoning, and a government mortgage. These depended on political connections.

Here, Donald had an advantage. His dad had known New York City mayor Abe Beame for thirty years and had been funding Beame's political career since Donald was causing trouble at his private elementary school. Fred's lawyer was also Beame's best friend. Penn Central took Donald's offer, and a bankruptcy court approved it. And with that, his career was launched, though in March 1975 a judge questioned whether Donald had been given an unfair edge.

Meanwhile, in 1974, Palmieri let Donald know about the Commodore Hotel, a once-grand structure next to Grand Central Station. The hotel was named for "Commodore" Cornelius Vanderbilt, the railroad tycoon who complained about the smell of Trump's grandfather and other immigrants arriving by ship. Vanderbilt owned Grand Central when his namesake hotel opened in 1919. At the time, the Commodore represented the height of elegance and modernity. A postcard from its early days touted the baths and "circulating ice water" in each of its two thousand rooms. But the intervening years and the struggles of the railroad industry had been hard on the place. New York City was also in a slump.

Donald knew this was an unbeatable location, right in the middle of Manhattan. Rivers of commuters coursed through this legendary travel hub every day. Anyone who couldn't make money off such a spot was a fool.

Donald wanted to make over this hotel, transforming it into something glossy, luxe, and sleek. Once again, though, he didn't have the cash. And once again, he was going to have to rely on a variety of taxpayer-funded plans, his father's bank account, partnerships with bigger players, connections—plus his own charm and persistence to pull it off.

> ## Once again, though, he didn't have the cash.

"I had to prove—to the real estate community, to the press, to my father—that I could deliver the goods," he said.

If all went according to plan, he and his partner would share profits from a successful hotel, while receiving an unprecedented forty years of tax breaks from New York City.

In the midst of this, he did impress at least one journalist, a *New York Times* reporter named Judy Klemesrud. Her piece reported that he graduated at the top of his class at Wharton. She also believed him when he told her he was the top real estate promoter of the age. He was nowhere near the top of either category. But he knew how to work a reporter, and the impression of Donald as a top student stuck.

Meanwhile, Donald was trying to deliver the goods more than just to the media and the players in the real estate industry. One night in 1976, he was grabbing dinner at Maxwell's Plum, a swank New York hotspot known for being a place you go to see stars and eat delicious chili and burgers. The place was packed but Donald couldn't help but notice a group of eight models. When the maître d' led the women to the bar and told them they'd have to wait for a table, Trump saw his opening. He walked to a leggy blonde in a red minidress and put a hand on her arm.

As Ivana wrote about it years later in her book about their life together, *Raising Trump*, he said, "I am so sorry to bother you. My name is Donald Trump, and I noticed that you and your friends are waiting for a table. I know the manager and I can get you one fast."

Within three minutes, he'd made good on his word and negotiated the best table in the house. He took a seat next to the blonde—Ivana was her name—and ordered a burger and iced tea. (He didn't drink alcohol, not after what had happened to Freddy.)

As the models finished their food, Donald slipped away and took care of the four hundred dollar tab. Then he raced home to get his black Cadillac limousine. He wanted to squire the women to their hotel in style. And he wanted to impress Ivana, who—like his mother and grandmother—was a beautiful immigrant. It worked. When she saw him sitting in the driver's seat, she laughed in delight. He did, too. He took her to the Americana hotel on Seventh Avenue, where the Beatles had once played and parts of *The Godfather* had been filmed. For his efforts, he got a kiss on the cheek.

The next day, he arranged to have a hundred roses sent to her room along with a card: "To Ivana, with affection. Donald."

When he knew they'd been delivered, he called her and invited her to lunch. Ivana couldn't make it because she had to work a fashion show. So he pitched dinner instead. She accepted, and they went back to Le Club.

"Have dinner with me tomorrow," he told her when they'd finished their meal.

But she couldn't. Her flight was the next evening.

They had lunch instead—at 21, a fancy club in midtown Manhattan. Donald negotiated a phone number out of Ivana, not knowing she was living with her boyfriend in Canada. Donald called her every day for months, and in October, flew to Montreal to watch her model fur. Later, he offered to sweep her away for Christmas. Ivana secured the blessing of her boyfriend and traveled first class to Aspen. Donald took her skiing, not knowing she'd been a competitive skier in her native Czechoslovakia. She pretended to be a novice on the slopes and then blew past him, humiliating him.

That time, he forgave her for making him look like a loser, and over dinner on New Year's Eve, he offered a proposal: "If you don't marry me, you'll ruin your life."

Ivana laughed, thinking he was joking. He wasn't. She paused, and then offered her answer. "My life is saved. I'll marry you."

On April 7, 1977, they married at the Marble Collegiate Church in front of six hundred people. He was thirty, and she was twenty-eight. Freddy, struggling deeply with alcoholism and living with their parents while he worked on a Trump maintenance crew, was the best man.

By the end of the year, Donald had given his wife two major projects. One was managing the interior design of the Grand Hyatt, where Donald had delivered the goods and partnered with the Hyatt Hotel to give new life to the old Commodore. The second was a child. They'd conceived on their honeymoon, and their baby boy was born on the anniversary of their engagement.

"What should we name him?" Trump asked his wife.

"Donald Junior."

Donald was initially skeptical. "You can't do that."

"Why not?"

"What if he's a loser?"

"What if he's a loser?" Donald had seen his brother Freddy, named for their father, flame out. It seemed risky.

Ivana overruled him. A second child came three years later, a girl. Ivana decided she'd name her daughter after herself, nicknaming her "Ivanka," which means "little Ivana."

Meanwhile, children weren't the only thing Trump was naming. He'd begun negotiating his biggest, most controversial deal yet, for a building he'd name after himself without hesitation: Trump Tower.

CHAPTER 5

KINGDOM of CARDS

AS A NEW FATHER, Trump continued his hunt for real estate. He found the perfect spot for something huge in Manhattan: a twelve-story department store near Central Park. The first time he made an inquiry about the historic building, which housed Bonwit Teller & Company, the corporate owners weren't interested. But he persisted, and eventually, when the company was in financial distress, they were willing to make a deal.

Trump still had to hustle to make his tower happen. Building in Manhattan is complicated. Sometimes one company owns the building and another owns the land beneath it, either of which might be leased (that is, rented for a certain period of time) by a separate company altogether. This was the case here with the land.

Trump also wanted to build a taller structure than was allowed. Here, he shrewdly mixed stores, offices, condominiums, and a public atrium to get around the regulations. He also negotiated the air rights of the famous Tiffany building next door, to increase the height of his building and to ensure no one erected anything higher there.

All of this, Trump had to make deals for: the building, the land, and the space to grow.

There was one remaining wrinkle.

Many considered the Bonwit Teller building a landmark, even though it didn't have official status as one.

The building opened in 1929, just before the historic stock market crash. Designed by the same firm that built Grand Central Station, the structure made a bold architectural statement for the era. The structure itself was plain limestone. But its entrance was spectacular. Crafted of platinum, bronze, hammered aluminum, and ceramics glazed in sunset hues, with tinted glass that lit up at night, the frieze was "a sparkling jewel in keeping with the character of the store," *American Architect* magazine wrote.

Sculptures of nearly naked women on top dancing with scarves were more controversial at first. But by the time Trump acquired the building, those rakish friezes were considered historically significant. The Metropolitan Museum of Art wanted them for its sculpture collection. A museum appraiser estimated they were worth around $200,000.

> ## Trump said he'd donate them to the museum. But he didn't.

Trump said he'd donate them to the museum. But he didn't. He ordered his workers instead to pulverize the dancing women with jackhammers. He also had the twenty-by-thirty-foot grillwork that had decorated the entrance cut into pieces.

The broken promise made the front page of the June 6, 1980, *New York Times*. When Trump talked to the reporter, he pretended to be a man named "John Baron," a vice president of the Trump Organization.

"The merit of these stones was not great enough to justify the effort to save them," he said, claiming he'd consulted three independent appraisers.

This was news to museum officials. A museum board member named Ashton Hawkins said, "How extraordinary. . . . Can you imagine the museum accepting them if they were not of artistic merit?"

Opinion writers at the *Times* let Trump have it: "Evidently, New York needs to make salvation of this kind of landmark mandatory and stop expecting that its developers will be good citizens and good sports." And, "Obviously big buildings do not make big human beings."

Two days later, Trump called the *Times* back, but this time as himself. He claimed that preserving the sculptures actually would

have cost $500,000 but that money wasn't even his biggest con-
cern. Public safety was.

"If one of those stones had slipped, people could have been
killed. To me, it would not have been worth that kind of risk."

But that wasn't all. "Let's say that I had given that junk to the
Met," Trump said. "They would have just put them in their base-
ment. I'll never have the goodwill of the Establishment, the taste-
makers of New York. Do you think, if I failed, these guys in New
York would be unhappy? They would be thrilled! Because they
have never tried anything on the scale that I am trying things in
this city. I don't care about their goodwill."

And in the end, Trump got the last laugh. Every time someone
wrote about the buildings, they'd say the destruction happened
"in order to make room for one of the world's most luxurious
buildings"—exactly the image he wanted.

The scandal over the friezes was just the beginning of trouble
Trump got himself into. He hired undocumented Polish immigrants
to demolish the building. They worked without hard hats, gloves, or
face masks to protect them from asbestos dust and other hazards
on the construction site. Trump's contractor paid them $4 to $5
an hour—less than a quarter of the going rate. He also didn't pay
into a pension fund as rules required.

"We worked in horrid, terrible conditions," a Polish worker told
the *New York Times*. "We were frightened illegal immigrants and
we did not know enough about our rights."

The workers filed suit and eventually settled in 1998 for $1.375
million. For years, the court kept the agreement secret from the
public. This is sometimes part of the terms of a settlement.

Other Trump business deals came under legal scrutiny. In 1979, a federal grand jury convened to study how Trump had gotten his Penn Central land option—and whether anything illegal had happened. FBI agents interviewed Trump twice, but the statute of limitations ran out and no charges were filed.

The next year, the US Attorney in Manhattan looked into Trump's Commodore deal, which some suspected had been too much of a gift to Trump. It also came to nothing.

And the FBI investigated the concrete supplier Trump used to build his tower, a felon and union leader named John Cody, an associate of Genovese mob boss Anthony "Fat Tony" Salerno.

Trump had built his tower using ready-mix concrete instead of steel. It would save him costs on fireproofing, but it was also risky. Workers had to pour the concrete quickly or it would harden and become useless. And in New York, concrete workers were notorious for being run by the mob, which made things hard for developers.

Although Trump usually bargained aggressively and sometimes didn't pay his employees what they were owed, he paid a premium for concrete, $8 million in all. Because Fat Tony was one of Roy Cohn's clients, Trump could be sure he wouldn't face a union strike, a competitive advantage.

A few years later, Fat Tony was brought down in what a prosecutor called "the largest and most vicious criminal business in the history of the United States." Trump was not charged with wrongdoing, although his building was part of the investigation.

The FBI also wanted to know whether Trump had secretly rewarded Cody with an apartment in Trump Tower in exchange for uninterrupted work. Trump said he hadn't. But later, an unemployed woman known to be cozy with Cody somehow managed to acquire three apartments downstairs from Donald and Ivana.

After Cody and the woman parted ways, Trump hit her with a $250,000 lawsuit, claiming she'd remodeled without permission. The woman filed a $20 million countersuit claiming Trump took kickbacks from contractors. Rather than face scrutiny from the courts, he settled for $500,000—twice what he'd sued her for in the first place.

In the midst of this, Trump sat down for a friendly television interview with a gossip columnist and TV personality named Rona Barrett. He wore his sandy-blond hair shoulder length and was dressed in a dark suit, white shirt, and striped, earth-tone necktie. The interview never aired, but Barrett asked a question he'd keep thinking about for the next twenty-five years.

"You're a mover. You are a doer," she said. "If you could make America perfect, how would you do it?"

Speaking softly, he said, "I think that much like the mind I think that America is using very, very little of its potential. I feel that this country, with the proper leadership, can go on to become what it once was, and I hope, and certainly hope, that it does go on to be what it should be."

She asked him what he'd do if he lost his fortune.

"Maybe," he said, "I'd run for president."

Trump wasn't as rich as people thought. His tax returns from 1978 and 1979 showed big losses: $406,379 and $3.4 million, respectively. His dad had to lend him $7.5 million in 1980 to cover his debts.

For now, Trump Tower was looking like a brilliant gamble. It had cost $200 million to build, but he made $300 million from the sales of the condominiums alone—and there was also office and retail space that would generate rent.

Though the building was marketed as having sixty-eight floors, it actually only has fifty-eight floors. This isn't the only Trump building that pads its height; at least seven of his buildings exaggerate their height by skipping numbers on the elevator buttons.

> **Trump's name, spelled in thirty-four-inch-high bronze letters, gleam on the wall.**

As much as Trump likes a tall building, he also likes glitz. Trump's name, spelled in thirty-four-inch-high bronze letters, gleam on the wall. The gold railings shimmer with the same shade Cadillac used. A soaring marble atrium in shades of pink and peach boasts a three-story waterfall and polished brass fittings.

Ivana influenced the interior design of the place, including overseeing the Trumps' 30,000-square-foot penthouse. She spared no expense or flourish, bragging that they imported a mountain's worth of Italian marble for the project.

"If something could be leafed in gold or upholstered with damask, it was," she said. "It was the eighties, and my aesthetic at the time was over-the-top glitz, glamour, and drama. My goal was to shock and amaze my guests when they walked into the space." The Trumps squabbled over what should be on the ceiling frescoes. Ivana wanted angels. Donald wanted warriors. He got his way. But

Ivana got a climate-controlled vault for her dozens of mink, sable, and chinchilla coats.

In their business, though, they were partners. She was driven, ambitious, and happy to be a mother. In addition to her work as a Trump organization executive, Ivana oversaw the children and their nannies, insisting her brood keep a tight schedule. She also wasn't afraid to spank a child who stepped out of line. At night, after helping her kids do their homework at the kitchen table, she and Trump would dress up for dinners and charity events. Tabloids loved covering the glamorous pair.

For his part, Trump focused on acquiring more properties. As Trump Tower went up, he also built Trump Plaza, a luxury co-op on the posh East Side of Manhattan. He got a tax break for the high-end housing after making a persuasive case the project would bring money back into the city.

In 1981, he picked up another pair of buildings: the Barbizon Plaza Hotel and the apartment building next to it. He planned to tear down both, but the people who lived in the rent-controlled apartment building objected. Enraged, Trump offered to move homeless people into the vacant apartments (the city declined his offer). He covered the windows in those vacant units with tinfoil and didn't make repairs. This amounted to harassment, a tenants' group argued. The fight continued for five years before Trump gave up and remodeled instead of replacing the buildings.

In 1982, he tried and failed to buy the *New York Daily News*. He also made a brand-new list *Forbes* magazine created: one of the wealthiest Americans. *Forbes* listed his net worth at $100 million (about $269 million in 2018 dollars). It was a feat of persuasion on his part that started with an all-afternoon meeting in Trump's huge office on Fifth Avenue.

First, Trump told a *Forbes* reporter the family was worth $900 million. The reporter, Jonathan Greenberg, had traveled the nation all year interviewing the super wealthy and was skeptical. Trump claimed he owned 80 percent of the Trump Organization's apartments—most of which, the journalist knew, Fred had built, not Donald.

"It amazed me when Donald claimed that he, and not his father, possessed 80 percent of the 23,000 apartments he said they had in Brooklyn, Queens and Staten Island," Greenberg said.

What's more, Trump said that those apartments "'were almost debt free and worth $40,000 each.'"

When Greenberg questioned the figure, "Trump shrugged and said, 'Okay, then $20,000 each.'"

Even that seemed high.

What's more, Trump had also fudged the location of his buildings in Queens, claiming they were in a more expensive neighborhood. Still, by Greenberg's revised figure of $9,000 per apartment, the Trump family would be worth $200 million.

Six weeks later, Trump's secretary called. She said she needed Greenberg's address so Trump could invite him to a party. Then Trump just happened to pass by, so she put him on the phone.

"I don't think that you have your facts 100 percent correct," Trump said. He argued he was worth more than the other developers in the category. "I mean, there's no contest."

Trump's pressure on Greenberg didn't end there. Trump's lawyer, Roy Cohn, called next. "Jon Greenberg . . . This is Roy.

Roy Cohn! You can't quote me! But Donny tells me you're putting together this list of rich people. He says you've got him down for just $200 million! That's way too low, way too low! Listen, I'm Donny's personal lawyer, but he said I could talk to you about this. I am sitting here looking at his current bank statement. It shows he's got more than $500 million in liquid assets, just cash. That's just Donald, nothing to do with Fred, and it's just cash." He concluded: "He's worth more than any of those other guys in this town!"

Greenberg wanted to take a look at the bank statement. He offered to send a messenger for it. Cohn wouldn't send the statement.

"Just trust me," he said.

Greenberg included Trump on the list that first year at $100 million. Trump's true net worth at the time was around $5 million, which would not have qualified him. Not by a long shot.

ABOVE: The Trump family attends the Horatio Alger Awards Dinner at the Waldorf Hotel in New York City, May 10, 1985. From left to right: Robert Trump, Fred Trump, Donald Trump, Ivana Trump, Elizabeth Trump, Mary Anne Trump, and Roy Cohn. *(Ron Galella/WireImage)*

Years later, when Greenberg thought about it, he realized that the hugeness of Trump's lies had an unexpected effect on him and his colleagues at Forbes. "Instead of believing that they were outright fabrications, my Forbes colleagues and I saw them simply as vain embellishments on the truth. We were so wrong."

One thing did have the potential to boost his wealth, and quickly: casino gambling. Gambling wasn't legal in New York State, or he'd have pushed for including it in the lobby of the Grand Hyatt New York. But in nearby Atlantic City, New Jersey, casinos were starting to generate stacks of cash. Trump wanted in . . . but he'd need land, and for land, he'd need money to leverage into loans. He'd made money on land sales in New York, his share of the Grand Hyatt was worth a lot . . . but his eyes were bigger than his bank account.

And money wasn't his only obstacle. To apply to own a casino, applicants couldn't have any ties to organized crime, and they couldn't have been charged with breaking any county, state, federal, or other laws. Trump had problems on both these counts: not only had he paid high prices for mob-delivered concrete, he'd been charged with discrimination in a federal housing suit, though he'd settled the matter.

At first, he simply didn't tell regulators about the racial bias suit. The regulators learned of it in the course of performing a background check on Trump. They also discovered Trump's Mafia ties. And by then, the New York concrete mob wasn't his only connection. Trump had leased property from associates of Philadelphia's Scarfo family for a potential casino. Regulators required he cancel the lease and buy the land instead from the Mafia associates. Trump put up $8 million for the property, almost triple what it had cost the sellers three years earlier.

Still, even though Trump was guilty of past discrimination and had mob ties, the commission was willing to look the other way. They also didn't mind that he had not yet lined up financing or that he lacked experience in the casino business. Atlantic City was struggling through desperate times, and the commission was willing to gamble on Trump if it meant the city had a shot at becoming great again. Trump got his casino license from the Casino Control Commission in March 1982.

Trump needed a partner, so he struck a deal with experienced Las Vegas casino people at Harrah's. Trump's job would be to supply the land and the casino license; Harrah's would pay for construction, arrange for financing, and manage the casino once it was built. For extra money, Trump also agreed to do construction, which started in 1983. Harrah's at Trump Plaza opened in the spring of 1984, just a few months after his son Eric was born.

> One thing Trump understood was that the wealthier he looked, the more likely it was that he could get in on big deals.

One thing Trump understood was that the wealthier he looked, the more likely it was that he could get in on big deals. With that aim, Trump played the role of John Barron again that same year (but this time, with two *R*s in *Barron*). In character, he argued with Greenberg, who was working on the magazine's annual ranking.

Their 1993 list had put his worth at $200 million. This wasn't nearly enough, "Barron" said, claiming that Trump was worth a billion dollars.

Greenberg was skeptical. He and "Barron" debated the numbers. In the end, Greenberg was no match for the salesmanship of "Barron," who told him once again that Donald now owned most of the family company.

"Most of the assets have been consolidated to Mr. Trump," Trump told Greenberg under the guise of John Barron. It wasn't true this time, either. But Fred didn't care what Donald told the media, and Donald got his way, creating the illusion of vast wealth. This strategy made him a more attractive lending target for banks. It also burnished his brand. Not only did *Trump* stand for luxury, it also stood for wild success.

Trump made other moves to expand his empire. In 1983, he bought the New Jersey Generals, a team in the United States Football League. The USFL was founded to give fans a spring football season. Trump wanted his league to compete directly with the NFL, hoping to ultimately force the two to merge. This could mean big money for people like him, who had bought USFL teams at a relatively bargain rate.

With this in mind, he helped launch an antitrust lawsuit against the NFL, arguing the league had a monopoly. The USFL won the case . . . and was awarded one dollar. Because it was an antitrust settlement, the fee was tripled to $3, not quite the riches he was seeking. When the USFL shut down before playing its 1986 season, largely as a result of Trump's aggressive tactics, the league was $163 million in debt.

That same year, his friend and mentor Roy Cohn was disbarred for dishonesty, fraud, deceit, and misrepresentation. Trump stuck by him. The men had often talked fifteen to twenty times a day on the phone. But when Cohn was critically ill with AIDS later that year, Trump—a self-identified germophobe—steered clear.

"I can't believe he's doing this to me. . . . Donald pisses ice water," Cohn said before he died.

TRUMP WAS IN A TIME OF TRANSITION. BECAUSE of his aggressive shenanigans and high media profile, Trump was no longer thought of as a young man on the rise. He was forty and entering middle age, and the public had formed opinions about him.

The city's tabloid newspapers loved Trump for his wealth, his brashness, and his knack for delivering stories that made for good ink even if they weren't strictly true. It was entertainment, and that's what the tabloids were all about.

Journalists at the *New York Times* saw him differently. They accused him of acting like a "petty" slumlord who harassed his tenants daily, actions that didn't receive equal coverage to the inches of newsprint devoted to his lavish lifestyle. He was also becoming known as a liar, but people found it amusing—the harmless exaggerations of a salesman.

Trump, who didn't care *what* people thought, as long as they were thinking about him, started looking overseas for conquests. After sitting next to a Russian ambassador at a luncheon, and then being visited by the ambassador, who flattered him, Donald and Ivana were invited on an all-expenses-paid trip to Moscow. Trump told people he was going to build a hotel across the street from the Kremlin. He even thought he might take a crack at international diplomacy.

Trump met with a doctor who'd won the 1985 Nobel Peace Prize (along with a Soviet physician). Querying the doctor for information about Soviet president Mikhail Gorbachev, Trump said, "I intend to call my good friend Ronnie (meaning President Ronald Reagan) to make me a plenipotentiary ambassador for the United States with Gorbachev."

"Those are the words he used," the doctor said. "And he said he would go to Moscow and he'd sit down with Gorbachev, and then he took his thumb and he hit the desk and he said, 'And within one hour the Cold War would be over!'"

Trump had long dreamed of staving off the possibility of nuclear holocaust and had told the *New York Times* in 1984 that his negotiating skills could bring that about.

The reporter was unimpressed and called it "the naive musing of an optimistic, deluded young man who has never lost at anything he has tried."

Trump and Ivana took the free trip to Russia, though, traveling on Independence Day in 1987. From their base in Lenin's suite at the National Hotel, they scouted potential hotel sites, intending to build something in partnership with the Soviet government.

Trump did not get a chance to negotiate the end of the Cold War, but he did start making his political views public after that trip. That fall, he spent almost $100,000 on full-page ads in three major newspapers, criticizing the United States' foreign policy toward the nation's allies, and arguing, according to the Associated Press, that America was paying to defend countries that could defend themselves. "The world is laughing at America's politicians as we protect ships we don't own, carrying oil we don't need, destined for allies who won't help."

Some suggested he was seeking the presidency.

Some suggested he was seeking the presidency.

"I'm not running for president," he said, "but if I did . . . I'd win. There, I said it. I didn't think I would, but I did." That October, he planned a trip to New Hampshire, where presidential campaigns are often launched.

In the meantime, his partnership with Harrah's had imploded. He bought them out and renamed the former joint operation Trump Plaza. But one casino wasn't enough. He snapped up a second one after the Casino Control Commission denied the Hilton Corporation a license because of the company's alleged ties with a mob lawyer. Trump bought the place without ever visiting it. He named this one Trump Castle Hotel & Casino, and he installed Ivana as vice president and chief operating officer. Neither Donald nor Ivana had any experience running casinos, so he brought in some pros, including a devout Mormon and family man named Steve Hyde, who was skilled at managing both casinos and Trump's moods and rough personal style.

Years later, Trump's business associates told a reporter at *Newsweek* that his characteristic aggression grew worse during this period. And, they said, he stopped treating the staff with thoughtfulness and care. He also became increasingly reckless and convinced of his own greatness. Around the time Trump got his casino license in 1982, he was reportedly diagnosed with a metabolic imbalance by a Manhattan endocrinologist, who prescribed a drug for treatment. The drug prescribed, diethylpropion, an amphetamine derivative, can cause delusions, hyperactivity, and paranoia. It is highly addictive if used for more than six months. According to the journalist, who said he obtained Trump's medical file and interviewed one of his friends, Trump took the drug for years.

In addition to acquiring casinos, Trump played the stock market. He took out loans and bought $70 million worth of shares of Holiday Inn, which owned Harrah's. Trump also spent $62 million on 10 percent of the Bally Manufacturing Corporation, which owned an Atlantic City casino. Both companies feared he'd attempt a hostile takeover. Instead, Trump sold his shares back to the companies.

This angered the Casino Control Commission, which saw Trump's actions as an unfair attempt to harm his competitors.

It seemed that Trump could not manage to stay out of trouble with the authorities, however. Although the Casino Control Commission renewed Trump's license, the Federal Trade Commission found that his actions in purchasing his rivals' stock violated federal antitrust laws when Trump failed to report the stock purchases of Holiday Inn and Bally Manufacturing. He ended up paying a $750,000 penalty in settlement . . . without admitting fault.

During this era, Trump was focused on acquiring trophies. A French-made helicopter. A huge yacht whose sinks and screws were plated in gold. An airline. A 118-room palace in Florida called

ABOVE: Trump promised he wouldn't use junk bonds to fund his crown jewel casino, the Trump Taj Mahal. He broke this pledge. *(John Margolies/Library of Congress)*

Mar-a-Lago. New York's legendary Plaza Hotel. He spent beyond his means, buying luxuries he didn't have the cash for. He borrowed the money, assuming he'd be able to pay it all back with casino profits.

Trump already owned two Atlantic City casinos, but he was legally allowed to have one more, so he sought to build his crown jewel, the Trump Taj Mahal. Building yet another casino would mean even more debt, and it was a risky time for that. The stock market crashed on October 19, 1987, six months after Trump's initial negotiation to purchase a controlling interest in the company that owned the Taj, which was only half completed at that time. Trump sought financing to complete construction and eventual purchase, arguing that the market crash wouldn't affect his ability to get bank loans, and he pressed on with the Taj, which would be the biggest casino in the world. He promised regulators he wouldn't use "ridiculous" junk bonds to finance the billion-dollar project.

Meanwhile, there was trouble at his second casino, the Castle. Against the advice of Trump's experts, but with Trump's permission, Ivana had invested $40 million in luxury suites to attract wealthy gamblers. The Castle was losing money and competing with Trump's first Atlantic City operation, causing tension.

> He sent Ivana back to New York to run the Plaza Hotel. Distraught, she wept at her good-bye party.

He sent Ivana back to New York to run the Plaza Hotel. Distraught, she wept at her good-bye party.

"Look at this," Trump told her employees. "I had to buy a $350 million hotel just to get her out of here and look at how she's crying. Now, that's why I'm sending her back to New York. I don't need this, some woman crying. I need somebody strong in here to take care of this place."

Ivana cried again when Trump held a press conference about Ivana's position at the Plaza. "My wife, Ivana, is a brilliant manager," he said. "I will pay her one dollar a year and all the dresses she can buy."

ABOVE: Donald and Ivana Trump with their children: Don Jr., Ivanka, and Eric. New York City, 1988. *(Norman Parkinson Achive/Iconic Images/Getty Images)*

Ivana was hardly a softie. She'd entered her first marriage to a fellow skier from Austria to escape communist Czechoslovakia. She was a demanding manager, working the same long hours as her husband while she also oversaw the raising of their children. But their marriage was in deep trouble.

Trump had begun an affair with a stunning blond woman he'd met in 1987 at the launch party for his bestselling book, *The Art of the Deal*. Marla Maples, a model and actress, was much younger than Ivana. She had a beautiful face and figure. Unlike Ivana, she had no major career aspirations, which he preferred.

Eventually, he made no secret of his relationship with Maples, who even followed the family on one of their ski vacations, provoking a public spat between the women.

Around the time the affair started, he and Ivana reportedly stopped being intimate. But in 1989, when he was recovering from plastic surgery on his scalp to hide his growing bald spot, he reportedly initiated violent sex with her, cursing her and claiming that her plastic surgeon had "ruined" him. Then he held back her arms, pulled out her hair, and forced himself on her. She described the incident under oath during their divorce trial, which is sealed and not available for public review. But a journalist named Harry Hurt III obtained a copy and described it in a book he wrote about Trump, writing that she told friends "he raped me." Trump denied both harming his wife and having had scalp surgery.

That same year, a white woman who was jogging in Central Park was raped and beaten and went into a coma for twelve days. A group of five black and Latino boys was arrested. The boys confessed and were found guilty, although DNA found at the crime scene belonged to a single assailant—not one of the boys. Nonetheless, they were convicted. Later they said they'd been coerced into confessing.

Trump took out expensive full-page ads in the *New York Times*, the *Daily News*, the *New York Post*, and *Newsday* calling for reinstatement of the death penalty for people like those boys.

> "Muggers and murderers . . . should be forced to suffer and, when they kill, they should be executed for their crimes," he wrote.

"Muggers and murderers . . . should be forced to suffer and, when they kill, they should be executed for their crimes," he wrote.

Most news coverage, though, Trump didn't have to pay for. Trump loved this. Advertising cost a fortune, and if he could stay in the media's spotlight without having to pay for it, all the better. The spectacular unraveling of his marriage generated many headlines for him, including one that quoted Marla Maples as saying Trump gave her the "Best Sex I've Ever Had."

Not all headlines were as flattering.

The Castle was awash in red ink, and he soon would be drowning in it. As financial disasters went, this one would be absolutely huge—and the whole world would be watching.

CHAPTER 6

PARTING a SEA of RED INK

AS HIS FINANCIAL EMPIRE teetered, Trump sat down with *Playboy* magazine for an interview that would be published in March 1990. Trump's finances were in tough shape, the worst of his life. Although he had assets worth $3.6 billion, he had $3.4 billion worth of debts, and only $17.1 million cash on hand. He was going to have a hard time paying the interest on his loans. He didn't let this on to the journalist, though.

Trump let the reporter believe his casino kingdom was gushing money. The reporter wrote that Trump had more than $900 million in cash lying around, with $50 million more a week churning in, not to mention assets of $3.7 billion. To Trump, lying to a reporter wasn't wrong. It was all about putting a good spin on things. He thought he was putting his best foot forward, the way any businessman or politician would.

In that interview, Trump fudged his cash situation and spoke of big deals, the biggest of which was an enormous development he wanted to build on New York's West Side. He'd call it "Trump City," an "architectural masterpiece" that would keep New York competitive with the New Jersey waterfront. There'd be housing galore. He'd construct the world's tallest building there. He wanted to let the reporter believe that great things seemed possible, including the presidency—not that he had any interest.

> "I don't want to be president," he told the magazine. "I'm one hundred percent sure. I'd change my mind only if I saw this country continue to go down the tubes."

"I don't want to be president," he told the magazine. "I'm one hundred percent sure. I'd change my mind only if I saw this country continue to go down the tubes."

But if he did become president, he'd believe in "extreme military strength," and "he wouldn't trust anyone." Not the Russians, and not our allies.

In addition to worrying about his finances and global politics, Trump worried about the fate of his kids.

"Statistically, my children have a very bad shot," he said. "Children of successful people are generally very, very troubled, not successful."

Despite their marriage ending, he and Ivana were raising their children to value work. He'd also shown them how to be competitors. On the ski slopes, for example, Trump would hook their jackets with his pole and zoom past them. Forget conventions. Winning was about finding leverage over the competition, wherever you could.

And his kids showed promise. Don, Ivanka, and Eric sold lemonade to their bodyguard and other household staff. They'd even chipped rocks to make them look like arrowheads, buried them in the woods, and sold them to their friends for $5 after "discovering" them. They were born entrepreneurs.

But the end of their parents' marriage had been hard on the three. Ivanka hadn't seen it coming. Don Jr. wouldn't talk with his father for a year.

These were dark days for Trump.

As his marriage ended and the extent of his financial troubles began to sink in, he was living in his tower by himself in an apartment, eating hamburgers and fries delivered from a nearby deli. He hardly left his room and spent evenings staring at his bedroom ceiling while he talked on the phone. His tawny hair nearly reached his collar. A friend compared him to Howard Hughes, the business tycoon, movie producer, and aviator who died as a gaunt recluse with overgrown hair and toenails. Trump told the friend that he didn't mind the comparison, because Hughes was a hero.

Trump had financial problems and they were largely of his own making. For one thing, even though he'd promised not to fund the Taj with junk bonds, he did anyway, signing a deal for $675 million at 14 percent interest, which he would need a heavy flow of cash to cover. What's more, his three casinos were competing against one another, cannibalizing revenue. About $58 million he'd been able to make earlier at the Castle and Plaza shifted to the Taj in 1990, its opening year.

And then there was the matter of the Trump Shuttle. Airlines were another business he knew nothing about, and here, he'd borrowed $380 million to purchase a route from a failing airline. He tricked the planes out with gold-plated bathroom fixtures, betting fliers would flock to his fancy lavatories. When they didn't, the business failed.

Also in 1990, another disaster in the air struck—a helicopter carrying three of his best casino executives crashed, killing them all. This meant he had to run the day-to-day operations. He alienated managers who remained, and things got so bad he was afraid that gamblers on lucky streaks would put him financially under.

Not long after his *Playboy* interview, Trump couldn't scrape up the cash to make a $43 million interest payment to people who'd invested in Taj junk bonds. The day after he missed that payment, he celebrated his forty-fourth birthday (which was actually two days earlier) in the Crystal Ballroom of the Trump Castle. He had only ten days to pay up, or he could lose the Taj.

The pressure was intense, and he had to put on a brave face surrounded by reminders of everything that was at risk. The party featured giant replicas of his casinos and a Trump Shuttle jet—

the latter large enough to conceal the *Lifestyles of the Rich and Famous* television host Robin Leach, who popped out to wish Trump a happy birthday. Meanwhile, the comedian Joe Piscopo impersonated Frank Sinatra and made jokes about Japanese people, and a George H. W. Bush lookalike told revelers that Trump should be president.

> But Trump had more immediate concerns. His total debt was $3.4 billion—way more than his dad could cover, even though he'd relied on his father to fix his money problems in the past.

But Trump had more immediate concerns. His total debt was $3.4 billion—way more than his dad could cover, even though he'd relied on his father to fix his money problems in the past. His debt was bigger than the gross domestic product of many countries at the time. And he was personally liable for $832.5 million, meaning he could lose his home. If Trump didn't pay back the loans, he could drag the banks down with him, too.

The banks weren't the only outside parties at risk.

During this time, Trump didn't pay many of the contractors who worked on his properties, bankrupting some. A report in *USA Today* found at least sixty lawsuits from people accusing Trump of stiffing them on their bills. These weren't big companies. They were often individuals: plumbers and painters. People who install chandeliers. Carpenters. Bartenders and waiters working at his resorts and clubs. Trump's companies were cited two dozen times for failure to pay workers overtime or minimum wage. On the Trump Taj Mahal alone, the New Jersey Casino Control Commission found at least 253 complaints by subcontractors— the people who built the walls and plumbed the bathrooms and hung the chandeliers.

In one typical strong-arm deal, Trump ordered $100,000 worth of pianos for the Taj and then refused to pay more than $70,000 of the tab. The difference came directly from the pocket of the owner of the small business, causing his business to stagnate for a couple of years until it could recover.

Trump used the legal system to his advantage, betting that most people didn't have the money to fight him. Trump claimed in many cases that the contractors had done inferior work. But in one of those cases, with a decades-old cabinet company, he immediately said they could work on future Trump projects. A real estate agent he'd shorted on commissions said he used "whimsy" to decide whether he wanted to pay people who worked for him. And in many cases, these people had to take pennies on the dollar or get nothing at all.

Trump fared far better than these creditors. Ironically, the sheer size of his debt actually helped him. It was better for the banks to keep his business limping along than for him to go bankrupt, because then even the banks wouldn't get paid at all. His creditors made him a deal: In addition to getting a $20 million loan and better terms for other money he'd borrowed, Trump would step down from his businesses and keep his personal expenses below $450,000 a month.

Even while being put on an allowance, Trump drove a hard bargain with the banks, said his friend Roger Stone, a roguish political strategist who'd helped Trump sniff out a run for the presidency. "The man has ice water in his veins. He says to the bankers: 'I'm worth more to you alive than dead, so you have two choices. You can get screwed and lose everything, or you can work with me, and we'll work our way out of this.' It's brilliant, and he's fearless. I mean, the guy is completely fearless."

Trump made it three months before he ran short of $1.1 million in interest that he owed. Once again, the banks were in a pickle. They made Trump put his airline and yacht up for sale. In return, they'd postpone $245 million in payments.

Three more months passed, and once again, Trump was short. He and his father came up with a plan. It wasn't legal for Trump to take a loan and not report it, so in mid-December, Fred Trump wrote a $3.35 million check that was used to buy 670 blackjack chips worth $5,000 each. Fred had no intention of playing those chips. The money could be kept by the casino. The next day, Fred sent over $150,000 more in exchange for thirty chips. With that $3.5 million total, Trump could make his payments. He didn't get away with the fraud; he ended up having to pay the Casino Control Commission $65,000 in fines for taking money from an unauthorized source.

Even a multimillion-dollar gift from his father wasn't enough to keep his life from falling apart. Ivana divorced him in 1991 for "cruel and inhuman treatment," stating that he "verbally abused and demeaned" her, and that he lied. And by 1992, all three of Trump's casinos had gone bankrupt. In addition, the Plaza Hotel filed for bankruptcy, which cost Trump 49 percent of the company. This, he had to turn over to his lenders. His debt was reorganized at better terms for Trump, and the consolidated company was renamed Trump Hotels and Casino Resorts. The Chapter 11 reorganization also helped reduce Trump's personal debt by about $750 million, or four-fifths of the total.

> ## Despite this, Trump didn't give up on himself.

Despite this, Trump didn't give up on himself.

In 1993, he tried making a deal with the Agua Caliente Band of Cahuilla Indians to run a casino for them. When this didn't work out, he complained to Congress that Indian casinos were unfair to "little guys" like him. He told the House Natural Resources Subcommittee on Native American affairs that he'd prepared a speech, but he wasn't going to give it because it was "boring."

Then he launched into a dramatic and unsupported claim: "Organized crime is rampant on Indian reservations," he said. "If it continues as a threat, it is my opinion that it will blow. It will blow sky high. It will be the biggest scandal ever or one of the biggest scandals since Al Capone."

Trump also said that the operators might be faking their claim to run casinos: "They don't look like Indians to me, and they don't look like Indians to Indians, and a lot of people are laughing at it," he said.

Trump's remarks about "looking Indian" did not land well. Representative George Miller, a California Democrat, scolded Trump:

ABOVE: Trump and Marla Maples wed in December 1993 before more than 1,000 guests, TV crews, gossip columnists, and paparazzi. *(Judie Burstein/Globe Photos/ZUMA Press, Inc./ Alamy Stock)*

"Thank God that is not the test of whether or not people have rights in this country or not."

Tribes have requirements for people to claim membership. At a minimum, a person must be a descendant of someone on the original tribal list of members or related to a tribal member who is a descendant.

Trump's inflammatory statements alienated at least one politician he needed as an ally for his projects.

But life went on, and eight days later, Trump and Maples had a daughter together, Tiffany. And two months later, in December, they were married. Over a thousand guests attended, including seventeen TV crews, assorted gossip columnists, and ninety paparazzi.

"There wasn't a wet eye in the place," one writer quipped.

TRUMP WAS LUCKY WITH THE TIMING OF HIS business disasters. In 1978, the United States updated its bankruptcy laws to give more leverage to the person in debt. Trump benefited directly. It would have cost the banks a fortune in legal fees to recoup their money. Making a deal was the safer, quicker bet.

Plus, Trump was a celebrity. It didn't matter that his fame generally came from outrageous statements and behavior. Trump put on a great show, and people loved watching it. He loved knowing he had an audience, even if he sometimes exaggerated its size. When he paid $200,000 to serve as grand marshal of a Veteran's Day parade in New York in 1995, newspapers reported a half a million people attended and 26,000 marched. Trump insisted the crowd size was even bigger: 1.4 million.

In his darkest days financially, his strategy to seek the spotlight paid off. By letting him continue being Trump, the banks minimized their catastrophic losses.

Trump, meanwhile, maximized them—at least when it came to the IRS. In 1995, he reported an astronomical loss on his tax return: $915.7 million. By reporting such a titanic loss, he was off the hook for federal income taxes on an equal amount of income for successive years, until his cumulative net gains exceeded this amount.

The same year he lost almost a billion dollars, he sold stock in his casinos to the public. Investors funneled $140 million into the company. In 1996 he sold two of his casinos to the public company for $100 million more than their market value, paying himself an $880,000 commission. This also shifted the debt on the casinos from himself to the Trump Hotels and Casino Resorts company.

It marked a big turning point in his personal fortune.

By October of 1996, Trump had sold his half of the Grand Hyatt, had for the time being managed his debt, and made his way back onto *Forbes*'s list, where his net worth was estimated to be $450 million. (Trump argued he was worth more than the tally—over $2 billion.)

Also in 1996, he made his first venture into television. After Maples cohosted the Miss Universe pageant, Trump invested in the broadcast rights for its parent company. The pageant combined two of his interests: beautiful women and real estate deals.

Under its auspices, he could travel to cities around the world, feeling them out for future Trump Towers and establishing himself as an international entrepreneur.

The pageant enterprise ultimately was not a success in the United States when it came to ratings, which dwindled during the time of his ownership. But it did help him get a foothold in global real estate ventures.

> **Russia remained a country he wanted to conquer.**

Russia remained a country he wanted to conquer. The year he bought the pageant, he traveled again to Moscow to see if he could strike a deal for Trump properties there. He showed up late for a meeting with representatives of Russian president Boris Yeltsin, and brought a pair of young Russian women. He did not close a deal, and his marriage to Maples would soon fall apart (a divorce would follow two years later, in 1999).

But he was still swinging for the fences as a real estate developer in the States. The West Side Yards he'd told *Playboy* about in 1990 were still in play, and a connection in Russia wanted to help him put a giant bronze statue of Christopher Columbus—taller than the Statue of Liberty—right on the river at the yards. The statue would be a gift from Moscow, Trump said. "It's got forty million dollars' worth of bronze in it."

Trump crossed paths with Russians at his casinos, too. By this time, the Taj Mahal had become a hotspot for Russian mobsters who lived in Brooklyn. In 1998, Trump had to pay the IRS $477,000

in settlement for allegedly breaking rules that required the casino to report gamblers who cashed out more than $10,000 a day. The fine was the largest ever that time for violations of the Bank Secrecy Act, which is intended to foil money launderers.

In November 1998, Trump caught his first glimpse of Melania Knauss, a Slovenian-born model, at a party during Fashion Week in New York.

"I went crazy," he said.

"He wanted my number," Melania said, "but he was with a date, so of course I didn't give it to him. I said, 'I am not giving you my number; you give me yours, and I will call you.' I wanted to see what

ABOVE: The Trump family gathers for Donald Trump's 50th birthday party at Trump Tower in New York City. June 13, 1996. From left to right: Eric Trump, Donald Trump Jr., Tiffany Trump, Ivanka Trump, Donald Trump, and Marla Maples. *(Ron Galella/Getty)*

kind of number he would give me—if it was a business number, what is this? I'm not doing business with you."

Trump gave Melania all of his numbers.

"It was a great chemistry and energy," she said. "We had a great time. We started to talk. And, you know, something was there right away."

Meanwhile, Trump's father died in 1999, presumably dividing his considerable estate among Trump and his three surviving siblings. It was a huge loss for Trump. His father had been his role model, his inspiration, and at times, his savior.

But Trump kept looking ahead. He was thinking seriously about pursuing the presidency.

In January 2000, Trump released a book called *The America We Deserve*, outlining his political vision for the nation. "Maybe our next great leader—one with the cunning of Franklin Roosevelt, the guts of Harry Truman, the resilience of Richard Nixon, and the optimism of Ronald Reagan—is walking down Fifth Avenue right now, straight through the heart of this land of dreamers and shakers—this land that I love."

Although Trump had contributed to both political parties and identified as a Republican, he was looking at the Reform Party for his run. They'd made a good showing in the 1992 and 1996 presidential elections, with businessman Ross Perot as a candidate. The Reform Party might be a shortcut to power, the way buying a USFL team might have been a novel way into NFL ownership.

Trump's "brief and flamboyant" run, as the *New York Times* described it, ended in conflict with the party.

The party's interim head accused Trump of using the party as a tool for self-promotion. "We're taking our party back to our very principles, and exploiters such as Donald Trump will not be able to exploit us again—and he realizes it."

Trump saw it differently. He said he didn't want to be in a party that had among its members former Ku Klux Klan leader David Duke.

Trump released a statement about his departure from the race on Valentine's Day 2000: "I have consistently stated that I would spend my time, energy and money on a campaign, not just to get a large number of votes, but to win," he said. "There would be no other purpose, other than winning, for me to run."

He returned his focus to building his business profile, sometimes in controversial ways.

On September 11, 2001, terrorists hijacked four planes and crashed them into the World Trade Center, the Pentagon, and a field in Pennsylvania after passengers fought back. That very day, Trump mentioned to a New York news station that the collapse of the Twin Towers meant he now had the tallest building in the borough.

> Trump was not correct.
> A building at 70 Pine Street
> became the tallest after the Twin
> Towers fell, according to the
> Council on Tall Buildings and
> Urban Habitat.

Trump was not correct. A building at 70 Pine Street became the tallest after the Twin Towers fell, according to the Council on Tall Buildings and Urban Habitat.

Trump also dreamed of rebuilding the Twin Towers, just as they were, only stronger and a little taller. He hated the design that ultimately was chosen. "The design for the Freedom Tower is an egghead design, designed by an egghead," he said.

The architect's spokesman speculated that Trump wanted that extra floor to "make room for his name."

By then, even with all his losses, Trump's name was poised to take a quantum leap forward. In May 2002, the wildly popular reality television show *Survivor* was shooting its finale at Trump Wollman Rink in Central Park, which Trump had managed to fix in 1986 in just four months after New York City's overly complex rehab plans had stalled out for six years. Trump had a front-row seat at the *Survivor* event, and the producer of the show, Mark Burnett, told the story of Trump's construction feat to the crowd.

Afterward, Trump buttonholed him and said they should "do something together sometime."

Later that year, while working in a Brazilian jungle, Burnett hatched the idea of a show about people seeking jobs and wealth in another jungle: New York City.

There would be thirteen weeks, and candidates would compete against each other until one lucky winner walked off with a dream job. Burnett would call it *The Apprentice*. And he knew just who ought to host.

On a trip to New York, Burnett called Trump from the airport, hoping to set up a meeting while he was in town.

Trump invited him to the tower immediately. "Just tell the door-man, and he'll send you right up."

Trump loved the idea, but when Burnett pitched Trump's agent, the agent balked. Dejected, Burnett went back to Trump, not sure how the mogul would take the news.

Trump directed his assistant to deliver the agent a note that said *You're fired.* Starting with the first season in 2003, this became the catchphrase to one of the highest-rated shows on television.

Not only had Trump rebounded from bankruptcy and divorce, he'd found love a third time, and in the midst of everything, he'd become the biggest television star in the nation, on a show that presented him as rich, savvy, commanding, and knowledgeable about America's obsession: money and how to make it.

CHAPTER 7

The ART of
an IMAGE

FORBES, 2005, WORLD'S Richest People list:

America's love affair with The Donald reaching impossibly new highs; his reality show, The Apprentice, *was prime-time television's highest-rated series last year. . . . After nearly defaulting on its debt obligations, Trump's gaming properties to reorganize . . . No matter. For Donald, real estate is where his real wealth lies. Over 18 million square feet of prime Manhattan space.*

Forbes was one thing: a respected business magazine with about a million subscribers. It was good for Trump to appear on their list of the world's wealthiest, which is why he took the time to argue that their valuations were too low.

But *The Apprentice* was something even better.

The prime-time television show launched Trump into a new orbit of fame. It cemented his image in the United States as a gifted and down-to-earth businessman, and in the 2003–2004 season, 20.7 million Americans were riveted weekly by his performance. The season finale that first year boasted 40 million viewers.

And little wonder. He'd had plenty of practice living his life as performance art for decades. He'd admitted as much back in 1990 in that interview with *Playboy*.

"The show is 'Trump,'" he said, "and it is sold-out performances everywhere."

Between September and November of *The Apprentice*'s second season, NBC generated $106 million in ad revenue. The show was

ABOVE: The TV show *The Apprentice* launched Donald Trump into celebrity status. Here, the Trump family walks the red carpet for *The Celebrity Apprentice* in 2015 in New York. From left to right: Lara Yunaska, Eric Trump, Melania Trump, Barron Trump, Donald Trump, Ivanka Trump, Donald Trump Jr., and Tiffany Trump. *(Debby Wong/Shutterstock)*

so popular that NBC executives told their advertisers Trump had saved the network after departure of the popular series *Friends*.

That was great news for NBC, but it didn't mean everything was going well for Trump's businesses.

When *The Apprentice* was soaring, Trump Hotels and Casino Resorts cratered. The company filed for bankruptcy in 2004 and Trump lost his job as the CEO, though he remained on the board of the company, which was renamed Trump Entertainment Resorts. Also, he was cut out of a casino management deal he'd made in 2000 with the Twenty-Nine Palms Band of Mission Indians. The twelve-member tribe determined that paying his company *not* to manage their business was the safer financial bet, so they paid him $6 million in 2004 to go away.

What's more, Trump had lost his shot at developing the West Side Yards when the Hong Kong investors in control of the property sold it. He earned management and construction fees, but New York would never have a Trump City with a giant bronze statue of Christopher Columbus on the shore.

Despite all this, people believed Trump had the golden touch, and that's what mattered the most. His brand was everything to him, and the television exposure was working wonders in building it.

He was also on a roll in his personal life. He and Melania married in 2005. The sparkling, sixty-pound dress she wore to the ceremony cost $100,000 (she changed into a lighter one for the reception at Mar-a-Lago). The guest list glittered, too, with attendees like Elton John, Heidi Klum, Shaquille O'Neal, Simon Cowell, Barbara Walters, Billy Joel, Chris Christie, and former president Bill Clinton and first lady Hillary Clinton.

Fame gave Trump a new way to make money without the same level of risk he'd faced as a builder. Glowing with celebrity, Trump lent his name to a dizzying variety of products, including eyeglasses, suits, neckties, cologne, deodorant, water, and steaks. Each one was packaged to make it sound as luxurious as possible.

He didn't stop at consumer goods. Because business schools were already talking about Trump's TV show in their classes, he trademarked Trump University, which promised students "the opportunity to learn directly from Donald J. Trump himself."

> "Trump University is going to be very big."

"Trump University is going to be very big," Trump told author Timothy L. O'Brien in 2005. "It's an investment in banking and education."

That same year, Trump entered into a one-year pact with a company called Bayrock, which had opened offices in Trump Tower, to build a luxury high-rise on the site of an abandoned pencil factory in Moscow. Nothing came of the deal, but it wouldn't be the last time he'd work with Bayrock.

In 2006, the year Trump released a vodka named after himself, his fifth child was born. Trump called the boy Barron, the name he'd sometimes use when talking with reporters about his business. Riding a wave of celebrity, he accepted invitations to participate in celebrity golf tournaments, like one in Lake Tahoe, where he met other famous people—everyone from professional athletes to adult film stars and Playboy models.

Trump had also started selling his name to buildings he did not construct in exchange for 8 to 15 percent of the gross sales price. This required no financial outlay for Trump. There was value in it for builders; in New York, Trump condominiums fetched a 36 percent premium in 2005.

Trump introduced one of those partnerships in 2006 from the set of *The Apprentice*.

Perched in a burgundy leather chair, he belted out a description of the glorious building to come: "When it's completed in 2008, this brilliant, $370 million work of art will be an awe-inspiring masterpiece."

Trump had two partners on Trump SoHo, Bayrock and the Sapir Organization, both of which had ties to Russia. The Trump organization would get money for the use of the Trump name, as well as management fees. He would also own a minority share. Don Jr. and Ivanka, both graduates of Wharton, handled sales and some marketing, as they'd become fully involved in Trump's business as senior executives.

Even as Trump had reduced his financial risk by only licensing his name to others, who'd in turn build his projects, this particular partnership introduced new risks to the organization. For one thing, his contact at Bayrock, Felix Sater, had a criminal record.

Sater, a Russian who emigrated to Brighton Beach as a child, lost his Wall Street trader license and went to jail for a year for stabbing a man in the face in 1991. In 1998 the former stockbroker was arrested for being part of a $40-million stock fraud and money-laundering scheme linked to Russian mobsters and four Mafia families. Authorities busted Sater after he neglected to pay the bill on a storage locker in Soho, coincidentally located right across the street from the future Trump tower.

Inside the locker, police found guns and a gym bag that had paperwork outlining the money-laundering scheme and the offshore accounts where Sater and his partners had stashed their loot.

Sater pleaded guilty and avoided jail because he had turned into a government informant. Sater was providing the government information when he became an executive at the Bayrock Group and started pitching Trump on real estate partnerships around the world.

Meanwhile, Trump had filed a lawsuit against Timothy O'Brien, author of *Trump Nation*, which pegged Trump's wealth at between $150 million and $250 million, rather than the $6 billion Trump sometimes claimed. Newspaper coverage of the book had embarrassed and enraged him. What's more, he believed it had harmed his reputation and cost him deals.

When the book came out, Trump had been telling people his brand was hotter than ever. O'Brien's writing undermined that, and Trump wanted O'Brien to pay.

Trump demanded $5 billion, claiming that O'Brien had purposely underestimated his fortune in order to harm him. In December of 2007, Trump was deposed in connection with the case, exposing that many times he'd exaggerated the soundness of his business and the size of his fortune.

Although his lawyers tried to keep the deposition secret, it became public during the course of the suit.

During his hours with lawyers, Trump was caught in numerous lies and unorthodox explanations of how he valued his own property.

"My net worth fluctuates, and it goes up and down with markets and with attitudes and with feelings, even my own feelings," he said.

His percentage of ownership in a property also depended on how he felt about the deal. For example, he'd sold the West Side Yards in 1994 to a development group from Hong Kong. Trump had bought the property for $115 million and sold it for $85 million, with the understanding that he'd get a 20 to 30 percent cut of the profits once it was developed and sold.

Trump valued this arrangement as being worth half the total value of the property. He reasoned that owning a 20- to 30-percent share without having to put anything down meant his share was worth more than 20 to 30 percent.

"And I've always felt I own 50 percent from that standpoint," he said. "I've always felt that. . . . And other people say said [sic] it's one of the best deals that they've seen made."

O'Brien wasn't the only journalist who challenged Trump's argument about his stake in the West Side Yards. During the deposition, Trump was forced to read a letter he'd written to a *New York Times* reporter named Peter Slatin, who'd written that "Trump has a small minority stake in the project."

"And what did you write?" the lawyer asked.

Trump read, "'Peter, you're a real loser. Thanks for the nice story.' And I wrote, 'Is 50 percent small?'"

He struggled in other ways to make the case for his own method of determining his net worth, which was not consistent with generally accepted accounting principles.

For example, Trump owned a golf course on the Pacific Ocean. Typically, the value of any property would consider the value of the land plus the revenue Trump earned, minus any expenses and debts. The value of a golf course can be affected by other things, like its design and maintenance. But this wasn't how Trump wanted to measure its value. He believed the land was worth whatever he might make by subdividing and building luxury homes on it. So, if he could build 75 homes for $12 million each, the land would be worth more. But he also admitted he had no intention of doing that, because he didn't want to sell off oceanfront property.

Ultimately, the case was dismissed as a matter of law, without a trial. To win a libel suit in New Jersey, a public figure like Trump would have to demonstrate that the author of the book acted with "actual malice," intentionally printing information he knew to be wrong or which he printed with reckless disregard as to its truth. Trump failed to do so.

What's more, the court said, Trump had long been suspected of playing fast and loose with his net worth. The ruling quoted newspaper and magazine articles to that effect. For example, the *Washington Post* reported in 2004, "There are skeptics out there who believe Trump has $300 million, tops. And the guy has a reputation for, let's say, shading the news in a light that reflects his enthusiasms."

The court also cited a *Fortune* magazine story where Trump said he purposely tried to make it harder for people to figure out what he was worth.

"It's always good to make things nice and complicated," Trump told *Fortune* in 2000, "so that nobody can figure it out."

Finally, the court was not persuaded that Trump's brand had a dollar value, no matter how convinced Trump was that it did.

"As Trump's accountants acknowledge in the 2004 Statement of Financial Condition, under generally accepted accounting principles, reputation is not considered a part of a person's net worth," the judgment read.

As challenging as it is to figure out what Trump's empire is worth, one thing is true: Had Trump invested everything his father gave him and simply sat on a Florida beach, he would be worth considerably more than he accumulated through his deal-making. Trump inherited an estimated $40 million worth of cash and real estate from his father, according to *Forbes* magazine. If he'd bought stocks that performed at average levels, he'd be worth between $2.9 billion and $13 billion. (He'd have had to borrow against his portfolio and invest to hit that higher number.) He had also underperformed against his peers in real estate, another *Forbes* analysis found.

> **Donald Trump's business efforts had left him worse off financially than if he'd never worked at all.**

Donald Trump's business efforts had left him worse off financially than if he'd never worked at all.

Around the time of Trump's revealing deposition, his organization was reeling along with the nation's housing and stock markets.

His bankruptcies—six in total, with the most recent occurring in 2009—represented an unprecedented level of failure in recent American business history. No major American company had filed for Chapter 11 bankruptcy more during the last thirty years.

The majority of companies that size—80 percent—avoided running aground even once.

Trump's history of bankruptcies also had made his organization a risky bet for banks, but one bank, Deutsche Bank, new to working with Trump, agreed to lend to him and financed several of his projects.

But in 2008, as the financial crisis hit, Trump fell behind on payments of a $640 million loan the company had taken out to build Trump International Hotel and Tower in Chicago, a project steered by Don Jr. and Ivanka.

In the midst of discussions for an extension, Trump sued Deutsche Bank for $3 billion, arguing that the economic downturn was the equivalent to a "force majeur"—an unexpected act of God outside of anyone's control or anticipation. The bank countersued, calling the move "classic Trump." Trump ended up getting extra time and a loan from one bank division to another to pay back what he owed.

And yet, even as Trump was struggling to make payments to Deutsche Bank, his company was plowing cash into fourteen luxury properties around the world: golf courses, homes, a winery, and more. The total tab from 2006 to 2014 topped $400 million, an unusual outlay for a real estate developer, and especially one struggling to keep up with loan payments.

What was the source of the money, particularly for the golf courses, which banks were not funding at that time? A lot of it came from people and companies connected to Russia.

In 2008, Trump sold a mansion in Florida to a Russian oligarch for $95 million. It was more than twice the $41 million Trump had paid for it four years before, appreciation that far exceeded the average gain in Florida real estate during the period. The buyer, who beat a murder rap and made his fortune in fertilizer, tore down the home.

That same year, Don told attendees of a New York real estate conference: "Russians make up a pretty disproportionate cross-section of a lot of our assets. . . . Say, in Dubai, and certainly with our project in Soho, and anywhere in New York. We see a lot of money pouring in from Russia."

Eric said something similar toward the end of the buying spree. "We have all the funding we need out of Russia," he told a golf journalist. (Eric Trump later denied saying this.)

In 2009, Trump opened a Twitter account. His kids had encouraged it, and the first person he followed was Ivanka.

His first tweet, on May 4, 2009, said: "Be sure to tune in and watch Donald Trump on *Late Night with David Letterman* as he presents the Top Ten List tonight!"

His next few tweets promoted an appearance on *The View*, another on *Letterman*, and a blog post about lessons he'd learned from *Celebrity Apprentice*.

But on May 12, 2009, Trump's singular Twitter personality emerged. "My persona will never be that of a wallflower," he said. "I'd rather build walls than cling to them."

Despite outward appearances, it was another challenging era for the family. Ratings of *The Apprentice* never matched its first season's popularity. It was still a hit, but it was losing viewers every year. And Trump Entertainment Resorts filed for Chapter 11 bankruptcy in 2009.

There was also a lawsuit over Trump Tower Tampa, one of the developments Trump had licensed his name to use. Buyers spent millions on something they thought Trump was building. The tower was never finished, and buyers lost their deposits.

In a deposition on September 20, 2010, lawyers asked Trump why he didn't return his $4 million license fee to buyers.

"Well, because I had no obligation . . . to give it back," he said.

Trump also claimed buyers who lost their deposits "were better off," because the housing market sank.

> Buyers who got scorched disagreed.
> They'd trusted his name.

Buyers who got scorched disagreed. They'd trusted his name. And they were meant to. In his deposition Trump said, "The name has a lot of value, and so any time I use my name, whether it is a licensing deal or whether it is something I own and build myself, it is very important."

In 2010, disgruntled Trump University customers filed suit, claiming they'd been given false promises in high-pressure sales situations, and didn't get the mentorships they'd paid for. The year also brought trouble with the SoHo deal—trouble that ensnared Don Jr. and Ivanka. Not only were some of the financing sources convicted felons and oligarchs in Russia and Kazakhstan, but in marketing the building, the siblings had lied about how many units had sold.

A lawyer filed suit in August 2010, saying the false numbers made investors think they were buying into a healthier project than they did, representing "a consistent and concerted pattern of outright lies."

Eventually, the case led to a criminal investigation of Don's and Ivanka's statements to potential buyers, particularly ones they'd made in e-mails they didn't expect outsiders to see. New York state law prohibits false statements in connection with the sale of real estate or securities.

The e-mails aren't public, but the liberal *New Yorker* magazine interviewed twenty people, four of whom had reviewed one of the e-mails in evidence. They said the Trumps talked about how to coordinate the fake stories they would tell prospective buyers. Don Jr. told a broker who was worried about the false statements that no one would ever find out because only company insiders and the broker knew about the deception.

It was deliberate deception to make sales, a person who saw the e-mails told the *New Yorker.* "They knew it was wrong."

In 2011, the Trumps settled the civil lawsuit with the buyers who felt cheated, and part of the settlement barred the buyers from talking with prosecutors unless they were subpoenaed by the court. In exchange, buyers got 90 percent of their deposits back plus attorneys' fees.

Trump admitted no wrongdoing.

In the midst of the investigation, one of Trump's lawyers, Marc Kasowitz, donated $25,000 to the campaign of Cyrus Vance, New York's District Attorney.

In August 2012, prosecutors abruptly dropped their investigation of Don Jr. and Ivanka, raising the eyebrows of some observers.

After scrutiny, Vance returned the money and defended closing the case. "At the end of the day, I felt if we were not going to charge criminally, we should leave it as a civil case in the posture in which it came to us," he said. When the case was closed, Kasowitz followed up with an even larger campaign contribution.

The criminal probe of the Trump children over the Soho building did not end the family's relationship with Felix Sater. Nor had a *New York Times* piece that came out in 2007, revealing Sater's questionable past. Sater left Bayrock and started working in 2010 as an unpaid consultant inside the Trump Organization offices, where he had Trump Organization e-mail and business cards that read: "Senior Advisor to Donald Trump."

Trump hadn't been bothered by Sater's criminal history. Nor had he been bothered by a separate suit filed against Bayrock over the Soho project. The suit did not name Trump but did name Sater. It claimed, "Bayrock does conduct legitimate real estate business, but for most of its existence it was substantially and covertly mob-owned and operated. [Management] operated it for years through a pattern of continuous, related crimes, including mail, wire, and bank fraud; tax evasion; money laundering; conspiracy; bribery; extortion; and embezzlement."

In the meantime, Trump had hired one of Sater's high school friends, a personal injury lawyer named Michael Cohen. In 2011, Cohen registered a website: Should Trump Run.

Thirty years after Trump told Rona Barrett he'd run for president if he lost all his money, he was once again on the edge of a deep dive into politics, and the site was meant to gauge how popular he was. Popularity was part of the equation. He also needed to get publicity, something that would be controversial enough to make a big splash so that this attempt to become president would achieve the necessary momentum.

Trump settled on attacking President Barack Obama, the nation's first black president and the son of a white woman from Kansas and a black man born in Kenya.

In 2008, supporters of Hillary Clinton floated a theory that Obama wasn't born in the United States. The Clinton campaign itself never advanced the idea, but Republicans embraced it. Many saw the notion as inherently racist. No white presidential candidate had been asked to prove they were born in the United States. Obama provided a birth certificate in 2008, proving he was born in Hawaii. Nonetheless, some people demanded the original long-form version.

Trump, no stranger to race-based controversies, was the most visible doubter. In March 2011, he appeared on *The View* and said, "Why doesn't he show his birth certificate? . . . There's something on that birth certificate that he doesn't like."

The strategy appeared to work.

The strategy appeared to work. An NBC poll showed Trump was a top Republican contender for president, so he kept on the offensive.

"I'm starting to think that he was not born here," Trump said in April on NBC News.

Trump also advanced the idea of his own candidacy. "I can make this country great again," he said in April. "This country is not great. This country is a laughingstock for the rest of the world."

But then came the night in May that President Obama evened the score. The White House Correspondents' Association dinner is an annual event that gathers the most powerful forces in the nation's capital to clink glasses, eat dinner, and enjoy a funny speech from the president. Dressed in matching black-and-white formal wear, Trump and Melania sat next to a socialite named Lally Weymouth, the daughter of Katharine Graham, who'd been the legendary publisher of the *Washington Post.*

> Obama occupied the seat of honor on a long table set high above the crowd.

Obama occupied the seat of honor on a long table set high above the crowd. Looking relaxed and in command before the thousands of guests, the president took to the lectern.

"Tonight, for the first time, I am releasing my official birth video," he said. The audience roared. Trump sat stone-faced at his table. He knew the spotlight was about to get hot.

Obama continued. "No one has seen this footage in fifty years. Not even me." The film rolled, and it was a scene from *The Lion King*, a children's movie set in Africa about a lion cub who overcomes tragedy to achieve his great destiny. The audience loved it.

Soon Obama unloaded on Trump himself.

"Now, I know that he's taken some flak lately," Obama said, "but no one is happier, no one is prouder to put this birth certificate matter to rest than the Donald. And that's because he can finally get back to focusing on the issues that matter—like, did we fake the moon landing? What really happened in Roswell? And where are Biggie and Tupac?"

Obama paused between each sentence, patient comic timing that gave the audience time to roar in laughter and even applaud. Trump rocked in his seat, smiling tightly. Thousands of people were laughing at him.

And Obama wasn't done. "But all kidding aside," he said, "obviously, we all know about your credentials and breadth of experience. For example—no, seriously, just recently, in an episode of *Celebrity Apprentice*—at the steakhouse, the men's cooking teams did not impress the judges from Omaha Steaks. And there was a lot of blame to go around. But you, Mr. Trump, recognized that the real problem was a lack of leadership. And so ultimately, you didn't blame Lil' Jon or Meatloaf. You fired Gary Busey. And these are the kind of decisions that would keep me up at night." The audience laughed and clapped. "Well handled, sir. Well handled."

People guffawed and cheered some more. They turned to stare at Trump, to see how he was handling it. Trump's grimace tightened. He was a laughingstock.

But Obama still wasn't done. "Say what you will about Mr. Trump, he certainly would bring some change to the White House." The screen revealed a White House redecorated to look like one of Trump's casinos, with gold-plated pillars and signs that read HOTEL & CASINO & GOLF COURSE and PRESIDENTIAL SUITE.

Trump, humiliated, left the party in a rush.

Since childhood, his favorite thing was to be cheered for. To be laughed at—repeatedly, by the elite of Washington, DC—was intolerable. Rather than move on from advancing conspiracy theories about Obama's place of birth, though, Trump stuck with it, in much the same way the younger version of himself insisted Antonino Rocca was "Rocky Antonino."

Trump stepped up the pace of the birther attacks, and Twitter emerged as a favorite media platform for his assaults on the president's identity as a native-born American.

Trump stepped up the pace of the birther attacks, and Twitter emerged as a favorite media platform for his assaults on the president's identity as a native-born American.

"Made in America?" Trump tweeted on November 18, 2011. "@BarackObama called his 'birthplace' Hawaii 'here in Asia.'"

On May 18, 2012: "Let's take a closer look at that birth certificate. @BarackObama was described in 2003 as being 'born in Kenya.'"

On August 6, 2012: "An 'extremely credible source' has called my office and told me that @BarackObama's birth certificate is a fraud."

On October 11, 2012: "Why does Barack Obama's ring have an Arabic inscription?" The tweet linked to an article on a conspiracy website claiming Obama's ring said, "There is no God except Allah."

On December 12, 2013: "How amazing, the State Health Director who verified copies of Obama's 'birth certificate' died in plane crash today. All others lived."

Trump's approach, as controversial as it was, worked splendidly.

As he attacked President Obama's legitimacy, he pummeled his way into the upper reaches of the Republican establishment. In part because of his continued appearance on *The Apprentice*, his reputation as a businessman remained largely intact despite a nearly two-decade-long string of bankruptcies.

If Trump was anything, he was a survivor. He'd crawled out of a deep hole of debt and come back, something he attributed to his positive attitude and his readiness to punch back.

"I knew conditions would change for the better," he once reflected, "and they certainly have."

ABOVE: April 6, 2011. Trump made his first speaking appearance after hinting at a run for the presidency in 2012 at the South Florida Tea Party's Tax Day Rally in Boca Raton, Florida. *(Storms Media Group/Alamy Stock Photo)*

CHAPTER 8

The BRASS RING

> "Barack Obama's delivery on Saturday night was excellent—cute mention of Trump—and I am flattered to be mentioned. @BarackObama"
>
> —@realDonaldTrump, April 30, 2012

SOON AFTER PRESIDENT Barack Obama turned him into a national laughingstock, Trump decided not to run after all. He'd given it a shot. He'd put up the website. He'd courted the media with the birther rumors. He'd met with pollsters, including one named Kellyanne Conway, who let him know that his negative ratings were high but not insurmountable.

Once again, he couldn't quite pull the trigger. Ultimately, Trump realized that front-runner Mitt Romney was going to be hard to catch. Romney had started earlier. He had experience in office. What's more, Romney was also a businessman, and one without a history of bankruptcies and broken marriages.

In February 2012, Trump stood by Romney in Las Vegas. "It's my honor, real honor, to endorse Mitt Romney," he said. "Mitt is tough, he's smart, he's sharp."

When it came to the presidency, Trump was going to bide his time. He'd learned this strategy with his real estate ventures. You sometimes had to hold on to land for a while before you could put together the zoning, financing, and tax benefits necessary to build at a profit. Likewise, a lot of things had to come together for Trump to be ready to win the White House.

The more immediate goal was to keep Obama from getting a second term. Trump tweeted about Obama more than 1,100 times before the 2012 election, calling him a "total disaster," accusing him of squandering taxpayer money on his vacations, and of enacting policies that would lead to a food-stamp crime wave.

Despite Trump's endorsement of Romney, Obama won easily, with 332 electoral votes to 206. That was it for Trump. The Republican Party had botched the job. Trump knew he could do better.

> "Our country is now in serious and unprecedented trouble . . . like never before."
>
> —@realDonaldTrump, election night 2012

T HIRTEEN DAYS AFTER OBAMA WON A SECOND term, Trump's lawyers paid a $325 fee and put in an application for a service mark for the phrase "Make America Great Again."

Echoing the "Let's Make America Great Again" slogan of the Republican icon Ronald Reagan, Trump angled to reach people who'd lost ground in an economy where manufacturing jobs had vanished, and people who felt threatened by cultural shifts around marriage, racial equality, and sex and gender identity. This population felt left behind by the economy and by progressive cultural values commonly viewed as belonging to the coastal elite. Despite his background as a New Yorker born to wealth and privilege, Trump knew he could put together a powerful coalition of people opposed to these "elites."

A couple of weeks before Obama was sworn in for his second term in front of a million-person-strong crowd, Trump's old friend Roger Stone dialed up Mar-a-Lago to wish Trump a happy New Year.

The subject immediately turned to politics. Trump wanted to know whether he could beat Jeb Bush and Hillary Clinton, and who else Stone thought might run.

"Romney's body isn't even cold yet, and he's already handicapping this election. It was clear to me then that he was going to run," Stone said.

Trump had a lot of reasons to do so. No matter what, it was great for his brand. He'd be larger than ever, and he wouldn't have to pay a penny for the media. Despite what generally accepted accounting principles and judges said, Trump's brand meant money. The bigger the brand, the more money he'd have.

Plus, Trump had been on TV regularly in a leather chair with his hair and makeup done. He looked presidential already.

"Politics is show business for ugly people," as Stone put it, and Trump, a bona fide celebrity, would make regular politicians look pale and weak.

> "The Miss Universe Pageant will be broadcast live from MOSCOW, RUSSIA on November 9th. A big deal that will bring our countries together!"
>
> —@realDonaldTrump, June 18, 2013

Even as he was aiming for the presidency, Trump kept trying to make a deal for a Trump Tower in Moscow. Early in 2013, he arranged for a meeting with an oligarch named Aras Agalarov, who'd accumulated almost $2 billion by importing luxury goods and developing shopping centers and residences for Russia's super-wealthy. The dark-haired, broad-faced billionaire became known as "Putin's Builder" for successfully completing projects at the Russian leader's behest, earning Putin's Order of Honor of the Russian Federation medal in the process.

In June, Agalarov and his son Emin, a pop star, met Trump in Las Vegas, where they'd traveled to take in the Miss USA pageant, part of Trump's beauty contest portfolio. Trump invited himself to

a dinner party the Russians were having and followed the group to a raunchy nightclub called The Act.

Trump and the Agalarovs each wanted something from each other. Emin wanted a career boost. Trump wanted his Moscow tower. The Russians proposed a deal. Agalarov could help Trump find a space for the pageant in Moscow—something tricky to do, given red tape in Russia. The pageant would take place in Crocus City Hall, the seven-thousand-seat entertainment center Agalarov had built. The Russian would also cover most of the $20 million production fee. And in exchange, Emin would get to perform two songs and get an appearance of the reigning Miss Universe in one of his music videos.

Not long after the meeting, Trump used Twitter to angle for a meeting with the Russian president: "Do you think Putin will be

ABOVE: Emin Agalarov, Donald Trump, and Aras Agalarov clown together on the red carpet at the 2013 Miss Universe pageant in Moscow. *(Victor Boyko/Getty Images)*

going to the Miss Universe Pageant in November in Moscow - if so, will he become my new best friend?"

Trump also continued to expand his real estate empire in the United States. In August, he signed an agreement to convert the old post office building in Washington, DC, into Trump International Hotel.

Not all business developments that month were good. New York Attorney General Eric Schneiderman filed suit against the now-defunct Trump University, following a similar suit in California. Trump punched back on Twitter: "Lightweight NYS Attorney General Eric Schneiderman is trying to extort me with a civil law suit."

But for Putin, Trump had only praise.

"Putin is having such a good time," Trump tweeted on September 11, after the Russian president published an op-ed in the *New York Times*. "Our President is making him look like the genius of all geniuses. Do not fear, we are a NATION OF POTENTIAL[.]"

"It really makes him look like a great leader," Trump said on Fox News.

Trump contended with civil lawsuits beyond the one for Trump University. He'd sued and been sued more than 4,000 times in thirty years—more than any other presidential nominee in history, according to a running tally kept by *USA Today*. About half the time, he was the defendant.

On November 5, 2013, Trump was back in the deposition seat again. This time, lawyers had questions about his relationship with mobster and FBI informant Felix Sater, with whom Trump had explored deals starting in 2002.

A 2007 story in the *New York Times* linking the two men revealed Sater's notorious past: "Felix H. Sater immigrated with his family to Brighton Beach when he was 8 years old. At 24 he was a successful Wall Street broker, at 27 he was in prison after a bloody bar fight, and at 32 he was accused of conspiring with the Mafia to launder money and defraud investors."

Trump said under oath he barely knew Sater. "If he were sitting in the room right now, I really wouldn't know what he looked like."

> "Success tip: Be ready for problems, and be patient—there are very few cases of instant gratification."
>
> —@realDonaldTrump, November 8, 2013

A few days after the deposition, Trump boarded a friend's private jet in Asheville, North Carolina.

He'd been there celebrating the ninety-fifth birthday of evangelist Billy Graham, a fellow Obama birther and an influential player in conservative Christian politics.

But that had been just a pit stop. Trump's real destination was Moscow's Vnukovo airport, an eleven-hour flight. The Miss Universe pageant was coming up, and Trump hoped the trip would help him finally seal the deal on a Moscow tower. What's more, he really hoped to meet Putin in person. No tower would be built without the Russian president's say-so.

After his flight landed in Russia on November 8, Trump headed to the Ritz-Carlton in Moscow, where he would stay in the presidential suite, the same room the Obamas once occupied.

His first order of business was to meet with Miss Universe executives and the Agalarovs to work on the final details of the show. During that meeting, someone approached Keith Schiller, Trump's bodyguard, with a curious offer: to send five prostitutes to Trump's suite.

Schiller said he declined. "We don't do that type of stuff."

Then came a sushi lunch with a crowd of oligarchs. Afterward, Trump stopped by his private room at the pageant venue, which had been stocked with all his favorites: unscented soap, rolled towels, Nutter Butters, white Tic Tacs, and Diet Coke. As was his custom, he retained the right to review videos of the contestants and overrule judges' decisions when he disagreed with them. (He often removed women of color for being "too ethnic.")

At the end of the day, Trump attended Agalarov's fifty-eighth birthday party, returning to his hotel room around 1:30 A.M. He and Schiller chuckled about the offer of prostitutes. Schiller guarded the door for a bit before turning in himself.

The next morning, Trump shot a fifteen-second cameo for the last scene in Emin's latest music video, using his catchphrase from *The Apprentice*: "You're fired!"

A meeting had been on Putin's calendar, but was canceled before the pageant. Even so, Trump still held out hope that Putin would at least attend the show. But the Russian president did not and instead sent a decorative black box and a sealed letter through the Agalarovs to Trump's NYC Miss Universe office.

Despite his failure to spend time in person with Putin, Trump was thrilled with his visit. "I was with the top level people, both oligarchs and generals, and top of the government people. I can't go further than that, but I will tell you that I met the top people, and the relationship was extraordinary."

> **After the trip, his dream was closer than ever.**

After the trip, his dream was closer than ever.

He tweeted Agalarov: "@AgalarovAras I had a great weekend with you and your family. You have done a FANTASTIC job. TRUMP TOWER-MOSCOW is next. EMIN was WOW!"

Two days later, Aras Agalarov spoke to journalists about the possibility of building a Trump-branded tower in Moscow. The state-owned Sberbank also announced they'd reached an agreement with Agalarov's Crocus Group to put up billions for a development that would potentially include a Trump Tower. If the plan came to fruition, Trump would be funded by the Russian government to build.

There was a problem, though. Corruption is rife in Russia and has been for decades. It's also pervasive, affecting the judicial system, law enforcement, and beyond. After a thirty-seven-year-old accountant named Sergei Magnitsky was beaten and tortured in prison, dying reportedly of heart failure and toxic shock from untreated pancreatitis, President Obama signed anti-corruption legislation.

The Magnitsky Act lets the United States freeze the assets of corrupt Russian oligarchs and prevent their travel into the country.

The Magnitsky Act could prevent Vladimir Putin from access-ing his money in Western banks. His fortune by some estimates is as much as $200 billion. This sum, allegedly stashed away and not reported, would make Putin the world's wealthiest man, and is a surprising fortune for someone who makes $112,000 a year as president.

Russia retaliated immediately, barring Americans from adopting Russian orphans. They claimed it was a human rights move, after an adopted Russian orphan died in an overheated car in the States.

Relations between the United States and Russia worsened in 2014, after Russia invaded Ukraine, annexed Crimea, and stole the country's assets. In retaliation, the United States and Euro-pean Union imposed sanctions on Russia. Some of Putin's closest associates were affected. And Sberbank—the state-owned bank that had offered to put up money for a Trump Tower Moscow—was on the list of companies not allowed to do business with the United States.

Once again, Trump had lost out on his tower in Moscow. This time, he had fallout from legislation signed by Obama to blame.

Trump kept up his attacks on the president throughout 2014, even pairing them with fear-mongering about Mexican immigrants and a perceived need for more security on the Mexico–US border.

That was the year the grisly Ebola virus broke out in West Africa. A few cases cropped up in Italy, Mali, Nigeria, Senegal, Spain, the United Kingdom, and the United States.

Trump, a germaphobe, was concerned. In October 2014, Trump expressed astonishment on an Iowa talk show that people didn't want to secure the US–Mexican border against Ebola:

"Now, especially with Ebola and how about when that starts happening down in that area and people just walk into the country," he said.

Later that month, Trump tweeted that Obama should step down after a traveling doctor risked contracting the virus. It was one of three times Trump called for Obama's resignation between August and October. And with one of those calls, Trump offered Obama a free lifetime membership at a Trump golf club—an attempt to ridicule the amount of time Obama spent on the links.

Trump had also written an op-ed piece in June about a settlement New York City made with the Central Park Five, the men who, as children, were falsely convicted of raping and beating a white woman. He thought the $40 million settlement, a million for each year the men wrongly spent in jail, was "a disgrace."

"These young men do not exactly have the pasts of angels," he wrote.

> As 2014 wound down, chatter increased about the chances that Trump might run for president again.

As 2014 wound down, chatter increased about the chances that Trump might run for president again. The timing was good for him: ratings for *The Apprentice* were lower than ever, averaging 7.6 million viewers per show during the 2014–2015 season, well below the 20 million who tuned in for the first season. And his Trump Tower Moscow hopes had been dashed.

As he deliberated whether to sign another contract with NBC, Trump threw some punches at Mitt Romney, who was considering another run.

Romney "choked," Trump said on Fox News. "He choked like a dog."

Trump also criticized Jeb Bush, the early front-runner. "The last thing we need is another Bush."

By February of 2015, Trump decided not to sign another *Apprentice* contract. Free from *Apprentice* duties, he'd have a few months to explore an official campaign announcement. He also hired his first staffers: Corey Lewandowski and Matt Ciepielowski. The men would coordinate Trump's campaign in New Hampshire, the state that kicks off the primary campaign season.

He also kept questioning President Obama's legitimacy, to the consternation of fellow Republicans. After a speech at a conservative conference in February, Trump held forth on the issue: "Hey look, [the president] wrote a book when he was a young man and it said 'born in Kenya,' blah blah blah. I don't know where he was born. I would like to see his college records, I think that's important.

"As far as the birth certificate, Hillary Clinton wanted his birth certificate. Hillary is a birther. She wanted it but she wasn't able to get it. John McCain fought really hard and really viciously to get his birth certificate. John McCain failed. Couldn't get it. Trump comes along—and I'm not a sitting senator, I'm not a sitting anything else, I'm a good businessman—but Trump comes along and I said, 'Birth certificate.' He gave a birth certificate.

"Whether or not that was a real certificate, because a lot of people question it, I certainly question it—but Hillary Clinton wanted it, McCain wanted it, and I wanted it. He didn't do it for them, he did it for me. So in one sense I'm proud of it. Now all we have to do is find out whether or not it's real."

In March, Trump formed an exploratory committee.

In April, he continued his volley against Mexican immigrants, and also took a shot against a Mexican he thought had stiffed him on a business deal as well as the Mexican judicial system:

"Rodolfo Rosas Moya and his pals in Mexico owe me a lot of money. Disgusting & slow Mexico court system. Mexico is not a US friend," he tweeted on April 16. "Mexico's court system is a dishonest joke. I am owed a lot of money & nothing happens."

The next day Trump tweeted that ISIS has a training camp in Mexico, a false rumor started by a conspiracy theorist who once tried to have Obama deported and has been barred from bringing new cases to court because he abused the judicial system so frequently.

On April 18, Trump denied ever declaring bankruptcy. "For all of the haters and losers out there sorry, I never went Bankrupt—but I did build a world class company and employ many people!"

It was essential for Trump to appear to be a business whiz. He would build a case for himself as president around his reputation as a successful negotiator. Instead of saying he'd gone bankrupt, he spun it as a shrewd business move on his part.

"What I've done is I've used, brilliantly, the laws of the country. And not personally, just corporate. And if you look at people like myself that are at the highest levels of business, they use—many of them have done it, many times," he said.

Trump traveled to Iowa and New Hampshire, key primary states for presidential candidates. And he continued to tweet on political issues of the day, ranging from race riots in Baltimore to his position on Iran sanctions.

On Memorial Day, Trump tweeted to honor the nation's fallen soldiers, calling them "our country's finest." As for everyone else, "I would like to wish everyone, including all haters and losers (of which, sadly, there are many) a truly happy and enjoyable Memorial Day!"

> By June 16, two days after his sixty-ninth birthday, Trump had made up his mind.

By June 16, two days after his sixty-ninth birthday, Trump had made up his mind.

Standing at the top of the escalator inside his original Trump Tower—the building where he'd spent his best and worst days—he gave two thumbs up to a gathered crowd. As Neil Young's song "Rockin' in the Free World" blasted, Trump glided down the escalator behind Melania, who was as poised as a statue as he waved to the crowd below.

Ivanka waited for her father at the bottom of the escalator, standing in front of navy blue cloth draped over the building's signature waterfall.

Trump took his spot in front of a cluster of American flags.

"Wow. Whoa!" he said into the microphone. "That is some group of people. Thousands."

There was a large crowd, some of whom had been promised $50 cash to be there, money they didn't get until a complaint was filed with the Federal Election Commission.

The speech that followed was unconventional in its informality and tone—not unlike the rude and brash tweets in the months leading up to the announcement.

Trump mocked former Secretary of State John Kerry for breaking his leg in a bicycle race.

He questioned the intelligence of Jeb Bush and the competence of Mario Rubio, two of his many opponents.

He talked at length about how rich he was, as proof he couldn't be bought by special interests.

"So the total is $8,737,540,000 . . . I'm not doing that to brag, because you know what? I don't have to brag. I don't have to, believe it or not."

He also made his controversial statement about Mexicans: "When Mexico sends its people, they're not sending their best. . . . They're sending people that have lots of problems, and they're bringing those problems. They're bringing drugs. They're bringing crime. They're rapists. And some, I assume, are good people."

And he made his promise to "build a great wall, and nobody builds walls better than me, believe me, and I'll build them very inexpensively, I will build a great, great wall on our southern border. And I will have Mexico pay for that wall."

He promised to repeal and replace Obamacare.

He said his negotiating skills would make corporate presidents beg him to reconsider his plans to ensure they stop building factories overseas. And he promised he would finance his own campaign.

"I don't care," he said.
"I'm really rich."

"I don't care," he said. "I'm really rich."

His speech had barely ended when it put the media into a frenzy over the shocking nature of some of the comments, particularly the ones about Mexico.

And that was exactly as Trump had planned for the months of campaigning ahead. He'd say what he wanted, he'd dominate the news cycle and drive its direction, and no one would be able to keep up.

CHAPTER 9

GOING NUCLEAR on NORMS

> "I'll do nearly anything within legal bounds to win. Sometimes, part of making a deal is denigrating your competition."
>
> —Donald Trump, *The Art of the Deal*

TRUMP WAS OFFICIALLY in the game—but his race looked like a long shot at best. At worst, it looked like a joke. It wasn't only that he had to beat the rest of the Republican field. He also had to beat the media, which was so cynical about his intentions and chances that they initially treated his campaign as a punch line.

A week before Trump announced his candidacy, the *New York Times* reported astonishment that Vegas bookies thought Trump was serious this time around:

"The market believes that Mr. Trump is for real this time, rating him a 62 percent chance to file paperwork with the Federal Election Commission sometime this month. Perhaps it is time to take him a bit more seriously. Or at least it's time to take seriously the idea that he intends to run."

It was true that Trump had flirted with running for decades. He'd paid for huge newspaper ads advancing his political views. He'd discussed the prospect with journalists, fans, and employees. He'd traveled to New Hampshire many times. He'd addressed conservative groups and rounded up volunteers and advisers. He'd done everything he could to advance the notion he was running—without actually running. Perhaps it was, in his view, a smart strategy. If he never officially declared, then he couldn't rightly be called a loser.

The notion that he stood no chance was tougher to surmount, but he was game. He'd been made a laughingstock by the sitting president. His rival Jeb Bush had also laughed at the idea of Trump's candidacy. Trump hated being laughed at. When he wanted to make the case that things in America were bad, he'd say other nations "are laughing at us." He'd used the expression more than a hundred times over the years.

So yes, there were "haters," as Trump called them. But he felt sure that he could beat his Republican rivals. He would show everyone he was not only not a joke, he was a winner. And he would do it *his* way, by smashing conventional campaign protocol into dust. Things were going to get rough, and that was fine by Trump.

No matter what, he'd generate massive amounts of free publicity for his brand. And if he won? He could finally offer the nation the sort of leadership he'd long thought would be effective. He'd seal the borders. Negotiate better deals with allies. Put America first.

Much of his campaign's core message he'd been saying for years. Some things would change, such as his position on abortion. He'd long been pro-choice, but the evangelical community would not support him if he remained so. But this was Trump's time to be himself and true to his deepest instincts. No one was going to tell him what to do, what to say, or how to say it.

His first political rally was a tiny one in New Hampshire on June 17, the day after he officially announced his run. New Hampshire, one of the smallest states in the nation, holds outsize importance in politics because it's where the second presidential primary is held. If a candidate is going to develop the momentum to get their party's nomination, doing well in contests in New Hampshire, Iowa, and other early bellwether states is vital.

> Reporters didn't make much of the event in their coverage, and Trump didn't do himself any favors with his remarks.

Reporters didn't make much of the event in their coverage, and Trump didn't do himself any favors with his remarks.

"I really am very smart and I'm very good at business and I can make this country so rich," Trump told the crowd. "Maybe people don't like my style. Maybe they don't like my hair, which is real, by the way."

Trump's hair, a source of frequent ridicule, had long been a touchy subject for the mogul. He'd made Ivana feel violated in their bedroom after painful surgery on his scalp. He'd also taken hair-growth medication to preserve what was left. The unmistakable style itself, a hair-sprayed whorl that covered a bald patch, had even become one of Trump's many superstitions. If he cut it, he believed he'd lose his wealth and power.

> ## Trump is also insecure about the size of his hands.

Trump is also insecure about the size of his hands. The editor of *Spy* magazine, which had pranked Trump earlier by sending him checks in diminishing amounts to see just how puny of one he'd cash (13 cents, ultimately), once described Trump as "a short-fingered vulgarian."

Trump hated the criticism, and for more than twenty-five years, he would occasionally send the editor photographs in an attempt to prove his fingers weren't short. He kept doing it, even when the editor, Graydon Carter, moved to *Vanity Fair*.

"There is always a photo of him," Carter said, "generally a tear sheet from a magazine. On all of them he has circled his hand in gold Sharpie in a valiant effort to highlight the length of his fingers. I almost feel sorry for the poor fellow because, to me, the fingers still look abnormally stubby."

Before Trump officially announced his candidacy, he sent yet another mailing to Carter, who said, "Like the other packages, this one included a circled hand and the words, also written in gold

Sharpie: 'See, not so short!' I sent the picture back by return mail with a note attached, saying, 'Actually, quite short.' Which I can only assume gave him fits."

Not all of Trump's relationships with the media were hostile, though. Every Monday, he had a spot on *Fox and Friends*. This he had to give up after announcing his campaign.

"This is because I am running for president and law prohibits. LOVE!" he tweeted.

(He still called the show every Monday morning during the primaries, though, because he was superstitious about breaking a routine that had worked so well for him.)

Even if his first rally was small, Trump's campaign started with a splash.

His speech—and especially the comments about Mexican immigrants—scandalized the media and political elite. The coverage was immense and intense, just what he wanted. It engaged voters, too. Of tweets mentioning Trump in the first ten months of his campaign, immigration was the top subject, with millions of tweets each week, overshadowing interest in foreign affairs, taxes, and health care, a Politico analysis found.

There were costs, though. NBC Universal cut ties with Trump. Macy's dropped his menswear line. Univision, a Mexican network, refused to air the Miss USA pageant, prompting a $500 million lawsuit in retaliation.

Even typically apolitical organizations jumped into the fray.

The PGA Golf Tour, which sometimes used Trump's courses, issued a statement: "In response to Mr. Trump's comments about the golf industry 'knowing he is right' in regards to his recent statements about Mexican immigrants, we feel compelled to clarify that those remarks do not reflect the views of our organizations," it read.

But coverage was coverage. Trump was happy to be the guy everyone was talking about. And even if the business and media worlds reviled his comments, Trump found support elsewhere.

The Daily Stormer, America's most popular site for neo-Nazi news, endorsed his candidacy:

"Trump is willing to say what most Americans think: it's time to deport these people." The Daily Stormer urged its readers to "vote for the first time in our lives for the one man who actually represents our interests."

Although most Americans do not support Trump's pledge to deport "millions and millions of undocumented immigrants," preferring a path to immigration for the young, Trump's rhetoric and attitudes appealed deeply to people who felt minimized by the growing diversity in the United States. Data collected by the US Census Bureau suggest that white people will make up less than half of the population by 2044. Because America has long had a white majority, whiteness has been seen by some as an American trait. For those who hold that view, growing diversity feels like a threatening loss.

The left-wing filmmaker Michael Moore called the phenomenon "The Last Stand of the Angry White Man."

The white supremacist leader Richard Spencer, who called Trump "refreshing," expressed a similar view:

"Trump, on a gut level, kind of senses that this is about demographics, ultimately. We're moving into a new America," he said.

While Trump didn't strike Spencer as a white nationalist, the candidate did embody "an unconscious vision that white people have—that their grandchildren might be a hated minority in their own country. I think that scares us. . . . I think that, to a great degree, explains the Trump phenomenon. I think he is the one person who can tap into it."

Deeply attuned to the resonance of the message, Trump continued to hammer on the issue of immigration. For his next rally, Trump traveled to Phoenix to address a crowd of five thousand people. Trump took the stage with a man whose son had been killed by an undocumented immigrant, underscoring Trump's factually baseless argument that undocumented immigrants are to blame for rising crime in America.

Trump's rhetoric appealed to the fears of certain voters. He began to climb in the polls. Even so, Trump's manipulation of facts alarmed many, including Senator John McCain, a Republican who'd run unsuccessfully for president in 2008.

"It's very bad," McCain told a reporter. "Because what he did was he fired up the crazies."

McCain wasn't the only Republican alarmed by Trump's claims about immigrants and crime. Republican senator Lindsey Graham, who was also running, called Trump "a wrecking ball for the future of the Republican Party with the Hispanic community, and we need to push back."

Characterizing Trump's performance as demagoguery, Graham predicted bad things for the party.

"If we don't reject it, we've lost the moral authority, in my view, to govern this country."

The Founding Fathers fretted about demagogues—political leaders who appeal to popular desires and prejudices rather than reasoned arguments. The electoral college was meant as a safeguard against the chance a demagogue might become president.

Criticism from establishment Republicans like McCain and Graham didn't faze Trump. Instead, and staying true to lessons he'd learned from Roy Cohn, Trump punched back. In an interview, he argued that McCain wasn't a war hero. It was an unprecedented attack on the integrity of a man who'd served in the military with honor. When he was serving in Vietnam, McCain was shot down, suffered grievous injuries, spent more than five years in captivity enduring torture, and turned down an opportunity to be released earlier than other prisoners because of his father's rank.

"I just knew that it wasn't the right thing to do," McCain has said. "I knew they wouldn't have offered it to me if I wasn't the son of an admiral."

> Trump argued that none of this behavior was heroic, and that McCain only had that reputation because he was captured.

Trump argued that none of this behavior was heroic, and that McCain only had that reputation because he was captured.

"I like people who weren't captured," Trump said.

Even conservative media were aghast. A *Wall Street Journal* editorial called Trump a "catastrophe."

Trump didn't care. If the Republicans rejected him, he could always run as a third-party candidate. Also, Trump understood that the approval of the elite didn't matter to the growing swath of voters who felt left behind culturally and financially.

Meanwhile, some members of the conservative media started encouraging Trump. A Fox commentator criticized the Republican party chairman, Reince Priebus, for telling Trump to tone it down.

An undocumented immigrant had killed a woman on July 1 in San Francisco, a sanctuary city that refused to enforce all federal immigration policies. For people who believe immigration is a threat to the American way, sanctuary cities are a source of resentment and fear.

"Trump needs to crank up the volume," the Fox journalist said.

And so, over the objections of party elites, Trump persisted. His approach hit the bull's-eye. Conservative talk show host Rush Limbaugh credited Trump with changing the debate on immigration.

"There is a bunch of us who have been saying similar things, doing similar things. But none of us is running for president and none of us has been covered by the media day in/day out," Limbaugh said.

As Trump drove the national dialogue according to his version of reality, he also created the signature image of his campaign: the Make America Great Again hat. He first wore one in July on a visit to the border in Laredo, Texas. Not only could the hat keep his hair in place on blustery airport tarmacs, it was the perfect populist touch, and something his supporters would want for themselves. It also played into the image Trump wanted to cultivate as an approachable Washington outsider, another vital facet of his campaign.

It wasn't a strictly accurate image. Trump had long cultivated political relationships, as had his father. He once boasted he could "buy" a senator for $200,000, and he regularly made political donations in order to grease the skids for his projects—and sometimes more questionable things. Just before Florida's attorney general was to decide whether to investigate Trump University, Trump used his foundation to make a $25,000 donation to her reelection campaign, an illegal use of the charity's funds. A few weeks later, the Florida attorney general opted not to join the suit, arguing it was unnecessary since New York State had filed suit on behalf of consumers nationwide.

Meanwhile, Trump traveled to Iowa, the state where the first primaries are held. He kicked off his speech there by commenting on the size of the crowd, and—previewing a coming war against the media—celebrated the fact that reporters from Iowa's largest

ABOVE: Trump started wearing his campaign's signature Make America Great Again hat in July 2015. It was populist and practical—his hair wouldn't get messy on airport tarmacs. *(LM Otero/Associated Press)*

newspaper had to stand outside. It was payback for an editorial in the Pulitzer Prize–winning *Des Moines Register* that suggested he "pull the plug on his bloviating sideshow."

"If he were merely a self-absorbed, B-list celebrity, his unchecked ego could be tolerated as a source of mild amusement. But he now wants to become president, which means that he aspires to be the leader of the free world and the keeper of our nuclear launch codes," the editorial said. "Trump, by every indication, seems wholly unqualified to sit in the White House."

Reporters dug into Trump's past, including the rape accusation Ivana made under oath in their divorce proceedings. Sometime after their divorce, she said she felt violated because his usual "love and tenderness" was absent that fateful night.

The Trump campaign responded with force to prevent any new airing of that long-ago incident. On July 27, Trump's lawyer, Michael Cohen, threatened a reporter who was looking into the story.

"I will make sure that you and I meet one day while we're in the courthouse. And I will take you for every penny you still don't have," Cohen said. "So I'm warning you, tread very f---ing lightly, because what I'm going to do to you is going to be f---ing disgusting. You understand me?"

Trump also fought to protect other aspects of his image. He wanted to convey the impression that he was too rich to be bought and influenced by lobbyists. So, Trump sparred with Forbes about his net worth, claiming now to be worth $10 billion. He suggested his Republican opponents were "puppets" of the Koch brothers, billionaires who fund conservative and libertarian political organizations.

This laid groundwork for a point he'd make a few days later in the first Republican debate: It was possible to buy a politician.

"When they call, I give," he said during the August 6 debate. "And you know what? When I need something from them two years later, three years later, I call them. They are there for me."

"Hillary Clinton: I said, 'Be at my wedding,' and she came to my wedding. She had no choice, because I gave to a foundation."

Offering himself up as proof of the corrupting effect of money in politics would have been viewed as a gaffe if a typical politician had said it. That old unwritten rule did not apply to Trump.

During the same debate, when Megyn Kelly, a Fox News anchor, pointed out he'd "called women you don't like 'fat pigs,' 'dogs,' 'slobs,' and 'disgusting animals,'" Trump tried to turn it into a joke.

"Only Rosie O'Donnell," he interrupted.

Kelly wasn't having it. "For the record, it went well beyond Rosie O'Donnell."

During the debate, Trump complained about Kelly's treatment of him, and said he might not be nice to her anymore as a result.

The next day, he kept grousing. "You could see there was blood coming out of her eyes, blood coming out of her wherever."

> **"You could see there was blood coming out of her eyes, blood coming out of her wherever."**

Some people inferred Trump was talking about menstruation, which led to more outraged coverage. The exchange turned off some potential Trump allies. The conservative RedState network's annual conference rescinded Trump's invitation to speak.

What critics failed to understand was that Trump wasn't playing by their rules. He was playing by his rules, and in Trump's game, it's all about dominance. If you stay on top in a conflict, you win. As if to prove the point, a few days later he insulted another woman, Carly Fiorina, the former CEO of Hewlett Packard.

"I just realized that if you listen to Carly Fiorina for more than ten minutes straight, you develop a massive headache. She has zero chance!"

A media bonanza followed, and this turned into Trump's formula. The more offensive he was, the more coverage he got, and the more his core supporters viewed it as a virtue—Trump's willingness to "tell it like it is."

As long as it was what his supporters wanted to hear, their support would not waver.

The August polls showed Trump taking a commanding lead in the Republican field. Emboldened by the effectiveness of his dominate-and-domineer strategy, he released a six-page immigration plan that promised toughness: large-scale deportation, confiscation of money that undocumented immigrants were sending home, and undoing the Fourteenth Amendment, which promises citizenship to everyone born on American soil.

"We will not be taken advantage of anymore," he said.

That same month, Trump met Michael Flynn, a retired US Army Lieutenant General who'd been director of the Defense Intelligence Agency until Obama fired him. Flynn, who'd started providing intelligence services for corporations and foreign governments, became an informal adviser to the campaign on international policy.

Meanwhile, Trump's rhetoric on immigration appeared to provoke violence in the streets. Before sunrise one August morning in Boston, a pair of brothers beat a homeless Hispanic man with a metal pole, urinated on him, and walked away laughing.

One of them explained the attack later: "Donald Trump was right. All these illegals need to be deported."

The man was not an undocumented worker; he had a Social Security number, which are issued to documented workers.

Trump's initial response was mild. "It would be a shame, but I haven't heard about that," he said. "I will say that people that are following me are very passionate. They love this country and they want this country to be great again. They are very passionate. I will say that."

Two days later, Trump finally condemned the attack.

It would not be the last time his words incited violent responses in others. At upcoming rallies, his fans would attack protesters, and Trump said things such as, "He should have been, maybe he should have been roughed up." He also said, "So if you see someone getting ready to throw a tomato, knock the crap out of them, would you? Seriously. Just knock the hell—I promise you, I will pay for the legal fees."

And Trump added another minority group to his list of targets. Picking up where his birther campaign against Obama had left off, Trump embraced anti-Muslim sentiment as well.

At a September 17 campaign event in Rochester, a man was invited to ask Trump a question.

"We have a problem in this country: It's called *Muslim*," the man said.

Rather than cut the man off, Trump nodded.

"You know our current President is one—" the man said.

"Right," Trump said.

"You know he's not even an American," the man said.

Rather than correct the man, as John McCain had done during a 2008 campaign stop, Trump said, "We need this question. This is the first question!"

The man continued: "But, anyway, we have training camps growing, where they want to kill us. . . . That's my question: When can we get rid of them?"

"We're going to be looking at a lot of different things," Trump replied. "And, you know, a lot of people are saying that, and a lot of people are saying that *bad things* are happening out there. We're going to be looking at that and many other things."

ABOVE: Lieutenant General Mike Flynn joined Trump on the campaign trail and led crowds in cheers of "lock her up!" *(Defense Intelligence Agency)*

That there are Muslim training camps in America is a conspiracy theory that originated in a 2005 report from the National White Collar Crime Center, a federally funded nonprofit seeking to understand how white-collar crime funds terrorism. Local law enforcement agencies where those two to three dozen camps allegedly are located say they've seen no such thing. But Trump not only didn't challenge the man's assertion that Obama was a Muslim and not an American, he gave credence to the man's conspiracy theory about Muslims being trained for violence on American soil.

Trump's rhetoric made both Muslim and Mexican immigrants and refugees seem more dangerous than they actually are to gain support for the policies he would propose. False information meant to deceive is known as disinformation. Trump's tendency to spread disinformation went beyond his claims about Obama's birth and the dangers posed by immigrants and refugees. Trump has also claimed global warming was a hoax on Twitter, and in 2012 said, "The concept of global warming was created by and for the Chinese in order to make US manufacturing non-competitive."

Trump's use of disinformation energized his base. This sharpened the polarization of voters. In the midst of Trump's birther campaign against Obama, for example, a *New York Times*/CBS poll indicated that 25 percent of Americans believed the president was born outside of the United States, and another 18 percent didn't know or had no opinion. But Republicans were much more likely to believe this false information. This persisted through the campaign; a 2016 NBC poll found that 72 percent of Republicans doubted Obama's citizenship. "The fact that more Republicans currently think that the president was not born in the US and that this belief does not depend on how knowledgeable they are about politics is surprising. The country may be divided both about facts and opinions," the report said.

And Trump—who would go on to lie, mislead, misinform, and disinform more frequently than he would tell the truth during the campaign—ramped up his hostility to a press corps trying to still hold him to the truth. In late November, Trump stood in front of a crowd at a Myrtle Beach convention center, and he mocked the movements of a *New York Times* reporter with a physical disability. The next day, Trump denied even knowing the reporter, whom he had met in person at least a dozen times.

Trump had a reason for attacking the press repeatedly. He explained it to Lesley Stahl, a correspondent with CBS's *60 Minutes*. "You know why I do it? I do it to discredit you all and demean you all so when you write negative stories about me, no one will believe you."

Trump's brash tactics were helping him win, and that is what Trump always liked to do.

But Trump wasn't the only one working to do this.

Even before Trump's campaign had started, Vladimir Putin had launched a secret disinformation war against the United States. US intelligence experts now believe that the Russian president's goal has been to erode the trust of Americans in presidential candidates and the US political system in general. Putin and his army of hackers and trolls had one man they hoped would become the next president of the United States: Donald Trump.

CHAPTER 10

The RUSSIA CONNECTIONS

"Thanks @piersmorgan! 'Trump is the most unpredictable, extraordinary, entertaining & massively popular candidate this country has ever seen.'"

—@realDonaldTrump, May 20, 2016

AS 2015 CAME TO AN end and nights grew darker and colder, Trump's rhetoric followed suit. He pledged to bring back torture, "bomb the shit" out of Islamic terrorists, and kill their families—a war crime. His supporters loved it, though, and he continued to dominate the media and climb in the polls.

He turned calls for torture into performance art at rallies like the one he held just before Thanksgiving in Ohio. Wearing a navy suit and powder-blue tie, Trump feigned weariness with the media.

"This morning, they asked me a question," he said. "'Would you approve waterboarding?'"

He repeated himself. "Would I approve waterboarding?"

> **He repeated himself.**
> **"Would I approve waterboarding?"**

He pointed to the cheering crowd, which knew its cue. More cheers erupted.

"Would I approve waterboarding?" he asked once more, before launching into a gruesome and detailed account of what the "other side" allegedly does.

"They chop off our young people's heads and they put 'em on a stick," Trump said. "They build these iron cages, and they'll put twenty people in them. And they drop them in the ocean for fifteen minutes and pull them up fifteen minutes later.

"Would I approve waterboarding? You bet your ass I would. In a heartbeat."

The crowd cheered again and waved *TRUMP: MAKE AMERICA GREAT AGAIN* signs.

But Trump wasn't finished.

"I would approve more than that," he said. "Don't kid yourself, folks. It works, okay? It works. Only a stupid person would say it doesn't work. It works."

He knew this, he said, because "very, very important people" had told him so, but were reluctant to say it out loud because of political correctness. "And you know what? If it doesn't work, they deserve it anyway for what they're doing to us."

His performance thrilled the crowd, even as it did not reflect research on interrogation methods, which shows that building rapport and relationships with detainees is the fastest and most effective means of getting reliable information. Also, no country permits torture, including the United States.

Trump wasn't concerned about truths demonstrated with research and data, or even the requirements of the law, despite his professed support of law and order. Trump appeared to be looking at the campaign the way a salesman looks at a product he wants to move. What do people want to hear? What do they feel in their gut? As long as he hit those targets, his fans would cheer him on at rallies and on social media. Trump knew his audience and how to move them, and he used misleading and false information to do so at a rate far higher than his competition.

> Trump knew his audience and how to move them, and he used misleading and false information to do so at a rate far higher than his competition.

As Trump flew from rally to rally on his private jet, he pushed ahead with his personal business, once again attempting to put a Trump Tower in Moscow. He had two intermediaries trying to set up a deal with a Russian builder: Felix Sater—whom Trump, under oath, testified he wouldn't recognize even if they were in a room together—and Michael Cohen, the lawyer who'd threatened a journalist who questioned Trump's treatment of his first wife.

If Trump's team could pull off the deal this time around, it would be a good one in many respects.

First, the tower would be large—at least 150 hotel rooms, 250 luxury condominiums, a spa and fitness center, high-end retail, and similarly posh office space. Trump wouldn't have to pay a dime to get in on it, and in exchange for the use of his name, he'd get $4 million up front; a percentage of the gross sales; approval of the building's design plans, sales, and marketing; and the rights to name the spa after Ivanka.

And finally, a successful project in Moscow could be used to bolster his political aims.

"Dear Michael," Sater wrote to Cohen on October 13, 2015, "Attached is the signed [letter of intent], by Andrey Rozov. Please have Mr. Trump counter-sign, signed [sic] and sent [sic] back. Lets [sic] make this happen and build a Trump Moscow. And possibly fix relations between the countries by showing everyone that commerce & business are much better and more practical than politics. That should be Putins [sic] message as well, and we will help him agree on that message.

"Help world peace and make a lot of money, [sic] I would say thats [sic] a great lifetime goal for us to go after."

Trump's swelling business empire gave ethicists much to ponder as they considered the possibility he might be elected. The US Constitution prohibits federal office holders to receive gifts, payments, or other things of value from foreign states or representatives. If the president could accept gifts from foreign governments, then foreign governments would essentially have a clear path for buying influence.

Given the size of Trump's holdings, the potential for abuse was vast. A *Washington Post* analysis found at least 111 Trump companies have operated in eighteen countries and territories across South America, Asia, and the Middle East. Trump's companies have more than eight hundred registered trademarks in eighty countries.

Nitty-gritty details of Trump's business were difficult for the public to assess. Trump refused to release his tax returns—making him the first major presidential candidate in forty years to do so. And while he had filled out a Personal Financial Disclosure form with the Federal Election Commission, those documents aren't as revealing as tax returns. What's more, Trump listed his net worth as $10 billion on his disclosure form—more than a billion higher than it had been just a few weeks before he filled it out. Given his past exaggerations and lies about his worth, people had reason to be skeptical of any claims Trump made.

Despite the potential for future conflicts, Trump continued to expand his empire and seek trademarks during his candidacy. It wasn't just the Moscow tower, either. Trump also signed eight deals apparently connected with a potential hotel in Saudi Arabia, the *Washington Post* reported.

The ethics issues would be unprecedented if Trump were to be elected. But no one in the Trump camp seemed concerned about the ethics of a business relationship between Trump and Putin. In fact, they viewed it as an advantage.

"Micheal [sic]," Sater wrote on November 3, "we can own this story. Donald doesn't stare down, he negotiates and understands the economic issues and Putin only want [sic] to deal with a pragmatic leader, and a successful business man is a good candidate for someone who knows how to negotiate. 'Business, politics, whatever [sic] it is all the same for someone who knows how to deal.'

"Our boy can become President of the USA and we can engineer it," Sater wrote. "I will get all of Putins [sic] team to buy in on this, I will manage this process."　．

As Trump's team angled to engineer the presidency with the assistance of Russian insiders, Russian propagandists under the direction of Putin were also working to advance Trump's campaign. The Russian intelligence arm that collects information for the nation's military—the GRU—hacked into the Democratic National Committee computer network in July of 2015, shortly after Trump announced his run.

> By December 2015, a Russian propaganda operation known as the Internet Research Agency had started boosting Trump as a candidate.

By December 2015, a Russian propaganda operation known as the Internet Research Agency had started boosting Trump as a candidate. Funded by a Putin crony, the St. Petersburg troll farm specialized in propaganda (biased information meant to promote a particular point of view) as well as disinformation (false information deliberately issued by a government). This was intended to widen the growing ideological divide between Americans.

Some disinformation was elaborate: websites that were functioning duplicates of mainstream media ones, reporting an alleged terror attack on US soil that never happened, as well as fake information about an Ebola outbreak in Atlanta. The trolls also posted comments online and made fake Facebook pages and Twitter accounts. Putin wanted to erode faith in the democratic process in the United States, help get Trump elected, or, failing that, harm Hillary Clinton's effectiveness as president of a deliberately divided nation.

Russia has long been hostile to the United States and to the US-led liberal democratic order in the world, but interfering directly with an election was more aggressive and ambitious than they'd ever been. Putin was angry about the Magnitsky Act and about painful and potentially destabilizing economic sanctions that followed his aggression in Ukraine. Russia had also lost its spot in an international political forum known as the Group of Eight (which was renamed the Group of Seven or G7 after the exit), a blow to Russian prestige.

Putin found a sympathetic ally in Lieutenant General Michael Flynn, the man Trump was leaning on as an informal foreign policy adviser. On December 10, Flynn traveled to Russia so he could attend the anniversary celebration for RT, a TV station funded by the Russian government whose purpose is to improve the appearance of Russia abroad. Other guests at the same dinner included Jill Stein, the Green Party presidential candidate who was, at the time, expected to siphon liberal votes away from Hillary Clinton, and Julian Assange—the editor of Wikileaks—who attended by satellite as he couldn't attend in person.

In Russia, Flynn sat down for a forty-five-minute chat with an RT interviewer.

Dressed in a gray suit, gray tie, and gray striped socks, Flynn criticized the foreign policy of the Obama administration, which had fired him as defense intelligence chief for insubordination. Flynn also spoke of wanting to work with Russia to combat ISIS. Both the United States and Russia, he said, had been acting like "two bullies on the playground," implying both sides were behaving equally badly.

"This is a funny marriage between Russia and the United States. But it's a marriage. It's a marriage whether we like it or not. And that marriage is very, very rocky right now . . . and what we don't need is, we don't need that marriage to break up."

For Flynn's efforts, he was paid up to $45,000, and as guest of honor, was seated next to Putin at a gala dinner. Flynn was supposed to disclose this income on federal forms, and had been informed of this at his retirement from the military. He did not.

Meanwhile, Trump kept up his tough rhetoric on immigrants—broadening his assault to include Muslims. On the seventy-fourth anniversary of the Japanese invasion of Pearl Harbor, in front of a rapt audience in South Carolina, and following a mass shooting of Americans by Muslim immigrants, Trump read a statement: "Donald J. Trump is calling for a total and complete shutdown of Muslims entering the United States until our country's representatives can figure out what the hell is going on," he said, to applause. "We have no choice. We have no choice."

Trump also advocated government surveillance of mosques, a potential database to track all Muslims in the country, and a ban on refugees from Syria, a Middle Eastern country that's been embroiled in a complicated civil war, pitting rebels against its brutal president.

Trump's statements about Muslim immigrants struck observers as being calculated bigotry—premeditated statements he knew would score political points based on the unfounded fear that Muslim immigrants pose a serious danger to Americans.

Ibrahim Hooper, national communications director at the Council on American-Islamic Relations, told the *Washington Post*, "We've always had anti-Muslim bigots, but they've always been at the fringes of society. Now they want to lead it. In saner times, his campaign would be over. In insane times, his campaign can gain support."

Not all of Trump's shows of toughness were political. The week after his Muslim ban, he wanted to demonstrate that he was physically tough, too, so he had his doctor release a letter describing his health. Although candidates typically release their health reports, Trump's letter was—like much of his campaign—one of a kind.

"To Whom My [sic] Concern," the letter began. "I have been the personal physician of Mr. Donald J. Trump since 1980. . . . Mr. Trump has had a recent complete medical examination that showed only positive results. Actually, his blood pressure, 110/65, and laboratory test results were astonishingly excellent."

The letter praised Trump's "physical strength and stamina" as "extraordinary" and said, "If elected, Mr. Trump, I can state unequivocally, will be the healthiest individual ever elected to the presidency."

As some reporters guessed, Trump dictated the letter for his doctor to sign.

The week after the physician's note made the news, Trump garnered more headlines by saying that Barack Obama had "schlonged" Hillary Clinton in the 2008 presidential race. People who recognized the Yiddish origins of the word—which refers to male genitalia—expressed surprise Trump would be so vulgar.

Trump argued the word wasn't crude.

"Once again, #MSM is dishonest," he tweeted. "'Schlonged' is not vulgar. When I said Hillary got 'schlonged' that meant beaten badly."

As 2015 turned into 2016, Trump's team was beaten badly in its attempt to negotiate a Moscow tower. The failure was not for lack of trying. Trump's lawyer Michael Cohen even reached out to Putin's spokesman, Dmitry Peskov. Cohen didn't have Peskov's contact information, so he sent his request to the Kremlin's general e-mail account for media inquiries.

"Over the past few months I have been working with a company based in Russia regarding the development of a Trump Tower-Moscow project in Moscow City," Cohen wrote. "Without getting into lengthy specifics, the communication between our two sides has stalled. As this project is too important, I am hereby requesting your assistance. I respectfully request someone, preferably you, contact me so that I might discuss the specifics as well as arranging meetings with the appropriate individuals. I thank you in advance for your assistance and look forward to hearing from you soon."

The Trump team got no response. Because the project could not go forward without Putin's support, they shelved the idea once more. Also, there were more pressing issues, including Trump's performance at the Iowa caucus on February 1. With the memory of Megyn Kelly's embarrassing questions in his Fox News interview still fresh, Trump shunned the pre-caucus Republican debate. After flying into town on his deluxe 757—where he loved nothing more than blasting Elton John's "Rocket Man" and "Tiny Dancer" at top volume as he ate fast food and Oreos from sealed packs—Trump held his own show three miles away, an event intended to raise money for military veterans and cost Fox ratings.

The show attracted a crowd of 700, and Trump claimed to have gathered more than $6 million in donations to the Donald J. Trump Foundation during the broadcast, including $1 million from his own pocket. He promised to distribute this money to charities that supported veterans, a promise journalists would track for months as part of escalating hostilities between Trump and a skeptical press.

> Despite his publicity stunt, Trump lost in Iowa, coming in behind Texas Senator Ted Cruz.

Despite his publicity stunt, Trump lost in Iowa, coming in behind Texas Senator Ted Cruz.

Trump was livid. "You don't know what you're doing," he told his campaign manager Corey Lewandowski. "This team is completely lost."

Trump also laid into Cruz, who had made an incorrect robocall blast claiming Dr. Ben Carson had dropped out of the race: "The State of Iowa should disqualify Ted Cruz from the most recent election on the basis that he cheated- a total fraud!" Trump tweeted on February 3.

Trump's team worried how his rage would affect voters. One evening, as Trump dined on a hamburger from McDonald's,

Lewandowski gave him a warning: "If you don't start talking about what your positive vision is for the country and stop complaining about Ted Cruz, you're going to lose."

Trump walked out of the room without saying a word. He continued to tweet angrily about Cruz dozens of times in the days that followed. But he still won in New Hampshire on February 9, a victory that struck observers as a bellwether. The conservative *National Review* called it "Armageddon for the GOP Establishment." Others predicted Trump had the party nomination in the bag.

Exit polls looked good for Trump. What he was saying on the stump aligned with what worried and frustrated New Hampshire's conservative voters. Almost half of them expressed anger at the federal government, which was the heart of Trump's campaign. Forty percent wanted to deport all undocumented immigrants, as Trump had pledged to do. Sixty percent expressed fear of terrorism. And even more, two thirds, favored Trump's temporary Muslim ban.

His political instincts had paid off like a slot machine. He could be crude and combative. He could say things that were offensive or even untrue. But as long as he criticized the government and his other favorite target, the media, he could draw thousands at rallies, dominate the headlines and airwaves, and eclipse every other candidate in the still-crowded field.

He was on track to win the nomination. But he was also going to need a more robust team to bring it home. The next two months transformed his operation in that regard, especially when it came to foreign policy.

Despite his long interest in foreign policy, he had no experience. Instead of turning to members of the conservative establishment—many of whom had considered him unfit to lead—Trump hired people with less diplomatic experience, putting them under the leadership of Alabama Senator Jeff Sessions, the first senator to endorse Trump's candidacy.

The team scooped up an energy consultant named George Papadopoulos from the defunct Carson campaign. Trump's team also picked up Carter Page, a consultant whose firm Global Energy Capital courted Russian businesses, including businesses subject to sanctions. Page also considered himself an "informal advisor to the staff of the Kremlin" on energy issues.

Unbeknownst to Trump, the FBI had been watching Page since at least 2013, when a wiretap of suspected Russian spies revealed they were trying to recruit Page, even as they thought he was a greedy "idiot."

Trump needed more than foreign policy expertise, though. He also needed a savvy political fixer in case the Republican elite forced Trump through a contested convention. For that insight, he turned to a veteran consultant and lobbyist named Paul Manafort, who'd sent a pair of memos to the campaign offering his services.

"I have managed Presidential campaigns around the world," Manafort wrote. "I have had no client relationships dealing with Washington since around 2005. I have avoided the political establishment in Washington since 2005."

That Manafort had no Washington baggage more recent than a failed Bob Dole campaign appealed to Trump. Manafort also had an apartment in Trump Tower, another pleasing fact. And there was one more factor that appealed to the deal-conscious Trump: Manafort was willing to work for free.

After Ivanka printed the memos so her father could read them, the campaign set up a meeting, and Trump liked what he saw.

"Wow, you're a good-looking guy," he told Manafort, who had wardrobe that he'd spent more than $1.3 million assembling, a large head crowned with thick brown hair, and deeply tanned skin.

Trump wasn't dissuaded by the brutes, dictators, and oligarchs on Manafort's client list. One of Manafort's clients, Viktor Yanukovych, had been elected president of Ukraine. His presidency ended in scandal, and he fled the country amid violent protests against his leadership. After Yanukovych's departure, Putin annexed Crimea, touching off sanctions from the United States and Europe. Yanukovych was hiding in Russia and wanted for treason when Manafort offered his services to Trump.

Another Manafort client was a Russian aluminum magnate and Putin ally named Oleg Deripaska. Manafort owed Deripaska nearly $19 million—money Deripaska wanted back. Manafort hoped his connection to Trump would help him solve that problem.

The extent of Trump's connections to Russia were hidden. But his bragging over the years of his relationship with Putin gave his primary opponents a target. They accused him of being soft on the Russian president. By the middle of his campaign, Trump began to downplay any connection he might have with Putin.

"I have no relationship with him other than he called me a genius," Trump said. "He said Donald Trump is a genius and he is going to be the leader of the party and he's going to be the leader of the world or something.

"These characters that I'm running against said, 'We want you to disavow that statement.' I said what, he called me a genius, I'm going to disavow it? Are you crazy? Can you believe it? How stupid are they?

"And besides that, wouldn't it be good if we actually got along with countries? Wouldn't it actually be a positive thing? I think I'd have a good relationship with Putin. I mean who knows?"

Even as Trump cultivated a good relationship with Putin, the relationship between Russia and the United States continued to deteriorate.

During the months Trump was staffing his foreign policy team with people who made their living in rubles, Putin authorized his Russian intelligence services to kick off a second phishing expedition of high-profile Democrats and Democratic Party officials, using fake e-mails meant to trick users into disclosing their passwords. A hacker group dubbed Fancy Bear raided the Democratic National Committee servers and stole thousands of e-mails, including the ones of John Podesta, Hillary Clinton's campaign manager.

Meanwhile, members of Trump's campaign reached out to the Kremlin repeatedly. Papadopoulos, the young newcomer from the Carson campaign, met with a pair of Russians in London, including a woman who falsely claimed to be Putin's niece. Papadopoulus wanted to set up a meeting between the Russian government and Trump's campaign.

The national co-chairman of Trump's campaign—a former Air Force colonel and Obama birther named Sam Clovis—was happy at the prospect.

"Great work," he told Papadopoulos.

Even without having a meeting, Trump had begun saying something Putin wanted to hear: that NATO was obsolete.

"We're dealing with NATO from the days of the Soviet Union, which no longer exists," he told Fox News.

The North Atlantic Treaty Organization was forged in 1949 to promote democratic values, peaceful resolution to conflict, as well as cooperative national security. Russia is not one of the twenty-nine nations that takes part in the treaty. Trump had long believed that the United States was paying more than its fair share to keep the world safe.

As Trump argued for a new balance of power in the world, he faced challenges balancing the power within his campaign.

His campaign manager, Corey Lewandowski, had allegedly manhandled and bruised a reporter from the far-right Breitbart News, lunging at her during a rally as she walked beside Trump and asked him questions. Lewandowski said he never touched her, and also claimed the reporter was a "nutjob" who leaped a barricade to get access to the candidate. Video footage contradicted his claim; the reporter does not jump a barrier and lunge at Trump. She's walking beside him, apparently asking questions. Battery charges were filed against Lewandowski, but later dropped.

What's more, Lewandowski wasn't thrilled with Manafort's presence. Trump's children, who were involved in his campaign as they were in other parts of his business, liked Manafort. When Trump lost the Wisconsin primary on April 5, coming in thirteen points behind Ted Cruz, it was only a matter of time before Manafort got the reins.

One of the first things Manafort did was to try to make Trump seem more presidential, as he'd done for Yanukovych in Ukraine. That meant no more freewheeling TV appearances.

Trump was traveling in his helicopter when he found out Manafort wanted to keep him off TV. He forced his pilot to lower the chopper enough to get cell service.

"Did you say I shouldn't be on TV on Sunday?" he asked Manafort. "I'll go on TV anytime I g--dam f---ing want and you won't say another f---ing word about me! Tone it down! I wanna turn it up! I don't wanna tone anything down!"

Despite this miscalculation, Manafort gained increasing control over the campaign, and increasing scrutiny from reporters, who were aware of his links to Russian and Ukrainian oligarchs. When reporters asked the campaign about Manafort's dealings with Deripaska and a Ukrainian businessman, he told spokeswoman Hope Hicks to ignore the questions. That turned into wishful thinking on his part.

Meanwhile, Trump delivered his first foreign policy speech, drafted with help from Papadopoulos, at the Mayflower Hotel in Washington, DC, on April 27. Wearing a dark suit, American flag pin, and brilliant red tie, Trump read from a teleprompter:

"America First will be the major and overriding theme of my administration," he said. "But to chart our path forward, we must first briefly take a look back. We have a lot to be proud of.

"In the 1940s we saved the world. The greatest generation beat back the Nazis and Japanese imperialists. Then we saved the world again. This time, from totalitarianism and communism. The Cold War lasted for decades but, guess what, we won and we won big.

Democrats and Republicans working together got Mr. Gorbachev to heed the words of President Reagan, our great president, when he said, 'tear down this wall.'"

As much as Trump intended to look back on proud moments in US history, the phrase "America First" is associated with policies that would have prevented those proud moments. In 1940, an America First Committee was founded to keep America from taking part in World War II. As many as a million joined the movement, including socialists, conservatives, future president Gerald Ford, Peace Corps founder Sergeant Shriver, and prominent anti-Semites, including the pilot Charles Lindbergh, automaker Henry Ford, and Avery Brundage, a former US Olympic Committee chairman who'd refused to let two Jewish track stars compete in the 1936 Olympics.

> **Trump's speech alarmed America's traditional allies in Europe.**

Trump's speech alarmed America's traditional allies in Europe. Hearing the echo of earlier US isolationism, some took the unusual step of criticizing the candidate's words.

A former Swedish prime minster, Carl Bildt, said Trump's speech sounded as if he was "abandoning both democratic allies and democratic values" while staying silent on Russian aggression in Ukraine.

One potential reason for Trump's silence on Russia's actions: the country's ambassador to the United States, Sergey Kislyak, was sitting in the front row during the speech.

Kislyak had already met with Sessions to discuss US policies of interest to Russia (though Sessions would later deny it had any relation to the campaign). At a reception before the speech, Kislyak met Ivanka's husband, Jared Kushner, one of Trump's chief advisers in his campaign, and a fellow real estate developer who, like Trump, had inherited a business from his father.

> The meetings might have seemed
> insignificant at the time.
> They would not seem that way
> later to the FBI.

The meetings might have seemed insignificant at the time. They would not seem that way later to the FBI.

Meanwhile, Trump was still trying to knock out his competition. A few days after his foreign policy speech at the Mayflower, he called *Fox & Friends* to share a conspiracy theory about his rival Ted Cruz. It was a tidbit about John F. Kennedy's assassin that Trump had read in the *National Enquirer*, a supermarket tabloid run by a Trump ally named David Pecker.

Trump told the hosts, "[Ted Cruz's] father was with Lee Harvey Oswald prior to Oswald's being—you know, shot. I mean, the whole thing is ridiculous. What is this, right prior to his being shot, and nobody even brings it up. I mean, they don't even talk about that. That was reported, and nobody talks about it."

"What was he doing with Lee Harvey Oswald shortly before the death? Before the shooting?" Trump said, implying that Cruz's father had something to do with the assassination, and that the collective media silence was a cover-up orchestrated by journalists around the globe. "It's horrible."

Cruz rejected the insinuation in blunt terms, calling Trump "a pathological liar."

The Texas senator had nothing to lose in saying that; he dropped out of the race that night, making Trump the presumptive Republican nominee.

During those same weeks, Papadopoulos kept pushing the prospect of meetings with the Kremlin, including with members of the Russian Ministry of Foreign Affairs, which he reported was "open for cooperation."

Clovis, the birther, wanted Papadopoulos to hold off: "There are legal issues we need to mitigate, meeting with foreign officials as a private citizen."

Clovis might have been referring to the Logan Act, a rarely prosecuted law passed in 1799 that makes it a crime for private citizens to negotiate with foreign governments that have disputes with the United States. No one has ever been convicted of violating the act.

Although he didn't get the meetings he wanted, Papadopoulos remained excited about the prospect of working with Russian officials to help Trump.

"It's history making if it happens," Papadopoulos wrote to one of his sources.

A couple weeks after Trump's speech, during a night of drinking in a cozy, brick-walled wine bar in London's Notting Hill neighborhood, the dark-haired Trump aide told Australia's top diplomat that the Russians had Clinton's e-mails and "dirt" on the candidate.

Months later, the diplomat would remember this conversation when stolen e-mails were released by Wikileaks, the organization run by Julian Assange, a host of a show on RT, which would participate in Russian efforts to influence the election.

As much as Trump's campaign wanted to meet Russians close to Putin, Russian oligarchs also wanted to lend support to Trump. Aras Agalarov, who worked with Trump on the Miss Universe pageant in Moscow, sent Don Trump Jr. a letter in February through his pop-star son's publicist, Rob Goldstone.

"Emin's father has asked me to pass on his congratulations . . . offering his support and that of his many important Russian friends and colleagues, especially with reference to US/Russia relations," it read in part.

Prominent Russians with close Putin connections wanted to meet Trump as well. A banker named Alexander Torshin tried to meet the candidate when he was in town as the guest of honor at the annual National Rifle Association convention in late May. The deputy governor of Russia's central bank—a suspected money launderer being wiretapped by Spanish authorities—met instead with Trump's son Don, a meeting noted by the Guardian Civil, Spain's national police.

FOLLOWING SPREAD: At the Republican National Convention in Cleveland, Ohio, Donald Trump accepts the party's presidential nomination. July 21, 2016. *(Nicolas Pinault/VOA)*

B Y SUMMER, THE NEARLY IMPOSSIBLE HAPPENED. Trump had gathered enough votes from delegates to win the Republican nomination. The journey had been a wild one, the culmination of a notion Trump had hatched as early as 1980, when he had that interview with Rona Barrett. Written off as a joke at first, Trump turned his campaign into a juggernaut, commanding billions of dollars in free media coverage with his blunt, blistering, and often baseless assertions. There was always a chance that delegates would refuse to cast their ballots for him, but that's why he had Manafort on board.

Trump's next challenge would be his biggest yet: On June 6, former Secretary of State Hillary Rodham Clinton had earned enough delegates to become the presumptive Democratic nominee. She was one of the most experienced candidates in history, and almost no one thought Trump could beat her.

A brutal campaign was about to get uglier in public.

A brutal campaign was about to get uglier in public. Behind the scenes, it was about to become the subject of an unprecedented investigation by the FBI.

CHAPTER 11

CROSSFIRE HURRICANE

"It is impossible for the FBI not to recommend criminal charges against Hillary Clinton. What she did was wrong! What Bill did was stupid!"

—@realDonaldTrump, July 2, 2016

AFTER A SUMMER OF Trump's bluster that Clinton should be in prison, the two nominees faced off in a series of three debates. Trump didn't perform well in the first two. Clinton had come highly prepared. Trump had preferred to go by instinct, and for some reason, he'd sniffed so much during their first two matchups that it had generated media coverage. Clinton crushed him in the polls.

"It was just announced-by sources-that no charges will be brought against Crooked Hillary Clinton. Like I said, the system is totally rigged!"

—@realDonaldTrump, July 2, 2016

"The new joke in town is that Russia leaked the disastrous DNC e-mails, which should never have been written (stupid), because Putin likes me"

—@realDonaldTrump, July 25, 2016

"The polls are close so Crooked Hillary is getting out of bed and will campaign tomorrow. Why did she hammer 13 devices and acid-wash e-mails?"

—@realDonaldTrump, September 4, 2016

> "The results are in on the
> final debate and it is almost
> unanimous, I WON! Thank you,
> these are very exciting times."
>
> —@realDonaldTrump, October 21, 2016

In the third matchup, despite a strong start on Trump's part, Clinton still found ways to get under his skin.

Anticipating he was going to lose the election, Trump repeatedly claimed the system was "rigged."

What's more, he refused to say whether he'd honor the results if Clinton won.

"I'll look at it at the time," he said.

This astonished the debate moderator, Chris Wallace of Fox News: "But, sir, there is a tradition in this country—in fact, one of the prides of this country—is the peaceful transition of power.... Are you saying you're not prepared now to commit to that principle?"

"What I'm saying is that I will tell you at the time," Trump said. "I'll keep you in suspense. Okay?"

"That's horrifying," Clinton shot back. "We've been around for 240 years. We've had free and fair elections. We've accepted the outcomes when we may not have liked them. And that is what must be expected of anyone standing on a debate stage during a general election."

Trump wouldn't budge, and Wallace had to switch topics.

When a quote from WikiLeaks came up, Clinton took the open-ing to hit Trump where he was weak—on his failure to condemn Russia for committing criminal hacking: "What's really important about WikiLeaks is that the Russian government has engaged in espionage against Americans. They have hacked American web-sites, American accounts of private people, of institutions," she said. "This has come from the highest levels of the Russian govern-ment, clearly, from Putin himself, in an effort, as seventeen of our intelligence agencies have confirmed, to influence our election."

ABOVE: Hillary Clinton and Donald Trump face each other in a 90-minute town hall meeting debate—the second of three presidential debates—at Washington University in St. Louis, October 9, 2016. *(AP Photo/Julio Cortez)*

Instead of condemning the attack, as Clinton challenged him to do, Trump said Putin didn't respect Clinton.

"Well, that's because he'd rather have a puppet as president of the United States," Clinton retorted.

"No puppet. No puppet," Trump said, talking over Clinton. "You're the puppet!"

When Wallace asked Trump if he condemned Russian interference, Trump said, "Of course I condemn. Of course I—I don't know Putin. I have no idea."

Wallace followed up: "I'm not asking—I'm asking do you condemn?"

> **Trump did not condemn the cyberattack. Not then, and not later.**

Trump did not condemn the cyberattack. Not then, and not later.

"I never met Putin," he said. "This is not my best friend. But if the United States got along with Russia, wouldn't be so bad."

It was a strange way to talk about a country that had just committed crimes against the United States.

But Trump had his reasons.

ONE MORNING ABOUT FOUR MONTHS EARLIER, AN e-mail arrived in the inbox of Trump's son Don Jr.— an e-mail that would have great significance in the years to come.

It was a message from Rob Goldstone, the bulldog-shaped publicist for the pop star Emin Agalarov, and it contained an offer of political assistance: A Russian government official wanted to give the Trump campaign "official documents and information that would incriminate Hillary in her dealings with Russia."

"This is obviously very high level and sensitive information but is part of Russia and its government's support for Mr. Trump," Goldstone wrote. "What do you think is the best way to handle this information and would you be able to speak to Emin about it directly? I can also send this info to your father via Rhona, but it is ultrasensitive. So wanted to send to you first."

Despite several laws that prohibit cooperation between private citizens and foreign governments, Don Jr. replied within twenty minutes: ". . . If it's what you say, I love it, especially later in the summer."

That was when dirt would be most useful to his dad.

Don Jr. would later swear under oath that he did not tell his father of the meeting.

But on June 7, Donald Trump gave a speech in California, hinting about something juicy on the way: "I am going to give a major speech on probably Monday of next week," he said, "and we're going to be discussing all of the things that have taken place with the Clintons. I think you're going to find it very informative and very, very interesting."

>>>>> What number he could call?
>>>>>
>>>>> This iphone speaks many languages
>>>>>
>>>>> On Jun 6, 2016, at 15:03, Donald Trump Jr. ████████████ wrote:
>>>>>
>>>>> Rob could we speak now?
>>>>> d
>>>>>
>>>>>
>>>>>
>>>>> Donald J. Trump Jr.
>>>>> Executive Vice President of Development and Acquisitions The Trump
>>>>> Organization
>>>>> 725 Fifth Avenue | New York, NY | 10022 p. █████████ | █
████████ | trump.com
>>>>>
>>>>>
>>>>>
>>>>> -----Original Message-----
>>>>> From: Rob Goldstone ████████████
>>>>> Sent: Monday, June 06, 2016 12:40 PM
>>>>> To: Donald Trump Jr. ████████████
>>>>> Subject: Re: Russia - Clinton - private and confidential
>>>>>
>>>>> Hi Don
>>>>> Let me know when you are free to talk with Emin by phone about this
>>>>> Hillary info - you had mentioned early this week so wanted to try
>>>>> to schedule a time and day Best to you and family Rob Goldstone
>>>>>
>>>>> This iphone speaks many languages
>>>>>
>>>>> On Jun 3, 2016, at 10:53, Donald Trump Jr.████████████ wrote:
>>>>>
>>>>> Thanks Rob I appreciate that. I am on the road at the moment but perhaps I just speak to Emin
first. Seems we have some time and if it's what you say I love it especially later in the summer. Could
we do a call first thing next week when I am back?
>>>>> Best,
>>>>> Don
>>>>>
>>>>>
>>>>> Sent from my iPhone
>>>>>
>>>>>> On Jun 3, 2016, at 10:36 AM, Rob Goldstone████████████ wrote:
>>>>>>
>>>>>> Good morning
>>>>>> Emin just called and asked me to contact you with something very interesting.
>>>>>> The Crown prosecutor of Russia met with his father Aras this morning and in their meeting offered
to provide the Trump campaign with some official documents and information that would incriminate Hillary
and her dealings with Russia and would be very useful to your father.
>>>>>> This is obviously very high level and sensitive information but is part of Russia and its
government's support for Mr. Trump - helped along by Aras and Emin.
>>>>>> What do you think is the best way to handle this information and would you be able to speak to
Emin about it directly?
>>>>>> I can also send this info to your father via Rhona, but it is ultra sensitive so wanted to send to
you first.
>>>>>> Best
>>>>>> Rob Goldstone
>>>>>>
>>>>>> This iphone speaks many languages
>>>>>
>>>>> This e-mail message, and any attachments to it, are for the sole use of the intended recipients,
and may contain confidential and privileged information. Any unauthorized review, use, disclosure or
distribution of this email message or its attachments is prohibited. If you are not the intended
recipient, please contact the sender by reply email and destroy all copies of the original message.
Please note that any views or opinions presented in this email are solely those of the author and do not
necessarily represent those of the company. Finally, while the company uses virus protection, the
recipient should check this email and any attachments for the presence of viruses. The company accepts no
liability for any damage caused by any virus transmitted by this email.
>

ABOVE: An extract of the e-mail exchange between Don Jr. and Rob Goldstone concerning a
meeting with a Russian government official offering incriminating materials on Hillary Clinton.
(Senate Judiciary Committee Inquiry into Circumstances Surrounding Trump Tower Meeting)

On June 9 at 4:00 P.M., Don Jr. was ready and waiting in the massive conference room on the twenty-fifth floor of Trump Tower, where giant windows offer spectacular views of Manhattan. An enormous stone-topped table dominates the floor. The conference table can seat dozens in its black leather chairs, but this meeting would not require even half of them.

Just two insiders from the Trump campaign had been invited to receive the high-level proof of Clinton's crimes that Don Jr. knew his father wanted: his brother-in-law, Jared Kushner, and Paul Manafort, the seasoned strategist who was being maneuvered into the top spot of the campaign.

They did not know whom they would be speaking with, only that incriminating evidence was coming.

When Goldstone arrived, he came with an entourage that included an interpreter and the following people:

- Natalia Veselnitskaya, who once worked as a prosecutor in Russia and defended Putin allies accused of corruption and also works as an informant to the Russian prosecutor general.

- Rinat Akhmetshin, a Soviet military veteran and a media consultant and DC lobbyist for Putin allies. He became a US citizen in 2009. He hadn't expected to come to the meeting, but accepted Veselnitskaya's invitation even though he'd been wearing a pink T-shirt and pink jeans with holes in them.

- Irakly Kaveladze, also an immigrant as well as a vice president at the Crocus Group and an accused money launderer, though he denies it.

After introductions and small talk about the beauty of the Manhattan view, Don Jr. addressed Veselnitskaya, who sat across the table from him: "So I believe you have some information for us."

> ## Through the interpreter, the lawyer spoke—but not about Clinton crimes.

Through the interpreter, the lawyer spoke—but not about Clinton crimes. Rather, she discussed a scheme by a hedge fund manager who allegedly dodged taxes in both Russia and the United States and also made donations to the DNC.

"So can you show us how does this money go to Hillary?" Don Jr. asked. "Like, specifically, do you have paperwork? Or just indicate how money goes to Hillary."

She did not have anything of the sort.

Kushner got impatient with her. "I really have no idea what you're talking about," he said. "Could you please focus a bit more and maybe just start again?"

Veselnitskaya gave her spiel again, word for word, infuriating Kushner, who left the meeting before it officially ended.

Meanwhile, Manafort leaned back in his chair, thumbing notes into his Blackberry. Although Kushner didn't understand what Veselnitskaya was talking about, Manafort—who was more politically savvy—did. Veselnitskaya was essentially arguing that the hedge fund manager who had employed Magnitsky was a tax cheat, and he and other wealthy people were supporting Democrats.

Eventually, Veselnitskaya got to her main point: advocating the repeal of the Magnitsky Act in exchange for ending the ban on adoptions of Russian orphans by Americans.

In short, she had no incriminating evidence against Clinton. There was nothing useful to the Trumps. When that was clear, Don Jr. abruptly cut off the meeting, inviting the Russians to return after his father was elected.

Afterward, Goldstone apologized to Don Jr. for the disappointing results. "I'm really embarrassed by this meeting," he said. "I don't know what that was about."

The "very, very interesting" Clinton news that Trump had promised to deliver in his speeches did not materialize.

But the *Washington Post* had a bombshell headline on June 14: "Russian government hackers penetrated DNC, stole opposition research on Trump."

The hack was a devastating security breach for the Democratic National Committee. Two teams of hackers—dubbed Cozy Bear and Fancy Bear—had been identified and kicked out, but the damage to the DNC was substantial. Hackers had plundered their correspondence for a year, with Cozy Bear focusing on e-mail and text messages and Fancy Bear stealing the DNC's opposition research on Trump. Their work had allegedly been authorized by Vladimir Putin.

Putin spokesman Dmitry Peskov, the architect of the strategy, denied it existed: "I completely rule out a possibility that the [Russian] government or the government bodies have been involved in this."

Likewise, the Trump campaign rejected the finding that Russia had hacked the DNC. "We believe it was the DNC that did the 'hacking' as a way to distract from the many issues facing their deeply flawed candidate and failed party leader," a news release said.

As Russia and the Trump campaign issued denials, someone named Guccifer 2.0 took credit for the hack, claiming to be a Romanian lone operative. On a WordPress blog, he posted about his exploits and invited people to send questions through Twitter.

But at one point Guccifer 2.0 messed up. Though he usually logged in through a virtual private network that hid his location, he once posted to social media without using the VPN. This left a Moscow-based IP address in the server logs on a site Guccifer used. Experts determined Guccifer 2.0 wasn't a Romanian hacktivist after all. "He" was a front for people working for Russian military intelligence.

The Russian intelligence agency's first release was a 237-page opposition-research report on Donald Trump. Compiled in December 2015, the report called him a disloyal, self-interested liar and provided extensive evidence in support of this argument. The research was meant to give Clinton substantiated ammunition to use in her speeches and at debates—for example, this broadside against his business chops: "[H]e has repeatedly run into serious financial crises in his career and his record raises serious questions about whether he is qualified to manage the fiscal challenges facing this country."

But, as nasty as this opposition research on Trump was, it was nowhere near the full story of the opposition research that had yet to arrive through a DC-based company called Fusion GPS. For clients who can afford their steep rates, Fusion GPS provides research and strategic intelligence. Most of their clients aren't political; they're trying to win lawsuits or "find out who ripped them off," cofounder Glenn Simpson said. Fusion mines public records, some of which they obtain using federal open-information laws. Fusion also has a network of contacts around the world for more elusive information.

A conservative news site had hired Fusion to look into Trump before it was clear he'd win the nomination. They stopped pursuing the information. But then the Clinton campaign moved in. Simpson is a former *Wall Street Journal* investigative reporter who covered corruption in Russia extensively. He describes himself as being "obsessed" with the country's kleptocracy and police state.

The Trump investigation was started in the fall of 2015 as a straightforward examination of Trump's business record, associations, bankruptcies, and suppliers—such as whether any of his branded products were made in sweatshops (they were).

The inquiry soon turned unusual, Simpson said, because of Trump's relationships to organized crime figures.

Felix Sater was of particular interest because of Sater's business relationship with a man named Semion Mogilevich, an organized crime boss. To Simpson, it was noteworthy and troubling that Trump had lied under oath about knowing Sater and continued to associate with him long after he'd learned of Sater's ties to mobsters.

Also, Fusion ran into roadblocks when they started looking at sources of Trump's income. Some money flowed in from Kazakhstan. Other income sources, they couldn't account for.

By June, when Simpson had exhausted public records searches, he reached out to a former British spy named Christopher Steele. Simpson was curious about the number of trips Trump had made to Russia, trips that had never materialized into a deal.

CONFIDENTIAL/SENSITIVE SOURCE

COMPANY INTELLIGENCE REPORT 2016/080

US PRESIDENTIAL ELECTION: REPUBLICAN CANDIDATE DONALD TRUMP'S ACTIVITIES IN RUSSIA AND COMPROMISING RELATIONSHIP WITH THE KREMLIN

Summary

- Russian regime has been cultivating, supporting and assisting TRUMP for at least 5 years. Aim, endorsed by PUTIN, has been to encourage splits and divisions in western alliance

- So far TRUMP has declined various sweetener real estate business deals offered him in Russia in order to further the Kremlin's cultivation of him. However he and his inner circle have accepted a regular flow of intelligence from the Kremlin, including on his Democratic and other political rivals

- Former top Russian intelligence officer claims FSB has compromised TRUMP through his activities in Moscow sufficiently to be able to blackmail him. According to several knowledgeable sources, his conduct in Moscow has included perverted sexual acts which have been arranged/monitored by the FSB

- A dossier of compromising material on Hillary CLINTON has been collated by the Russian Intelligence Services over many years and mainly comprises bugged conversations she had on various visits to Russia and intercepted phone calls rather than any embarrassing conduct. The dossier is controlled by Kremlin spokesman, PESKOV, directly on PUTIN's orders. However it has not as yet been distributed abroad, including to TRUMP. Russian intentions for its deployment still unclear

Detail

1. Speaking to a trusted compatriot in June 2016 sources A and B, a senior Russian Foreign Ministry figure and a former top level Russian intelligence officer still active inside the Kremlin respectively, the Russian authorities had been cultivating and supporting US Republican presidential candidate, Donald TRUMP for at least 5 years. Source B asserted that the TRUMP operation was both supported and directed by Russian President Vladimir PUTIN. Its aim was to sow discord and

CONFIDENTIAL/SENSITIVE SOURCE

ABOVE: The first page of the first report compiled by former British spy Christopher Steele. *(Senate Judiciary Committee Inquiry into Circumstances Surrounding Trump Tower Meeting)*

"That struck me as a little bit odd and calling for an explanation," Simpson said.

Simpson gave Steele, who now runs a private intelligence firm, an open-ended assignment: find out what Donald Trump had been doing on those trips—whom he'd done business with, where he'd stayed, and whether anyone had ever offered him anything. Steele, as a former spy stationed in Russia, had sources Simpson didn't, people whose trust he had cultivated during his intelligence work and afterward.

Steele's first report, dated June 20, was a shocker:

Putin's regime had been cultivating, supporting, and helping Trump since at least 2011, with a goal of shattering Western alliances.

Trump had declined real estate deals offered by Russia but had accepted "a regular flow of intelligence from the Kremlin."

Trump had engaged in sexual activities in a Russian hotel room that could make him subject to blackmail.

The Kremlin had a dossier of compromising material on Clinton, too, mostly intercepted phone calls rather than documentation of embarrassing conduct.

The memo was explosive, but Simpson trusted Steele, who had been the lead Russian expert for MI6, where he worked for twenty-two years.

"He's basically a Boy Scout," Simpson said.

Despite Steele's sterling reputation, it was still possible that the report contained errors and even disinformation, a favorite Russian tool meant to sow confusion.

Also, human intelligence—information gathered from people—isn't like public records. You can't file a lawsuit based on human intelligence. But you *can* develop judgments and make informed decisions when the information is credible.

Simpson was concerned with the possibility of Russian meddling with an American election. In 1996, when Simpson was still at the *Wall Street Journal*, he covered Chinese government interference in the US election, something that triggered an investigation and numerous prosecutions. To Simpson, it was credible that the Russian government would want to do the same thing. It also fit a pattern of increasing Russian intelligence operations in Western capitals.

But the DNC hack—which made the news right around the time he got the report—wasn't like anything he'd seen before. Instead of keeping it quiet, the Russians had leaked the information, turning it into a weapon meant to erode Americans' faith in their electoral system. This was "extraordinary" and "criminal," Simpson said.

Simpson and Steele talked it over. From Steele's perspective, there was a chance Trump was being blackmailed, a significant national security threat. Simpson thought there might be an illegal conspiracy between Trump and Russia's government. Steele wanted to tell the FBI, but Simpson wanted to think it over. He had no idea how he might report it, nor did he think it was his role as someone working for the Clinton campaign. What's more, Clinton was still under investigation by the FBI herself over her use of private e-mail servers for government business. The campaign would not want him to approach the bureau.

Steele, who had a contact at the FBI, said he'd take care of making the report. By late June or early July, the former spy began sharing what he knew with the bureau.

This wasn't the first the FBI had heard of troubling information about Trump, his campaign, and its worrisome Russian ties.

Intelligence agencies from the Netherlands and the United Kingdom had provided similar information. What's more, after WikiLeaks released twenty thousand e-mails stolen from the DNC on the eve of the Democratic National Convention, Australian intelligence agents reached out to their American counterparts with word that a Trump adviser, George Papadopoulos, had gotten drunk in London with Australia's top diplomat and bragged about the "dirt" that the Russians had on Clinton.

To confirm this, the FBI secretly sent a pair of agents to London to interview the diplomat, Alexander Downer. Such interviews required a breach of protocol that had to be delicately negotiated by the US and Australia.

But the report seemed credible, and with that, the FBI had opened an investigation into the Trump campaign, which they named Crossfire Hurricane after a Rolling Stones lyric. The FBI would keep an especially tight lid on the investigation, which involved several members of Trump's campaign. Only a select few at the bureau knew the probe was underway at all.

On July 25, the FBI publicly confirmed another investigation, though: this one of the DNC hack.

"A compromise of this nature is something we take very seriously, and the FBI will continue to investigate and hold accountable those who pose a threat in cyberspace," a news release said.

Don Jr. scoffed at the idea of the Russian government meddling in the election. It was a plot cooked up by Democrats, he said. "It's disgusting. It's so phony . . . I mean, I can't think of bigger lies, but that exactly goes to show you what the DNC and what the Clinton camp will do. They will lie and do anything to win."

Donald Trump also refused to acknowledge the possibility of a hack directed by Putin. He was aware that people were scrutinizing his links with Russia, though. "For the record," he tweeted on July 26, "I have ZERO investments in Russia."

Then the next day, at his last press conference for nearly two years, Trump did something astonishing:

Standing in front of the flags of the United States and Florida, Trump encouraged Russia, a nation hostile to the United States, to keep at its criminal hacking efforts.

"Russia, if you're listening," he said, "I hope you're able to find the thirty thousand e-mails that are missing. I think you will probably be rewarded mightily by our press."

It was one of the most surreal moments in a decidedly unusual election: A candidate inviting a hostile foreign nation to commit a crime against Americans.

> It was one of the most surreal moments in a decidedly unusual election: A candidate inviting a hostile foreign nation to commit a crime against Americans.

On or around that day, hackers under the direction of the Russian government made their first attempt to access the e-mails of Hillary Clinton's personal office, as well as seventy-six e-mail addresses for her campaign.

Despite Trump's bravado, his campaign was in another rough patch.

During the Republican National Convention on July 18, Melania delivered a speech plagiarized from one Michelle Obama had delivered in 2008. Ted Cruz refused to endorse Trump on July 21. And overall, Trump's television ratings weren't great. More people had tuned in to watch John McCain accept the Republican nomination in 2008. Trump would have loved to beat McCain in the ratings.

There had also been leaks to the media when Trump was choosing a vice presidential candidate. Trump hadn't wanted to go with Mike Pence; that had been Manafort's idea. Leaks created a perception Trump could be pushed around, and Trump never wanted to look weak.

Meanwhile, Steele's investigation into Trump and his team continued. The ex-spy sent memo after memo to Simpson. Fifteen additional confidential reports would come before Election Day, and one afterward.

Steele reported on July 30 that he'd found evidence of "extensive conspiracy" between Trump's campaign team and the Kremlin, as well as a two-way flow of information. This was exactly the sort of thing Don Jr. had demonstrated a willingness to participate in by hosting the Trump Tower meeting on June 9.

What's more, Steele reported, Trump was aware that Russia had *kompromat* on him. But he understood that the Kremlin wouldn't use this embarrassing information against him because his team had been helpful and cooperative for years, "and particularly of late," the memo said.

The memo also said sources close to Trump and Manafort indicated the men were happy that Russia was being made out as a "bogeyman," because this took the spotlight off numerous corrupt business ties in China and other emerging countries.

On August 10, Steele filed another report. This one claimed the campaign was worried about the bad publicity. The memo also said it had been Carter Page's idea to release the first batch of WikiLeaks memos right before the Democratic National Convention, to drive Democrats who'd liked Sanders toward Trump, but the campaign had underestimated the blowback from this strategy. Also, the Trump campaign was angry that Putin had gone beyond the objective of weakening Clinton and boosting Trump by also undermining the US government and democratic system.

Meanwhile, the Trump campaign was about to take a big public blow. Now that he was running Trump's campaign, Paul Manafort came under increasing media scrutiny. The *New York Times* reported on a ledger discovered in Ukraine that revealed Manafort had received $12.7 million in secret—and illegal—cash payments from the pro-Russia political party of his client Viktor Yanukovych.

Although Manafort denied receiving the money, he was done for with Trump. Manafort resigned on August 19. Kellyanne Conway took over as campaign manager, and former Breitbart executive chairman Steve Bannon became the campaign's chief executive officer.

By mid- to late September, Steele had given a full briefing to the FBI. It was obvious to Fusion GPS's Simpson that a crime had occurred—hacking. Reporters had begun calling him, wondering

U.S. Department of Justice

Federal Bureau of Investigation

Washington, D.C. 20535

October 28, 2016

Honorable Richard M. Burr
Chairman
Select Committee on Intelligence

Honorable Devin Nunes
Chairman
Permanent Select Committee on Intelligence

Honorable Charles E. Grassley
Chairman
Committee on the Judiciary

Honorable Robert Goodlatte
Chairman
Committee on the Judiciary

Honorable Richard Shelby
Chairman
Committee on Appropriations
Subcommittee on Commerce, Justice, Science
  and Related Agencies

Honorable John Culberson
Chairman
Committee on Appropriations
Subcommittee on Commerce, Justice,
  Science and Related Agencies

Honorable Ron Johnson
Chairman
Committee on Homeland Security and
  Governmental Affairs

Honorable Jason Chaffetz
Chairman
Committee on Oversight and
  Government Reform

Dear Messrs Chairmen:

   In previous congressional testimony, I referred to the fact that the Federal Bureau of Investigation (FBI) had completed its investigation of former Secretary Clinton's personal email server. Due to recent developments, I am writing to supplement my previous testimony.

   In connection with an unrelated case, the FBI has learned of the existence of emails that appear to be pertinent to the investigation. I am writing to inform you that the investigative team briefed me on this yesterday, and I agreed that the FBI should take appropriate investigative steps designed to allow investigators to review these emails to determine whether they contain classified information, as well as to assess their importance to our investigation.

   Although the FBI cannot yet assess whether or not this material may be significant, and I cannot predict how long it will take us to complete this additional work, I believe it is important to update your Committees about our efforts in light of my previous testimony.

Sincerely yours,

James B. Comey
Director

ABOVE: Then–FBI director James Comey's letter to Congress, dated October 28, 2016, regarding reopening the inquiry into Hillary Clinton's e-mail server. *(Senate Judiciary Committee Inquiry into Circumstances Surrounding Trump Tower Meeting)*

whether the FBI was investigating the Trump campaign. Simpson encouraged the journalists to ask the FBI directly. At the end of September, he and Steele briefed reporters from the *New York Times*, the *Washington Post*, Yahoo News, the *New Yorker*, and CNN. Steele talked with reporters again in mid-October, after hackers had released the e-mails of Clinton's campaign chairman, John Podesta. In late October, he spoke with a journalist from *Mother Jones*, a liberal newsmagazine.

Inside the Trump campaign, people were frantic, and not just because of Trump's poor debate performances and the specter of Russian election interference.

The *Access Hollywood* video publicized on October 7, in which Trump bragged about grabbing women by their genitalia, wasn't

ABOVE: Earlier that year, on July 5, 2016, Comey addressed reporters during a press briefing at FBI Headquarters about the investigation. *(FBI)*

the only sexual misconduct dogging the candidate. Numerous women publicly accused him of harassment and worse. Trump's team was cleaning it up as well as they could. One challenging task was to complete a nondisclosure agreement about Trump's extramarital affair with an adult film star. Trump had met Stephanie Clifford—known onscreen as Stormy Daniels—at a charity golf tournament when Barron was just a baby, and their relationship lasted a few months.

Cohen negotiated to buy her silence, but he failed to pay her, so she threatened to talk to the press. After he wired her $130,000, she signed the agreement on October 28. But Cohen didn't quite finish the job. Trump, using the alias David Dennison, never signed the deal. That same day, FBI Director James Comey wrote a letter to Congress reopening the inquiry into Clinton's e-mail server, turning the spotlight back on her.

Three days later, on Halloween, Trump got another lucky break, this one from the *New York Times*. Although *Mother Jones* published a piece headlined, "A Veteran Spy Has Given the FBI Information Alleging a Russian Operation to Cultivate Donald Trump," the less liberal *New York Times* ran a story that said the FBI's investigation so far had found no conclusive or direct link between Trump and the Russian government:

"And even the hacking into Democratic emails, F.B.I. and intelligence officials now believe, was aimed at disrupting the presidential election rather than electing Mr. Trump."

The FBI had cautioned reporters from the *Times* not to draw any conclusions from the Steele dossier—a message that led them to discount its contents. The FBI had an agenda in conveying such a message. They were concerned that any "overt actions" they might take related to the Trump campaign would fuel charges that the election was rigged to favor Clinton, a charge Trump had made repeatedly.

But then the utterly unexpected happened. Trump won, probably due in part to the letter Comey sent Congress. The news about the reopened inquiry shifted between 1 and 4 percent of the vote toward Trump. Clinton lost Michigan, Pennsylvania, and Wisconsin each by less than one point.

"The Comey letter probably cost Clinton the election," statistician Nate Silver said.

> "This will prove to be a great time in the lives of ALL Americans. We will unite and we will win, win, win!"
>
> —@realDonaldTrump, November 12, 2016

T RUMP WAS ELECTED NOVEMBER 8, 2016. HE'D be inaugurated as president on January 20, 2017, giving him seventy-three days to transition into his new role. In the meantime, he had a court date on the calendar: On November 28, the class-action lawsuit against Trump University was set to go to trial. The amount of work he faced was overwhelming.

Trump was ill-prepared for the coming transition. He hadn't wanted to jinx himself by planning for a win that almost no one thought would happen. But it wasn't just his superstitious nature that had left him behind schedule: He had no government experience and had never served in the military—the only president to lack either qualification. He had little understanding of what the job would take.

When Trump and Obama met in the White House on November 10, Obama explained the duties of the presidency to Trump, who was surprised by how big the job was. He also didn't know he'd need to replace every West Wing staffer—up to five hundred people. Obama would spend extra time with Trump to get him up to speed.

> He also didn't know he'd need to replace every West Wing staffer—up to five hundred people. Obama would spend extra time with Trump to get him up to speed.

Trump was slower than Obama had been in choosing key staff, and the process was chaotic. Trump had an advisory board of

sixteen, including Ivanka, Don Jr., and Eric, as well as Ivanka's husband, Jared Kushner.

Kushner was no fan of New Jersey Governor Chris Christie, Trump's transition team leader. As a federal prosecutor, Christie had sent Kushner's father to jail for tax evasion, illegal campaign donations, and witness tampering (the elder Kushner had hired a sex worker to entrap and humiliate his wife's brother for testifying against him). Christie lost his job as leader of the transition team on November 11. Trump replaced him with Vice President-elect Mike Pence.

Despite the slow rate of appointments, Trump was pleased with the process, which he teased as if it were a reality television show.

ABOVE: On November 10, 2016, just two days after the election, President Barack Obama meets with President-elect Donald Trump in the Oval Office. *(Official White House Photo by Pete Souza)*

Sixty-five days before the inauguration

"VERY ORGANIZED PROCESS TAKING PLACE AS I decide on Cabinet and many other positions," he tweeted. "I am the only one who knows who the finalists are!"

Although Trump distrusted Republican party leaders, he appointed Republican National Committee Chairman Reince Priebus as his chief of staff—which some observers read as a sign that Trump would become more traditional in his approach to the presidency than he had been as a candidate. Trump chose Priebus over Steve Bannon, who'd been a driving influence on his campaign. But Bannon still had a spot near Trump; he would be Trump's chief strategist and senior counselor.

While most in Trump's circle dressed neatly and conservatively, Bannon stood out as a slob with his layered shirts, stubbled chin, and shabby jackets. But he and Trump had simpatico world views that could be surprising in their darkness.

"Darkness is good," Bannon told journalist Michael Wolff. "Dick Cheney. Darth Vader. Satan. That's power. It . . . helps us when they get it wrong. When they're blind to who we are and what we're doing."

He viewed the world as hurtling toward a crisis. The Trump administration would destroy "the administrative state" and eventually lead to fifty years of Republican political domination.

This rationale drove Trump's cabinet appointments over the weeks that followed.

For secretary of education, he chose Betsy DeVos, a billionaire with no experience working in schools or attending public schools.

DeVos advocated allowing parents to use school vouchers to pay for education in religious and for-profit institutions, giving parents "choice" while undermining public education.

He chose Scott Pruitt to head the Environmental Protection Agency, a man who'd sued the EPA many times as Oklahoma's attorney general and who does not accept the scientific consensus on climate change.

For secretary of housing and urban development, Trump chose Dr. Ben Carson, a former rival for the Republican presidential nomination and, like Trump, someone with no government background and no experience running a large bureaucracy. Trump, a big believer in business experience as the ultimate qualifier, would later appoint his son's wedding planner to run the agency's New York and New Jersey operations.

For his national security adviser, Trump chose the one man Obama told him not to hire: Lieutenant General Mike Flynn.

Sixty-two days before the inauguration

ON NOVEMBER 19, TRUMP SETTLED THE CLASS-action lawsuit against Trump University for $25 million. He admitted no wrongdoing in the settlement, which gave a 90 percent refund to customers he'd defrauded.

". . . As President I have to focus on our country," he tweeted.

That same day, Trump vented his spleen at the cast of *Hamilton*. Mike Pence had watched the show when he was in New York, and afterward, the actor who played Vice President Aaron Burr had addressed Pence from the stage afterward: "We, sir—we—are the diverse America who are alarmed and anxious that your new administration will not protect us, our planet, our children, our parents, or defend us and uphold our inalienable rights," he said. "We truly hope that this show has inspired you to uphold our American values and to work on behalf of all of us."

Trump couldn't stand it: "Our wonderful future V.P. Mike Pence was harassed last night at the theater by the cast of Hamilton, cameras blazing. This should not happen!"

Meanwhile, Trump didn't want his victory to look anything less than legitimate. So he turned to Twitter and praised the electoral college, where he won 305 of a possible 538 votes. He also tweeted that he would have won the popular vote, too, if elections were based on that.

"I would have campaigned in N.Y. Florida and California and won even bigger and more easily," he said.

Several times he suggested that millions of fraudulently cast ballots had given Clinton the popular vote win.

> Several times he suggested that millions of fraudulently cast ballots had given Clinton the popular vote win.

And he still refused to believe Russia was behind hacks on the DNC. On November 28, he told *Time* magazine, "It could be Russia. And it could be China. And it could be some guy in his home in New Jersey."

Fifty days before the inauguration

EVEN AS THE ROLE RUSSIA HAD PLAYED IN HIS VIC-
tory was in the news, members of Trump's transition team, including Kushner and Flynn, met secretly with Russian ambassador
Sergey Kislyak in the Trump Tower on December 1.

They discussed the possibility of setting up a "secret and secure"
way for the transition team to communicate with the Kremlin
before Trump officially became president. Kushner suggested using
the Russian embassy for these secret chats.

When Kislyak informed his superiors in Moscow of Kushner's
request, US agents were listening in—something that would cause
trouble down the road for Kushner.

And Kushner wasn't just making forbidden diplomatic overtures.
He also met with Sergey N. Gorkov, the chief of a Russian state-run
bank that had been sanctioned in 2014 by Obama, making it illegal
for American entities and the bank to conduct business together.
And although the Trump administration would later claim Kushner
was filling in until Trump could get the State Department in order,
the bank released a statement that said Kushner was actually representing his family real estate empire in the meeting.

In the meantime, the *Washington Post* had reported the CIA's
view of Russian election meddling: It was meant to help Trump win.

Still, Trump refused to accept it. "These are the same people
that said Saddam Hussein had weapons of mass destruction," he
said. "The election ended a long time ago in one of the biggest
Electoral College victories in history. It's now time to move on and
'Make America Great Again.'"

Obama ordered a review of the hacks, and on December 29, announced retaliatory sanctions against the Russian government for its cyberattack on the 2016 election. Obama also sent home thirty-five Russian diplomats and seized two compounds they had used.

Flynn and Kislyak talked secretly about those sanctions the same day, and would do so several more times. On December 30, Putin announced he wouldn't return fire.

That same day, Trump praised the Russian president on Twitter. "Great move on delay (by V. Putin)-I always knew he was very smart!"

Fourteen days before the inauguration

ON JANUARY 6, 2017, THE OFFICE OF THE DIRECTOR of National Intelligence released a declassified version of its report on the hack.

"Russian President Vladimir Putin ordered an influence campaign in 2016 aimed at the US presidential election," the report said. The goal was "to help President-elect Trump's election chances."

The report made no mention of cooperation between Trump's campaign and the Kremlin—something asserted in the Steele dossier.

But Trump was about to get a look at these findings.

Intelligence agencies suspected it was only a matter of time before the Steele dossier became public, and they knew they had to brief both President Obama and President-elect Trump on its contents.

The dossier hadn't been fully verified. But it had been put together by someone considered reliable—even as some material struck FBI Director James Comey as being "wild stuff."

In that category, Comey counted the portion of the Steele dossier that said Trump had been recorded engaging in unusual sexual behavior that could be used to blackmail him, specifically that Trump had hired a number of sex workers to urinate on a bed in a hotel room that the Obamas had once occupied.

Even though this had not been verified—presumably because any footage that might exist had not been leaked—it was widely known that Russian intelligence put cameras in hotel rooms. Russia also has a history of gathering sex-based *kompromat*, making the contents credible human intelligence.

Comey and his colleagues from the CIA and National Security Agency rode in a fleet of fully armored SUVs through Manhattan on their way to meet Trump. The FBI director felt uneasy. He hadn't met the incoming president yet, but Trump had not struck Comey as a man of sound judgment. Trump was not going to enjoy the conversation, and yet it had to take place.

"How on earth could we brief the man about Russian efforts and not tell him about this piece?" Comey thought. He planned to tell Trump privately, to minimize the embarrassment. Comey worried that Trump might think he was blackmailing him or trying to get leverage.

Comey and his colleagues did not meet Trump in the grand conference room Don Jr. had used the day he was hoping to get evidence of Clinton crimes delivered to him from the Russian government. They met instead in a small conference room with heavy gold curtains hung over its window to obscure the view from the hallway. They were joined by Trump's senior team, as well as directors and representatives of various US intelligence agencies.

Trump was shown highly classified text messages and e-mails that revealed Putin had ordered cyberattacks meant to throw the election to Trump, undermine Clinton, and divide the nation along partisan lines. The messages came from Russian military officers and a top-secret source in Putin's inner circle, and the source described how the Kremlin's hacking and disinformation plan had been enacted.

Trump seemed convinced. But he had concerns, though not about what measures could be taken to prevent future attacks on America's digital infrastructure. Rather, Trump wanted reassurance that Russia's meddling hadn't affected the outcome.

"You found there was no impact on the result, right?" he said.

James Clapper, the director of national intelligence, told Trump no such analysis had been made. Neither Trump nor anyone on his team asked what might be done to ward off any future threat from Russia. Instead, and in front of the intelligence personnel, they started talking about how they'd spin the press statement. Comey said he was taken aback.

The time came for Comey to deliver Trump the difficult information. The two men waited for the others to leave the room.

"You've had one heck of a year," Trump told Comey when they were alone. He praised Comey and said he hoped the FBI director would remain in his job. It was perhaps a strange thing for Trump to say. Comey had been appointed for a ten-year term. Trump would have to fire him for him to leave. That had only happened once before in the history of the FBI.

Comey started to explain about the embarrassing material in the dossier. He didn't include the most salacious details. But Trump interrupted him before he'd finished, eager to argue the allegations were false. Trump asked Comey whether he seemed like a guy who needed the services of sex workers, and then started talking about all the women who'd accused him of sexual assault, something entirely unrelated to the dossier. As Trump grew ever more defensive, Comey said, "We are not investigating you, sir."

"This was literally true," Comey later said. "We did not have a counterintelligence case file open on him. We really didn't care if he had cavorted with hookers in Moscow, so long as the Russians weren't trying to coerce him in some way."

When Trump released a statement about the briefing the next day, he stressed he'd been legitimately elected—and implied the attacks were commonplace, when really they were unprecedented in their scope and maliciousness. He also falsely claimed there had been "absolutely no effect on the outcome of the election;" the report did not address that question.

Trump said nothing at all about the mortifying content of the report.

Trump said nothing at all about the mortifying content of the report.

Ten days before the inauguration

THE CEREMONY MARKING TRUMP'S ASCENSION TO the presidency was harder to plan than had been anticipated. Although a committee for the inauguration event had raised $106.8 million, almost two times what Obama's first inauguration committee raised, Trump couldn't get any A-list performers to agree to come. Obama had attracted dozens.

The best Trump could do was the Mormon Tabernacle Choir and an alumna of *America's Got Talent*, Jackie Evancho. The Radio City Rockettes were booked to perform, but many women in the dance troupe were unhappy to do so.

One posted on her Instagram account: "The women I work with are intelligent and are full of love and the decision of performing for a man that stands for everything we're against is appalling."

Trump, grumpy that big stars didn't want to celebrate his election, had complained a few weeks earlier on Twitter. "The so-called 'A' list celebrities are all wanting tixs to the inauguration, but look what they did for Hillary, NOTHING. I want the PEOPLE!"

The celebrity snub was demoralizing. But it was not as upsetting as what happened on January 10. That day, CNN reported on the two-page summary of the briefing intelligence agencies had given to Obama and Trump. Worse—far worse—an upstart online news source called BuzzFeed did what no mainstream news source had dared: It published the entire Steele dossier.

"These Reports Allege Trump Has Deep Ties To Russia," the BuzzFeed headline read.

"A dossier making explosive—but unverified—allegations that the Russian government has been 'cultivating, supporting and assisting' President-elect Donald Trump for years and gained compromising information about him has been circulating among elected officials, intelligence agents, and journalists for weeks," the story said.

The website posted the entire report so that Americans could decide for themselves what they thought of the information. Buzz-Feed characterized the report as unverified, and pointed out some errors, such as the misspelling of Alfa Group as "Alpha Group."

The next day, Trump was up early. He took to Twitter to mount a defense.

At 4:13 A.M. on January 11, he said, "Russia just said the unverified report paid for by political opponents is 'A COMPLETE AND TOTAL FABRICATION, UTTER NONSENSE.' Very unfair!'"

At 4:44 A.M., he blamed unnamed adversaries: "I win an election easily, a great 'movement' is verified, and crooked opponents try to belittle our victory with FAKE NEWS. A sorry state!"

At 4:48 A.M., he laid into intelligence agencies: "Intelligence agencies should never have allowed this fake news to 'leak' into the public. One last shot at me. Are we living in Nazi Germany?"

He also called Comey to complain about the "leak," but this was a misnomer. Because the dossier wasn't a government document, it wasn't classified. It had been compiled by private individuals and shared widely. That meant it wasn't something that *could* be leaked, Comey told him.

Trump switched tactics. He'd been thinking more about his Moscow weekend. He falsely claimed he hadn't stayed overnight in Moscow, and that he'd flown from New York.

As far as the most lurid allegation in the dossier, well, it couldn't be true Trump said. "I'm a germaphobe."

Nine days before the inauguration

ON JANUARY 12, MORE BAD NEWS CAME FROM THE *Washington Post.*

The paper revealed Flynn and the Russian ambassador had spoken shortly after Obama announced sanctions in retaliation for the election interference.

Trump's spokesman, Sean Spicer, downplayed the exchange. "The call centered on the logistics of setting up a call with the president of Russia and the president-elect after he was sworn in," Spicer said. "And they exchanged logistical information on how to initiate and schedule that call. That was it, plain and simple."

This was untrue. What none of Trump's team yet knew was that US intelligence officers had been listening in.

Five days before the inauguration

VICE PRESIDENT–ELECT MIKE PENCE STOOD BEHIND the false statement. "They did not discuss anything having to do with the United States' decision to expel diplomats or impose censure against Russia," Pence said.

One day before the inauguration

PENCE'S STATEMENT DID NOT END THE MATTER.

Obama's deputy attorney general, Sally Yates, knew what Flynn had really said to Kislyak. She held a meeting with FBI Director James Comey, outgoing CIA Director John Brennan, and outgoing Director of National Intelligence James Clapper to figure out how to handle the information. Should they tell Trump or other White House officials?

Yates, Brennan, and Clapper thought Trump ought to know Flynn had discussed sanctions. Comey disagreed. It could complicate the FBI investigation into Trump's campaign.

Without being able to reach an agreement, the group decided silence was the best route. At the request of Trump's incoming administration, Yates agreed to stay on as acting attorney general until Alabama senator Jeff Sessions could be sworn in.

She would not last that long.

CHAPTER 12

The MAN WHO WOULD BE KING

> "The forgotten men and women of our country will be forgotten no longer. From this moment on, it's going to be #AmericaFirst 🇺🇸"
>
> —@realDonaldTrump, January 20, 2017

NAUGURATION DAY arrived, slinging thin silver clouds over Washington, DC.

Trump woke in a foul mood. He hadn't liked staying in the guest quarters across the street from the White House and wished he'd ignored the staff who had told him not to stay in Trump International Hotel. He carped at Melania, and then news cameras caught him getting out of their limousine without holding the door for her, making him look like less than a gentleman. He also failed to wait for her as he climbed the steps to the White House, leaving her to make her way out of the limousine alone bearing a wrapped gift from Tiffany and Co., a silver picture frame for the always loving and composed Obamas, with whom the Trumps were to drink tea before traveling as a foursome to the inauguration.

Trump had wanted an absolutely huge event to celebrate his inauguration, and despite having raised and spent more than any other president on such a party—nearly $107 million—record-setting crowds did not materialize. The presidential limousine, a pair of flags on its hood snapping in the wind, passed block after block of empty bleachers on its way to the Capitol. Closer to the west face of the Capitol, where the inauguration would take place, a respectable mass had gathered: as many as twenty-eight thousand law enforcement officers and six hundred thousand civilians, many wearing Make America Great Again hats.

> The presidential limousine, a pair of flags on its hood snapping in the wind, passed block after block of empty bleachers on its way to the Capitol.

This far exceeded the number of people who'd attended the first inauguration of Ronald Reagan in 1981 but was significantly smaller than the throng that showed up for Barack Obama's first inauguration.

In a way, this was unsurprising.

Trump had lost the popular vote by millions, and he started his presidency with the worst approval rating of any incoming president ever polled. A divisive figure all along, his popularity had not been helped by the controversy over Russian election interference, nor by the contents of his widely covered Twitter feed, which he had used to launch attacks against the media, the actress Meryl

Streep, and Congressman John Lewis, a civil rights legend, as well as to falsely allege widespread voter fraud.

Without A-list celebrities performing contemporary music, Trump's inauguration was also less of a draw. It relied instead on the efforts of the more staid United States Marine Band and the Mormon Tabernacle Choir, who together performed "America the Beautiful" before Supreme Court Chief Justice John Roberts administered Trump's oath of office.

In the company of his nemesis Hillary Clinton, four past presidents, and his supportive family, Trump took the oath of office with his hand on two bibles—one from his family, the other used by President Abraham Lincoln at his inauguration. His oath to uphold the Constitution sworn, Trump embraced his family, accepted congratulations, and pumped a fist in front of the crowd.

ABOVE: Donald Trump takes the oath as President of the United States of America.
(Official White House Photo by Shealah Craighead)

Then, with his dark overcoat unbuttoned to reveal a red necktie that dangled below his belt, Trump delivered an unusually grim inaugural address written by Steve Bannon and Stephen Miller, who'd been an aide to Alabama senator Jeff Sessions.

Gone was the soaring rhetoric of Ronald Reagan. Gone was the spirit of service embraced by John F. Kennedy. In Trump's view, the country was in a state of "American carnage."

He rattled off the nation's ills: "Mothers and children trapped in poverty in our inner cities; rusted-out factories scattered like tombstones across the landscape of our nation; an education system, flush with cash, but which leaves our young and beautiful students deprived of knowledge; and the crime and gangs and drugs that have stolen too many lives and robbed our country of so much unrealized potential.

"From this day forward, a new vision will govern our land," he promised. "From this moment on, it's going to be America First."

Trump was happy with his performance. "Nobody will forget this speech," he said after he finished.

Former president George W. Bush, standing nearby, agreed—in a way. "That's some weird shit," he observed.

> Former president George W. Bush, standing nearby, agreed—in a way. "That's some weird shit," he observed.

Trump's speech did not unite Americans behind his vision for the nation.

IN HONOR OF THOSE MEMBERS
OF THE CENTRAL INTELLIGENCE AGENCY
GAVE THEIR LIVES IN THE SERV⋯⋯ THEIR COUNTRY

The next day, more than 4 million people in 915 locations around the country—mostly women enraged by his behavior and the revelations made during the campaign—marched to protest Trump's inauguration. It was the largest political march in the nation's history, and a remarkably peaceable one: No arrests were reported in the largest cities, where hundreds of thousands gathered.

As millions protested his election, Trump gave a speech in front of the CIA's Memorial Wall, which honors 117 unnamed intelligence officers killed in the line of duty. The event was a politically calculated one, meant to mend fences Trump had been battering by consistently rejecting the conclusion of America's intelligence agencies that the Russian government had interfered with the 2016 election. Worse, he'd compared America's intelligence agencies to Nazis on Twitter only nine days before his inauguration.

ABOVE: President Trump makes a speech in front of the CIA's memorial wall.
(Official White House Photo by Shealah Craighead)

Rather than apologize, he blamed the press.

"And the reason you're my first stop is that, as you know, I have a running war with the media. They are among the most dishonest human beings on Earth," he said. "And they sort of made it sound like I had a feud with the intelligence community. And I just want to let you know, the reason you're the number-one stop is exactly the opposite—exactly."

Trump had a speech prepared for this first official appearance of his presidency, one meant to repair relations with the CIA and other intelligence agencies he'd been insulting. But he set his text aside in favor of a tangent about his inauguration and the size of the crowd he'd drawn. Despite evidence to the contrary, Trump was adamant more people had attended his big day than actually had, and the fight would make headlines for months.

"We had a massive field of people," he said. "You saw them. Packed. I get up this morning, I turn on one of the networks, and they show an empty field. I say, wait a minute, I made a speech. I looked out, the field was—it looked like a million, million and a half people. They showed a field where there were practically nobody standing there."

Trump also praised his incoming national security adviser, Lieutenant General Mike Flynn—who unbeknownst to Trump was under investigation by the FBI.

"What a good guy," Trump said.

Flynn had been a key asset at Trump's rallies. Flynn had led the crowd at the Republican National Convention in a chant of "Lock her up!" about Hillary Clinton, arguing she should go to jail for using a private server for government e-mails, including some that were classified, despite an investigation that turned up no evidence of criminal behavior.

Trump attempted to excite the CIA about his appointment for the agency's new director, Mike Pompeo, who'd graduated first in his class at West Point. In praising Pompeo, Trump couldn't resist referring to his own intelligence as well:

"Now, I know a lot about West Point. I'm a person that very strongly believes in academics. In fact, every time I say I had an uncle who was a great professor at MIT for thirty-five years who did a fantastic job in so many different ways, academically—was an academic genius—and then they say, is Donald Trump an intellectual? Trust me, I'm like a smart persona," he said.

The remarks did not go over well with former CIA director John Brennan, who thought it was a despicable display of self-aggrandizement, especially in front of the memorial for the agency's fallen heroes. Brennan, already privy to classified information about Trump and the conduct of members of his campaign, would later give Congress a blunt assessment of the Trump team: "Frequently, people who go along a treasonous path do not know they are on a treasonous path until it is too late."

Trump was pleased with his talk, though. The next day he tweeted, "Had a great meeting at CIA Headquarters yesterday, packed house, paid great respect to Wall, long standing ovations, amazing people. WIN!"

Trump was struggling to transcend his insecurity about the election and his inauguration. Twelve minutes after he praised his own CIA speech, he tweeted about the protesters and celebrities who'd scorned him: "Watched protests yesterday but was under the

impression that we just had an election! Why didn't these people vote? Celebs hurt cause badly."

Trump had bigger problems than his unpopularity, though. That same morning, the *Wall Street Journal* reported that US counterintelligence officials had recorded calls Flynn had made on December 29 to the Russian ambassador. It meant that Trump's press secretary, Sean Spicer, would have to spend part of his first full press briefing addressing Flynn's conduct instead of Trump's policy priorities.

"I talked to General Flynn about this again last night," Spicer said. "One call, talked about four subjects. One was the loss of life that occurred in the plane crash that took their military choir, two was Christmas and holiday greetings, three was to—to talk about a

ABOVE: Press Secretary Sean Spicer fields questions from reporters.
(Official White House Photo by Shealah Craighead)

conference in Syria on ISIS and four was to set up a—to talk about after the inauguration setting up a call between President Putin and President Trump."

This wasn't true, and FBI agents knew it. The next day, investigators visited Flynn at the White House. They had questions about the conversations he'd had with the Russian ambassador. They knew what had been discussed. But they were testing Flynn, who lied to them in the interview, a felony that can carry a five-year prison sentence.

On January 25, the FBI gave acting Attorney General Sally Yates a report. She and others at the Justice Department thought the White House needed to know Flynn had deceived investigators, the vice president, and the American people. That meant Flynn was at risk of blackmail.

"To state the obvious," Yates said, "you don't want your national security adviser compromised with the Russians."

She met with White House counsel Don McGahn on January 26. McGahn then informed Trump, who maintained Flynn had done nothing wrong.

Yates talked with McGahn again January 27. This time, McGahn wanted to know why the Justice Department cared about one White House official lying to another, whether Flynn could be prosecuted, and whether the White House could look at the evidence of Flynn's dishonesty, which Yates shared with them.

Meanwhile, Trump and his relatively inexperienced staff wanted to kick off their legislative agenda.

Eager to get going on a long list of executive orders to issue during the first hundred days of his presidency, that same day Trump signed an executive order regarding travelers and immigrants.

Drafted by Bannon and Miller, the order suspended the entry of Syrian refugees indefinitely, barred all other refugees for 120 days, and prohibited the entry of people from seven mostly Muslim countries for 90 days. Though Trump had pledged to ban Muslims while on the campaign trail, he said the executive order was "not a Muslim ban." The travel restrictions took effect immediately, throwing major US airports into chaos, which had been Bannon's plan.

> The travel restrictions took effect immediately, throwing major US airports into chaos, which had been Bannon's plan.

That same evening, Trump had a private dinner with James Comey. The two men sat together in the Green Room at the White House, the place where President James Madison had declared war on England in 1812 and a heartbroken Lincoln had laid out his young son's body for viewing in 1862.

Trump and Comey occupied a small oval table set for two. A pair of retired Navy submariners were the only others present; they served and cleared the plates as Trump and Comey ate.

Trump did most of the talking, touching on a wide range of topics, including the size of the crowd at the inauguration, the value of the media coverage he got during the campaign, the luxury of the White House, how tall his son Barron was, and his innocence of the allegations that he had assaulted women or mocked a handicapped reporter.

Then Trump settled into business. He told Comey a lot of people wanted to lead the FBI—as many as twenty others. Trump said he would understand if Comey wanted to walk away, given all he'd been through, though he warned it would make Comey seem guilty of wrongdoing. Trump also let Comey know he could fire him if he wanted to. Trump, making it clear who had the power in their relationship, told Comey that he "needed" and "expected" loyalty.

Comey didn't respond. Then Trump brought up the Steele dossier, in particular the most lurid portion, which described the alleged encounter he had had with Russian sex workers in a Moscow hotel. It wasn't the only incident with sex workers alleged in the dossier, but it was the one that bothered Trump most because of the "one percent chance" Melania might think it was true. Trump told Comey he'd considered asking the FBI to investigate the whole thing to prove it was a lie.

"It's very difficult to disprove a lie," Comey said.

"Maybe you're right," Trump replied.

Then they talked once more about Comey's job.

"I need loyalty," Trump said.

Comey, uncomfortable, promised the president that he'd always get honesty.

That was what Trump wanted, he said: "honest loyalty."

Then Trump brought up the topic of Mike Flynn's judgment. Trump pointed at his own head and said, "the guy has serious judgment issues."

Comey, whose agency was investigating Flynn, said nothing. The dinner ended with a handshake.

Trump's executive order on travel didn't last the weekend. A federal judge in New York granted an injunction that blocked the deportation of people who'd been stranded in US airports by Trump's ban, ruling that it effectively violated a part of the Constitution that guarantees people due process and equal protection under the law. Four other courts also blocked implementation of the ban.

On Monday, January 30, Sally Yates sent a memo to the Justice Department staff letting them know not to defend Trump's executive order in court; she wasn't convinced it was lawful. Trump fired her immediately, accusing her of being "weak" on borders and "very weak" on illegal immigration.

"The acting Attorney General, Sally Yates, has betrayed the Department of Justice," a White House press release said.

The next day, Trump racked up a public victory by announcing the nomination of federal appellate judge Neil Gorsuch to fill the vacancy on the Supreme Court that Republicans had denied to Obama. After Gorsuch gave his acceptance speech, Trump could not resist giving the nominee a forceful handshake—a gesture that had become so notable various media observers described Trump's behavior in such instances as a show of dominance.

In private, Trump had wavered on Gorsuch. He wanted to give the job to a friend, perhaps onetime New York mayor Rudy Giuliani, who'd wanted to be secretary of state but was passed over for former ExxonMobil chief executive Rex Tillerson. Later, Trump almost withdrew the nomination after Gorsuch objected to the way Trump had criticized the courts.

Over the next few days, Michael Flynn maintained the lie that he hadn't talked about sanctions with Kislyak, but his deception was unraveling. Flynn told a *Washington Post* reporter on February 8 that he hadn't talked to Russia about sanctions. That same day, though, a spokesman called the reporter back to soften Flynn's claim.

"While he had no recollection of discussing sanctions, [Flynn] couldn't be certain that the topic never came up," the spokesman said.

It wasn't until February 9 that Vice President Pence—who'd vouched for Flynn in public—learned that the Justice Department knew Flynn had lied to the FBI.

Trump pretended to know nothing of the subject, although the White House counsel had already obtained the evidence of Flynn's deception from Sally Yates.

"I don't know about that. I haven't seen it," Trump said as he embarked on a trip to Mar-a-Lago to meet with the Japanese prime minister.

> ## The Mar-a-Lago weekend turned out to be a busy one.

The Mar-a-Lago weekend turned out to be a busy one. North Korea launched a missile just as Prime Minister Shinzo Abe and Trump were about to eat their iceberg lettuce salads. Rather than head to a secure location, Trump and Abe reviewed classified documents by the light of their cell phones, while servers and other Mar-a-Lago guests looked on. Some guests even posted Facebook photos, and one took a selfie with the military aide holding the satchel of codes and other gear needed for the president to launch a nuclear weapon.

Security officials outside the administration were dumbstruck that these events had unfolded in front of unscreened onlookers at the private club.

"I don't think this team has any appreciation about the vulnerabilities they are creating for themselves and how dangerous this is," said Julianne Smith, deputy national security adviser to Vice President Joe Biden in the Obama White House.

Secure communications were not a Trump priority. Trump also gave his personal cell number to world leaders. Usually, presidents make calls using a secure line in the White House or presidential limousine. Though presidents are issued government phones, even these can be spied on. A private phone is particularly vulnerable.

Despite Trump's indifference to Flynn's conduct, the general stayed under the media microscope. The day after Trump's Mar-a-Lago display, the *Washington Post* reported that Yates had in fact warned the White House counsel about Flynn.

That night, February 13, Flynn delivered his resignation letter, which claimed he had "inadvertently briefed the Vice President–Elect and others with incomplete information regarding my phone calls with the Russian Ambassador."

Trump's Valentine's Day schedule was busy. In the afternoon he had a meeting to deal with ongoing litigation over the travel ban followed by a homeland-threat briefing, which Comey attended. After that meeting ended, Trump told Comey that he wanted a word in private. Everyone left the room except Jared Kushner, who lingered by Comey's chair for a handshake and some chat about the investigation of Clinton's e-mail. But even Kushner had to go.

Trump wanted to talk about Mike Flynn, claiming the former national security adviser "hadn't done anything wrong" in his call with the Russians. The real problem, Trump said, was all the leaks to the media. Trump suggested jailing journalists to pressure them into revealing their sources.

"They spend a couple days in jail, make a new friend, and they are ready to talk," Trump said.

> "They spend a couple days in jail, make a new friend, and they are ready to talk," Trump said.

Comey agreed with Trump that the leaks were bad, and said he'd like to "nail [a leaker] to the door" to send a message to anyone considering leaking in the future. But he thought Trump's idea of jailing journalists was "tricky, for legal reasons and because [the Department of Justice] tends to approach it conservatively."

Trump then put the pressure on Comey: "I hope you can see your way clear to letting this go, to letting Flynn go. He is a good guy. I hope you can let this go."

The meeting unsettled Comey, who felt as though Trump was interfering with an investigation of the former national security adviser. The next day, Comey told Sessions he did not want to be left alone with Trump again.

It had been a rough first few weeks of the Trump presidency, marked by massive public protests and an inquiry into a Russian attack on American democracy that might have involved members of his campaign team, combined with Trump's own behavior, particularly on Twitter, where he made baseless claims that voter fraud had robbed him of the popular vote and attacked the media and private companies, sometimes even temporarily affecting their stock prices.

In rejecting the norms of campaigning, he'd won the presidency. In rejecting the norms of presidential behavior, he seemed to many to be unpresidential.

There was growing division among his staff, particularly between Steve Bannon, who was used to using chaos to his advantage, and Ivanka and Jared, who preferred a less divisive approach to governing.

On February 28, Trump gave a speech to Congress. He used a teleprompter—and couldn't ad-lib because his speech had been handed out beforehand.

He impressed the media at last.

"This is Trump at his absolute best so far," CNN pundit Chris Cillizza said. "VERY nice grace note about our shared humanity to start speech."

Fox News host Chris Wallace said, "I feel like tonight Donald Trump became the president of the United States."

But troubling headlines kept coming. The day after Trump's well-received speech, the *Washington Post* reported that Sessions hadn't told the truth to Congress during his confirmation hearings. Sessions was asked, "Have you been in contact with anyone connected to any part of the Russian government about the 2016 election, either before or after election day?"

Sessions said, "No."

But this was not true. He'd met twice with Kislyak, the Russian ambassador, once in July 2016 and again in September. Although senators may have meetings with ambassadors, Sessions at the time was also the head of the national security advisory committee for the Trump campaign. Many observers felt Sessions should have disclosed those meetings during his confirmation hearing. Trump disagreed; in his view, Sessions had been acting in his capacity as a senator during those meetings, not as a campaign surrogate.

Some Democrats called for Sessions to resign. Instead, on March 2, Sessions announced he'd recuse himself from any investigation of Trump's campaign.

"A proper decision, I believe, has been reached," Sessions said.

That evening, Trump defended his attorney general and attacked Democrats in a series of four tweets that took him sixteen minutes to type: "Jeff Sessions is an honest man. He did not say anything wrong. He could have stated his response more accurately, but it was clearly not . . ."

". . . intentional. This whole narrative is a way of saving face for Democrats losing an election that everyone thought they were supposed . . ."

". . . to win. The Democrats are overplaying their hand. They lost the election, and now they have lost their grip on reality. The real story . . ."

". . . is all of the illegal leaks of classified and other information. It is a total 'witch hunt!'"

Trump's fury raged the next day. Trump demanded investigations of top Democratic leaders, and he vented his fury in front of aides instead of working with them to revise his travel order. He was also angry at Sessions. After Sessions had been the first senator to endorse his campaign, they'd shared meals and talked frequently on the phone, and Trump had rewarded Sessions with a job. Where was the loyalty?

Sessions had to follow Trump to Mar-a-Lago that weekend to beg him to sign the revised travel order to meet legal deadlines. Trump kept after Sessions to change his mind, but he wouldn't.

Sunday morning, Trump was up early with unfounded allegations that President Obama had spied on him.

"Terrible!" Trump tweeted at 3:35 A.M. "Just found out that Obama had my 'wires tapped' in Trump Tower just before the victory. Nothing found. This is McCarthyism!"

At 4:02 A.M., Trump followed up: "How low has President Obama gone to tapp [sic] my phones during the very sacred election process. This is Nixon/Watergate. Bad (or sick) guy!"

No evidence supported this claim.

No evidence supported this claim.

Despite his best efforts, Trump couldn't make the Russia situation go away. He continued to deny that Russia had interfered with the election, and his team maintained—without evidence either way—that the hacking and other measures had not changed anyone's votes.

Trump insiders also rejected the idea that the campaign had colluded with Russia. According to Trump's chief strategist, Steve Bannon, such a conspiracy was beyond the skills of Trump's team.

Over time, Trump grew angry that he wouldn't have an attorney general willing to protect him from the scrutiny of law enforcement.

"If he would have recused himself before the job, I would have said, 'Thanks, Jeff, but I can't, you know, I'm not going to take you.'" Trump said. "It's extremely unfair, and that's a mild word, to the president."

Meanwhile, Comey continued to frustrate Trump.

On March 20, the FBI director testified at a hearing of the House Intelligence Committee, confirming that the bureau was investigating the Russian government's efforts to interfere in the election, "and that includes investigating the nature of any links between individuals associated with the Trump campaign and the Russian government and whether there was any coordination between the campaign and Russia's efforts."

But Comey wouldn't say in public what he'd said in private, that Trump wasn't under investigation.

On March 22, Trump collared CIA Director Mike Pompeo and Dan Coats, the nation's newly confirmed director of national intelligence. He wanted the two men to intervene with the FBI and shut down the investigation of Flynn. He also pressed Admiral Mike Rogers, director of the National Security Agency, to say there was no evidence of a conspiracy. But he couldn't get anywhere with them—particularly when it came to getting them to make false statements about an ongoing investigation.

As Trump tried to influence the nation's intelligence directors, Jared Kushner came into the investigative crosshairs. The Senate Intelligence Committee informed the White House it had questions about Kushner's meetings in December with Kislyak.

What's more, Trump had put Kushner, a political novice, in charge of relationships with countries in the Middle East and beyond. Critics considered this a possible violation of nepotism laws, which prevent presidents and other public officials from hiring their relatives. In any case, Kushner needed security clearance to take the lead on international relations. To get clearance, Kushner had to fill out a form describing the contacts he'd had with representatives of foreign governments over the past seven years. The day after he first filed his security form, Kushner let the FBI know it was incomplete.

Among the meetings he'd left off: those with Kislyak and the Russian banker subject to sanctions, as well as the June meeting with Natalia Veselnitskaya.

> But this wasn't all. Dozens of foreign contacts were omitted.

But this wasn't all. Dozens of foreign contacts were omitted. Kushner ended up revising his form several times, fixing the one hundred meetings he'd omitted on the original one—an unprecedented number of errors.

This left Kushner open to charges he was concealing contacts that would aid his business, which generated at least $70 million for him in 2017 while he was working full-time at the White House. In March, ethics watchdogs helped sink a deal between the Kushner family and a bank with close ties to the Chinese government to bail out the Kushners' struggling flagship building at 666 Fifth Avenue in New York.

As Trump's family came under attack and the Russia investigation lingered, Trump called Comey on the morning of March 30. Trump considered the investigation a "cloud" preventing him from focusing on policy initiatives. And parts of it—especially the salacious bits—were personally embarrassing.

"Can you imagine me, hookers?" he said. "I have a beautiful wife, and it has been very painful."

He wanted to know what he could do to lift the cloud.

"We [are] running it down as quickly as possible," Comey said. "There would be great benefit, if we didn't find anything, to our Good Housekeeping seal of approval, but we have to do our work."

Comey reminded Trump he wasn't under investigation, and Trump again urged the FBI director to make that public.

The conversation disturbed Comey enough that he documented it in a memo.

Meanwhile, Trump continued his relentless Twitter assault on the investigation. The next day, at 4:04 A.M., he tweeted, "Mike Flynn should ask for immunity in that this is a witch hunt (excuse for big election loss), by media & Dems, of historic proportion!"

> Meanwhile, Trump continued his relentless Twitter assault on the investigation.

Trump was desperate to end this inquiry, which was, in his mind, baseless and impeding his ability to succeed as president. He'd made promises to the nation—to build a wall on the southern border, to dismantle Obamacare and replace it with something better, and to lower taxes and reduce regulations that businesses didn't like. He couldn't do that if his legitimacy was under attack.

Trump had always used his positive attitude to weather bankruptcies, divorces, and other painful events. His staff had taken to compiling folders of positive news coverage, tweets, and flattering photographs to deliver to Trump at 9:30 A.M. and 4:30 P.M. each day. Having positive coverage—called the "propaganda document" by more cynical staff—helped him keep his chin up.

One legitimate boost came on April 6 when he ordered the launch of a missile strike in Syria in retaliation to a chemical attack waged by forces loyal to the Syrian president. Trump had promised isolationism as a candidate but was moved by pictures of dead children, their mouths covered in foamy spittle.

The media raved about the leadership he showed.

"I think Donald Trump became president of the United States last night," CNN host Fareed Zakaria said. "I think this was actually a big moment. For the first time really as president, he talked about international norms, international rules, about America's role in enforcing justice in the world."

But adherence to certain norms wouldn't last.

Trump kept after Comey, phoning him on the morning of April 10. It was a short call, about four minutes, but Trump wanted to know whether Comey had done what he'd asked: getting the word out that Trump was not under investigation. Trump told Comey that he was trying to do work for the country and visit with foreign leaders, and "any cloud, even a little cloud gets in the way of that."

Comey wouldn't, and Trump reminded him, "I have been very loyal to you, very loyal, we had that thing, you know."

Trump meant he'd let Comey keep his job.

On April 27, Rod Rosenstein was confirmed as deputy attorney general. He took over the Justice Department's Russia investigation, which had spread to include separate investigations by the intelligence committees of both the House and Senate. On April 28, the Senate Intelligence Committee asked Flynn for any documents related to their inquiry. He refused to provide them, but he wasn't going to be able to hold out for long.

Meanwhile, Comey was in the hot seat on May 3. He testified about decisions he'd made in the Clinton e-mail investigation, and he also discussed the ongoing investigation of Russia's illegal hacking operations—directly challenging Trump's consistent rejection of the truth.

"In many circumstances, it's hard to do attribution of a hack, but sometimes the intelligence is there. We have high confidence ... that the Russians did the hacking of the DNC and the other organizations," Comey testified.

It was a fraught time for the president. A key promise—to repeal and replace Obamacare—was up for a vote in the House of Representatives the day after Comey's testimony, which Trump considered "showboating."

The measure squeaked by in a 217–213 vote after a bumpy few weeks of negotiations. But the Russia investigation continued to be a distraction. The day after the successful House vote, a report from the National Security Agency was leaked; it said Russian efforts to penetrate the nation's voting systems were worse than initially thought, including hacks on eight companies that supply voting machines. The report did not claim votes were changed. That wasn't something investigators could determine.

On May 8, Sally Yates and James Clapper, the former director of national intelligence, testified before Congress about the hacking.

Clapper, whom Trump considered an ally, said under oath, "Russia's influence activities in the run-up to the 2016 election constituted the high-water mark of their long running efforts since the 1960s to disrupt and influence our elections. They must be congratulating themselves for having exceeded their wildest expectations with a minimal expenditure of resource."

Clapper also implied that the lack of response from the Trump administration was a problem: "I believe they are now emboldened to continue such activities in the future both here and around the world, and to do so even more intensely. If there has ever been a clarion call for vigilance and action against a threat to the very foundation of our democratic political system, this episode is it."

That day, Trump resolved to fire Comey. His team drafted a memo that alarmed White House counsel Don McGahn, so the new deputy attorney general, Rod Rosenstein, wrote a replacement memo outlining disagreements he had with the way Comey had handled aspects of the investigation into Hillary Clinton's e-mail server.

On May 9—the same day federal prosecutors subpoenaed Flynn's records and the Senate Intelligence Committee asked the Treasury Department for some of Trump's financial records—the president had his private bodyguard deliver a humiliating letter in a manila envelope to the FBI. Comey wasn't there, and he learned of his dismissal from television. The letter, which made no mention of the Clinton e-mail investigation, read in part:

"While I greatly appreciate you informing me, on three separate occasions, that I am not under investigation, I nevertheless concur with the judgment of the Department of Justice that you are not able to effectively lead the Bureau."

Trump allies cheered the move.

"Comey Fired!!! Finally," tweeted Sean Hannity of Fox News.

Trump's lawyer, Michael Cohen, tweeted, ".#ComeyFired #Hallelujah! Need anyone say more?"

Others saw it as a huge and unnecessary tactical error, reminiscent of the one President Richard Nixon had made when he fired the special prosecutor investigating the Watergate break-in and potential links to Nixon and his campaign.

For his part, Trump felt a cloud had been lifted.

The next day, he invited several Russian officials into the Oval Office. Trump barred American reporters from the meeting but permitted Russian journalists and a photographer for a state-run news agency called TASS to attend—a way for him to needle the national news media.

Trump confessed his relief to his Russian guests, who included ambassador Sergey Kislyak.

"I just fired the head of the FBI," Trump said. "He was crazy, a real nut job. I faced great pressure because of Russia. That's taken off."

> "I just fired the head of the FBI," Trump said. "He was crazy, a real nut job. I faced great pressure because of Russia. That's taken off."

Perhaps with relationship-building in mind, Trump also disclosed extremely sensitive raw intelligence about ISIS terrorists that had been gathered by Israeli intelligence allies. The disclosure jeopardized spies and would make American allies less likely to share vital information, intelligence veterans said.

It also looked bad. Not only did the visitors represent the government that had interfered with the 2016 election to put him in office, meetings with Kislyak had also become the subject of the FBI probe.

Trump didn't like the criticism that followed this and the Comey firing.

"James Comey better hope that there are no 'tapes' of our conversations before he starts leaking to the press!" Trump tweeted the morning of May 12.

What's more, Trump maintained it had been his "absolute right" to share the intelligence materials with Russia.

To Trump, the presidency granted him absolute power in many areas. He'd also claimed shortly after the election that the presidency protected him from any conflict-of-interest charges with his business, for example.

"The law is totally on my side," Trump said.

Less than four months into his presidency, though, the limits of his power would face a new test.

Less than four months into his presidency, though, the limits of his power would face a new test.

Without telling Trump beforehand, Rod Rosenstein appointed a special prosecutor to take over the Russia investigation. Rosenstein informed White House counsel Don McGahn once the order was signed, and at 5:35 P.M. on May 17, McGahn found Trump in the Oval Office and told him the news.

Trump handled it better than his aides expected. He was calm. He didn't scream. He told his team they had nothing to hide. And as he'd done all his life, he vowed to fight back.

His enemy this time, Robert Mueller, was a Republican, a war hero, a former FBI director, a former prosecutor, and a lifelong public servant with a spotless reputation.

He would be, without a doubt, the most formidable opponent Trump had ever faced.

CHAPTER 13

"The FISH STINKS from the HEAD DOWN"

> "The big story is the 'unmasking and surveillance' of people that took place during the Obama Administration."
>
> —@realDonaldTrump, June 1, 2017

O**N THE SURFACE, TRUMP** and Mueller had much in common. They shared German and Scottish ancestry. Each had four siblings and affluent parents. Both excelled at sports in their youth. As much as they had in common, even more separated them.

While Trump learned the art of selling from his father, sometimes straying from the strict truth in the process, this was not the Mueller family way.

"A lie was the worst sin," Mueller said. "The one thing you didn't do was to give anything less than the truth to my mother and father."

Unlike Trump, Mueller continued his athletic pursuits in college—a decision that changed his life. At Princeton, where the motto was "In the nation's service and in the service of all nations," Mueller played varsity lacrosse with a student who was later killed by a sniper's bullet in Vietnam.

Inspired by his teammate's sacrifice, Mueller enlisted for service weeks after he graduated. A knee injury prevented him from qualifying for service right away. As Mueller healed, he earned his master's degree in international relations at New York University. After he finally passed the military's physical examination in August 1967, Mueller headed to Officer Candidate School at

ABOVE: Robert Mueller *(FBI)*

Quantico, Virginia. Then came an elite, eight-week Ranger training program in which he learned skills that would be essential to his survival in Vietnam.

In 1968, Mueller arrived at the Dong Ha combat base near the dividing line between North and South Vietnam. That was a tumultuous year for Americans. Martin Luther King Jr. and Robert Kennedy were assassinated, and the war in Vietnam was beginning to look like an insatiable sinkhole filled with the blood of thousands of young men—a stalemate at best. It was also the deadliest year of the war to date.

> It was also the deadliest year of the war to date.

Mueller led twenty Marines in a regiment known as the "Magnificent Bastards." His men had neither his wealth nor his elite education, but he rapidly won their respect with his laser-sharp focus on their mission and his knowledge of the myriad details they'd need to master to survive.

That December, a team of highly skilled North Vietnamese soldiers packing machine guns, mortars, and rocket-propelled grenades ambushed Mueller and his men. In the devastating eight-hour conflict that followed, Mueller braved gunfire to rescue injured men, including one who would die from his wounds. He won a Bronze Star for his courage.

Around that same time, Trump graduated from Penn. He'd been declared medically unfit for service except "in time of national emergency" in October 1968.

As Trump would later tell the radio personality Howard Stern, his heroics during that era—his "personal Vietnam"—were of a different sort: avoiding STDs.

Vaginas are "potential landmines," he told Stern. "There's some real danger there."

Just a few months after Mueller won a Bronze Star, as Trump and his father settled a Swifton Village housing discrimination claim, Mueller took a bullet through the thigh from a Russian-designed AK-47. Afterward, he received a Navy Commendation Medal for courage, leadership, and devotion "in the face of great personal danger." In all, Mueller brought home thirteen awards from the war, including a Purple Heart, two Bronze Stars, badges for marksmanship, and ribbons for combat and valor.

After Vietnam, Mueller attended law school at the University of Virginia. He worked briefly in the private sector before securing government jobs in California and Massachusetts, focusing on major financial fraud, drug conspiracies, international money laundering, and public corruption. As an assistant attorney general, Mueller oversaw the investigations of the mob boss John Gotti, the Lockerbie airplane bombers, and the Panamanian military dictator Manuel Noriega. In 2001, after George W. Bush was elected president, he picked Mueller to lead the FBI.

Before he was selected, Mueller had disclosed he had cancer. He underwent surgery to remove a cancerous prostate gland on August 2, 2001, the day the Senate unanimously confirmed him to the position. Four days later, Mueller was back at his desk—much faster than a typical patient—and his doctors were confident he'd been cured.

On September 11 of that year, hijackers crashed planes into the World Trade Center towers, the Pentagon, and—after passengers fought back—a Pennsylvania field. The attack did not come out of the blue. In July and August, the Federal Aviation Administration had warned airlines twice that terrorists planned to hijack planes. By then the nation's various intelligence agencies had also received urgent word from the CIA. And the day before the attack, the National Security Agency picked up a pair of messages sent between Afghanistan and Saudi Arabia.

One said, "Tomorrow is zero hour."

The other said, "The match begins tomorrow."

Translators got to the messages on September 12.

The nation's intelligence agencies, including the FBI, needed a radical overhaul. During his term, Mueller updated the bureau's data operations systems and broadened its focus to fight crime globally instead of just nationally. His tenure as FBI director was criticized by some subordinates, who said he was gruff and didn't like to admit errors. In one case, his investigation of a man wrongly suspected of sending poisonous anthrax through the mail led to a $5.8 million suit against the government.

In 2013, when Mueller retired from public service, a guest at his retirement party joked that the event meant Mueller would "depart Justice for the last time, hopefully."

Fate had something else in store.

In 2017, three years after Mueller had joined a private law firm, Deputy Attorney General Rod Rosenstein called on Mueller to serve again. The appointment of Mueller as special counsel delighted prominent Republicans; Democrats praised the move as well.

Office of the Deputy Attorney General
Washington, D.C. 20530

ORDER NO. 3915-2017

APPOINTMENT OF SPECIAL COUNSEL
TO INVESTIGATE RUSSIAN INTERFERENCE WITH THE
2016 PRESIDENTIAL ELECTION AND RELATED MATTERS

By virtue of the authority vested in me as Acting Attorney General, including 28 U.S.C. §§ 509, 510, and 515, in order to discharge my responsibility to provide supervision and management of the Department of Justice, and to ensure a full and thorough investigation of the Russian government's efforts to interfere in the 2016 presidential election, I hereby order as follows:

(a)　Robert S. Mueller III is appointed to serve as Special Counsel for the United States Department of Justice.

(b)　The Special Counsel is authorized to conduct the investigation confirmed by then-FBI Director James B. Comey in testimony before the House Permanent Select Committee on Intelligence on March 20, 2017, including:

(i)　any links and/or coordination between the Russian government and individuals associated with the campaign of President Donald Trump; and

(ii)　any matters that arose or may arise directly from the investigation; and

(iii)　any other matters within the scope of 28 C.F.R. § 600.4(a).

(c)　If the Special Counsel believes it is necessary and appropriate, the Special Counsel is authorized to prosecute federal crimes arising from the investigation of these matters.

(d)　Sections 600.4 through 600.10 of Title 28 of the Code of Federal Regulations are applicable to the Special Counsel.

_5/17/17_
Date

Rod J. Rosenstein
Acting Attorney General

ABOVE: The letter appointing Robert Mueller as special counsel "to investigate Russian interference with the 2016 presidential election and related matters." *(Department of Justice)*

But Trump's initial calm quickly frothed into rage. At a speech at the Coast Guard Academy on May 17, he told the new graduates, "Look at the way I've been treated lately, especially by the media. No politician in history—and I say this with great surety—has been treated worse or more unfairly. You can't let them get you down. You can't let the critics and the naysayers get in the way of your dreams."

Trump couldn't sleep off his anger either. At 4:52 A.M. the next day, he tweeted, "This is the single greatest witch hunt of a politician in American history!"

In June, Trump resolved to fire Mueller, even though firing James Comey from the FBI had led to the appointment of the special counsel in the first place. Trump listed three reasons why this was fair: Mueller had once quit Trump National Golf Club in an alleged dispute over fees while he was FBI director, Mueller had worked for a law firm that represented Jared Kushner, and Mueller had interviewed to lead the FBI again the day before his appointment as special counsel.

Trump ordered his White House counsel, Don McGahn, to make the Justice Department fire Mueller. McGahn wouldn't, and instead threatened to quit himself in protest. Firing Mueller would be ruinous for Trump's presidency, McGahn said.

It was a tough spot for Trump.

Mueller had brought down foreign leaders, mobsters, and terrorists. Mueller could end Trump's presidency if Trump *didn't* fire him.

Meanwhile, Mueller quickly assembled a team of seventeen experts in a breadth of areas: fraud, criminal law, organized crime, cybersecurity, Ponzi schemes, foreign bribes, terrorism, money laundering, corruption, asset forfeiture, national security, and espionage. The makeup of his team gave some indication to the range of issues Mueller was investigating—far beyond obstruction of justice in the firing of James Comey.

Trump's Twitter feed reflected his obsessions and frustrations. For the next month, Trump frequently defended his travel ban, which continued to take hits in the courts. He underscored the importance of his tax and health-care legislation, which he'd promised on the campaign trail.

The Mueller investigation threatened everything Trump wanted to accomplish. It also cast a shadow over his legitimacy as president, particularly since Clinton had beaten him so soundly in the popular vote. That fact bothered Trump enough that his Presidential Advisory Commission on Election Integrity requested massive amounts of voter data from states: names, birth dates, voting histories, and party identifications. He gave state election commissioners sixteen days to comply. Many refused outright, some because state laws prohibited it, and others because the commission was founded on a baseless premise that many people voted illegally.

On July 7, the *New York Times* turned up the heat on the Russia controversy. Reporters there had learned of the June 2016 meeting in Trump Tower, where Don Jr. expected help from the Russian government for the campaign. For weeks, Jared Kushner had known this meeting could be a problem. Congressional investigators had asked him for information about any meetings he'd had with Russians, and he'd given his lawyers the e-mail chain setting up this particular one.

The team of lawyers and communication specialists in charge of figuring out how to explain the meeting agreed that the best strategy was to tell the truth about what happened with a conservative website, Circa. This was the plan until the plane ride home from an international financial summit on July 8. Then Trump changed his mind about the strategy. Instead of telling the truth, he dictated a misleading statement for his son to release:

"It was a short introductory meeting. I asked Jared and Paul to stop by. We primarily discussed a program about the adoption of Russian children that was active and popular with American families years ago and was since ended by the Russian government, but it was not a campaign issue at the time and there was no follow up. I was asked to attend the meeting by an acquaintance, but was not told the name of the person I would be meeting with beforehand."

The statement did not include the discussion of the Magnitsky Act. What's more, adoption was not the primary focus of the meeting. The initial promise of the meeting had been to receive information from the Russian government that would help Trump defeat Clinton.

Meanwhile, Trump continued to act with unusual deference toward Putin. During a dinner at the financial summit, Trump had an hour-long private conversation with the Russian president. Because Trump's interpreter did not speak Russian, the two leaders depended on Putin's. No American was part of the discussion, nor were notes taken. It was a departure from normal diplomatic procedures, worrying some experts. Leaders of other nations also thought it strange that Trump singled out Putin for such extended attention, especially in the presence of traditional US allies. Meanwhile, just such a meeting was good strategy for Putin.

Afterward, Trump again cast doubt over the intelligence community's assessment that Russia had engaged in cyberwarfare against the United States in order to help Trump win the presidency.

"I said to [Putin], were you involved in meddling with the election? He said, absolutely not. I was not involved. He was very strong on it."

Trump was also intrigued by a curious notion: that proof of Russian hacking was *actually* proof there had been no hacking. "Somebody said later to me . . . let me tell you, if they were involved, you wouldn't have found out about it. Okay, which is a very interesting point."

The private dinner conversation and aftermath renewed the impression that Trump trusted the Russian president more than his own intelligence agencies.

Trump kept fighting the Mueller investigation. In an interview on July 19 with the *New York Times*, Trump said it would be a "violation" for the special counsel to look into his finances. Even so, Trump tried to convey the notion that his mind was fully focused on the presidency, and that he wasn't at all worried about what Mueller might find if he reviewed past business deals.

"So I think if he wants to go, my finances are extremely good, my company is an unbelievably successful company," Trump said. "And actually, when I do my filings, people say, 'Man.' People have no idea how successful this is. . . . . . But I don't even think about the company anymore. I think about this. 'Cause one thing, when you do this, companies seem very trivial. Okay? I really mean that. . . . . .

But I have no income from Russia. I don't do business with Russia."

Trump was secretive about his finances. He'd refused to release his tax returns, the only presidential candidate in forty years to do so. He'd claimed that he couldn't release them because he was being audited. He promised to release them if he won. Then he said he wouldn't release them, because no one cared but journalists.

Although his lawyers were trying to figure out how to contain the scope of Mueller's inquiry on behalf of their client, drawing red lines for Mueller was wishful thinking on Trump's part. He probably knew it on some level, which is why he also asked his lawyers for more information about his power to pardon his aides, relatives, and even himself.

Trump was still hopeful he could fire Mueller, and his lawyers hunted for potential conflicts of interest the special counsel might have, because those could be a legitimate grounds for dismissal.

Meanwhile, Trump's behavior and claims had posed challenges for his staff to handle.

Trump press secretary Sean Spicer—who'd had to defend his boss's meeting with Putin as "pleasantries and small talk"—had become a punchline. Spicer had defended Trump's claims about the size of crowds at inauguration. He'd claimed Syria's president Bashar al-Assad was worse than Hitler because Assad had used chemical weapons, when Hitler had used deadly gas on millions. Spicer performed so badly that the movie star Melissa McCarthy lampooned him repeatedly on *Saturday Night Live*, portraying him as a gum-chewing "Spicy" who liked to chase the press with a motorized lectern.

When Trump hired a new boss for Spicer on July 21, a former

hedge fund manager named Anthony Scaramucci, Spicer quit. So did Chief of Staff Reince Priebus, though he expected to take a few weeks and make a dignified exit.

High turnover of key staff like Spicer and Priebus defined much of Trump's first months as president. Trump lost six times as many senior West Wing staff as Obama, and nine times as many as George W. Bush had in the same time period.

In the midst of this chaos, Mueller's Russia investigation barreled ahead. Before dawn on July 26, the FBI raided Paul Manafort's $2.7 million brick condominium unit in Alexandria, Virginia.

So vital was the secrecy of the raid that agents didn't even knock on Manafort's door. They entered bearing a search warrant giving them license to collect tax, banking, and other finance-related records Manafort might have on hand. Agents could have obtained

ABOVE: Paul Manafort *(Shutterstock)*

the search warrant only if they'd proved to a judge they had reason to believe a crime had been committed.

The raid slung an ominous shadow over the Trump campaign, which Manafort had worked on and eventually run, for months.

The raid wasn't yet public knowledge, but that same morning, Trump tweeted something that seemed to come from nowhere:

"After consultation with my Generals and military experts, please be advised that the United States Government will not accept or allow. . . . ."

". . . . Transgender individuals to serve in any capacity in the US Military. Our military must be focused on decisive and over-whelming. . . ."

". . . . victory and cannot be burdened with the tremendous medical costs and disruption that transgender in the military would entail. Thank you"

It reversed a decision Obama made in 2016 permitting transgender military members to serve. Conservatives had objected to Obama's policy, and Trump's sudden announcement on Twitter left his team scrambling to explain its implications, which would affect an estimated 15,500 transgender people on active duty or in the reserves and potentially an additional 149,800 veterans.

Meanwhile, legislation vital to Trump—the partial repeal of Obama's Affordable Care Act—was up for a vote that night. At around 1:30 A.M. on July 27, it failed in a 49-51 vote. Trump had promised to "repeal and replace" Obamacare. This meant he'd failed.

It was a huge political blow for Trump.

THE SAME DAY, THE *NEW YORKER* RAN A FOUL-mouthed interview with Trump's new communications director, Anthony Scaramucci, who was in a lather about a small dinner party that had been leaked to the media. Such a leak was "a major catastrophe for American citizens," he said.

Scaramucci also called Trump's chief of staff, Reince Priebus, a "paranoid schizophrenic," and said that senior adviser Steve Bannon's desire for media attention was like "trying to suck [his] own cock."

The astonishing interview revealed the intensity of turmoil inside Trump's West Wing. Scaramucci made yet more headlines that day when he told CNN, "The fish stinks from the head down. I can tell you two fish that don't stink, and that's me and the president."

> The astonishing interview revealed the intensity of turmoil inside Trump's West Wing.

That night brought more drama.

At 7:00 P.M., a Trump campaign adviser, George Papadopoulos, arrived at Dulles Airport near Washington, DC. Before Papadopoulos could even get through customs, FBI agents intercepted him.

By 1:45 A.M. on July 28, Papadopoulos was booked into a detention center in Alexandria, Virginia. Authorities charged him with lying to FBI agents during an interview in January about contacts he'd had with Russian advocates during the campaign. Papadopoulos was also charged with obstruction of justice for deleting his

Facebook account the day after another FBI interview in February. The account had contained some of the exchanges he'd lied about.

That afternoon, Trump shook up his inner circle, ousting his chief of staff Reince Priebus and introducing his replacement, John Kelly, who had been serving as the secretary of homeland security. Trump revealed the change on Twitter.

> ## Behind the scenes, danger loomed for Trump.

Behind the scenes, danger loomed for Trump. With the raid on Manafort's home on July 26 and the arrest of Papadopoulos on July 27, Mueller's team was moving swiftly. Many special counsel investigations took more than a year before charges were filed; these came in just a few months.

And Papadopoulos, detained by authorities, had a significant decision to make: cooperate with Mueller's investigation, or resist on behalf of the president. Either choice would change the course of history.

CHAPTER 14

A SEASON of STORMS

> "... Russia was against Trump in the 2016 Election-and why not, I want strong military & low oil prices. Witch Hunt!"
>
> —@realDonaldTrump, July 29, 2017

PAPADOPOULOS CHOSE to cooperate.

In a sealed record, prosecutors told a federal judge that Papadopoulos would be "proactive." That meant he might be fitted with a wire to record conversations—a major hazard for the Trump administration.

August arrived, and reporters were still probing the statement attributed to Don Jr. about his meeting with Russians in Trump Tower.

Had the president tried to change the story, a reporter asked at a press briefing? The new White House press secretary, Sarah Huckabee Sanders, dismissed the idea out of hand.

"Look, the statement that Don Jr. issued is true," she said. "The president weighed in as any father would, based on the limited information that he had. He certainly didn't dictate, but he—like I said, he weighed in, offered suggestion like any father would do. This is all discussion, frankly, of no consequence."

Neither assertion was true.

Reporters would not forget this.

As rocky as things were inside the White House, Trump also faced major challenges overseas.

> As rocky as things were inside the White House, Trump also faced major challenges overseas.

In July, US intelligence officials issued a confidential report that North Korea had succeeded in making a nuclear warhead small enough to fit inside a missile, meaning the country was close to becoming a full-fledged nuclear power. Another report revealed North Korea had enough nuclear material for up to sixty warheads. While this was far fewer than the 6,550 possessed by the United States and the 6,800 estimated to be in Russia's arsenal, just one nuclear warhead is capable of catastrophic damage.

When this news became public in August, Trump threatened the North Korean dictator during a briefing at Trump National Golf Course in Bedminster, New Jersey.

"North Korea best not make any more threats to the United States," he said. "They will be met with fire and fury . . . and frankly power, the likes of which this world has never seen before."

Trump had said similar things to aides in private, but those public remarks surprised them and indicated that Trump's new chief of staff, John Kelly, hadn't completely succeeded in keeping the president's messages disciplined.

In return, North Korea's leader, Kim Jong-un, threatened to shoot missiles at Guam, a US territory.

The verbal duel continued when Trump, a longtime critic of North Korea's leadership, nicknamed the dictator "Rocket Man." Kim released a statement that said, among other things, "I will surely and definitely tame the mentally deranged US dotard with fire."

Trump's difficulties weren't just with North Korea. They hit him at home, too.

On August 2, Congress passed legislation that not only leveled new sanctions against Russia but also included measures that would prevent Trump's ability to ease them. Trump, who still refused to criticize Putin for his cyberattack on the US election, called the legislation "seriously flawed," "unconstitutional," and in violation of Trump's "constitutional authority to conduct foreign relations."

The next day, still fuming, Trump tweeted, "Our relationship with Russia is at an all-time & very dangerous low. You can thank Congress, the same people that can't even give us HCare!"

Eight days later, the troubles at home grew worse. White supremacists and separatists who'd been invigorated by Trump's rhetoric converged for a torchlight march on the University of Virginia campus in Charlottesville.

Charlottesville had already been the site of two far-right rallies in 2017. Unite the Right held its first there without a permit in May.

Another racist organization, the Ku Klux Klan, got a permit for its July 8 rally. That one ended in violence as protesters perceived the city's law enforcement to be protecting the Klan members while threatening those who had gathered in protest of racism.

Trump bore responsibility for these rallies. Former Ku Klux Klan leader David Duke said they were meant "to fulfill the promises of Donald Trump, and that's what we believed in, that's why we voted for Donald Trump, because he said he's going to take our country back."

> ## Trump bore responsibility for these rallies.

The night of August 11, a crowd of 250 white men wearing white polo shirts and khaki pants—a uniform Trump favored for his many golf outings—lit kerosene-fueled torches and marched across the University of Virginia's Nameless Field yelling, "Blood and soil!" and "You will not replace us!" and "Jews will not replace us!" The nighttime march was meant to kick off a weekend-long protest of the decision to remove a statue of Confederate general Robert E. Lee erected in 1924.

The white supremacists crossed the campus and approached a statue of the university's slave-owning founder, Thomas Jefferson. There, a group of thirty university students—some white, some people of color—locked arms around the statue's base. The white supremacists made monkey noises at the black students while chanting "White lives matter!" Violence broke out, injuring protesters and marchers alike. Both sides blasted pepper spray at each other. Marchers flung torches at protesters. Police officers were slow to intervene.

The next day, things grew worse. Downtown Charlottesville stores and restaurants had, for the most part, closed in anticipation of danger.

Protesters and anti-fascists arrived long before noon, when the white supremacist rally was scheduled to begin. Likewise, the white supremacists showed up early with banners, shields, clubs, and guns, which are legal to carry openly in Virginia. A third group, a self-described militia of three dozen men, arrived with semiautomatic rifles and pistols. They claimed to be peacekeepers welcomed by local police, but this was not true. They'd been told to stay away.

The white supremacists deviated from their original plan for the event. Instead of entering through a single entrance, they instead came in from many spots, putting them in direct contact with protesters. Police had been warned not to let this happen. Then when violence exploded, police did not intervene because they were not wearing protective gear and they had not received proper field training.

Thirty-eight minutes before the event officially started, it was declared an unlawful gathering. That did not end things, and at 1:14 P.M., a white supremacist drove his car through a crowd of pedestrians, reversed, and struck more people. He injured nineteen and killed a thirty-two-year-old protester from Charlottesville, Heather Heyer.

Trump's first statement did not condemn white nationalists for their protest. He seemed to blame both the white supremacists and the protesters equally for the horrifying outcome. "We condemn in the strongest possible terms this egregious display of hatred, bigotry and violence, on many sides," he said.

It wasn't until later that Trump spoke against racism. "We ALL must be united & condemn all that hate stands for. There is no place for this kind of violence in America. Lets [sic] come together as one!"

Some saw it as too little too late. But David Duke, the former Klan leader, saw Trump's words as ungrateful.

"I would recommend you take a good look in the mirror & remember it was White Americans who put you in the presidency, not radical leftists," Duke tweeted.

Three days later, Trump reversed his condemnation of racists, casting equal blame on people protesting the gathering: "I think there's blame on both sides, and I have no doubt about it."

On September 5, Trump kept at his campaign promise to end an Obama-era immigration program called Deferred Action for Childhood Arrivals. DACA protected young, undocumented immigrants from deportation; ending it would put nearly 690,000 young people at risk of deportation starting as early as March 2018.

After immediate protests and criticism of the decision as "cruel," Trump seemed to backtrack, tweeting that same night, "Congress now has 6 months to legalize DACA (something the Obama Administration was unable to do). If they can't, I will revisit this issue!"

More action against undocumented immigrants would come, but first, Trump faced more scrutiny related to Russia. On September 7, the Senate Judiciary Committee questioned Don Jr. about the statement attributed to him describing the June 2016 meeting in

Trump Tower. The stakes were high for the president's son. Lying to Congress is a crime.

"The *Washington Post* has since reported that your father was involved in drafting your July 8th statement. Is that correct?"

"I don't know," Don Jr. said. "I never spoke to my father about it."

The president was not only involved in drafting the statement, he'd dictated it. Months later, Trump's lawyers would acknowledge this in a confidential memo they sent to Mueller. Until that point, though, many—including Trump's son—had said misleading things to protect the president. The Trump camp intended to keep the president as far from perceived legal jeopardy as possible, even if it led to potentially problematic testimony by his son.

Between his election and the beginning of September, Trump had withstood an astonishing number of metaphorical storms: the Steele dossier; the raid on his campaign manager's home; the arrest of a campaign staffer; a special counsel investigation and investigations by the House and Senate into some of the same issues; unprecedented staff turnover, including the August dismissal of chief strategist Steve Bannon; and even the fraught testimony of his son before the Senate Judicial Committee.

But the next storms Trump faced were literal.

By early September, three deadly hurricanes named Harvey, Irma, and Maria had caused $265 billion in damage in Texas, Louisiana, Florida, the US Virgin Islands, and Puerto Rico. All three were among the top five costliest storms in the nation's history.

Initially, Trump received praise for his response to Hurricane Harvey, which hit land on August 26. Then Hurricane Maria hit the

US commonwealth of Puerto Rico on September 20. The Category 4 storm wiped out a great deal of the island's infrastructure, making it far worse than the hurricanes that hit other locations.

What's more, Puerto Rico wasn't easy to help. As Trump put it, "It's on an island in the middle of the ocean . . . You can't just drive your trucks there from other states."

The administration failed to rise to the challenge, and the people of Puerto Rico, who are American citizens, suffered. As long as one hundred days after the storm, seventy-six thousand island residents were still drinking water contaminated with sewage. It took nearly eleven months for power to be fully restored on the island. Although the official death count provided by the Puerto Rican government was sixty-four, other estimates were much higher—on average around one thousand by October 2017.

ABOVE: Trump is briefed on the devastation of Hurricane Maria in Puerto Rico.
(Official White House Photo by Shealah Craighead)

As Puerto Rico endured the catastrophic storm, Trump zeroed in on an issue closer to home: criticizing NFL players who chose to kneel instead of stand during the national anthem to protest police brutality and racism. Two days after Maria hit land, Trump attended a political rally in Alabama and attacked players who chose to protest.

"Wouldn't you love to see one of these NFL owners . . . say, 'Get that son of a bitch off the field right now. Out! He's fired!'" Trump said.

> "Wouldn't you love to see one of these NFL owners . . . say, 'Get that son of a bitch off the field right now. Out! He's fired!'" Trump said.

In Trump's view, football players earning millions of dollars should be required to stand during the national anthem as a show of respect for military veterans.

"If not, YOU'RE FIRED. Find something else to do!"

Kneeling during the anthem wasn't a new form of protest. It had started in 2016, when San Francisco 49ers quarterback Colin Kaepernick knelt as "The Star-Spangled Banner" played. Trump's throwaway political riff in support of struggling Alabama senator Luther Strange resonated with the crowd.

Trump—under siege for ignoring Puerto Rico and mollycoddling Putin—hammered the point for months. On its surface, it looked like a fight for patriotic respect for soldiers. But the players were not protesting the military or the flag. They were protesting racism and police brutality against black people. Trump's hesitance to condemn white supremacists with torches compared to his vociferous criticism of football players peacefully protesting racial injustice did nothing to dispel Trump's reputation as a racist or the reality of the threat he posed to the First Amendment right to free speech.

"Protest is patriotism," said Senator Cory Booker, a black Democrat who represents New Jersey.

Meanwhile, Mueller's team had reportedly summoned at least twenty people from Trump's orbit for interviews as Trump's first year wore on. Mueller scored his first guilty plea on October 5, when Papadopoulos—the one who'd promised the Russians had "dirt" on Clinton—pleaded guilty to lying to the FBI. It wasn't public knowledge yet that the former Trump adviser had been arrested, and Trump, anxious about the fate of his tax cuts he'd promised on the campaign trail, was worried.

"All of this 'Russia' talk right when the Republicans are making their big push for historic Tax Cuts & Reform. Is this coincidental? NOT!" Trump tweeted on October 29.

The next day, Mueller—who had made no public statements about his team's investigation—unsealed Papadopoulos's guilty plea. Along with that came a twelve-count indictment against Trump's former campaign manager, Paul Manafort, and Manafort's business partner Rick Gates, who had remained on Trump's campaign team after Manafort resigned, even making $100,000 for working on the president's inauguration.

Manafort and Gates were charged with laundering millions of dollars, making false statements, and not reporting fees earned

for lobbying on behalf of foreign governments. Both men pleaded not guilty and were released to home confinement on bond: $10 million for Manafort and $5 million for Gates.

Once the news broke, Trump's team tried to downplay Papadopoulos's significance to the campaign. Trump had called him an "excellent guy" in 2016, when he told the *Washington Post* that Papadopoulos had joined his team. But on October 30, when news about Papadopoulos's guilty plea became public, another former Trump adviser went on national television and called Papadopoulos a volunteer "coffee boy."

Trump also brushed off the significance of the charges against Manafort. "Sorry, but this is years ago, before Paul Manafort was

ABOVE: Rick Gates *(Shutterstock)*

part of the Trump campaign. But why aren't Crooked Hillary & the Dems the focus?????" he tweeted.

". . . Also, there is NO COLLUSION!"

No matter how many times Trump defended his innocence on Twitter, the questions about Russia, his finances, and his campaign's interactions with Kremlin actors remained.

This angered Trump. He thought he'd done nothing wrong, and he perceived the issue as an attack on his legitimacy as president and the investigation as a threat to the promises he'd made to the people who voted for him. On the campaign trail, he'd promised an immigration crackdown, the end of Obamacare, and tax cuts for "everybody across the board."

Many Republicans in Congress shared these priorities. The Mueller investigation could cost the Republicans their majority in the House and Senate. Even with the majority of seats in Congress, Republicans had so far failed to "repeal and replace" Obamacare, and any reduction in seats would make it even harder to achieve conservative legislative victories in the future.

Things got worse for Trump on December 1, when Mike Flynn pleaded guilty to lying to the FBI about his many calls with Russia's ambassador, Sergey Kislyak.

On or around the day Obama signed an executive order announcing sanctions against Russia in response to its cyberattack on the 2016 election, Kislyak had contacted Flynn. Afterward, Flynn called someone on the Trump transition team to discuss the communication strategy about the sanctions and their effect on the Trump administration's foreign policy goals. Then Flynn called Kislyak back and asked that Russia "not escalate the situation."

Flynn reported the call back to the transition team official—meaning the transition team knew about the call all along. Flynn also had calls with officials of foreign governments, including Russia, about voting strategy on a UN Security Council resolution condemning Israeli settlements in East Jerusalem and the West Bank.

The Logan Act makes it illegal for unauthorized citizens to negotiate with foreign governments. It's an old, rarely prosecuted law from 1799, when it was passed to prevent citizens from undermining the US government. Flynn's plea did not admit to violating the Logan Act; he admitted only that he'd lied about having the conversations when the FBI had asked about them.

But Trump didn't think Flynn was wrong to negotiate with the Russian ambassador. "I had to fire General Flynn because he lied to the Vice President and the FBI. He has pled guilty to those lies. It is a shame because his actions during the transition were lawful. There was nothing to hide!"

The Mueller investigation moved ever closer to Trump, interviewing White House counsel Don McGahn on November 30 and communications director Hope Hicks on December 7 and 8.

In the midst of these interviews, a private lie caught up with Trump—one about his assertion that he had grabbed women by their crotches without their consent. Even though his statement had been captured on the *Access Hollywood* video, he'd started privately telling people maybe it hadn't been him after all.

"We don't think that was my voice," he told allies, a senator, and aides.

The *New York Times* caught wind of it, detailing Trump's revisionist history on November 28. A few days later, the *Access*

Hollywood host who'd been with Trump when he said the words wrote an editorial confirming Trump had bragged about grabbing "pussy."

It was brazen of Trump to lie about something that had been recorded on tape—something that he'd apologized for doing, something that had been witnessed as it happened. And yet it was part of a pattern for Trump, who'd lied so frequently during his campaign and afterward that the *New York Times* started a "definitive list" of public falsehoods he'd told since he took his oath of office.

A few days after this attempt to rewrite reality became public, Trump heard a news report that Mueller was subpoenaing his financial records from Deutsche Bank.

The president raged. This was exactly what he'd said was off-limits in his *New York Times* interview. He told his aides, once again, to shut down the Mueller investigation. The order sent his aides and lawyers on a hurried mission to find out whether Mueller's team really *had* sought those records. The special counsel's office informed them they had not, which defused the situation for the time being.

In the midst of this, time was running out for Republicans to pass Trump's promised tax cuts. Trump considered this a once-in-a-generation opportunity.

Overall, his first year as president had been a legislative bust. His travel ban had hit legal obstacles. The "repeal and replace" of Obamacare failed. He had signed twenty-eight pieces of legislation in his first hundred days—a high number. But it was deceptively so. Thirteen documents he'd signed were simple rollbacks of

Obama-era regulations, including one that would have prevented states from withholding funding from Planned Parenthood.

After those first hundred days, Trump's productivity had plummeted. For Trump to have a shot at passing his last hope, big tax cuts, he would need to keep Republicans in office. He turned his attention again to the Alabama special election to fill the Senate seat vacated by Jeff Sessions.

> After those first hundred days, Trump's productivity had plummeted.

A former judge named Roy Moore had beaten Trump's previous pick, Luther Strange, in the primary. Moore was a candidate with heavy baggage. He had twice been removed from his post as Alabama's chief justice for disobeying federal laws, a violation of the state's judicial ethics codes. Also, four women had accused Moore of sexual misconduct when they were teenagers, including one who was just fourteen when Moore, then thirty-two, had initiated a sexual encounter with her. Moore had used ethnic slurs for Native Americans and Asian Americans, calling them "reds" and "yellows," and he called homosexuality "inherent evil."

Moore's opponent, Doug Jones, meanwhile, was a former US Attorney for the Northern District of Alabama who had led a team that convicted two Ku Klux Klan members of murdering four black children in a church bombing.

Nonetheless, Trump actively backed Moore, apparently preferring a racist, law-breaking sexual harasser to another Democrat in the Senate. Moore lost.

Meanwhile, on November 2, the first draft of the Tax Cuts and Jobs Act had been released. Cutting taxes, especially the rate corporations pay, had been a longtime goal of Republicans. After attempts to end Obamacare had failed in July, Republicans pivoted immediately to securing tax cuts.

The first hurdle: Find a way to cut taxes without increasing the budget deficit. They couldn't do it. And then they decided it didn't matter, though the size of the nation's budget deficit had been a frequent Republican criticism of Obama's performance.

Trump and his fellow Republicans were willing to gamble that cutting taxes would spur the economy enough to make up the lost revenue. They decided they could live with a $1.5 trillion budget deficit—higher than any one-year shortfall under the Obama administration.

In November, the House and Senate each introduced their versions of tax-cut legislation. The Senate version had two key features: tax cuts for individuals that would expire in 2025 and permanent corporate tax cuts. And—in a blow to what remained of Obamacare—the Senate eliminated a rule that required everyone to get insurance coverage, a decision that would mean higher rates and a reduction in the number of Americans with insurance.

Working at speeds typically seen only in national emergencies, the Republicans finalized their tax bill by December 15. It was the biggest one-time corporate tax cut in American history, a huge windfall for the nation's wealthiest, and a $1.46 trillion addition to the annual budget deficit.

Trump and his fellow Republicans were thrilled. This was the kind of victory they longed for, although the GOP tax cuts were not popular with voters. Polls showed only 32 percent of Americans approved of the GOP's plan, making it the least popular tax bill since 1981. Bill Clinton's tax hike in 1993 had had a higher approval rate.

Trump signed it into law on December 22.

As he sat in the Oval Office at 10:45 that morning with the legislation on his desk, he stressed how important it was that he kept his promise to sign the bill before Christmas.

"We were going to wait until January seventh or eighth and do a big, formal ceremony, but every one of the networks was saying, 'Will he keep his promise? Will he sign it before Christmas?' And so I immediately called, I said, let's get it ready."

He was proud of what he'd accomplished, saying "corporations are literally going wild over this."

But he couldn't help but leak resentment at what he perceived was unfair perception of his accomplishments in his first year.

Speaking about himself in the third person, he said, "A lot of people say he needed this because he has had no legislative approvals. Well . . . we have more legislative victories than any other President."

This was not true. Every president since World War II had signed more legislation in his first year than Trump did.

This was not true. Every president since World War II had signed more legislation in his first year than Trump did.

But this was a win. A huge one.

A major legislative victory under his belt at last, Trump boarded Air Force One and headed to Mar-a-Lago for his tenth visit of the year to his private club.

It was a heady time for Trump.

He'd been telling his friends that more good news would be coming. Robert Mueller, he told them, was going to write a letter exonerating him. Trump would wave it around Washington and blow away the heavy cloud of the Russia investigation. Landing in Palm Beach, Trump stepped off the plane still sharply dressed in a navy-blue suit with a red tie. He walked down the stairs to the tarmac, pumping his fist against the bright blue curve of the sky.

Even if he didn't get that letter from Mueller, Trump and his lawyers had a plan in the works to contain the investigation, a confidential, twenty-page memo that they would deliver by hand to the special counsel in the new year. The missive made an argument, among other things, for unprecedented presidential power to shut down the investigation into the possibility that Trump had obstructed justice. If that effort failed, the memo asserted he could potentially pardon himself.

Trump was gearing up to argue that if there was any law preventing what he'd done, as president, he was above it.

CHAPTER 15

"I HAVE DONE NOTHING WRONG"

> "As has been stated by numerous legal scholars, I have the absolute right to PARDON myself, but why would I do that when I have done nothing wrong?"
>
> —@realDonaldTrump, June 4, 2018

TRUMP SPENT CHRISTmas and New Year's Day at Mar-a-Lago, his private, for-profit club. Tradition dictates that presidential travel, even vacation, is funded by taxpayers. Trump added a new complexity to the equation: His privately held companies were profiting from his trips. This hadn't happened before with a president, and Trump traveled often to Mar-a-Lago and other properties he owned.

In 2017, he'd taken ten trips there for a total of forty-four days. He made more than ninety visits to his own golf clubs. And he took still more trips to other Trump properties. In his first year in office, Trump spent one in three days at a property his company owns.

Travel by Obama and his family had cost on average $1 million a month during his presidency. The Trump family's travel costs during his first year as president were higher; a conservative watchdog group tracked his spending at $13.5 million for just the Air Force One portion of travel.

All presidential travel is costly, in part because of security requirements. Golf cart rental for the Secret Service cost $150,000 by late 2017, an expense Trump is not legally allowed to reimburse because of conflict-of-interest rules. Trump took special heat because his businesses were profiting at the expense of taxpayers, and because his presidency was possibly giving Trump properties an unfair advantage over his competitors.

Unlike other presidents, Trump did not sever his relationship with his businesses. Although his sons Don Jr. and Eric were put in charge, Trump still owned them and profited when his businesses do.

> Unlike other presidents, Trump did not sever his relationship with his businesses.

The Constitution has two clauses that prohibit "emoluments," or payments and gifts from foreign or domestic governments.

With this in mind, the District of Columbia and State of Maryland filed suit against Trump. It was new legal ground; never in the nation's history had a federal court been asked to determine what a ban on emoluments means when it comes to the president. The Justice Department, which represents the president, had argued unsuccessfully in federal court that the case should be dismissed.

But it was not just that Trump's visits to his properties, paid for by the public, enriched him. The Trump Organization does business in many countries around the world. It was conceivable that his business interests and American foreign policy might at some point be in conflict. Some argued this position left him open to bribery and even blackmail by foreign governments.

Trump rejected the suggestion that his ongoing business interests presented a conflict of interest.

"The law's totally on my side," he said. "The president can't have a conflict of interest."

It's more of a gray area than Trump made out. Generally, officials who work in the executive branch are breaking the law if they participate in government business where they, their families, or their business partners have financial interests. But the president and vice president have traditionally gotten a pass from Congress. There isn't a legal requirement for a president to give up a business because of a conflict of interest. The president and vice president have been trusted to do the right thing.

In the past, the men holding these offices made efforts to avoid conflicts of interest and even the appearance of them.

When Nelson D. Rockefeller, a wealthy man, was being considered as Gerald Ford's vice president, Congress scrutinized

Rockefeller's business. Trump withheld his tax returns, so no such examination could be made. Past presidents also separated themselves completely from their businesses. President Jimmy Carter put his peanut farm into a blind trust that allowed an independent manager to operate, sell, or rent portions of it without Carter's approval, for example.

Just as Trump had no interest in being like other candidates, he had no interest in being like other presidents.

Likewise, as 2017 became 2018, he wasn't going to follow diplomatic protocol. Aggression had always worked for him, and so in the second year of his presidency, he turned up the dials as soon as he was back in Washington.

On January 2, he responded to a tweet from North Korea's dictator:

"North Korean Leader Kim Jong Un just stated that the 'Nuclear Button is on his desk at all times.' Will someone from his depleted and food starved regime please inform him that I too have a Nuclear Button, but it is a much bigger & more powerful one than his, and my Button works!"

The same day, Trump called for the jailing of Comey and a Clinton aide. He criticized the Department of Justice. And he announced he'd be giving awards to the most "dishonest and corrupt" members of the media.

While some people viewed those tweets as an example of Trump being Trump—calling things as he saw them and being a strong leader—experts on authoritarian governments considered the sentiments embedded in tweets like these to be warning signs of assaults on democracy.

Dictators threaten and sometimes imprison their opponents. They stack the courts and interfere with an independent judiciary. They also intimidate, threaten, and censor the free press.

During his campaign rallies, he'd reveled in chants of "Lock her up!" directed at Clinton, even after the FBI had found no criminal intent with her use of a private e-mail server for public business.

As president, he criticized the US judicial system as being "broken and unfair." Having not forgiven Attorney General Jeff Sessions for recusing himself from the Russia investigation, Trump frequently insulted Sessions and even attorneys in the Justice Department for how they did their jobs, especially when it came to the Mueller investigation. Trump expected the Justice Department to protect him, and he believed he had an "absolute right" to do what he wanted with the nation's top law-enforcement agency and its investigations.

Trump's threats on the media were also relentless and grave. During the campaign, Trump banned reputable media outlets from covering his rallies. As a candidate and as president he criticized journalists for being the "most dishonest" people. He tweeted hundreds of times about "fake news" in an attempt to diminish the credibility of information that he considered unflattering. He also tweeted about changing the nation's libel laws, an assault on the First Amendment.

Trump's threats on the media were also relentless and grave.

Although this extreme behavior was new for an American president, there is historical precedent elsewhere.

In Germany before World War II, Adolf Hitler was both hostile to the press and a master of the dark art of propaganda. Trump had long been familiar with Hitler's propaganda tactics. When Trump and Ivana were in the midst of their divorce, she wrote that Trump kept a book of Hitler's speeches by his bed. Titled *My New Order*, the speeches illuminated how Hitler had used propaganda to lead his nation to the murders of six million Jews, as well as millions more communists, gay people, disabled people, Jehovah's Witnesses, and members of the Roma ethnic group. Hitler also tarred his critics as *Lügenpresse*, which means "lying press." The term carried an anti-Semitic connotation, much like Trump's "America First" proclamation—associations that aren't evident to people unaware of those moments in history.

Trump also borrowed an insult from the Soviet dictator Joseph Stalin, calling the press "the enemy of the people." This was the exact phrase Stalin used to justify putting his opponents to death. Stalin used a state news outlet called Pravda—which means "truth"—to create a fact-free reality fueled by hysteria and maintained by gaslighting, an intentional manipulation of facts to make a person doubt their memory, perceptions, and even reality itself. His use of propaganda, biased information meant to mislead people, led to the purges and deaths of millions.

T WAS IN TRUMP'S INTEREST TO DISCREDIT the media.

The job of the political press is to fairly and accurately cover what members of the government say and do, and to correct reporting errors when they occur. When Trump, his campaign, and his family business were under investigation, and when that investigation regularly appeared in the news, discrediting the press was a strategy for self-preservation.

What's more, Trump enjoyed praise. He liked people to be "nice" to him, and he criticized the journalists and media outlets who did not meet this expectation as "horrendous," "fake news," and "failing." He also called journalists "sick people."

Although the media typically cover presidents critically, Trump created many of his own problems with the media by failing to tell the truth.

During his first hundred days in office—before the Mueller investigation began—Trump lied repeatedly. The *Washington Post*'s fact checkers tallied 492 lies for Trump's first hundred days, an average of 4.9 lies per day. He lied more frequently afterward, bringing his average for the first year and a half of his presidency to more than six lies per day. In June and July 2018, he averaged sixteen lies per day.

Trump's record of deception has no presidential precedent.

Obama also lied, but far less often. In his eight-year presidency, journalists caught him in eighteen public falsehoods. By early 2018, Trump was uttering that many false and misleading statements every two days. By mid-2018, Trump was lying almost twice that often. It is true that both presidents have said untrue things, but during the first half of his presidency, Trump lied 1,230 times as often as Obama did. That is, for each lie Obama told, Trump told 1,230.

Trump's lies carried consequences.

His lies about Obama's birthplace, for example, meant that in 2017, 57 percent of Republicans still believed Obama had been born outside the United States. While this had been a politically useful lie for Trump, it also meant some people would not be able to shed misinformation Trump had aggressively advanced for years. Trump had created a new and false reality for many voters.

Trump also frequently characterized inquiries into Russia's cyberattack on the election as a "witch hunt." He persisted in calling Russian interference in the election "fake news." He disregarded consensus among the intelligence agencies of the United States and the nation's allies, and he dismissed classified e-mail evidence he'd seen proving that the Russian government had hacked servers and spread disinformation and misinformation meant to divide voters, undermine Clinton, and elect Trump.

His assault on people's perceptions of reality was effective.

In October 2017, the conservative-leaning polling agency Rasmussen Reports found that 52 percent of voters believed Mueller's investigation was honest. By April 2018, only 46 percent trusted the investigation. Forty percent considered it a "partisan witch hunt," up from 32 percent over the same period.

Republicans were especially inclined to believe misinformation Trump provided. So, even if Trump could not shut down the Mueller investigation without political consequence, he could undermine the public's faith in it, especially with people likely to vote for his reelection.

RUMP'S FLURRY OF NEWS-MAKING TWEETS CON-
tinued on January 6, when he was at Camp David, the rustic
presidential retreat in Maryland. Trump had traveled there
to discuss his legislative priorities for the year, but the day before,
a book called *Fire and Fury* came out, and it raised questions about
Trump's mental state.

The book's author, Michael Wolff, said White House insiders
were having regular conversations about the Twenty-fifth Amendment, which can be used to remove a mentally unfit president from
office. The amendment was put in place in response to the Kennedy
assassination, and it specifies who replaces a president who has
died or resigned or is experiencing "an inability to discharge the
powers and duties of the office."

"The Twenty-fifth Amendment is a concept that is alive every
day in the White House," Wolff said. "It's that bad. I mean, it's an
extraordinary moment in time."

Such talk threw Trump into a state of outrage. Instead of focusing on his legislative priorities, he took to Twitter, his means of
talking with people without interference from his aides and without filter from the media.

"Now that Russian collusion, after one year of intense study, has
proven to be a total hoax on the American public, the Democrats
and their lapdogs, the Fake News Mainstream Media, are taking out
the old Ronald Reagan playbook and screaming mental stability
and intelligence. . . . . ," he tweeted.

". . . . Actually, throughout my life, my two greatest assets have
been mental stability and being, like, really smart. Crooked Hillary
Clinton also played these cards very hard and, as everyone knows,

went down in flames. I went from VERY successful businessman, to top T.V. Star.....

".... to President of the United States (on my first try). I think that would qualify as not smart, but genius. . . . and a very stable genius at that!"

Trump provided no evidence to prove the Russia investigation was a "total hoax." To the contrary, his campaign manager and national security adviser, among others, had been charged with crimes. So had Russian citizens and businesses. Less significantly, Trump had also once been a Reform Party candidate for president and therefore could not accurately claim he'd won on his first try, regardless of how big of an upset his victory had been. But Trump, being Trump, wanted to construct another reality he and his loyalists could inhabit. Anyone who challenged his version of it, whether it was the press, his political opponents, or the courts, could expect a fight. The media was "fake news." Opponents in government were the "deep state." The court system was "broken and unfair."

Immigration, particularly of people of color, remained an intensely frustrating subject for him, too. In a meeting to hammer out a bipartisan deal on DACA, which was intended to remove the threat of deportation for nearly 690,000 people brought to the United States as children, Trump told lawmakers he wanted more immigrants from places like Norway.

"Why are we having all these people from shithole countries come here?" he reportedly asked.

He was referring to immigrants from some countries in Africa, and also earthquake refugees from Haiti and El Salvador, hundreds of thousands of whom had been protected from deportation by President George W. Bush and President Obama. Trump's administration had just ended those protections when he described poor countries using crude language. His description of these poor nations struck many as another example of the president's disdain for people of color. He took to Twitter to deny having made the remarks, and a few days later, before a dinner at Trump International Golf Club, he defended himself to reporters: "No, I am not a racist. I'm the least racist person you have ever interviewed."

Soon the reality of the remarks had become a question. Had Trump made them?

Republican senator Lindsey Graham and Democratic senator Dick Durbin both said Trump had. But two other Republican senators, Tom Cotton and David Perdue, put out a joint statement implying the language was not used.

"In regards to Senator Durbin's accusation, we do not recall the President saying these comments specifically," the statement said.

Later the men said they'd heard the term "shithouse" instead of "shithole," which allowed them to defend the president and support his version of reality.

Lindsey Graham split from his fellow Republicans here.

"My memory hasn't evolved," he told reporters. "I know what was said and I know what I said."

For some Republicans, this was the bargain they faced with Trump in the Oval Office. Either stand with him or run the risk of threatening the political majority that would allow them to pass their legislation and put conservative judges on the nation's courts.

Sometimes, the reality in dispute was greater than whether Trump said a word that ended with "house" or "hole."

Representative Devin Nunes, a Republican from California and chairman of the House Select Intelligence Committee, set to work on a four-page memorandum called "Foreign Intelligence Surveillance Act Abuses at the Department of Justice and The Federal Bureau of Investigation." The memo was meant to discredit an FBI investigation of Carter Page and therefore the ongoing Mueller investigation into Trump's campaign.

Nunes was not a wholly impartial source. He'd been a part of Trump's presidential transition team. The FBI issued a statement saying it had "grave concerns" about the accuracy of the Nunes memo. Democrats who objected to the memo wrote a ten-page rebuttal.

But Trump's supporters waged a social media campaign urging public release of the Nunes memo. Russian propaganda bots on Twitter embraced it, along with Don Jr. and other prominent conservatives. Trump permitted the release of the Nunes memo and initially blocked the release of the Democrats' rebuttal.

Then Trump tweeted that Nunes's "memo totally vindicates 'Trump' in probe.

"But the Russian Witch Hunt goes on and on. . . . This is an American disgrace!"

It would be easy to write this off as partisan bickering, or as a government agency resisting criticism. This is where provable facts matter. The Republican memo claimed the surveillance warrant was tantamount to spying on the Trump campaign. But Carter Page was no longer part of the campaign when the FBI applied for the warrant. The FBI had also had Page in its sights for years before he joined the Trump campaign.

The Nunes memo also asserted the FBI did not tell the court issuing the warrant that it had received information from a British spy paid by a firm that had been hired by Democrats—the reports that became the Steele dossier.

This was also false. The FBI application disclosed the political origins in a lengthy footnote, and it noted that Steele—identified as Source #1—had a history of credibility with the bureau.

It's one thing to make a partisan argument based on different political philosophies. But it's another thing to ignore or misstate facts to protect a political party or its leader. To chip away at objective truth is to threaten the bonds that hold a society together.

"Sociologists say that a belief in truth is what makes trust in authority possible," said Timothy Snyder, a professor of European history at Yale. "Without trust, without respect for journalists or doctors or politicians, a society can't hang together. Nobody trusts anyone, which leaves society open to resentment and propaganda, and of course to demagogues."

Disregarding and distorting truth is also dangerous, he said. "Post-truth is pre-fascism. To abandon facts is to abandon freedom."

Trump continued his assault on facts and notions of American liberty and patriotism.

In Cincinnati on February 5, during a speech about tax cuts, Trump bemoaned a lack of applause from some Democrats to his State of the Union address. He called it "un-American."

"Somebody said 'treasonous,'" he said. "I mean, yeah, I guess. Why not? Can we call that treason? Why not. They certainly don't seem to love our country very much."

Trump's definition of treason diverges from the legal description: when someone who owes allegiance to the country wages war against it or gives its enemies "aid and comfort within the United States or elsewhere."

Not clapping for the president falls short of that threshold.

Less than two weeks later, on February 16, the Mueller investigation made its first charges against thirteen Russians and three Russian companies believed to be responsible for the attacks on the American electoral system.

The allegations went beyond hacking into e-mail accounts and servers. Russians also traveled to the United States to disrupt democracy, prosecutors said. The indictment alleged that Yevgeny Prigozhin, an oligarch known as "Putin's Cook" for his proximity to the Russian president, funded the Internet Research Agency which, starting as early as 2014, hired thirteen Russians to pose as Americans, create fake social media identities, post inflammatory social media, and host fake political rallies. They also allegedly stole the identities of real Americans as part of their criminal scheme.

Their goal was to sow political discord, support Trump, and disparage Clinton, the thirty-seven-page indictment said. The Russians capitalized on inherently divisive issues: immigration, religion, and race. They also targeted certain states, such as Texas and Tennessee, with fake social media groups that had hundreds of thousands of followers. Using false identities, they communicated with unwitting Trump campaign staff to get signs for their fake rallies, and in one case paid an American to dress up as Hillary Clinton in a prison uniform at a rally. Mueller also charged an

American, Richard Pinedo, with illegally selling bank account numbers over the internet.

On February 18, more charges came. A Dutch attorney named Alex van der Zwaan was indicted for lying to the FBI about his interactions with Manafort's associate, Rick Gates. Van der Zwaan pled guilty, served thirty days, and was deported.

On February 22, Mueller filed new charges against Manafort and Gates. The indictment listed thirty-two charges, including tax and bank fraud. Gates pled guilty the next day and agreed to cooperate with the special counsel.

Trump persisted in trashing the investigation despite the number of serious charges and guilty pleas.

> **"WITCH HUNT!" he tweeted on February 27.**

"WITCH HUNT!" he tweeted on February 27.

He also continued making comments that violated American democratic norms.

On March 3, in a private speech given to Republican donors at Mar-a-Lago, Trump complained about a decision not to investigate Clinton after the election, called the system "rigged," and suggested China's president, Xi Jinping, had achieved something noteworthy: "He's now president for life. President for life. No, he's great," Trump said. "And look, he was able to do that. I think it's great. Maybe we'll have to give that a shot someday."

Even if he was kidding during the conversation, which CNN described as "upbeat" and "peppered with jokes," Trump's words gave critics one more instance of a time Trump expressed admiration of an authoritarian leader. And given the number of times he'd called Clinton "crooked" and pressed for her incarceration, it's hard to make a case that threats of prison for a political enemy were entirely in jest.

Trump was often less than upbeat with his staff. He could be abusive to them, as he had been on the campaign trail and at times with employees of the Trump organization. He excoriated Secretary of Homeland Security Kirstjen Nielsen when data showed undocumented border crossings were rising, much as he'd humiliated Attorney General Jeff Sessions after the appointment of Mueller as special counsel.

This wasn't the only way Trump's behavior defied presidential norms. He also had a habit of tearing up papers after he was done with them. As a candidate, he'd done this after a debate with Clinton. Presidents aren't supposed to do this. The Presidential Records Act requires the preservation of all documents the president touches. Trump was especially zealous in tearing up a letter written to him by Chuck Schumer, a Democratic senator from New York.

Aides had to spend their days taping sheets of paper back together—including some that had been torn into confetti-like bits. The behavior contrasted starkly with that of Trump's predecessors, especially Obama, whose staff had had an organized and color-coded system for preserving presidential documents.

"It was the craziest thing ever," said Solomon Lartey, a records-management analyst with thirty years' experience. "He ripped papers into tiny pieces."

As rocky as February was for Trump, March was no better. Because Trump announced and signed tariffs on imported steel and aluminum in early March, his chief economic adviser, Gary Cohn, resigned. On March 13, Trump fired Rex Tillerson as secretary of state, putting CIA chief Mike Pompeo in the job. Tillerson and Trump hadn't gotten along for months; in 2017, Tillerson reportedly called Trump "a moron" within earshot of cabinet members and Trump's national security team. Later, Trump tweeted that Tillerson was "wasting time trying to negotiate with Little Rocket Man."

Trump did score a political victory against Andrew McCabe, the former FBI deputy director. Attorney General Jeff Sessions fired McCabe for an alleged lack of candor.

"The FBI expects every employee to adhere to the highest standards of honesty, integrity, and accountability," Sessions said.

McCabe, who'd worked for the FBI for twenty-one years, was fired on March 16, two days before he was eligible for a government pension. He denied being dishonest.

"This is part of an effort to discredit me as a witness" in an obstruction of justice investigation of Trump, he said.

Meanwhile, relations with Russia crackled with tension.

In early March, a Russian double-agent and his daughter were found slumped on a park bench in Salisbury, England. They'd been poisoned with a nerve agent developed in the former Soviet Union, a substance so toxic it sickened police officers who were investigating the deaths, putting one in intensive care for two weeks.

Putin denied responsibility. Had it been a military-grade nerve agent, he said, the victims "would have died on the spot."

Though Putin dismissed any link to him or the Kremlin, his critics had sometimes ended up dead. The same poison later killed another British woman on July 9.

"A very sad situation," Trump said. "It certainly looks like the Russians were behind it. Something that should never, ever happen. And we're taking it very seriously, as I think are many others."

America's traditional allies—Britain, France, and Germany—denounced the attack. The White House imposed sanctions on Russian companies and individuals for this and the election interference. But Trump still called the Mueller investigation a hoax, setting him apart not only from the nation's foreign allies but also from factions inside his own White House.

That same day new sanctions were announced, March 15, the FBI and the Department of Homeland Security jointly issued a warning that Russian hackers were targeting critical US infrastructure, including power and nuclear facilities. Hackers had also managed to get remote access to energy facilities. The chances of an attack on the nation's electrical grid were low; this would be an act of war. But the intrusions were an indication that Russia was gathering an understanding of how to do this.

Vladimir Putin was reelected on March 18 to another six-year term as Russia's president. It wasn't a clean election. One of his opponents was barred from the ballot, and reports were made of employers forcing their employees to vote for him. Nonetheless, Putin won 77 percent of the vote, despite putting the barest effort into a campaign.

Despite the fresh round of sanctions, Putin wanted Trump to offer his congratulations. He went about getting them in an indirect way; his spokesman, Dmitry Peskov, said Putin didn't consider it "unfriendly" that Trump hadn't called.

"Tomorrow's another day," Peskov said.

Trump resolved to telephone Putin. Before the call, his aides wrote briefing materials with specific instructions.

"DO NOT CONGRATULATE," the briefing said in capital letters.

Trump's national security adviser, H. R. McMaster, also told Trump in person to withhold his congratulations. There were reasons for this. It wasn't just that the Russian election was suspect. Putin's leadership did not warrant praise.

Nevertheless, Trump congratulated Putin.

Trump also failed to mention the nerve-agent poisoning or Russian interference in the US election. Nor did he condemn the hacks on the nation's infrastructure.

"We had a very good call," Mr. Trump said afterward. "We will probably be meeting in the not-too-distant future."

Trump's critics pounced.

"An American president does not lead the Free World by congratulating dictators on winning sham elections," Senator John McCain said.

The next day, McMaster resigned as national security adviser; he and Trump had long butted heads. John Bolton, the former ambassador to the United Nations, took McMaster's place.

Despite Trump's deference to Putin, the United States expelled sixty Russian diplomats and closed the Russian consulate in Seattle on March 26, calling all of the ousted diplomats spies. The diplomatic expulsion was part of a joint response to the poison attack by the US, Canada, Ukraine, and European Union states. Russia was not pleased.

The official White House statement was brief and measured, calling the expulsion an "appropriate response" to the deadly attack: "Russia's response was not unanticipated, and the United States will deal with it."

Meanwhile, as attempted crossings of the United States' southern border rose, Trump's administration had begun dealing more aggressively with immigrants. On April 6, Jeff Sessions announced a new policy that directed federal prosecutors to criminally prosecute all adult migrants entering the country without documentation.

"The situation at our Southwest Border is unacceptable. Congress has failed to pass effective legislation that serves the national interest—that closes dangerous loopholes and fully funds a wall along our southern border," Sessions said.

Trump repeatedly exaggerated the danger immigration posed to citizens. He said immigrants bring "death and destruction . . . They are thieves and murderers and so much else." This is a widely held misbelief—almost half of Americans think immigrants worsen crime. Both undocumented and documented immigrants commit less crime less often than citizens.

What's more, while border crossings rose from 2017 to 2018, they were far lower than they had been in 2000. Since that peak, border crossings had diminished sharply. Very few of the people who crossed the border illegally were gang members. Many who attempted to gain entry to the US were families seeking safety from gang violence or to escape from poverty. It is also legal for immigrants to seek and apply for asylum.

Although an international law passed after World War II established a human right to seek asylum, the Trump administration sought to make refuge harder to obtain, and the new policy sub-jected all undocumented border-crossers to criminal prosecution, including those legally seeking safety from danger.

The policy meant that parents and children—even babies—were separated from one another. The Trump administration had been considering doing exactly this for months. In March 2017, then–Secretary of Homeland Security John Kelly—later Trump's chief of staff—said it was intended to "deter more movement along this terribly dangerous network." Not long after that, Kelly said parents and children would be separated at the border only "if the child's life is in danger."

This was not true.

> **The administration started separating families in October 2017.**

The administration started separating families in October 2017. Groups that advocate for immigrants complained about the prac-tice in December 2017. A lawsuit later alleged that some of these detained children were being forcibly administered powerful drugs meant to act as "chemical straitjackets."

Before the family separation policy, families seeking asylum could cross the border or show up at a port of entry and request asylum. Then they would be taken to a family detention center and interviewed to determine whether their fear of returning home was credible. Most families seeking asylum—77 percent—proved their fear of home was real. At that point, they could pay a bond or wear an ankle monitor while awaiting their case in court.

But under the Trump administration, this policy changed drastically. Between April 19 and May 31, nearly two thousand children were taken from their parents.

The Trump administration expressed no remorse for separating families.

"We have to do our job," Secretary of Homeland Security Kirstjen Nielsen said. "We will not apologize for doing our job. This administration has a simple message—if you cross the border illegally, we will prosecute you."

The public outcry was intense. In the face of it, Trump signed an executive order that would keep migrant families together. The administration failed to reunite all of the families it had separated, despite a court order to do so, leaving hundreds of children effectively orphaned.

In the midst of the Trump administration's efforts to ramp up law enforcement at the border, the FBI brought law enforcement closer than ever to Trump himself.

On April 9, federal authorities raided the office of Trump's longtime lawyer, Michael Cohen. Among other things, Cohen had arranged payoffs to Stormy Daniels and other women to keep their sexual affairs with Trump secret. Trump initially denied knowledge of the hush money to Daniels, money paid weeks before the election to ensure her silence about the adulterous relationship they had had in 2006. But in 2017, Trump had disclosed the payments as federal law required.

Cohen did more than block disclosure of potential sex scandals for Trump. Cohen also helped pursue business deals for the Trump

Organization in Georgia, Kazakhstan, and Russia—including the Trump Tower Moscow deal Cohen had tried and failed to launch when Trump was a candidate. In seizing documents from Cohen, Mueller had crossed the "red line" of Trump's business dealings. It also meant Mueller's team—with deep expertise in criminal law, organized crime, corruption, and money laundering—would have access to a great deal of information about Trump's business and its practices.

The raid infuriated Trump.

The raid infuriated Trump.

"Attorney-client privilege is dead!" he tweeted.

Rather than say the raid threatened the Trump Organization, Trump claimed Mueller's "Fake & Corrupt" investigation was harming the nation's relations with Russia.

"Our relationship with Russia is worse now than it has ever been, and that includes the Cold War . . . Russia needs us to help with their economy, something that would be very easy to do, and we need all nations to work together. Stop the arms race?"

Trump's claim that the Russian economy was in trouble was true. Russia produces a lot of oil, and prices had cratered between 2013 and 2016. But sanctions Russia received for annexing Crimea and interfering with Ukraine had also hobbled the country's economy by blocking international funding sources for Russia's businesses. Putin's actions led to the original sanctions. Putin responded to these sanctions by interfering with the 2016 election and working to sow political divisions among Americans, resulting in more sanctions. Even if no bombs were dropped, this represented an attack on the United States.

> ## Even if no bombs were dropped, this represented an attack on the United States.

And it was an attack Trump knew about even before he took office. Not only did the nation's intelligence agencies agree on that fact in early 2017, a bipartisan Senate report confirmed that assessment in 2018. The report also concluded Russia's interference had not stopped.

There was no doubt that the Russian government disliked Mueller's investigation. But Putin's acts of aggression had resulted in the investigation. To blame the investigation for deteriorating relations was a bit like saying the burglar resented the home-owner for pressing charges.

What's more, the investigation that Trump had called fake and corrupt had led to real criminal charges and guilty pleas. Trump's language amounted to an attack on the judicial system, a pillar of the nation's democracy. Trump's statements were designed to diminish public opinion of the courts, and they amounted to a violation of the Constitutional principle of separation of powers.

Meanwhile, Mueller filed another charge against Manafort on June 8—this time for obstruction of justice. He also indicted Manafort's Russian business partner, Konstantin Kilimnik, on the same charge. That same day, Trump traveled to the G7 summit in Quebec, a meeting of the United States and key economic partners.

Russia had once been part of the group but was kicked out after it illegally annexed Crimea. At the summit, Trump argued that Russia should be brought back into the group. He also blasted trade deficits America has with other countries—something he had tried to remedy by imposing tariffs on imports. Trump's views represented departure from traditional American policies, which had favored free trade. What's more, his tariffs and rhetoric incensed traditional US allies and trade partners.

Trump's positions had caused a rift, French President Emmanuel Macron said. "The American President may not mind being isolated, but neither do we mind signing a 6 country agreement [without the United States] if need be . . . [T]hese 6 countries . . . represent an economic market which has the weight of history behind it and which is now a true international force."

A few days later, Trump traveled to Singapore for a summit with North Korean dictator Kim Jong-un. The move was a gamble. Kim was considered a pariah among world leaders. He'd ordered the assassinations of his uncle and half-brother and spent money on developing nuclear weapons even as his people starved. His record on human rights was riddled with abuses. No sitting US president had met with a North Korean head of state. For Trump to meet with him would transform Kim from a pariah into a peer. In exchange for this, the United States asked nothing in return.

Trump had hoped to make progress on a deal to disarm North Korea. This did not happen. But the meeting did reduce rising tensions and the name-calling the two men had engaged in, diminishing the chance of war between the two nations.

Trump considered that a win.

"If I have to say I'm sitting on a stage with Chairman Kim and that's going to get us to save thirty million lives, maybe more than that, I'm willing to sit on the stage. I'm willing to travel to Singapore very gladly."

As Trump was smashing diplomatic norms, his former campaign manager, Paul Manafort, had his bail revoked and was sent to jail on June 15 for attempting to coerce witnesses in his pending trial.

Trump once again criticized the court. "Wow, what a tough sentence for Paul Manafort," Trump tweeted. "Didn't know Manafort was the head of the Mob. What about Comey and Crooked Hillary and all of the others? Very unfair!"

Not long after that, Supreme Court justice Anthony Kennedy announced he'd retire, giving Trump a second court seat to fill. Trump announced the nomination of Brett Kavanaugh on July 9. Kavanaugh was a federal appeals court judge who earlier in his career had participated in the investigation of President Bill Clinton. After he helped impeach Clinton, Kavanaugh wrote an article that suggested a sitting president should not be subject to the distraction of a civil lawsuit or criminal investigation or prosecution. His nomination raised the possibility that Trump was appointing a judge who might protect him from the Mueller investigation.

Mueller, meanwhile, indicted a dozen Russian intelligence officers on July 13 for their roles in hacking the DNC, the Clinton campaign, and the Democratic Congressional Campaign Committee, and for leaking stolen e-mails and other documents. Significantly, the charging papers also described how Guccifer 2.0—the front for Russian intelligence officers—communicated with the Trump team. Guccifer 2.0 exchanged messages with an unnamed "US person" who was "in regular contact with senior members of the presidential campaign of Donald J. Trump."

Roger Stone, a political dirty trickster who was Trump's long-time confidante, acknowledged on CNN that he was probably that unnamed source.

"It's benign, it's innocuous," Stone said of his exchanges.

Not everyone saw it that way. The ongoing nature of Russia's cyberwarfare alarmed intelligence experts. Dan Coats, the director of national intelligence, likened the urgency of the situation to the months just before the September 11, 2001, terrorist attacks on American soil, when there were ample signs the nation was in danger.

"And here we are nearly two decades later, and I'm here to say the warning lights are blinking red again," Coats said. "Today, the digital infrastructure that serves this country is literally under attack."

It wasn't just the nation's digital infrastructure.

At least one Russian allegedly succeeded in infiltrating American political organizations, as well. On July 16, the Justice Department charged a Russian woman named Maria Butina with conducting a covert operation against the United States on behalf of the Russian government.

The charges—for conspiracy and failing to register as a foreign agent—were not part of the Mueller investigation; the FBI had been already scrutinizing Butina before Mueller came on the scene. The red-haired Russian agent came to the United States

ostensibly to study and during that time infiltrated the National
Rifle Association and other conservative organizations. She'd even
started a sexual relationship with a much older Republican operative as part of her covert operations. Butina's boss, Alexander
Torshin, had been the one to arrange a meeting at the NRA's
National Prayer Breakfast with Don Jr., after Trump himself was
not available. When investigators arrested Butina, she'd been just
about to flee for Russia.

The day her arrest became public, Trump was in Helsinki, the
capital of Finland, a city only an hour flight from Moscow, preparing for a private summit with Putin.

Trump had already been in Europe for a NATO meeting. It had
not gone smoothly. He'd threatened to leave the organization over
a funding dispute with America's allies. The cooperation of these

ABOVE: President Donald J. Trump and President Vladimir Putin of the Russian Federation
shake hands. July 16, 2018. *(Official White House Photo by Shealah Craighead)*

allies had helped contain Soviet aggression during the Cold War, and Putin, who'd been a KGB officer during that time, was no doubt pleased to see NATO bonds strain under Trump's pugilistic diplomatic style.

People in Finland protested the meeting with signs criticizing both Trump and Putin. The summit also caused concern in the States. Democrats and some Republicans implored Trump to cancel.

Nebraska senator Ben Sasse, a Republican, issued a statement that read, "All patriotic Americans should understand that Putin is not America's friend, and he is not the President's buddy. We should stand united against Putin's past and planned future attacks against us."

Rather than stand against Putin's onslaughts, Trump turned on the United States.

ABOVE: Trump and Putin hold a joint press conference in Helsinki, Finland. July 16, 2018.
(Official White House Photo by Shealah Craighead)

"Our relationship with Russia has NEVER been worse thanks to many years of US foolishness and stupidity and now, the Rigged Witch Hunt!"

Trump and Putin had their private meeting July 16. There were no reporters. No aides. The only American besides Trump was a US government interpreter. Only Trump, Putin, and their interpreters knew what was said in the meeting. No one else ever would, at least not for certain. Interpreters don't take notes that are meant to be long-term records, and their code of ethics prevents them from sharing what was exchanged.

But whatever was said in the meeting, the words said afterward were explosive.

At a joint press conference with both Putin and Trump, a reporter asked Trump about interference in the 2016 election: Whom did Trump believe? Putin or American intelligence agencies?

It was an opportunity for Trump, once and for all, to show his allegiance to the United States and the intelligence officers who serve the nation. It was also an opportunity for Trump to confront a foreign adversary who'd launched information warfare against America—to fight back, as presidents had done after the Japanese attack on Pearl Harbor and the terrorist attack on 9/11.

He did neither.

"My people came to me," Trump said. "Dan Coats came to me and some others and said they think it's Russia. I have President Putin. He just said it's not Russia. I will say this. I don't see any reason why it would be."

Trump's remarks were met with two reactions: silence from his allies, and astonishment from others.

House Speaker Paul Ryan said: "There is no question that Russia interfered in our election and continues attempts to undermine democracy here and around the world. That is not just the finding of the American intelligence community but also the House Committee on Intelligence. The president must appreciate that Russia is not our ally."

Jeff Flake, a Republican senator from Arizona, called Trump's performance "shameful."

"I never thought I would see the day when our American president would stand on the stage with the Russian president and place blame on the United States for Russian aggression."

John Brennan, director of the CIA under Obama, said the performance rose to the level of high crimes and misdemeanors, an impeachable offense.

"It was nothing short of treasonous," he tweeted. "Not only were Trump's comments imbecilic, he is wholly in the pocket of Putin. Republican Patriots: Where are you???"

In the days that followed, Trump briefly claimed he'd misspoken. He'd meant to say he didn't know why it *wouldn't* be Russia engaging in cyberwarfare.

But his historical revisionism didn't last.

By July 22, Trump was back in the ring throwing rhetorical jabs and hooks that had no basis in reality. The whole thing was a "big hoax." It was Obama's and Clinton's faults. And worse, they'd spied on his campaign for political gain.

A few hours later, Trump was once again banging the drums of war. Not against North Korea, nor against Russia, who had waged information warfare against the nation he'd sworn to serve.

This time, Iran was in Trump's crosshairs, because the Iranian president had the audacity to tell Trump not to "play with the lion's tail, because you will regret it eternally."

Not one to let a punch go unanswered, Trump hit back.

He hit back firmly, swiftly, and in a way no president ever had: by threatening war on Twitter in capital letters.

"NEVER, EVER THREATEN THE UNITED STATES AGAIN OR YOU WILL SUFFER CONSEQUENCES THE LIKES OF WHICH FEW THROUGHOUT HISTORY HAVE EVER SUFFERED BEFORE. WE ARE NO LONGER A COUNTRY THAT WILL STAND FOR YOUR DEMENTED WORDS OF VIOLENCE & DEATH. BE CAUTIOUS!"

It was an astounding moment in American history, and at the same time, it hardly made a splash in the history of Trump's presidency.

It was a day on which Trump trafficked in conspiracy theories, partisan sniping, threats, and lies. A day on which Trump accused law enforcement agencies investigating him of betraying their principles for the sake of politics. A day on which threats to destroy the world passed for attempts to keep the nation secure.

It was a day on which reality could be torn as easily as a sheet of paper that others would have to reassemble for the sake of history.

It was a day like many others in the Trump White House. It was unprecedented.

And Donald Trump, the nation's forty-fifth president, was not yet halfway through his term.

OPPOSITE: President Donald J. Trump *(Department of Defense)*

DONALD J. TRUMP MILESTONES

Born in Queens, New York
JUNE 14, 1946

Attends New York Military
Academy
1959–1964

Studies at Fordham
University
1964–1966

Graduates from University
of Pennsylvania
1968

Trump Management
Corporation sued by
United States Department
of Justice for violating the
Fair Housing Act of 1968
by allegedly discriminating
against black applicants.
Trump countersues
for $100 million. Loses
countersuit and settles
Justice Department suit
in 1975.
OCTOBER 15, 1973

Marries Ivana Zelnícková
Winklmayr
APRIL 7, 1977

Donald John Trump Jr.
is born.
DECEMBER 31, 1977

Grand Hyatt New York
opens.
SEPTEMBER 25, 1980

Ivana "Ivanka" Marie
Trump is born.
OCTOBER 30, 1981

Trump Tower in
Manhattan opens.
JULY 26, 1982

Makes inaugural Forbes
list of 400 wealthiest
Americans.
His wealth is estimated
at $100 million. A later
review pegged his wealth
then at $5 million—not
enough to have qualified.
1982

Sued for knowingly hiring
undocumented, nonunion
workers to raze building
on site of future Trump
Tower. Settles in 1999.
1983

Buys New Jersey Generals
SEPTEMBER 1983

Eric Frederic Trump is
born.
JANUARY 6, 1984

Harrah's at Trump Plaza
opens in Atlantic City.
MAY 15, 1984

Trump's Castle opens in
Atlantic City.
JUNE 17, 1985

Travels with Ivana to
Moscow for the first time
hoping to build hotel in
partnership with Soviet
government, the only way
such a venture could take
place.
JULY 4, 1987

First book, *Art of the Deal*,
is published
Becomes a *New York
Times* bestseller beginning
December 20, 1987
NOVEMBER 1987

Trump buys Eastern Air
shuttle and renames it the
Trump Shuttle.
OCTOBER 19, 1988

Removed from Forbes
400 list
1990

Separates from Ivana after
having started affair with
Marla Maples
FEBRUARY 1990

Trump Taj Mahal Casino
Resort opens
APRIL 1990

Trump Taj Mahal Casino
Resort files for Chapter 11
bankruptcy.
1991

Trump Shuttle shuttered
1992

Trump Plaza Hotel files for
Chapter 11 bankruptcy.
1992

Testifies before Congress
that organized crime on
Indian reservations is
rampant, and that Native
Americans running casinos
"don't look like Indians"
to him
1993

Tiffany Ariana Trump is
born.
OCTOBER 13, 1993

Marries Marla Maples
DECEMBER 20, 1993

Reports $916 million loss on his tax return. Potentially off the hook for federal income taxes until around 2013
1995

Sells stake in Grand Hyatt, returns to Forbes 400 list
1996

Buys Miss Universe Organization
1996

Separates from Marla Maples
MAY 1997

Trump Taj Mahal pays IRS $477,000 for violating the Bank Secrecy Act, which is intended to foil money launderers
1998

Meets Melania Knauss
1998

Divorces Marla Maples
1999

Fred Trump dies.
JUNE 25, 1999

Runs for president as Reform Party candidate
1999-2000

The Apprentice debuts.
JANUARY 8, 2004

Trump Hotels and Casino Resorts files for Chapter 11 bankruptcy.
2004

Marries Melania Knauss
JANUARY 22, 2005

Opens Trump University
2005

Barron Trump is born.
MARCH 20, 2006

Trump announces Trump SoHo.
Condo-hotel was built in partnership with Russia-connected company that employed a man who was part of a stock scam linked to Russian mobsters and Mafia families.
2006

Trump Organization spends $400 million in cash on new properties.
2006-2015

Trump falls behind on payments to Deutsche Bank.
2008

Trump Entertainment Resorts files for Chapter 11 bankruptcy.
2009

Trump files $5 billion defamation suit against author who estimated his fortune to be $150 million to $250 million. Loses lawsuit.
2009

Trump's first tweet
MAY 4, 2009

Trump University students in California, and later the New York state attorney general, file fraud suits against Trump.
2010

Trump SoHo buyers file suit. Settles in 2011
2010

ShouldTrumpRun.com website is registered.
DECEMBER 2010

Obama roasts Trump at White House Correspondents' Dinner in Washington, DC.
APRIL 2011

Trump advances already-debunked conspiracy theory that Barack Obama was born outside the United States.
APRIL 2011-
SEPTEMBER 2016

Trump registers "Make America Great Again" service mark.
NOVEMBER 2012

Trump travels to Moscow for Miss Universe pageant.
NOVEMBER 2013

Trump Entertainment Resorts files for Chapter 11 bankruptcy again (Trump owns 10 percent but does not run the organization).
2014

Trump hires first campaign staffers.
FEBRUARY 2015

Announces he is running for president
JUNE 16, 2015

Elected president of the United States
NOVEMBER 8, 2016

Settles three Trump University lawsuits
NOVEMBER 18, 2016

Sworn in as nation's forty-fifth president.
JANUARY 20, 2017

TRUMP PRESIDENCY TIMELINE

TRUMP'S AGENDA MILESTONES

STAFF DEPARTURES

MUELLER INVESTIGATION

JANUARY 21, 2017

Trump signs executive order intended to begin dismantling of Affordable Care Act (known as Obamacare).

JANUARY 25, 2017

Trump orders immediate construction of border wall between US and Mexico.

JANUARY 26, 2017

Trump signs two anti-immigrant orders: one that withholds money from sanctuary cities and announces plans to build a border wall, and a second to make it easier to deport immigrants believed to have broken any law (without needing to be charged or convicted).

JANUARY 27, 2017

Trump issues what he calls a "Muslim ban," a halt on travel for Muslim refugees and immigrants. It faces nearly immediate court challenges.

JANUARY 30, 2017

Acting Attorney General Sally Yates fired for refusing to enforce Trump's "Muslim ban."

JANUARY 31, 2017

Trump nominates Neil Gorsuch to fill Supreme Court seat vacant since death of Justice Antonin Scalia.

FEBRUARY 10, 2017

Robin Townley, senior director for Africa on the National Security Council, resigns after CIA revokes her security clearance. Replaced by Cyril Sartor.

FEBRUARY 13, 2017

National Security adviser Michael Flynn resigns after misleading White House about conversations with Russian ambassador.

MARCH 6, 2017

Trump signs new version of "Muslim ban"; it blocks entry into US from six predominantly Muslim countries. (Iraq is now off the list, and refugees who already hold a valid visa are allowed to enter, regardless of their country of origin, including Syria.)

MARCH 6, 2017

House Republicans release their plan to repeal and replace the Affordable Care Act.

MARCH 23, 2017

Trump signs $1.3 spending bill he'd threatened to veto because it did not fully fund his promised border wall.

MARCH 30, 2017

Deputy chief of staff Katie Walsh, formerly chief of staff at the Republican National Committee, resigns under pressure. She is succeeded by Kirstjen Nielsen.

APRIL 6, 2017

Senate Republicans reduce threshold for approving a Supreme Court nominee from 60 to 51.

APRIL 7, 2017

Gorsuch approved as Supreme Court Justice, 54–45.

APRIL 26, 2017

White House proposes tax rates that are especially advantageous to the wealthy. Does not yet offer plan for paying for the cuts.

MAY 4, 2017

Vote to repeal and replace parts of the ACA passes by narrow margin.

MAY 9, 2017

Trump fires FBI Director James Comey.

MAY 17, 2017

Robert Mueller III named special counsel, takes over FBI's Russia investigation.

MAY 18, 2017

Communications director Michael Dubke resigns but remains on staff until May 30 when Trump completes international trip; is replaced by Anthony Scaramucci on July 21.

JUNE 8, 2017

James Comey testifies before Senate Intelligence Committee, claiming Trump pressured him.

JUNE 14, 2017

Washington Post reports Mueller is investigating Trump for possible attempt to obstruct justice.

SUMMER 2017

Mueller removes Peter Strzok from Russia probe after biased (pro-Clinton, anti-Trump) texts found.

SUMMER–FALL 2017

As Mueller interviews many Trump associates during the summer and fall, his team and the president's lawyers discuss the possibility of Trump testifying.

JUNE 2017

Around this time, Trump orders staff to fire Mueller. White House counsel Donald McGahn refuses to ask the Department of Justice to do this, threatening to leave instead.

JUNE 15, 2017

Mueller orders Trump transition team to retain documents related to Russia and Ukraine.

JULY 20, 2017

Bloomberg News reports the Mueller investigation has expanded to include Trump's business transactions.

JULY 21, 2017

Press secretary Sean Spicer resigns after Trump hires Scaramucci. Sarah Huckabee Sanders, who worked on the Trump campaign, is promoted.

JULY 25, 2017

Trump tells *Wall Street Journal* he is considering firing Attorney General Jeff Sessions; Trump is angry Sessions isn't protecting him against Mueller investigation.

JULY 26, 2017

FBI raids Paul Manafort's condominium in Virginia.

JULY 27, 2017

Senate rejects repeal of parts of the Affordable Care Act, 49–51.

JULY 27, 2017

Mike Pence's chief of staff, Josh Pitcock, announces he will resign August 1.

JULY 28, 2017

Chief of staff Reince Priebus ousted. John Kelly replaces him.

AUGUST 18, 2017

Steve Bannon, former campaign CEO and chief strategist to Trump, resigns.

SEPTEMBER 1, 2017

Trump's former personal bodyguard and director of Oval Office operations, Keith Schiller, announces he will resign in September or October.

SEPTEMBER 15, 2017

Facebook provides information on Russian political ads to Mueller.

OCTOBER 5, 2017

Former foreign policy adviser George Papadopoulos pleads guilty to lying to FBI. Agrees to cooperate with Mueller investigation.

OCTOBER 30, 2017

Mueller investigation leads to charges against Paul Manafort and his deputy Richard "Rick" Gates, who also worked on Trump campaign. The men face many counts, including conspiracy against the US, conspiracy to money launder, making false statements, failing to register as foreign agents, and seven counts of failing to file reports of foreign bank and financial accounts. They plead not guilty.

NOVEMBER 16, 2017

House of Representatives passes tax cut bill, 227–205.

NOVEMBER 28, 2017

Deputy assistant and White House counsel Greg Katsas resigns to serve on Washington DC Circuit Court of Appeals.

DECEMBER 1, 2017

Former National Security adviser Michael Flynn pleads guilty to lying to the FBI. He will cooperate with Mueller investigation.

DECEMBER 1, 2017

Senate passes its version of tax bill, 51–49.

DECEMBER 8, 2017

Deputy national security adviser Dina Powell, formerly of Goldman Sachs, announces her return to private sector.

DECEMBER 13, 2017

Omarosa Manigault Newman, a former *Apprentice* villain, resigns under pressure. She had been assistant to the president and director of communications for the Office of Public Liaison.

DECEMBER 15, 2017

Paul Winfree, deputy director of the Domestic Policy Council and director of budget policy, resigns.

DECEMBER 20, 2017

House votes on reconciled version of tax plans, passing bill 224–201.

DECEMBER 22, 2017

Trump signs tax bill into law. Bill eliminates coverage mandate in Affordable Care Act. It also lowers corporate tax rate dramatically. It temporarily lowers tax rates on individuals, with most of the reductions going to the wealthiest taxpayers.

DECEMBER 21, 2017

Deputy chief of staff Rick Dearborn announces he will resign early in 2018.

JANUARY 2018

Convicted pedophile George Nader is questioned by Mueller about alleged meetings in the Seychelles between a Trump intermediary and representatives of the UAE and Russia.

JANUARY 8, 2018

More conversation between Trump's attorneys and Mueller's team about the possibility Trump will testify.

JANUARY 29, 2018

Trump lawyers John Dowd and Jay Sekulow send a memo to Mueller. The memo argues Trump's actions could not constitute obstruction because he had the power to shut down any investigation and could also pardon its subjects, possibly even himself.

FEBRUARY 7, 2018

Staff secretary Rob Porter resigns under pressure after surfacing of domestic abuse allegations made by two former wives. The White House chief of staff John Kelly initially defends him.

FEBRUARY 12, 2018

A California man named Richard Pinedo pleads guilty to charges of identity fraud after he sold bank account numbers online.

FEBRUARY 16, 2018

Justice Department charges thirteen Russians and three companies for building a network designed to help elect Trump, promote discord, and undermine Americans' confidence in the nation's democracy.

FEBRUARY 20, 2018

Dutch Lawyer Alex van der Zwaan, who worked for Manafort and Gates, pleads guilty to lying to investigators about conversations he had with Gates.

FEBRUARY 22, 2018

Mueller's team brings a second indictment against Manafort and Gates. This one has thirty-two counts, and it includes new allegations of tax and bank fraud.

FEBRUARY 23, 2018

Rick Gates pleads guilty to two charges. Begins cooperating with Mueller investigation.

FEBRUARY 23, 2018–APRIL 2018

Starting around February 23, Manafort tries to influence witnesses in the government's case against him.

FEBRUARY 28, 2018

Hope Hicks, communications director, announces pending resignation the day after she testified before the House Intelligence Committee for eight hours, admitting her job sometimes required her to tell "white lies" on behalf of Trump.

MARCH 2018

Trump's personal lawyer John Dowd says he hopes Rod Rosenstein, the deputy attorney general, shuts down Mueller investigation.

MARCH 6, 2018

Gary Cohn, director of the National Economic Council, resigns.

MARCH 17, 2018

Trump's personal lawyer John Dowd says he hopes deputy attorney general shuts down Mueller investigation.

MARCH 22, 2018

Dowd resigns.

MARCH 23, 2018

Trump signs $1.3 trillion spending bill he'd threatened to veto because it did not fully fund his promised border wall. He also noted the bill did not fund DACA.

MARCH 28, 2018

The Department of Justice's inspector general begins an investigation of the FBI and DOJ to see if they abused their surveillance and wiretap powers. Trump criticizes the attorney general's action as "disgraceful"; he wanted a criminal investigation by the Department of Justice.

APRIL 9, 2018

FBI raids Trump attorney Michael Cohen's home, office, and hotel room. He is under investigation for alleged bank fraud and violations of campaign finance laws.

APRIL 10, 2018

Homeland Security adviser Thomas Bossert pushed out by National Security adviser John Bolton.

APRIL 26, 2018

In Fox News interview, Trump criticizes the Mueller investigation, the FBI, and the DOJ.

MAY 2, 2018

White House lawyer Ty Cobb leaves his post as point man for Mueller investigation. Former Clinton impeachment defense lawyer Emmet Flood replaces him.

MAY 8, 2018

Trump announces withdrawal of U.S from nuclear agreement between Iran and other world powers, and the reintroduction of sanctions.

MAY 15, 2018

White House eliminates top cyber policy adviser role. Critics say the move decreases the nation's security against cyberattacks.

MAY 16, 2018

Senate Intelligence Committee reports that Russia interfered in the 2016 election on Trump's behalf.

MAY 17, 2018

Manafort's son-in-law, charged in a real estate Ponzi scheme, "might be required by a plea deal to cooperate with Mueller."

MAY 20, 2018

Trump demands the DOJ investigate whether the DOJ or FBI infiltrated or spied on his campaign.

JUNE 4, 2018

Echoing his lawyers' arguments, Trump tweets he can pardon himself and that Mueller's appointment is unconstitutional: "As has been stated by numerous legal scholars, I have the absolute right to PARDON myself, but why would I do that when I have done nothing wrong? In the meantime, the never ending Witch Hunt, led by 13 very Angry and Conflicted Democrats (& others) continues into the midterms!"

JUNE 8, 2018

Mueller files new obstruction of justice charge against Manafort and includes charges against Manafort's associate Konstantin Kilimnik.

JUNE 15, 2018

Trump defends Manafort and says Michael Flynn "maybe . . . didn't lie."

JUNE 15, 2018

Marc Short, White House director of legislative affairs, tells staff he will resign by the end of summer.

JUNE 26, 2018

Supreme Court upholds Trump's ban on travel from several predominantly Muslim countries.

JUNE 26, 2018

Everett Eissenstat, an important trade adviser, announces he will resign in July. Eissenstat had worked on both the National Economic Council and the National Security Council.

JULY 3, 2018

Senate Intelligence Committee concludes that the previously released report from the FBI, CIA, and NSA is sound, noting that Russia intensified its longstanding attempts to undermine the US democratic process during the 2016 election, and in particular, to harm Clinton and help Trump.

JULY 5, 2018

Scott Pruitt, head of EPA, resigns after reports of ethical lapses and questionable spending.

JULY 9, 2018

Trump nominates Brett Kavanaugh to fill Supreme Court seat to be vacated by Justice Anthony M. Kennedy.

JULY 13, 2018

Mueller accuses twelve Russian intelligence officers of hacking into Clinton campaign, Democratic organizations, state election systems, and more.

TRUMP'S CAMPAIGN TEAM
KEY PLAYERS

Donald Trump ran an unorthodox presidential campaign in many respects. In addition to high turnover, especially in the last few months of the campaign, the campaign was relatively low budget. It also did not pay several key staffers, an unusual arrangement. Trump had 130 people on his payroll by the end of August 2016, far fewer than Clinton's 800 paid staffers.

KEY CAMPAIGN STAFF

Paul Manafort

Campaign chairman and chief strategist starting May 19, 2016. Was convention manager starting March 29, 2016. Resigned August 19, 2016.

Manafort was a veteran campaign strategist and consultant for American candidates, foreign candidates and governments, and corporations. He also is alleged to have worked as an unregistered lobbyist for Ukraine. Manafort was not paid by the Trump campaign. He was charged with thirty-two counts of financial crimes, including falsified income tax returns, failure to file foreign bank and

(Shutterstock)

financial accounts, bank fraud conspiracy, and bank fraud. Initially released on bail, he was sent to jail while he awaited trial because he allegedly tried to get witnesses to lie on his behalf.

ABOVE: (Left to right) Former football star, Fox production assistant, and Trump "body man" John McEntee, with Dan Scavino, Jared Kushner, Stephen Miller, Hope Hicks, and Donald Trump aboard Air Force One. *(White House/ Wikimedia Commons)*

Rick Gates

Deputy campaign manager, May 2016. Deputy chair of Trump inauguration committee.

Gates, a lobbyist, political consultant, and long time associate of Paul Manafort's, joined the Trump campaign as its second-in-command in spring 2016. Gates was not paid for his work on the Trump campaign but made $100,000 for his work on the inauguration. In February 2018 Gates pleaded guilty to conspiracy and lying to the FBI, and he agreed to provide information to the special counsel's investigation into Russia's interference in the 2016 election.

(Shutterstock)

Stephen K. Bannon

Campaign chief starting August 17, 2016. Trump's chief strategist until August 2017.

Bannon was the chairman of Breitbart News Network, a website that specializes in news and commentary from the far right end of the political spectrum. Bannon worked for Goldman Sachs, was a producer in Hollywood, and was an officer in the United States Navy.

Kellyanne Conway

Joined Trump campaign as senior adviser on July 1, 2016, and became campaign chair on August 19, 2016, when Manafort resigned. A pollster and strategist, she worked for a political action committee that supported Trump's rival Ted Cruz. The campaign did not pay her, but Trump's political action committee did. She is the first woman to run a presidential campaign. In the Trump White House, she is counselor to the president.

(Gage Skidmore)

Hope Hicks

Communications director for the Trump campaign starting in January 2015. Left White House in 2018.

One of Trump's most trusted aides, Hicks is a former model who worked for Ivanka Trump and then briefly for the Trump Organization before she joined the campaign in its early stages. She remained one of Trump's most trusted aides until she left the White House in February 2018.

Corey Lewandowski

Campaign manager, June 2015–June 2016.

A lobbyist and conservative strategist and unsuccessful state congressional candidate himself, Lewandowski's campaign motto for the Trump campaign was "Let Trump Be Trump." He was charged with battering a reporter at a campaign event; those charges were later dropped.

Roger Stone

Adviser, left campaign in August 2015, but continued to provide Trump support afterward.

A lobbyist and longtime Trump confidant, Stone is described as a dirty trickster and master of the political dark arts and is a self-professed GOP hitman. He has a tattoo of Richard Nixon on his back and worked for the Committee to Re-Elect the President, which he called CREEP. His political rules are "admit nothing, deny everything, launch counterattack." He reportedly sought dirt on Clinton from Russian sources but balked at the $2 million price tag.

Sam Nunberg

Political consultant for Trump, on and off, starting in 2014.

Nunberg, a protégé of Roger Stone, helped Trump with communications. He had a history of posting controversial things on social media, including racial slurs. Trump once left Nunberg in a McDonald's after his special-order burger was taking too long. After Nunberg left the Trump campaign he endorsed Trump's rival Ted Cruz.

Michael Glassner

National political director hired in July 2015, later served as deputy campaign manager.

Glassner was an adviser to John McCain's former vice-presidential candidate Sarah Palin. He was in charge of the campaign's strategic planning operations. He is now the chief operating officer of Trump's reelection campaign.

Roger Ailes

Debate adviser, August 2016.

Ailes was the chairman of Fox News but lost his job following allegations of sexual harassment. He advised Trump on debate strategy, though the campaign insisted the disgraced media mogul and experienced debate adviser had no role in preparing Trump.

David Bossie

Deputy campaign manager, August 2016, and deputy executive director for Trump presidential transition team.

Bossie is president of Citizens United, a political action committee that sued the Federal Elections Commission and won a Supreme Court decision that protects the act of speech of corporations and unions as though they were individual citizens.

Sam Clovis

Policy adviser, August 2015, eventually becoming national co-chair of Trump's election campaign.

A former Air Force fighter pilot, he became a college professor, talk show host, and birther conspiracy theorist. He selected George Papadopoulos for the Trump campaign.

Brad Parscale

Started work building websites with the Trump organization in 2011. Was digital director during 2016 election campaign. Appointed campaign manager of 2020 reelection campaign.

Parscale's company, Giles-Parscale, received $94 million from the Trump campaign, which was used to take out online ads and pay subcontractors for Trump's online presence. Parscale headed digital strategy, and also oversaw data collection, fundraising, and advertising.

KEY CAMPAIGN POLICY ADVISERS

Stephen Miller

Senior policy adviser beginning in January 2016, national policy director for the Trump transition team, and then senior White House adviser for policy. A former communications director for then-Senator Jeff Sessions of Alabama, Miller helped write Trump's inaugural address, drafted the original White House ban on Muslim immigrants, and also endorsed a zero-tolerance approach to preventing undocumented border crossings, which included separating infants and children from their parents.

George Papadopoulos

Joined the Trump campaign as foreign policy consultant in March 2016.

Selected by Sam Clovis to join the Trump campaign, Papadopoulos had briefly worked for Ben Carson's presidential campaign. Trump identified Papadopoulos as an "energy and oil consultant, excellent guy." Papadopoulos repeatedly attempted to make connections between the Trump campaign and the Russian government, and on October 5, 2017, pleaded guilty to making "material false statements and material omissions" to the FBI about contacts he'd had with Russian government officials.

Carter Page

Foreign policy adviser, announced as a member of Trump's campaign team in March 2016.

He'd been of interest to the FBI since 2013, when he was caught on a wiretap talking with suspected Russian spies who were trying to recruit him. Page also described himself in a letter as "an informal adviser to the staff of the Kremlin." He has denied being a Russian agent.

TRUMP FAMILY INVOLVED IN CAMPAIGN

Jared Kushner

Ivanka Trump's husband since 2009, Kushner is an heir to a real estate empire who joined the campaign initially to help research tax and trade policy positions. But he assumed more control and influence over the campaign, focusing eventually on data and digital marketing. In the White House, he is a senior adviser to Trump.

Ivanka Trump

Introduced Trump at June 2015 launch of his campaign. Advised his campaign on issues relating to women.

She stepped down from her role as executive vice president in the Trump Organization in early 2017 earning $3.9 million that year from her share in Trump International Hotel in DC, and an additional $2 million in severance. She works as an unpaid senior adviser in the Trump White House.

Don Trump Jr.

On June 3, 2016, Trump's oldest son was sent an e-mail offering "official documents and information that would incriminate Hillary and her dealings with Russia and would be very useful to your father." He accepted the meeting and was disappointed not to receive useful information. He later testified before the Senate Judiciary Committee about the meeting and provided a misleading description of the meeting to journalists, a description Trump himself dictated while on board Air Force One.

TRUMP'S LEGAL TEAM

Donald Trump has had many lawyers:

FOR TRUMP ORGANIZATION BUSINESS AND PERSONAL MATTERS

Roy Cohn

Represented Trump and his father in the Justice Department suit against the Trumps and their organization for discriminatory housing practices. Served as Trump's mentor and confidant for more than a decade. Previously worked with Wisconsin senator Joe McCarthy during the nation's Red Scare, investigations now considered baseless witch hunts. Disbarred for "dishonesty, fraud, deceit, and misrepresentation" shortly before his death in 1986.

Michael Cohen

Former personal injury lawyer who joined the Trump Organization around 2007. Was executive vice president and special counsel to Donald Trump. Arranged confidentiality agreements with and payments for women who'd had sexual relationships with Trump. Remained Trump's personal attorney after 2016 presidential election, charging corporations six- and seven-figure sums for "insight" into Trump administration. Office raided by FBI on April 9, 2018.

Marc Kasowitz

An outside attorney for the Trump Organization for both marital and business matters. Led defense team in fraud suit against Trump University. Trump's "personal lawyer" in early months of Trump presidency, focusing on the Russia investigation. Resigned on July 21, 2017, a week after sending threatening e-mails to a stranger who'd advised him to resign as Trump's attorney.

FOR MATTERS RELATED TO THE RUSSIA INVESTIGATION

John Dowd

A prominent white-collar defense attorney. Lead personal lawyer for Russia investigation. Quit March 22, 2018.

Rudolph "Rudy" Giuliani

Former U.S. Attorney and mayor of New York City. Ran for president in 2008 and considered another try in 2012. Hired by Trump April 19, 2018.

(Gage Skidmore)

Jay Sekulow

Seasoned appellate litigator who has argued twelve times before the Supreme Court, with a special focus on religious liberty.

Jane Raskin and Martin Raskin

A married couple with experience in the Department of Justice and a focus on white-collar criminal defense. Joined Trump team in April 2018 after Dowd departed.

Ty Cobb

A former federal prosecutor. Joined Trump's legal team in July 2017. Left May 2018.

Emmet T. Flood

Represented President Bill Clinton during his impeachment. White House lawyer during President George W. Bush's second term. Represented former Vice President Dick Cheney in Flood's private practice. Joined Trump team May 2, 2018.

FOR THE PRESIDENCY ITSELF

Don McGahn

Appointed White House Counsel by president and in this role provides legal support on matters relating to the presidency and its administration. Was Trump's campaign counsel in 2016 election. Before that, worked in private practice, for the Federal Election Commission, and the National Republican Congressional Committee.

(Gage Skidmore)

TRUMP'S RUSSIA CONNECTIONS

Donald Trump has long aspired to do business in Russia.

He took his first trip to Moscow in 1987. He has done business with Russian immigrants in the United States.

He has been fined for violating an anti-money laundering law by failing to properly report transactions at the Trump Taj Mahal.

Members of his campaign also have or had ties to Russia, some of which have raised flags for the FBI. Members of his cabinet also have business connections with Russia.

These descriptions explain Trump's many and sometimes complex ties with Russia.

TRUMP BUSINESS PARTNERS

FELIX SATER is a Russian immigrant, former felon, longtime government informant, and longtime business partner of Trump's.

Jailed for slashing a man in the face with the stem of a broken margarita glass, Sater also pleaded guilty to a stock fraud scheme run with members of the Russian mafia, which flourishes in Russia with Putin's consent.

Operating out of a Trump-owned building, Sater and his partners bilked elderly investors, some of whom were Holocaust survivors, out of about $40 million. He became a government informant in exchange for leniency.

The Trump family launched Trump SoHo with Sater when he worked for Bayrock, a company founded by a former Soviet official named Tevfik Arif and funded with a $10 million investment from Arif's brother in Russia.

ARAS AGALAROV is a Russian billionaire known as "Putin's Builder" for completing projects at the Russian leader's behest. Putin awarded Agalarov an Order of Honor medal. Agalarov helped Trump secure permission and a location to host the Miss Universe pageant in Moscow in 2013.

ABOVE: Russian pop star Emin Agalarov, Donald Trump, and Aras Agalarov, a Russian billionaire known as "Putin's builder." *(Victor Boyko/Getty Images)*

EMIN AGALAROV is son to Aras. He is a pop star who performed at the Miss Universe pageant in Moscow and featured a Trump cameo in one of his videos. His manager offered the Trump campaign, through the Agalarovs, information from the Russian government that would allegedly incriminate Hillary Clinton.

TRUMP AND THE RUSSIAN MOB

In 1998, Trump paid a $477,000 fine for breaking anti-money laundering rules at his Trump Taj Mahal casino.

Casinos are supposed to report gamblers who cash out more than $10,000 in a single day, and the Trump Taj Mahal failed to do this 106 times in its first eighteen months, when the Taj Mahal was where Russian mobsters living in Brooklyn liked to gamble.

WHO ATTENDED JUNE 9, 2016, TRUMP TOWER MEETING

Trump's business associate Aras Agalarov, through an intermediary, offered assistance to the campaign from the Russian government. Don Trump Jr. scheduled a meeting to receive the information. Here's who attended:

- DON TRUMP JR.
- JARED KUSHNER, Trump's son-in-law
- PAUL MANAFORT, Trump's campaign manager
- ROB GOLDSTONE, Emin Agalarov's publicist
- NATALIA VESELNITSKAYA, a Russian attorney who acts as an informant to the Russian prosecutor general
- RINAT AKHMETSHIN, a Russian-American lobbyist and Soviet military veteran
- IKE KAVELADZE, vice president of the Crocus Group, the Agalarovs' company. Also investigated for money laundering; he denies wrongdoing.
- ANATOLI SAMOCHORNOV, intepreter

TRUMP CAMPAIGN STAFF WITH CONNECTIONS TO RUSSIA

- PAUL MANAFORT, Trump's unpaid campaign manager. Manafort has worked with:
  - VIKTOR YANUKOVYCH, former president of Ukraine and political ally of Putin
  - OLEG DERIPASKA, Russian oligarch with ties to Putin (Manafort owed Deripaska millions of dollars)
  - KONSTANTIN KILIMNIK, Russian-Ukrainian political operative who once was part of the GRU, Russia's military intelligence agency. Kilimnik, an employee of Manafort's, has been charged by special counsel Robert Mueller with obstruction of justice for alleged witness tampering.

- **CARTER PAGE**, foreign policy adviser to Trump campaign; also oil and gas consultant. The FBI had been watching Page since at least 2013, when a wiretap of suspected Russian spies revealed they were trying to recruit Page.

- **GEORGE PAPADOPOULOS**, an energy expert/foreign policy adviser to Trump campaign. Pleaded guilty on October 3, 2017, for lying to FBI about contacts he had with foreign nationals connected to the Russian government. He'd been promised "dirt" on Hillary Clinton to benefit the campaign.

- **MICHAEL FLYNN**, informal adviser to Trump campaign and then Trump's national security adviser. Was paid for his appearance on Russian propaganda network. As director of Defense Intelligence Agency, made an unusual visit to the GRU in 2013. Resigned as national security adviser after caught lying to the vice president and White House officials about his contacts with Russian ambassador Sergey Kislyak.

- **JARED KUSHNER**, Trump son-in-law and senior adviser. Met secretly with Flynn and Kislyak after election but before Trump was inaugurated. Tried to set up "secret and secure" way for transition team to communicate with Kremlin. Also met with Sergey Gorkov, head of a Russian state-owned bank prohibited from doing business in the United States because of sanctions.

ENDNOTES

xi. Glum, Julia. "Poll Shows 57 Percent of Trump Voters Still Think Obama Was Born in Kenya." *Newsweek*. December 15, 2017. Accessed August 3, 2018. https://www.newsweek.com/trump-birther-obama-poll-republicans-kenya-744195.

1. Donald J. Trump (@realDonaldTrump), Twitter, October 8, 2016, 10:48 a.m., https://twitter.com/realDonaldTrump/status/784767399442653184.

2. Corey R. Lewandowski and David N. Bossie. *Let Trump Be Trump: The Inside Story of His Rise to the Presidency*. Nashville: Center Street, 2017, 197.

2. President Ford, who replaced President Nixon following his resignation after Watergate, tripped going down the steps of Air Force One in 1975, as he was guiding his wife Betty off the plane on a rainy day. After other stumbles, he blamed a high school football knee injury. He became the butt of jokes of the comedian Chevy Chase.

3. Michael Isikoff and David Corn, *Russian Roulette: The Inside Story of Putin's War on America and the Election of Donald Trump*. New York: Twelve, 2018, 242.

3. Statement from Donald J. Trump, Trump Pence Campaign (October 7, 2016), archived at https://web.archive.org/web/20170429192721/https://www.donaldjtrump.com/press-releases/statement-from-donald-j.-trump.

5. Donald J. Trump (@realDonaldTrump), Twitter, October 7, 2016, 9:19 p.m., https://twitter.com/realdonaldtrump/status/784609194234306560.

6. Donald J. Trump (@realDonaldTrump), "I have a judge in the Trump University civil case, Gonzalo Curiel (San Diego), who is very unfair. An Obama pick. Totally biased—hates Trump." Twitter, May 30, 2016, 5:45 p.m. https://mobile.twitter.com/realdonaldtrump/status/737399475509985280?lang=en. *See also* Brent Kendall, "Trump Says Judge's Mexican Heritage Presents 'Absolute Conflict,'" *Wall Street Journal*, June 3, 2016, https://www.wsj.com/articles/donald-trump-keeps-up-attacks-on-judge-gonzalo-curiel-1464911442.

6. "Paul Ryan: Trump Made 'Textbook Definition of a Racist Comment,'" Washington Week, PBS online, June 7, 2016, video (0:45) and transcript available at http://www.pbs.org/weta/washingtonweek/web-video/paul-ryan-trump-made-textbook-definition-racist-comment. (accessed February 18, 2018).

6. https://www.youtube.com/watch?v=c2xBCVsp3mI This video on YouTube shows Trump at a rally making a promise that he'd build a wall on the border between the United States and Mexico. He initiates a call-and-response. "Who's gonna pay for the wall?" he asks. The crowd replies, "Mexico!" In the end, he and his fans chant, "Build that wall! Build that wall!"

6. Alan Rappeport, "Donald Trump Says He May Pay Legal Fees of Accused Attacker from Rally,"

New York Times, First Draft, March 13, 2016, https://www.nytimes.com/politics/first-draft/2016/03/13/donald-trump-says-he-may-pay-legal-fees-of-accused-attacker/.

6. Jeremy Diamond, "Trump: I Could 'Shoot Somebody and I Wouldn't Lose Voters,'" CNN online, January 24, 2016, https://www.cnn.com/2016/01/23/politics/donald-trump-shoot-somebody-support/index.html.

7. Steve Turnham, "Donald Trump to Father of Fallen Soldier: 'I've Made a Lot of Sacrifices,'" ABC News online, July 30, 2016, http://abcnews.go.com/Politics/donald-trump-father-fallen-soldier-ive-made-lot/story?id=41015051; Maggie Haberman and Richard A. Oppel, "Donald Trump Criticizes Muslim Family of Slain U.S. Soldier, Drawing Ire," *New York Times*, July 30, 2016, https://www.nytimes.com/2016/07/31/us/politics/donald-trump-khizr-khan-wife-ghazala.html.

7. The First Amendment of the Constitution states, in part, that "Congress shall make no law respecting an establishment of religion." The idea behind this was to maintain a separation of church and state in the United States, because state-sponsored religion had led to persecution in the past. US Const., Amend I.

According to some interpretations, banning Muslims is the equivalent of having a state-sponsored religion. *See, for example*, "SPLC Tells Supreme Court: President Trump's Muslim Ban Is an Unconstitutional Violation of Religious Freedom," Southern Poverty Law Center website, September 18, 2017, https://www.splcenter.org/news/2017/09/18/splc-tells-supreme-court-president-trumps-muslim-ban-unconstitutional-violation-religious (accessed April 22, 2018).

7. Jeremy Diamond, "Donald Trump: Ban All Muslim Travel to U.S.," CNN online, December 8, 2015, https://www.cnn.com/2015/12/07/politics/donald-trump-muslim-ban-immigration/index.htl.

7. John S. McCain, "John McCain, Prisoner of War: A First-Person Account," *U.S. News*, January 28, 2008, https://www.usnews.com/news/articles/2008/01/28/john-mccain-prisoner-of-war-a-first-person-account.

7. Scott Neuman, "Trump Lashes Out at McCain: 'I Like People Who Weren't Captured,'" NPR online, July 18, 2015, https://www.npr.org/sections/thetwo-way/2015/07/18/424169549/trump-lashes-out-at-mccain-i-like-people-who-werent-captured.

7. Lisa Desjardins, "All the Assault Allegations Against Donald Trump, Recapped," PBS Newshour online, October 14, 2016, https://www.pbs.org/newshour/amp/politics/assault-allegations-donald-trump-recapped.

7. Sarah Fitzpatrick, "Stormy Daniels Sues Trump, Says 'Hush Agreement' Invalid Because He Never Signed," NBC News online, March 6, 2018, updated March 7, 2018, https://www.nbcnews.com/politics/donald-trump/stormy-daniels-sues-trump-says-hush-agreement-invalid-because-he-n854246.

8. Lewandowski and Bossie, 203.

8. Donald J. Trump (@realDonaldTrump), Twitter, October 28, 2016, 3:20 p.m., https://twitter.com/realdonaldtrump/status/792083605405171712?=lang=en.

9. Everett Rosenfeld, "FBI's Comey Says 'No Reasonable Prosecutor' Would Bring a Case Against Clinton for Emails," CNBC online, July 5, 2016 (as updated), https://www.cnbc.com/2016/07/05/fbi-director-james-comey-has-concluded-the-investigation-into-clintons-emails.html.

9. Hillary Clinton's aide, Huma Abedin, was married to Anthony Weiner, a former Democrat representing New York's Ninth Congressional District. Weiner resigned following a sexting scandal. In a separate incident years later, he was fined and sentenced to twenty-one months in prison for texting obscene images to a minor, and he must register as a sex offender for the rest of his life. Andy Campbell, Sebastian Murdock, and Sam Levine, "Anthony Weiner Pleads Guilty to Sexting a Minor, Will Register as Sex Offender," *HuffPost*, May 19, 2017, updated May 22, 2017, https://www.huffingtonpost.com/entry/anthony-weiner-sexting-minor_us_591ee9fde4b034684b0ba34f.

9. James Comey. *A Higher Loyalty: Truth, Lies, and Leadership*, New York: Flatiron Books, 2018, pp. 194–195.

9. Pete Williams, Kasie Hunt, and Corky Siemaszko, "Emails Related to Clinton Case Found in Anthony Weiner Investigation," NBC News online, October 28, 2016 (as updated), https://www.nbcnews.com/news/us-news/fbi-re-open-investigation-clinton-email-server-n674631. Comey recently stated that he wanted to make sure that when Hillary Clinton won, which victory he anticipated, it was an untainted victory. Lauren Effron and Meghan Keneally, "Comey Says His Assumption Clinton Would Win Was 'a Factor' in the Email Investigation," ABC News online, April 14, 2018, http://abcnews.go.com/Politics/comey-assumption-clinton-win-factor-email-investigation/story?id=54467459.

9. Luke Harding. *Collusion: Secret Meetings, Dirty Money, and How Russia Helped Donald Trump Win.* New York: Vintage Books, 2017, p. 35.

FBI Director James Comey opened a formal investigation into the relationship of the Trump campaign with Russia when WikiLeaks began releasing emails hacked from Democratic party officials around July 22, less than three weeks after the Clinton investigation had been resolved.

9. *New York Times.* "Harry Reid's Letter to James Comey." *DocumentCloud*, www.documentcloud.org/documents/3035844-Reid-Letter-to-Comey.html.

9. Former *Wall Street Journal* reporter Glenn Simpson, who runs a research business called Fusion GPS, hired Christopher Steele, a former British intelligence officer, as part of a contract to gather information about Donald Trump by his political opponents. As part of this project, Steele wrote a series of memos that came to be known as the Steele Dossier. Simpson testified about the work before Congress on August 22, 2017, and this portion of his testimony relates to an exchange he and Steele had

after Comey reopened his investigation into Hillary Clinton's e-mails.

"There was some sort of interaction, I think it was probably telephonic that occurred after Director Comey sent his letter to Congress reopening the investigation into Hillary Clinton's e-mails. That episode, you know, obviously created some concern that the FBI was intervening in a political campaign in contravention of long-standing Justice Department regulation.

"So it made a lot of people, including us, concerned about what the heck was going on at the FBI. So, you know, we began getting questions from the press about, you know, whether they were also investigating Trump and, you know, we encouraged them to ask the FBI that question."

10. Donald J. Trump (@realDonaldTrump), Twitter, November 6, 2016, 4:09 p.m., https://twitter.com/realdonaldtrump/status/795417907476000768.

10. Eric Bradner, Pamela Brown, and Evan Perez, "FBI Clears Clinton—Again," CNN online, November 7, 2016, https://www.cnn.com/2016/11/06/politics/comey-tells-congress-fbi-has-not-changed-conclusions/index.html.

10. Lucy Westcott, "Presidential Election Polls," *Newsweek*, November 7, 2016, http://www.newsweek.com/polls-presidential-election-trump-clinton-november-7-2016-517857.

10. Ibid.

10. Donald J. Trump (@realDonaldTrump), Twitter, November 8, 2016, 1:18 p.m., https://twitter.com/realdonaldtrump/status/796099494442057728.

11. "Exclusive Look Inside Donald Trump's Campaign War Room," Fox News online, November 8, 2016, video, 2:32, http://video.foxnews.com/v/5201610541001/?#sp=show-clips.

11. Michael Wolff, *Fire and Fury: Inside the Trump White House.* New York: Henry Holt and Co., 2018, 11.

11. Nolan D. McCaskill, "Trump Tells Wisconsin: Victory Was a Surprise," Politico, December 13, 2016, https://www.politico.com/story/2016/12/donald-trump-wisconsin-232605.

11. Lewandowski and Bossie, 8.

11. McCaskill.

12. Lewandowski and Bossie, 9.

The fifteenth floor of the Trump Tower is actually the fifth floor. *See* Dennis Green, "Trump Tower Is Actually 10 Floors Shorter than Donald Trump Says It Is," *BusinessInsider*, October 25, 2016, http://www.businessinsider.com/trump-tower-is-not-as-tall-as-trump-says-2016-10. Many Trump buildings exaggerate their size. It's a signature Trump marketing move that many builders have since copied.

The Trump Tower has 58 floors, but the elevators go up to 68. The Trump SoHo has 43 real floors, but the elevator buttons top out at 46. The Trump International Hotel and Tower, remodeled by Trump from 1995 to 1997, went from 44 floors to 52 floors without getting a single inch taller. The Trump World Tower has 90 *stories* according to Trump, but 70 according to New York's building records. Vivian Yee, "Donald Trump's Math Takes His Towers to Greater Heights," *New York Times*, November 1, 2016, https://www.nytimes.com/2016/11/02/nyregion/donald-trump-tower-heights.html.

12. Lewandowski and Bossie, 9.

12. He made this statement at a December 2016 political rally in Wisconsin. McCaskill.

12. U.S. Const. art. II, § 1.

12. Tessa Berenson, "Donald Trump Wins the 2016 Election," *Time*, November 9, 2016, http://time.com/4563685/donald-trump-wins/; Associated Press, "The Latest: Trump Promises 'I Will Not Let You Down,'" November 9, 2016, https://elections.ap.org/content/latest-trump-promises-i-will-not-let-you-down.

12. "Presidential Election Results: Donald J. Trump Wins," *New York Times*, as updated August 9, 2017, http://www.nytimes.com/elections/results/president.

13. Wolff, 18.

13. Ibid., 15.

13. Tessa Brenson, "Here's What Donald Trump Says Will Happen if He Loses on Tuesday," *Time*, November 7, 2016, http://time.com/4560707/donald-trump-election-loss-rigged/.

13. Walsh, Joe. "On November 8th, I'm Voting for Trump.On November 9th, If Trump Loses, I'm Grabbing My Musket.You In?" Twitter. October 26, 2016. Accessed September 05, 2018. https://twitter.com/walshfreedom/status/791369493809201152.

13. Berenson.

13. Presidents, WhiteHouse.gov, https://www.whitehouse.gov/about-the-white-house/presidents/ (accessed April 15, 2018).

19. Gwenda Blair, *The Trumps: Three Generations of Builders and a President*. New York: Simon & Schuster, 2015, 31.

19. Kevin Hagen and Maria Feck, "Calling in Kallstadt: A Visit to Donald Trump's Ancestral Home," Spiegel Online, January 20, 2016, www.spiegel.de/international/germany/a-visit-to-the-german-ancestral-home-of-the-trump-family-a-1072975.html.

19. "History of Germany," Germany-Deutschland.com, http://kallstadt.germany-deutschland.com/germany/english/history_of_germany/.

20. Blair, 31.

20. Ibid., 29.

20. Ibid., 31.

20. Ibid.

20. Ibid.

21. The Homestead Act of 1862 opened up settlement in the western United States (following a period when indigenous people were forcibly removed from their land as part of the Indian Removal Act). The Homestead Act permitted any American, including formerly enslaved people, to put in a claim for up to 160 free acres of federal land. Eventually, 1.6

million people claimed 420,000 square miles of land. "The Homestead Act of 1862," National Archives website, https://www.archives.gov/education/lessons/homestead-act (accessed April 15, 2018).

For more information on the Removal Act: "Removing Native Americans from Their Land," Library of Congress, www.loc.gov/teachers/classroommaterials/presentationsandactivities/presentations/immigration/native_american2.html.

21. Blair, 27.

22. Ted Widmer, "An Immigrant Named Trump," *The New Yorker*, October 1, 2016, https://www.newyorker.com/culture/culture-desk/an-immigrant-named-trump.

22. A photocopy of the customs list is available at "Donald Trump's Ancestry: How His Immigrant Family Made It in America," Sheaffer Genealogy, October 11, 2016, https://sheaffergenealogy.com/2016/10/11/donald-trumps-ancestry-how-his-immigrant-family-made-it-in-america/ (accessed April 15, 2018).

22. "Disasters: The Great Fire of 1776," Baruch College website, http://www.baruch.cuny.edu/nycdata/disasters/fires-1776.html (accessed April 15, 2018).

22. J. S. T. Stranahan, *Opening Ceremonies of the New York and Brooklyn Bridge, May 24, 1883*. New York: Brooklyn, 1883, https://archive.org/details/openingceremonie00stra.

22. Jim Talbot, "The Brooklyn Bridge: First Steel-Wire Suspension Bridge," *Modern Steel Construction*, June 2011, https://www.aisc.org/globalassets/modern-steel/archives/2011/06/2011v06_brooklyn_bridge.pdf.

23. Greg Lang, "Seattle's Great Fire," January 16, 1999, HistoryLink, Essay 715, http://www.historylink.org/File/715.

23. "The Great Seattle Fire of June 6, 1889," United States History (website), http://www.u-s-history.com/pages/h3179.html (accessed April 15, 2018).

23. Blair, 31.

23. "Express train crosses the nation in 83 hours," This Day in History: June 4, 1876, History.com, https://www.history.com/this-day-in-history/express-train-crosses-the-nation-in-83-hours.

23. Rob Ketcherside, "Frederick Trump in Pioneer Square, Seattle," ba-kground (blog of Rob Ketcherside), http://www.ba-kground.com/frederick-trump-seattle/. The address of Trump's restaurant was 208 Washington Street.

23. Ketcherside.

23. Blair, 86.

24. Blair, 53–78.

25. Blair, 86 (quoting *Yukon Sun*, April 17, 1900, as reprinted in *Atlin Claim*, May 5, 1900, page 2, available at https://open.library.ubc.ca/collections/bcnewspapers/xatlin/items/1.0169737#p0z-5r0f:).

25. Michael Kranish and Marc Fisher, *Trump Revealed: an American Journey of Ambition, Ego, Money and Power*. New York: Scribner, 2017, 24.

27. Friedrich Trump. "The Emigrants." Translated by Austen Hinkley, Harper's Magazine, Mar. 2017, harpers. org/archive/2017/03/the-emigrants/.

28. Blair, 113.

28. "Immigration . . . Shadows of War," Library of Congress website, https://loc.gov/teachers/classroommaterials/presentationsandactivities/presentations/immigration/german8.html (accessed April 21, 2018).

28. "Frederick Christ 'Fred' Trump Sr.," Find a Grave website, https://www.findagrave.com/memorial/40736522/frederick-christ-trump (accessed April 21, 2018).

30. Tracie Rozhon, "Fred C. Trump, Postwar Master Builder of Housing for Middle Class, Dies at 93," *New York Times*, June 26, 1999, as corrected July 16, 1999, https://www.nytimes.com/1999/06/26/nyregion/fred-c-trump-postwar-master-builder-of-housing-for-middle-class-dies-at-93.html.

32. Jason Horowitz, "Fred Trump Taught His Son the Essentials of Showboating Self-Promoting," *New York Times*, August 12, 2016.

32. Colby Thompson, "Fred Trump and the Destruction of Steeplechase Park," Odyssey, Sept. 7, 2016 https://www.theodysseyonline.com/fred-trump-steeplechase-park.

33. Blair, 172.

34. Blair, 173.

34. About $37 million in 2018 dollars.

34. Brooklyn Daily Eagle: June 12, 1954, Page 1. *Brooklyn Public Library*, bklyn.newspapers.com/image/53870134/?terms=Charge%2B%244%2B million%2BWindfall%2Bto%2BBuilder%2Bof%2B Beach%2BHaven.

35. William McKenna, Report to the Senate Committee on Banking and Currency, 6/29/54.

35. Hearings, Senate Banking and Currency Committee, August 24, 1954, 409.

35. Blair, 182.

35. FHA Investigation: Hearings Before the Committee on Banking and Currency, United States Senate, 409 https://www.washingtonpost.com/wp-stat/graphics/politics/trump-archive/docs/fha-investigation-1954-part-1.pdf

35. Ibid., 410.

36. Ibid., 409.

36. *New York Times*, January 25, 2016. https://www.nytimes.com/politics/first-draft/2016/01/25/woody-guthrie-sang-of-his-contempt-for-his-landlord-donald-trumps-father/

36. Michael Kranish and Robert O'Harrow Jr., "Inside the Government's Racial Bias Case Against Donald Trump's Company, and How He Fought It," *Washington Post*, January 23, 2016, https://www.washingtonpost.com/politics/inside-the-governments-racial-bias-case-against-donald-trumps-company-and-how-he-fought-it/2016/01/23/fb90163e-bfbe-11e5-bcda-62a36b394160_story.html.

39. Blair, 231.

40. Paul Schwartzman and Michael E. Miller, "Confident. Incorrigible. Bully: Little Donny Was a Lot like Candidate Donald Trump," *Washington Post*, June 22, 2016, https://www.washingtonpost.com/lifestyle/style/young-donald-trump-military-school/2016/06/22/f0b3b164-317c-11e6-8758-d58e76e11b12_story.html.

40. Ibid.

41. Jason Horowitz, "For Donald Trump, Lessons from a Brother's Suffering," *New York Times*, January 2, 2016, https://www.nytimes.com/2016/01/03/us/politics/for-donald-trump-lessons-from-a-brothers-suffering.html.

42. Michael E. Miller, "50 Years Later, Disagreements Over Young Trump's Military Academy Record," *Washington Post*, January 9, 2016, https://www.washingtonpost.com/politics/decades-later-disagreement-over-young-trumps-military-academy-post/2016/01/09/907a67b2-b3e0-11e5-a842-0feb51d1d124_story.html.

42. "New York Military Academy," Military School USA website, https://militaryschoolusa.com/new-york/military-academy/ (accessed April 22, 2018).

42. Schwartzman and Miller.

44. *New York Times*, March 7, 1964. https://timesmachine.nytimes.com/timesmachine/1964/03/08/106944098.pdf

44. Miller.

45. "Donald Trump: The Early Years," *Newsday*, https://www.newsday.com/news/nation/young-donald-trump-pictures-1.11583814 (accessed April 22, 2018).

45. Horowitz.

45. Michael Kranish and Marc Fisher, *Trump Revealed: The Definitive Biography of the 45th President*. New York: Scribner, 2016, 93.

45. Gwenda Blair. *Donald Trump: the Candidate*. New York: Simon & Schuster, 2015, 19.

46. "1964 New York Military Academy Yearbook." *Explore 1964 New York Military Academy Yearbook, Cornwall On Hudson NY - Classmates*, www.classmates.com/yearbooks/New-York-Military-Academy/32008

46. "How the Draft Has Changed Since Vietnam," Selective Service System website, https://www.sss.gov/About/History-And-Records/How-The-Draft-Has-Changed-Since-Vietnam (accessed April 22, 2018).

46. Spencer C. Tucker, ed., *The Encyclopedia of the Vietnam War: A Political, Social, and Military History*, 2nd ed. (Santa Barbara, Cal: ABC-CLIO, 1998), 9. This reality struck hard in the African American community. Furthermore, "African Americans were woefully underrepresented on local draft boards. In 1966 blacks accounted for slightly more than 1 percent of all draft board members, and seven state boards had no black representation at all." Ibid.

47. Blair, *The Trumps: Three Generations*, 239.

47. Glenn Kessler, Trump's False Claim He Built His Empire with a 'Small Loan' from His

Father," *Washington Post*, March 3, 2016, https://
www.washingtonpost.com/news/fact-checker/
wp/2016/03/03/trumps-false-claim-he-built-his-
empire-with-a-small-loan-from-his-father/. He also
received about $2,000 annually from a second trust
established in 1949 by his grandmother, $6,000
annually as a gift from his parents, and beginning in
1976, much larger trust amounts from a 1976 trust.
Ibid.

47. Blair, *The Trumps: Three Generations*, 241.

47. Ibid., 241.

47. http://media.pennlive.com/news/photo/2017/02/19/
trump-commencementpng-c8cfb2506f7ec1cd.png

47. Steve Chapin, "Donald Trump's Biggest Flaw:
He's Not That Bright," *Chicago Tribune*, Column,
November 3, 2017, http://www.chicagotribune.com/
news/opinion/chapman/ct-perspec-chapman-donald-
trump-dumb-20171103-story.html.

47. Steve Eder and Dave Philipps, "Donald Trump's
Draft Deferments: Four for College, One for Bad Feet,"
New York Times, August 1, 2018, https://www.nytimes.
com/2016/08/02/us/politics/donald-trump-draft-
record.html.

47. Beth J. Harpaz, "Trump and Wharton: A
Complicated Relationship," *Seattle Times*,
April 16, 2016, updated April 18, 2016,
https://www.seattletimes.com/nation-world/
trump-and-wharton-a-complicated-relationship/.

47. "Heel Spurs and Plantar Fasciitis." WebMD,
www.webmd.com/pain-management/
heel-spurs-pain-causes-symptoms-treatments#1.

47. Hechmi Toumi, et al. "Changes in Prevalence
of Calcaneal Spurs in Men & Women: A Random
Population from a Trauma Clinic." *BMC
Musculoskeletal Disorders* 15 (2014): 87, http://doi.
org/10.1186/1471-2474-15-87 (also available at https://
www.ncbi.nlm.nih.gov/pmc/articles/PMC3995580/)
(accessed April 22, 2018).

48. Blair, 246 and 513 n.2.

48. Ibid., 247.

48. Ibid., 513 n. 4.

49. Ibid., 247.

51. Michael Paulson, "For a Young Donald J. Trump,
Broadway Held Sway," *New York Times*, March 6, 2016,
https://www.nytimes.com/2016/03/07/theater/for-a-
young-donald-j-trump-broadway-held-sway.html.

52. Donald J. Trump with Tony Schwartz, *Trump: The
Art of the Deal*. New York: Ballantine, 1987, 94.

52. Wayne Barrett. *Trump: the Greatest Show on
Earth: The Deals, the Downfall, the Reinvention*, New
York: Regan Arts, 2016, 90–91.

53. Trump with Schwartz, 96.

53. Michael Kranish and Marc Fisher, *Trump
Revealed: An American Journey of Ambition, Ego,
Money, and Power*. New York: Simon & Schuster,
2016, 106.

54. Albin Krebs. "Roy Cohn, Aide to McCarthy and
Fiery Lawyer, Dies at 59." *The New York Times*,

archive.nytimes.com/www.nytimes.com/library/
national/science/aids/080386sci-aids.html.

54. Michael Kranish and Robert O'Harrow Jr.,
"Inside the Government's Racial Bias Case Against
Donald Trump's Company, and How He Fought
It," *Washington Post*, January 23, 2016, http://
www.washingtonpost.com/politics/inside-the-
governments-racial-bias-case-against-donald-
trumps-company-and-how-he-fought-it/2016/01/23/
fb90163e-bfbe-11e5-bcda-62a36b394160_story.html.

54. Ibid.

54. Morris Kaplan, "Major Landlord Accused of
Antiblack Bias in City," *New York Times*, October 16,
1973, http://www.nytimes.com/1973/10/16/archives/
major-landlord-accused-of-antiblack-bias-in-city-us-
accuses-major.html.

55. Ibid.

55. Ibid.

55. Trump with Schwartz, 96.

56. Blair, 251.

56. Jonathan Mahler and Matt Flegenheimer, "What
Donald Trump Learned from Joseph McCarthy's Right-
Hand Man," *New York Times*, June 20, 2016, https://
www.nytimes.com/2016/06/21/us/politics/donald-
trump-roy-cohn.html. One of Roy Cohn's significant
others, Peter Fraser, said, "That bravado, and if you
say it aggressively and loudly enough, it's the truth—
that's the way Roy used to operate to a degree, and
Donald was certainly his apprentice." Ibid.

56. Blair, 251.

57. From the FBI files, in an affidavit dated October
10, 1974: "[Redacted] told me that if a black person
came to 2650 Ocean Parkway and inquired about an
apartment for rent, and he, that is [redacted] was not
there at the time, that I should tell him that the rent
was twice as much as it really was, in order that he
could not afford the apartment."

57. From the FBI files, in an affidavit dated October
23, 1974: "I asked Fred Trump what his policy was
regarding minorities and he said it was absolutely
against the law to discriminate. At a later time during
my two weeks at Tysens Park, Fred Trump told me not
to rent to blacks. He also wanted me to get rid of the
blacks that were in the building by telling them cheap
housing was available for them at only $500 down
payment, which Trump would offer to pay himself.
Trump didn't tell me where this housing was located.
He advised me not to rent to persons on welfare."

57. Kranish and O'Harrow Jr.

The testimony of the former emloyees, available
through the National Archives, reads, "The Schefflins
advised that Mr. Fred Trump and other agents,
including Mr. Wiss, wanted them to rent only to 'Jews
and Executives' and discouraged rental to blacks. They
advised that a racial code was in effect, blacks being
referred to as 'No. 9.'"

Full Text of "Donald Trump Archive," Internet
Archive, archive.org/stream/DonaldTrumpArchive/
Discrimination%20case%20%20US%20v%20
Trump%20case%20via%20National%20Archives%20
FOIA_djvu.txt

57. In an August 1974 affidavit, Justice Department lawyer Elyse Goldweber said under oath, "Mr. Miranda also stated to me during this interview that he was afraid that the Trumps would have him 'knocked off,' or words to that effect, because he told me about their allegedly discriminatory practices. He was reluctant to have his name disclosed." Accessed via National Archives, USA v. Fred Trump and Donald Trump and Trump Management, case 75-C-1529.

57. This summary is in a FBI document dated November 6, 1972.

57. Kranish and Fisher, 51.

57. Kranish and O'Harrow Jr.

57. Blair, 252.

57. Joseph P. Fried. "Trump Promises To End Race Bias." *The New York Times*, 11 June 1975, www.nytimes.com/1975/06/11/archives/trump-promises-to-end-race-bias-realty-management-concern-reaches.html.

58. Kranish and O'Harrow Jr.

58. Ibid.

58. Letter from Drew S. Days III, Assistant Attorney General, Civil Rights Division, and Harvey Handley III, Attorney, Housing and Credit Section, to Roy Cohn, *US v. Trump Management*, Civ. A. No. 73-1529, January 23, 1978, available at https://www.clearinghouse.net/chDocs/public/FH-NY-0024-0038.pdf.

58. "Trump Charged With Rental Bias." *The New York Times*, March 7, 1978, www.nytimes.com/1978/03/07/archives/trump-charged-with-rental-bias.html.

58. Goodman, George W. "For Starrett City, An Integration Test." *The New York Times*, 16 Oct. 1983, www.nytimes.com/1983/10/16/realestate/for-starrett-city-an-integration-test.html?scp=4&sq=trump%2Bdiscrimination&st=nyt&pagewanted=all.

The story in the *Times* read, "Brightwater and the Trump developments both have white majorities of at least 95 percent, according to estimates by the Division of Housing and Community Renewal."

59. Kranish and Fisher, 55.

59. Barrett, 85–86.

60. Ibid., 38, 48.

60. Simon Van Zuylen-Wood. "Trump and the Artifice of the Deal." *POLITICO Magazine*, May 12, 2016, www.politico.com/magazine/story/2016/05/donald-trump-2016-father-artifice-of-the-deal-213888.

60. Kranish and Fisher, 73.

60. Trump with Schwartz, 134.

60. "The Commodore: New York's Newest Hotel." *Ephemeral New York*, Dec. 15 2014, ephemeralnewyork.wordpress.com/tag/new-york-city-in-the-1920s/.

61. Trump with Schwartz, 121.

61. Judy Klemesrud, "Donald Trump, Real Estate Promoter, Builds Image as He Buys Buildings," *New York Times*, November 1, 1976, https://www.nytimes.com/1976/11/01/archives/donald-trump-real-estate-promoter-builds-image-as-he-buys-buildings.html.

61. As he put it a few years later in *Trump: The Art of the Deal* at page 56: "One thing I've learned about the press is that they're always hungry for a good story, and the more sensational, the better ... [I]f you do things that are bold or controversial, the press is going to write about you. I've always done things a little differently, I don't mind controversy, and my deals tend to be somewhat ambitious."

61. Bryan Miller. "Maxwell's Plum, a 60's Symbol, Closes." *The New York Times*, July 11, 1988, www.nytimes.com/1988/07/11/nyregion/maxwells-plum-a-60-s-symbol-closes.html.

61. Ivana Trump, *Raising Trump*. New York: Gallery Books, 2017, p. 41.

62. Ivana Trump, 41.

62. Ivana Trump, 43.

62. There's more than one story about their first meeting. Trump claimed in *The Art of the Deal* that he first laid eyes on her at the summer Olympic Games in Montreal in 1976, and he also claimed that she'd been on the Czechoslovakian Olymic team as an alternate (32). There is no record of this, although she was a competitive skier.

Small details vary about their Maxwell's Plum meeting. Another version says he introduced himself to her in the line outside the bar, and then sent her three dozen roses the next day—not the 100 Ivana tells in her version.

63. Marie Brenner. "After the Gold Rush." *Vanity Fair*, Sept. 1, 1990, www.vanityfair.com/magazine/2015/07/donald-ivana-trump-divorce-prenup-marie-brenner.

63. Ivana Trump, 63-64.

63. Ibid., 57.

63. Horowitz.

63. Michael Shnayerson. "Inside Ivana's Role in Donald Trump's Empire." *Vanities*, *Vanity Fair*, Jan. 2, 1988, www.vanityfair.com/news/1988/01/ivana-trump-business-empire.

64. Ivana Trump, 63.

67. Christopher Gray, "The Store that Slipped Through the Cracks," *New York Times*, October 3, 2014, www.nytimes.com/2014/10/05/realestate/fifth-avenue-bonwit-teller-opulence-lost.html.

67. Blair, Chapter 17.

68. Gray.

69. Robert D. McFadden, "Developer Scraps Bonwit Sculptures; Builder Orders Bonwit Art Deco Sculptures Destroyed," *New York Times*, June 6, 1980, available at timesmachine.nytimes.com/timesmachine/1980/06/06/120997165.html?action=click&contentCollection=Archives&module=ArticleEndCTA&region=ArchiveBody&pgtype=article&pageNumber=1.

69. Ibid.

69. Quoted in Christopher Gray, "The Store That Slipped Through the Cracks."

69. Quoted in Dan Merica, "The Time Donald Trump Wasn't Worried About the 'History and Culture' of

Sculptures," CNN online, August 18, 2017, https://www.cnn.com/2017/08/18/politics/donald-trump-history-culture-sculptures/index.html.

70. Kranish and Fisher, *Trump Revealed*, chapter 5.

Borchers, Callum, "Donald Trump Hasn't Changed One Bit Since His First Media Feud in 1980," *Washington Post*, March 18, 2016, https://www.washingtonpost.com/news/the-fix/wp/2016/03/18/donald-trumps-first-media-controversy-is-a-really-great-story-just-a-really-fabulous-story/?postshare=5251458315517113&utm_term=.479bbe727d55.

70. Quoted in Borchers, "Donald Trump Hasn't Changed One Bit Since His First Media Feud in 1980," *Washington Post.*

70. Marie Brenner, "After the Gold Rush."

70. Trump and Schwartz, 175.

Blair, *The Trumps*, chapter 17 and note III.

70. Marie Brenner, "After the Gold Rush."

Charles V. Bagli, "Trump Paid Over $1 Million in Labor Settlement, Documents Reveal," *New York Times*, November 27, 2017, https://www.nytimes.com/2017/11/27/nyregion/trump-tower-illegal-immigrant-workers-union-settlement.html.

70. Selwyn Raab, "After 15 Years in Court, Workers' Lawsuit Against Trump Faces Yet Another Delay," *New York Times*, June 14, 1998, http://www.nytimes.com/1998/06/14/nyregion/after-15-years-in-court-workers-lawsuit-against-trump-faces-yet-another-delay.html.

71. David Cay Johnston, *The Making of Donald Trump*. London: Melville House, 2016, 43.

71. Wayne Barrett, *Trump: The Greatest Show on Earth*. New York: Regan Arts, 2016, chapter 4.

71. Johnston 43-44

71. David Cay Johnston, "Just What Were Donald Trump's Ties to the Mob?" *Politico*, May 22, 2016, https://www.politico.com/magazine/story/2016/05/donald-trump-2016-mob-organized-crime-213910

71. Ibid.

71. Johnston, *The Making of Donald Trump*, 43.

72. Johnston, "Just What Were Donald Trump's Ties to the Mob?"

72. See Donald Trump interview 1980 (Rona Barrett) [Reelin' In The Years Productions, Archives] 4:23 excerpt, published January 14, 2017, https://www.youtube.com/watch?v=nAgJAxkALyc. A full transcript of this interview is available at https://www.washingtonpost.com/wp-stat/graphics/politics/trump-archive/docs/rona-barrett-1980-interview-of-donald-trump.pdf, accessed July 4, 2018.

72. Ibid., p. 33.

72. Ibid.

72. John Santucci and Corinne Cathcard, "Four Years of Tax Returns All Show Donald Trump Did Not Pay Federal Taxs," ABCNews, October 2, 2016, http://abcnews.go.com/Politics/years-tax-returns-show-donald-trump-pay-federal/story?id=42512200;

Kurt Eichenwald, "Donald Trump's Many Business Failures, Explained," *Newsweek*, August 2, 2016, http://www.newsweek.com/2016/08/12/donald-trumps-business-failures-election-2016-486091.html?amp=1&_twitter_impression=true

73. Jerome Tuccille, *Trump: The Saga of America's Most Powerful Real Estate Baron*. Washington D.C.: Beard Books, rep. ed. 2004, 197.

73. See discussion above, Chapter 1, note 33.

73. Ibid.

73. Vivian Yee, "Donald Trump's Math Takes His Towers to Greater Heights," *New York Times*, November 1, 2016, https://www.nytimes.com/2016/11/02/nyregion/donald-trump-tower-heights.html.

73. John Cantwell, "Trump, The Logo," Design Observer, Essay, May 7, 2009, https://designobserver.com/feature/trump-the-logo/8477/.

73. William E. Geist, "The Expanding Empire of Donald Trump," *New York Times Magazine*, April 8, 1984, http://www.nytimes.com/1984/04/08/magazine/the-expanding-empire-of-donald-trump.html?pagewanted=all.

73. Barrett, *Greatest Show on Earth*, chapter 7.

Trump Tower website, http://www.trumptowerny.com/about (accessed July 4, 2018).

73. Ivana Trump, 68.

73. Marie Brenner, "After the Gold Rush."

74. Ivana Trump, 69.

74. Blair, *The Trumps*, 327.

In his career, Trump has received at least $885 million in tax breaks, grants, and other public subsidies for his luxury projects, according to an analysis of tax, housing, and finance records by the *New York Times*. Such tax abatement meant lower costs and higher selling prices for him—while the public picked up the tab in forfeited taxes. Charles V. Bagli, "A Trump Empire Built on Inside Connections and $885 Million in Tax Breaks," *New York Times*, September 17, 2016, https://www.nytimes.com/2016/09/18/nyregion/donald-trump-tax-breaks-real-estate.html.

74. See Kranish and Fisher, *Trump Revealed*, chapter 5.

Tracie Rozhon, "A Win by Trump! No, by Tenants!; Battle for the 80's Ends, with Glad-Handing All Round," *New York Times*, March 26, 1998, https://www.nytimes.com/1998/03/26/nyregion/win-trump-no-tenants-battle-80-s-ends-with-glad-handing-all-around.html; 100 Central Park South website, 100centralparksouth.com.

74. Callum Borchers, "Rupert Murdoch Introduced 'My Friend Donald J. Trump.' Their Friendship Is Kind of Rocky." *Washington Post*, May 5, 2017, https://www.washingtonpost.com/news/the-fix/wp/2017/05/05/rupert-murdoch-introduced-my-friend-donald-j-trump-their-friendship-is-kind-of-rocky/?utm_term=.2270b9b64f38.

74. Sean Kilachand, "The Forbes 400 Hall of Fame: 36 Members of Our Debut Issue Still in Ranks," *Forbes*, September 20, 2012, https://www.forbes.com/sites/

seankilachand/2012/09/20/the-forbes-400-hall-of-fame-36-members-of-our-debut-issue-still-in-ranks/#1ca312474113.

75. Jonathan Greenberg, "Trump Lied to Me about His Wealth to Get onto the Forbes 400. Here Are the Tapes." *Washington Post*, April 20, 2018, www.washingtonpost.com/outlook/trump-lied-to-me-about-his-wealth-to-get-onto-the-forbes-400-here-are-the-tapes/2018/04/20/ac762b08-4287-11e8-8569-26fda6b404c7_story.html?utm_term=.97e2e0c17b43.

75. Ibid.

75. Ibid.

75. Ibid.

75. Ibid.

76. Ibid.

77. Ibid.

77. Kranish and Fisher, *Trump Revealed*, 89–90.

78. Ibid., 127.

78. Ibid.

78. Ibid.

79. Jonathan Greenberg, "Trump Lied to Me about His Wealth to Get onto the Forbes 400. Here Are the Tapes."

79. Ibid.

79. Drew Jubera, "How Donald Trump Destroyed a Football League," *Esquire*, January 13, 2016, https://www.esquire.com/news-politics/a41135/donald-trump-usfl/.

79. Ibid.

80. Margot Hornblower, "Roy Cohn Is Disbarred by New York Court," *Washington Post*, June 24, 1986, https://www.washingtonpost.com/archive/politics/1986/06/24/roy-cohn-is-disbarred-by-new-york-court/c5ca9112-3245-48f0-ab01-c2c0f3c3fc2e/?utm_term=.62432cf49e02.

80. Brenner, "After the Gold Rush."

80. Dan Mangan, "Donald Trump Says He's a 'Germaphobe' as He Dismisses Salacious Allegations," CNBC online, January 11, 2017, as updated, https://www.cnbc.com/2017/01/11/donald-trump-says-hes-a-germaphobe-as-he-dismisses-salacious-allegations.html.

80. Barrett, chapter 9.

80. Susan Mulcahy, "Confessions of a Trump Tabloid Scribe," *Politico*, May/June 2016, https://www.politico.com/magazine/story/2016/04/2016-donald-trump-tabloids-new-york-post-daily-news-media-213842

80. Sydney H. Schanberg, "New York; Doer and Slumlord Both," *New York Times*, op-ed, March 9, 1985, archived at http://www.nytimes.com/1985/03/09/opinion/new-york-doer-and-slumlord-both.html.

80. William E. Geist, "The Expanding Empire of Donald Trump," *New York Times Magazine*, April 8, 1984, archived at http://www.nytimes.

com/1984/04/08/magazine/the-expanding-empire-of-donald-trump.html?pagewanted=all.

81. Paula Span, "From the archives: When Trump Hoped to Meet Gorbachev in Manhattan," *Washington Post*, December 3, 1988, http://www.washingtonpost.com/lifestyle/style/from-the-archives-when-trump-hoped-to-meet-gorbachev-in-manhattan/2017/07/10/3f570b42-658c-11e7-a1d7-9a32c91c6f40_story.html.

81 "Journalist Investigating Trump and Russia Says 'Full Picture Is One of Collusion,'" Fresh Air, NPR, 37:12 (November 21, 2017, 2:47 p.m.), podcast and transcript available at https://www.npr.org/2017/11/21/565654507/journalist-investigating-trump-and-russia-says-full-picture-is-one-of-collusion.

81. Scott Feinberg, "Donald Trump Angled for Soviet Posting in 1980s, Says Nobel Prize Winner (Exclusive)," *Hollywood Reporter*, May 26, 2017, https://www.hollywoodreporter.com/news/donald-trump-angled-soviet-posting-1980s-says-nobel-prize-winner-1006312

81. William E. Geist, "The Expanding Empire of Donald Trump."

81. Trump with Schwartz, 364.

82. John Shanahan, "Trump: U.S. Should Stop Paying to Defend Countries That Can Protect Selves," AP News, September 2, 1987, http://www.apnews.com/05133dbe63ace98766527ec7d16ede08.

82. "The Other Time Trump Was Huge: Newsweek's 1987 Look at the Presidential Candidate," July 30, 2015, *Newsweek*, http://www.newsweek.com/rise-trump-357533.

82. Mark Makela, "How Donald Trump Bankrupted His Atlantic City Casinos, but Still Earned Millions," *New York Times*, June 11, 2016, https://www.nytimes.com/2016/06/12/nyregion/donald-trump-atlantic-city.html.

82. Kranish and Fisher, *Trump Revealed*, 129.

82. Ibid.

83. *Newsweek* opted not to publish the story, but the reporter tweeted part of a draft, which was also uploaded to SCRIBD. Kurt Eichenwald (@kurteichenwald), 2018, "Ah, what the hell. . . . this is the portion on Trump's drug use from the Newsweek story that set off a war. Matt Mccallaster, soon fired under sex discrimination cloud, said he was 2 frightened to publish despite push by every other editor. I've left Newsweek." Twitter, March 1, 2018, 10:20 a.m. https://mobile.twitter.com/kurteichenwald/status/969230789283020800; "According to Medical Records Obtained by *Newsweek*," Draft article, uploaded to SCRIBD by kurtewald on March 1, 2018, https://www.scribd.com/document/372716093/According-to-Medical-Records-Obtained-by-Newsweek.

83. "Diethylpropion," National Institutes of Health website, https://pubchem.ncbi.nlm.nih.gov/compound/diethylpropion (accessed July 5, 2018).

83. "According to Medical Records Obtained by *Newsweek*," Draft article, uploaded to SCRIBD by kurtewald on March 1, 2018, https://www.scribd.com/document/372716093/

According-to-Medical-Records-Obtained-by-Newsweek.

83. Kranish and Fisher, *Trump Revealed*, chapter 7.

83. Ibid.

83. Ibid.

83. Glenn Plaskin, "The Playboy Interview with Donald Trump," *Playboy*, March 1, 1990, available at https://www.playboy.com/read/playboy-interview-donald-trump-1990.

85. Blair, *The Trumps*, chapter 20.

85. "Opening the Books on Donald Trump's Business Deals in Atlantic City," NPR, Fresh Air, 33:36, March 17, 2016, 1:14 p.m., podcast and transcript available at www.npr.org/2016/03/17/470806232/opening-the-books-on-donald-trumps-business-deals-in-atlantic-city.

85. Kranish and Fisher, *Trump Revealed*, chapter 7.

86. "This isn't just a building, it's the ultimate work of art," Trump said when he bought The Plaza in 1988 for $407.5 million.

https://www.trump.com/real-estate-portfolio/new-york-past/the-plaza-hotel/.

86. Kranish and Fisher, *Trump Revealed*, 137.

86. "7 Takeaways from *Vanity Fair*'s 1990 Profile of Donald Trump," *Vanity Fair*, August 12, 2015, http://www.vanityfair.com/news/2015/08/donald-trump-marie-brenner-ivana-divorce.

87. Ivana Trump, 26.

87. Brenner, Marie. "After the Gold Rush."

87. Harry Hurt III, *Lost Tycoon: The Many Lives of Donald J. Trump*. Vermont: Echo Points Books & Media, reprint ed. 2016. Trump denied having scalp reduction surgery. He also denied harming Ivana, saying that the journalist who wrote the book, *Newsweek* and *Texas Monthly* reporter Harry Hurt III, "is a guy that is an unattractive guy who is a vindictive and jealous person."

Brandy Zadrozny and Tim Mark, "Ex-Wife: Donald Trump Made Me Feel 'Violated' During Sex," Daily Beast, July 27, 2015, https://www.thedailybeast.com/ex-wife-donald-trump-made-me-feel-violated-during-sex (citing original *Newsday* article).

87. Ibid. In a statement that was also included in the book, Ivana claimed that she'd felt violated because the "love and tenderness he normally exhibited" was absent. She admitted that she'd referred to this as "rape" in her deposition but added that she didn't want her words "to be interpreted in a literal or criminal sense."

87. Brandy Zadrozny and Tim Mak. "Ex-Wife: Donald Trump Made Me Feel 'Violated' During Sex."

Shortly before his inauguration in 2017, Trump kicked Hurt off of the Trump International Golf Club in West Palm Beach after Hurt introduced himself on the practice range.

Liptak, Kevin, Kevin Bohn, and Eric Bradner. "Biographer Says Trump Booted Him from Golf Course." CNN. January 2, 2017. Accessed July 16, 2018.

https://www.cnn.com/2017/01/01/politics/donald-trump-biographer-golf-course/index.html.

87. Trisha Meili, *I Am the Central Park Jogger: A Story of Hope and Possibility*. New York: Scribner, 2003, 25.

88. Benjamin Weiser, "5 Exonerated in Central Park Jogger Case Agree to Settle Suit for $40 Million," *New York Times*, June 19, 2014, https://www.nytimes.com/2014/06/20/nyregion/5-exonerated-in-central-park-jogger-case-are-to-settle-suit-for-40-million.html.

The boys were freed 15 years later after a man in jail for murder and rape, whose DNA matched that found at the scene, confessed to the crime.

88. Lisa W. Foderaro, "Angered by Attack, Trump Urges Return of the Death Penalty," *New York Times*, May 1, 1989, archived at https://www.nytimes.com/1989/05/01/nyregion/angered-by-attack-trump-urges-return-of-the-death-penalty.html.

88. See Blake Fleetwood, "Trump Was 'The Best Sex I've Ever Had'—Marla Maples," *HuffPost*, The Blog, March 11, 2016, updated December 6, 2017, https://www.huffingtonpost.com/blake-fleetwood/marla-maples-trump-was-th_b_9438540.html.

91. Glenn Plaskin, "The Playboy Interview with Donald Trump."

92. Mr. Trump is asked about these numbers during his deposition, although he denies their accuracy in retrospect. Deposition of Donald J. Trump, December 19, 2007, *Donald J. Trump v. Timothy L. O'Brien, Time Warner Book Group Inc., and Warner Books Inc.*, No. CAM-L-545-06 (N. J. Sup. Ct., Camden County), transcript p. 96, uploaded to SCRIBD by Rachel D. Lamkin on March 4, 2016, and available at https://www.scribd.com/doc/302208690/Trump-Depo-Tr-2007.

92. Glenn Plaskin, "The Playboy Interview with Donald Trump."

93. Ibid.

93. *New York* Magazine: http://nymag.com/nymetro/news/people/features/10610/

93. Ivanka Trump, *The Trump Card: Playing to Win in Work and Life*. New York: Touchstone, 2009, 40.

93. Ibid., 60.

93. Brenner, Marie. "After the Gold Rush."

93 Ibid.

94. Buettner, Russ, and Charles V. Bagli. "How Donald Trump Bankrupted His Atlantic City Casinos, but Still Earned Millions." *The New York Times*. June 11, 2016. Accessed July 16, 2018. www.nytimes.com/2016/06/12/nyregion/donald-trump-atlantic-city.html.

94. Ibid.

94. Peterson, Barbara. "The Crash of Trump Air." The Daily Beast. October 4, 2015. Accessed July 16, 2018. https://www.thedailybeast.com/the-crash-of-trump-air.

94. Kranish and Fisher, *Trump Revealed*, 175.

94. Barrett, 689.

94. Kranish and Fisher, *Trump Revealed*, 178–79.

94. Barrett, 52; Kranish and Fisher, 172.

95. Barrett, chapter 1.

95. Kranish and Fisher, *Trump Revealed*. 172.

95 "GDP (Current US$)." GDP Growth (Annual %) | Data, World Bank, data.worldbank.org/indicator/ NY.GDP.MKTP.CD?end=2015.

95. Russ Buettner and Charles V. Bagli, "How Donald Trump Bankrupted His Atlantic City Casinos, but Still Earned Millions."

95. Ibid.

95. Steve Reilly, "*USA Today* Exclusive: Hundreds Allege Donald Trump Doesn't Pay His Bills," *USA Today*, June 9, 2016, https://www.usatoday.com/story/ news/politics/elections/2016/06/09/donald-trump-unpaid-bills-republican-president-lawsuits/85297274/.

96. Ibid.

96. Hallie Jackson, Hannah Rappleye, and Talesha Reynolds, "Hundreds Claim Donald Trump Doesn't Pay His Bills in Full," ABC News online, June 9, 2016, updated June 10, 2016, https://www.nbcnews.com/ news/us-news/hundreds-claim-donald-trump-doesnt-pay-his-bills-n589261.

96. J. Michael Diehl, "I Sold Trump $100,000 Worth of Pianos. Then He Stiffed Me." *The Washington Post*, September 28. 2016, www.washingtonpost. com/posteverything/wp/2016/09/28/i-sold-trump-100000-worth-of-pianos-then-he-stiffed-me/?utm_ term=.6b29ccc3c203.

96. Steve Reilly, "*USA Today* Exclusive: Hundreds Allege Donald Trump Doesn't Pay His Bills."

96. Blair, 411.

97. Jason M. Breslow, "The *Frontline* Interview: Roger Stone." PBS online, https://www.pbs.org/wgbh/ frontline/article/the-frontline-interview-roger-stone/.

97. Hylton, Richard D. "$1.1 Million Loan Payment Missed by Trump on Shuttle." *The New York Times*, Sept. 21, 1990, www.nytimes.com/1990/09/21/business/ company-news-1.1-million-loan-payment-missed-by-trump-on-shuttle.html.

97. Alan Sloan, "From Father Fred to the Donald Cashing in Chips Off the Old Block," *Washington Post*, January 29, 1991, https://www.washingtonpost.com/ archive/business/1991/01/29/from-father-fred-to-the-donald-cashing-in-chips-off-the-old-block/40928ac7-ce98-46b8-b257-b6a5893461fb/?utm_term=. b29129a34c72.

97. Ibid.

97. Kranish and Fisher, *Trump Revealed*. 185.

97. Barbara Ross and Stephen Rex Brown, "EXCLUSIVE: Court Docs from Ivana Trump's Prenuptial Challenge Reveal Donald's 'Cruel and Inhuman' Treatment, but Little Else as Lots of Pages Were Suspiciously Concealed," *New York Daily News*, September 17, 2016, http://www.nydailynews.com/ news/politics/court-docs-reveal-donald-trump-cruel-treatment-ivana-article-1.2796179.

98. Kranish and Fisher, *Trump Revealed*. 185–68.

98. Mikkelson, David. "Donald Trump's Bankruptcies." Snopes.com. August 1, 2016. Accessed July 13, 2018. https://www.snopes.com/news/2016/08/01/ donald-trumps-bankruptcies/.

98. Blair, 462.

98. David S. Hilzenrath and Michelle Singletary, "Trump Went Broke, But Stayed on Top," *Washington Post*, November 29, 1992, www.washingtonpost. com/archive/politics/1992/11/29/trump-went-broke-but-stayed-on-top/e1685555-1de7-400c-99a8-9cd9c0bca9fe/?utm_term=.faa3681aba9e.

98. Kurt Eichenwald, "A Brief History of Donald Trump's Many Business Failures," *Newsweek*, August 3, 2016, https://theweek.com/articles/640462/ brief-history-donald-trumps-many-business-failures.

98. Canty, Jennifer. "Transcript: Donald Trump Testifies Before Congress About Indian Gaming Act— October 5, 1993." Factbase, Candymedia, factba.se/ transcript/Donald-trump-testimony-congress-Indian-gaming-October-5-1993.

98. Ibid.

Colman McCarthy, "Trumped-Up Assault on Indian Gambling," *Washington Post*, October 26, 1993, https://www.washingtonpost.com/ archive/sports/1993/10/26/trumped-up-assault-on-indian-gambling/beece94f-3c59-481d-9174-84808b288fa1/?utm_term=.568f3f70683e.

98. Colman McCarthy, "Trumped-Up Assault on Indian Gambling."

98. Kurt Eichenwald, "A Brief History of Donald Trump's Many Business Failures."

98. Joseph Tafani and Noah Bierman, "Trump's Art of the Deal with Native Americans: Racial Insults or Flattery, Whichever Was Good for Business," *Los Angeles Times*, June 17, 2016, http://www.latimes.com/ politics/la-na-pol-trump-american-indians-20160617-snap-story.html#.

100. Ibid.

100. Tribal Enrollment Process, U.S. Department of the Interior website, www.doi.gov/tribes/enrollment (accessed July 6, 2017).

100. Trump and Connecticut's governor, Lowell Weicker Jr., got in an insult war after the testimony. Weicker, disgusted by Trump's performance, called him a "bigot" and a "dirtbag." Trump retaliated, Cohn-style, calling Weicker "a fat slob who couldn't get elected dog catcher in Connecticut." Kurt Eichenwald, "A Brief History of Donald Trump's Many Business Failures."

Weicker replied to Trump: "I've got another message for you. I can lose weight a lot faster than a bigot can lose bigotry." Associated Press, "Weicker Apologizes in Feud with Trump," *New York Times*, December 5, 1993, archived at https://www.nytimes.com/1993/12/05/ nyregion/weicker-apologizes-in-feud-with-trump.html.

Trump has used the insult "Couldn't get elected dog catcher" frequently since lobbing it at Weicker. He's said it about Hillary Clinton, Michael Bloomberg, Marco Rubio, Lindsey Graham, and Bob Corker. Denis Slattery, "Sen. Corker Joins List of Many Politicians Trump Has Said Couldn't 'Get Elected Dog Catcher,'"

New York Daily News, October 24, 2017, http://www.
nydailynews.com/news/politics/corker-joins-long-list-
pols-hit-trump-dog-catcher-dig-article-1.3585115.

100. Georgia Dullea, "VOWS; It's a Wedding Blitz for
Trump and Maples," *New York Times*, December 21,
1993, archived at http://www.nytimes.com/1993/12/21/
nyregion/vows-it-s-a-wedding-blitz-for-trump-and-
maples.html.

Although his parents had wanted him to reconcile
with Ivana (Klein, Edward. "Donald Trump Battles
Back from Collapse." *Vanity Fair*. August 26, 2016.
Accessed July 16, 2018. https://www.vanityfair.com/
news/1994/03/donald-trump-family-bankruptcy.),
Trump wanted to reward Maples's loyalty, though he
also saw the marriage as a marketing decision. Blair,
464.

The new couple failed to register at Tiffany & Co.
until two days after they'd tied the knot. Not a single
one of the 48 soup bowls they'd registered for were
purchased, and only four of 24 white dinner plates
with gold rims had been purchased. However, several
much more expensive gifts were purchased, including
a $550 crystal sail sculpture from Howard Stern.

Tripucka, Jennifer Casson. "Donald Trump and
Marla Maples' Wedding Registry Leaked And You
Won't Believe What's On It." Brides. May 26, 2017.
Accessed July 16, 2018. https://www.brides.com/story/
donald-trump-marla-maples-wedding-registry.

100. Georgia Dullea, "VOWS; It's a Wedding Blitz for
Trump and Maples."

100. David S. Hilzenrath and Michelle Singletary,
"Trump Went Broke, but Stayed on Top."

101. Douglas Martin, "Veterans Day Parade Tries
for a Comeback," *New York Times*, November 10,
1995, archived at http://www.nytimes.com/1995/11/10/
nyregion/veterans-day-parade-tries-for-a-comeback.
html.

101. "26,000 Veterans Proudly March in
'Nation's Parade' Reinvigorated N.Y. Event Among
Hundreds in U.S.," *Baltimore Sun*, November
12, 1995, articles.baltimoresun.com/1995-11-12/
news/1995316010_1_veterans-day-war-ii-parade.

101. Mark Singer, "Trump Solo," *New Yorker*, May
19, 1997, www.newyorker.com/magazine/1997/05/19/
trump-solo.

101. "Pages from Donald Trump's 1995 Income Tax
Records," *New York Times*, October 1, 2016, https://
www.nytimes.com/interactive/2016/10/01/us/politics/
donald-trump-taxes.html.

101. Max J. Rosenthal, "How Donald Trump Went
Bust and Got Rich Using Other People's Money: A
Timeline," *Mother Jones*, October 14, 2016, http://
www.motherjones.com/politics/2016/10/how-donald-
trump-destroyed-his-empire-and-dumped-ruins-
others-timeline/.

101. Ibid.

101. Jonathan Greenberg, "Trump Lied to Me about
His Wealth to Get onto the Forbes 400. Here Are the
Tapes."

He also repeatedly tried to make the case that he was
the biggest developer in New York. But others had

built more, owned more, and were worth far more
money.

Craig, Susanne, and David W. Chen. "Donald Trump
in New York: Deep Roots, but Little Influence." *The
New York Times*, February 23, 2016. Accessed July 16,
2018. https://www.nytimes.com/2016/02/24/nyregion/
donald-trump-nyc.html.

Kaczynski, Andrew. "Trump Often Claimed To Be
'The Largest Real Estate Developer In New York.' He
Isn't." BuzzFeed. Accessed July 16, 2018. https://www.
buzzfeed.com/andrewkaczynski/trump-often-claimed-
to-be-the-largest-real-estate-developer?utm_term=.
eeqPmaAB3.

101. "Ain't That a Beauty: Marla to Co-Host 'Miss
Universe,'" *New York Daily News*, April 1, 1997, http://
www.nydailynews.com/archives/entertainment/
ain-beauty-marla-co-host-universe-article-1.758304.

101. Lisa de Moraes, "Pageants May Move from
CBS," *Washington Post*, April 3, 2002, https://www.
washingtonpost.com/archive/lifestyle/2002/04/03/
pageants-may-move-from-cbs/f287f1f3-c0ff-4d5f-
a0bd-2b28df407798/?resType=accessibility&
utm_term=.3aaadf3c0e7c.

102. Jeffrey Toobin, "Trump's Miss Universe
Gambit," *New Yorker*, February 26, 2018, http://
www.newyorker.com/magazine/2018/02/26/
trumps-miss-universe-gambit.

102. Ibid.

102. Elizabeth Johns, "Donald and Marla
Trump Split," *E! News*, May 2, 1997, https://www.
eonline.com/news/34465/donald-and-marla-
trump-split; Dareh Gregorian, "Donald & Marla
Set to $ettle on Divorce Deal," *New York Post*,
April 25, 1999, https://nypost.com/1999/04/25/
donald-marla-set-to-ettle-on-divorce-deal/.

102. Singer, Mark. "Trump Solo," *The New
Yorker*, May 19, 1997 Issue, www.newyorker.com/
magazine/1997/05/19/trump-solo.

102. "The Russian Gangster Who Loved Trump's Taj
Mahal." Trump / Russia. December 21, 2017. Accessed
July 13, 2018. https://trump-russia.com/2017/10/06/
the-russian-gangster-who-loved-trumps-taj-mahal/.

103. Jose Pagliery, "Trump's Casino Was a Money
Laundering Concern Shortly After It Opened," CNN
online, May 22, 2017, http://www.cnn.com/2017/05/22/
politics/trump-taj-mahal/index.html.

103. Joseph Milord, "How Did Donald and Melania
Trump Meet?" *Elite Daily*, June 21, 2017, https://www.
elitedaily.com/news/politics/story-donald-melania-
trump-met-started-dating-fitting/1998686.

Interview with Donald, Melania Trump, CNN
online, *Larry King Live* (air date May 17, 2015, 9
EST), transcript available at http://edition.cnn.com/
TRANSCRIPTS/0505/17/lkl.01.html (accessed July 6,
2018).

104. Ibid.

104. Ibid.

104. Amy Sherman, "Did Donald Trump Inherit
$100 Million?" PolitiFact, March 7, 2016, http://

www.politifact.com/florida/article/2016/mar/07/
did-donald-trump-inherit-100-million/

104. Donald Trump and Dave Shiflett, *The America We Deserve*. Los Angeles: Renaissance Books, 2000, epilogue.

104. Adam Nagourney, "Reform Bid Said to Be a No-Go for Trump," *New York Times*, February 14, 2000, http://www.nytimes.com/2000/02/14/us/reform-bid-said-to-be-a-no-go-for-trump.html.

105. Ibid.

105. Ibid.

105. Michael Kruse, "What Trump and Clinton Did on 9/11," *Politico*, September 10, 2016, https://www.politico.com/magazine/story/2016/09/trump-hillary-clinton-september-11-911-attacks-nyc-214236#ixzz4JrLrKNb4

(includes WWOR-TV video interview with Trump, 9:55).

106. Fredric U. Dicker, "TRUMP: BUILD 'TWINS'—WANTS OLD WTC BACK—& HIGHER," *New York Post*, May 6, 2005, http://www.nypost.com/2005/05/06/trump-build-twins-wants-old-wtc-back-higher/.

106. Ibid.

106. Steve Cuozzo, "Saving Wollman Rink Made Trump a New York City Hero," *New York Post*, January 22, 2017, https://nypost.com/2017/01/22/saving-wollman-rink-made-trump-a-new-york-city-hero/.

106. Ivana Trump, *The Trump Card: Playing to Win in Work and Life*, 171.

106. Ibid.

106. Ibid.

Kranish and Fisher, "The Inside Story of How 'The Apprentice' Rescued Donald Trump," *Fortune*, September 8, 2016, http://fortune.com/2016/09/08/donald-trump-the-apprentice-burnett/.

106. Ivana Trump, *The Trump Card*, p. 172.

106. Ibid.

107. Ibid., 173.

107. Kranish and Fisher, "The Inside Story of How 'The Apprentice' Rescued Donald Trump"

Tony Maglio, "'Celebrity Apprentice': Just How 'Yuge' Were Those TV Ratings Anyway?" The Wrap, January 1, 2017, updated January 1, 2017, https://www.thewrap.com/celebrity-apprentice-trump-tv-ratings-arnold/.

109. https://www.forbes.com/static/bill2005/LIRU5WX.html (accessed July 6, 2018).

109. Top paid circulation data, as reported by *AdAge*: Top 200 Magazines by Circulation, December 31, 2004, AdAge, http://www.adage.com/datacenter/datapopup.php?article_id=106861 (accessed July 6, 2018).

110. ABC Prime-Time rankings archived at ABC Medianet, https://web.archive.org/web/20070930155240/http://www.abcmedianet.com/Web/progcal/dispDNR.aspx?id=060204_11 (accessed July 6, 2018).

110. Bill Carter, "'The Apprentice' Scores Ratings Near Top for the Season," *New York Times*, April 17, 2004, https://www.nytimes.com/2004/04/17/us/the-apprentice-scores-ratings-near-top-for-the-season.html.

110. Glenn Plaskin, "The Playboy Interview with Donald Trump."

110. Timothy L. O'Brien, *TrumpNation: The Art of Being The Donald* (New York: Grand Central Publishing, 2016), 25.

111. Ibid., 20, 26.

111. Russ Buettner and Charles V. Bagli, "How Donald Trump Bankrupted His Atlantic City Casinos, but Still Earned Millions."

111. Brett Kelman and Jesse Marx, "How Donald Trump Got Fired by a California Casino." *Desert Sun*, March 21, 2016, http://www.desertsun.com/story/news/politics/2016/03/21/donald-trump-spotlight-29/81860676/.

111. Timothy L. O'Brien, "How Trump Bungled the Deal of a Lifetime," Bloomberg, op-ed, January 26, 2016, https://www.bloomberg.com/view/articles/2016-01-27/donald-trump-s-track-record-on-deals.

111. Blair Donovan, "The 15 Most Expensive Wedding Dresses of All Time," *Brides*, February 6, 2018, http://www.brides.com/story/the-most-expensive-wedding-dresses-of-all-time.

112. Michael Callahan, "Flashback: When Hillary and Bill Hit the Wedding of Donald and Melania," *Hollywood Reporter*, April 7, 2016, https://www.hollywoodreporter.com/features/trumps-wedding-melania-bill-hill-880088

Joseph O'Neill, "Memories of Trump's Wedding," *New Yorker*, August 1, 2016, https://www.newyorker.com/news/news-desk/memories-of-trumps-wedding.

112. See Trump.com, Merchandise, https://www.trump.com/merchandise/signature-collection/ (accessed July 6, 2018).

112. See Sasha Talcott, "'The Apprentice': A Case Study," Boston.com archives, April 15, 2004, https://archive.boston.com/business/globe/articles/2004/04/15/the_apprentice_a_case_study?pg=full.

112. O'Brien, *TrumpNation*, 35.

112. Rosalind S. Helderman and Tom Hamburger, "Former Mafia-Linked Figure Describes Association with Trump," *Washington Post*, May 17, 2016, https://www.washingtonpost.com/politics/former-mafia-linked-figure-describes-association-with-trump/2016/05/17/cec6c2c6-16d3-11e6-aa55-670cabef46e0_story.html?utm_term=.cfa73726f84c.

112. Max Abelson, "On the Rocks: The Story of Trump Vodka," Bloomberg, April 20, 2016, https://www.bloomberg.com/features/2016-trump-vodka/.

113. Malika Andrews, Joe Drape, and Karen Crouse, "In Tahoe, a Wild Intersection of Golf and Celebrities," *New York Times*, January 27, 2008, https://www.nytimes.com/2018/01/27/sports/golf/stormy-daniels.html.

113. Rob Walker, "Trumped," *New York Times Magazine*, October 14, 2007, https://www.nytimes.com/2007/10/14/magazine/14wwln-consumed-t.html.

113. Alex Williams, "Trump Jr.: Finally Trading on a Famous Name," *New York Times*, November 21, 2006, http://www.nytimes.com/2006/11/21/arts/21iht-trump.3611735.html.

113. Trump SoHo from The Apprentice, YouTube (0:34), published by BobbyDay, September 12, 2007, www.youtube.com/watch?v=INe_2FaBVAO.

113. Helderman and Hamburger, "Former Mafia-Linked Figure Describes Association with Trump."

113. The sponsor of the Trump SoHo site, according to marketing materials, was "Bayrock / Sapir Organization LLC," and there was a Russian-language website for the property, now archived at https://web.archive.org/web/20111126050509/http://trumpsoho.ru/ (accessed July 6, 2018). Philip Bump, "Here's How Trump SoHo Was Marketed to Russians," *Washington Post*, April 12, 2018, https://www.washingtonpost.com/news/politics/wp/2018/04/12/heres-how-trump-soho-was-marketed-to-russians/?utm_term=.63dc752430f0.

113. Gary Silverman, "Trump's Russian Riddle," *Financial Times*, August 14, 2016, https://www.ft.com/content/549ddfaa-5fa5-11e6-b38c-7b39cbb1138a.

113. Timothy L. O'Brien, "Trump, Russian and a Shadowy Business Partnership," Bloomberg, op-ed, June 21, 2017, https://www.bloomberg.com/view/articles/2017-06-21/trump-russia-and-those-shadowy-sater-deals-at-bayrock.

113. Bump, "Here's How Trump Soho Was Marketed to Russians."

113. https://www.biography.com/people/donald-trump-jr-020317

113. Charles V. Bagli, "Real Estate Executive with Hand in Trump Projects Rose from Tangled Past," *New York Times*, December 17, 2007, https://www.nytimes.com/2007/12/17/nyregion/17trump.html

Chris Sommerfeldt, "Shady Businessman Engangled in Trump-Russia Investigation Claims He Doubled as American Spy," *Daily News*, March 12, 2018, http://www.nydailynews.com/news/politics/businessman-entangled-trump-russia-probe-doubled-u-s-spy-article-1.3870344.

114. Bagli, "Real Estate Executive with Hand in Trump Projects Rose from Tangled Past."

114. Ibid.

114. Helderman and Hamburger, "Former Mafia-Linked Figure Describes Association with Trump."

114. "Trump Picked Mafia-Linked Stock Fraud Felon as Senior Adviser," *Chicago Tribune*, December 4, 2015, http://www.chicagotribune.com/news/nationworld/politics/ct-trump-felix-sater-felon-adviser-20151204-story.html.

114. Goodman, Peter S. "Defamation Suit Filed by Donald Trump Is Dismissed." *The New York Times*. July 15, 2009. Accessed July 13, 2018. https://www.nytimes.com/2009/07/16/business/media/16trump.html.

114 Deposition of Donald J. Trump, December 19, 2007, *Trump v. O'Brien*, No. CAM-L-545-06 (N. J. Sup. Ct., Camden County), uploaded to SCRIBD by Rachel D. Lamkin on March 4, 2016, and available at https://www.scribd.com/doc/302208690/Trump-Depo-Tr-2007.

115. "In 2007, Trump Was Forced to Face His Own Falsehoods. And He Did, 30 Times." *The Washington Post*. Accessed July 13, 2018. https://www.washingtonpost.com/graphics/politics/2016-election/trump-lies/?utm_term=.4efd14cc23a3.

115. Deposition of Donald J. Trump, December 19, 2007, *Donald J. Trump v. Timothy L. O'Brien, Time Warner Book Group Inc., and Warner Books Inc.*

115. *Trump v. O'Brien*, 29 A.3d 1090 (N.J. Super. Ct. App. Div. 2011), available at https://www.courtlistener.com/opinion/2318710/trump-v-obrien/ (quoting *TrumpNation*).

115. Deposition of Donald J. Trump, December 19, 2007, 63–64.

115. Ibid., 64.

115. Ibid., 61.

115. Ibid., 61–62.

116. "What to Look for in a Golf Course Appraisal." Golf Property Analysts New Golf Industry Numbers: What Do They Mean for the Game's Future? Accessed July 13, 2018. http://golfprop.com/uncategorized/what-to-look-for-in-a-golf-course-appraisal/.

116. Ibid., 216, 228.

116. See *Trump v. O'Brien*, 29 A.3d 1090 (N.J. Super. Ct. App. Div. 2011), available at https://www.courtlistener.com/opinion/2318710/trump-v-obrien/.

116. David Segal, "He's the Top," *Washington Post*, September 9, 2004, https://www.washingtonpost.com/archive/lifestyle/2004/09/09/hes-the-top/69e9be62-93f0-46e2-8d88-75182dc08761/?utm_term=.7a4df6eb5221, quoted in *Trump v. O'Brien*, 29 A.3d 1090 (N.J. Super. Ct. App. Div. 2011), available at https://www.courtlistener.com/opinion/2318710/trump-v-obrien/.

Docket No. A-6141-08T3

117. Jerry Useem, "What Does Donald Trump Really Want?" *Fortune*, April 3, 2000, http://www.fortune.com/2000/04/03/what-does-donald-trump-really-want/, quoted in *Trump v. O'Brien*, 29 A.3d 1090 (N.J. Super. Ct. App. Div. 2011), available at https://www.courtlistener.com/opinion/2318710/trump-v-obrien/.

117. *Trump v. O'Brien*, 29 A.3d 1090 (N.J. Super. Ct. App. Div. 2011), available at https://www.courtlistener.com/opinion/2318710/trump-v-obrien/.

117. Stalter, Kate. "Would Donald Trump Be Better Off Investing In Stocks?" *Forbes*. September 1, 2016. Accessed July 13, 2018. https://www.forbes.com/sites/katestalter/2016/09/01/would-donald-trump-be-better-off-investing-in-stocks/.

"What's More Lucrative: 'The Apprentice' or the S&P 500?" *Fortune*. Accessed July 13, 2018. http://fortune.com/2015/08/20/donald-trump-index-funds/.

117. Forum, Forbes Leadership. "Has Donald Trump Underperformed In The Real Estate Business?" *Forbes.* March 3, 2016. Accessed July 13, 2018.

118. "Fact Check: Has Trump Declared Bankruptcy Four or Six Times?" *The Washington Post.* Accessed July 13, 2018. https://www.washingtonpost.com/politics/2016/live-updates/general-election/real-time-fact-checking-and-analysis-of-the-first-presidential-debate/fact-check-has-trump-declared-bankruptcy-four-or-six-times/.

118. "I Have Used the Laws of This Country . . . the [bankruptcy] Chapter Laws. "Donald Trump Bankruptcy: Everything You Want to Know." CNNMoney. Accessed July 13, 2018. https://money.cnn.com/2015/08/31/news/companies/donald-trump-bankruptcy/index.html.

118. Ibid.

118. Alan Smith, "Trump's Long and Winding History with Deutsche Bank Could Now Be at the Center of Robert Mueller's Investigation," *Business Insider*, December 8, 2017, http://www.businessinsider.com/trump-deutsche-bank-mueller-2017-12.

118. Ben Protess, Jessica Silver-Greenberg, and Jesse Drucker, "Big German Bank, Key to Trump's Finances, Faces New Scrutiny," *New York Times*, July 19, 2017, http://www.nytimes.com/2017/07/19/business/big-german-bank-key-to-trumps-finances-faces-new-scrutiny.html.

118. Susan Diesenhouse, "Trump Jr. Builds on Roots," *Chicago Tribune*, September 18, 2005, http://www.chicagotribune.com/chi-0509180214sep18-story.html.

118. Emily Nunn, "The Daughter Also Rises," *Chicago Tribune*, January 5, 2007, http://articles.chicagotribune.com/2007-01-05/features/0701050009_1_trump-tower-donald-trump-ivanka-trump.

118. Ben Protess, Jessica Silver-Greenberg, and Jesse Drucker, "Big German Bank, Key to Trump's Finances, Faces New Scrutiny."

118. Ibid.

119. "All-Transactions House Price Index for Florida." FRED. May 24, 2018. Accessed July 14, 2018. https://fred.stlouisfed.org/series/FLSTHPI/.

119. "Dmitry Rybolovlev," *Forbes* Profile, https://www.forbes.com/profile/dmitry-rybolovlev/ (accessed July 7, 2018).

119. Robert Frank, "Only in Palm Beach: The $95 Million Tear-Down," *New York Times*, August 27, 2016, http://www.nytimes.com/2016/08/28/business/only-in-palm-beach-the-95-million-tear-down.html.

119. Brennan Weiss, "Trump's Oldest Son Said a Decade Ago That a Lot of the Family's Assets Came from Russia," *Business Insider*, February 21, 2018, http://www.businessinsider.com/donald-trump-jr-said-money-pouring-in-from-russia-2018-2?op=1.

119. Bill Littlefield, "A Day (And A Cheeseburger) with President Trump," WBUR, May 11, 2017, audio (9:57) and transcript at http://www.wbur.org/onlyagame/2017/05/05/james-dodson-donald-trump-golf.

119. Eric Trump (@EricTrump), 2017, "This story is completely fabricated and just another example of why there is such a deep distrust of the media in our country. #FakeNews" Https://T.co/YZMUnniw7Z." Twitter, May 8, 2017, 3:32 a.m. https://twitter.com/erictrump/status/861529156701564929?lang=en.

119. Donald J. Trump (@realDonaldTrump), 2009, Twitter, May 4, 2009, 11:54 a.m. https://twitter.com/realdonaldtrump/status/1698308935.

119. "Trump Twitter Archive." Trump Twitter Archive. Accessed July 14, 2018. http://www.trumptwitterarchive.com/.

119. Donald J. Trump (@realDonaldTrump), 2009, "'My persona will never be that of a wallflower-I'd rather build walls than cling to them'—Donald J. Trump" Twitter, May 12, 2009, 7:07 a.m. https://twitter.com/realdonaldtrump/status/1773561338.

120. "Trump Entertainment Resorts Files for Chapter 11 Bankruptcy Protection," CNBC, September 9, 2014, as updated, https://www.cnbc.com/2014/09/09/trump-entertainment-resorts-files-for-chapter-11-bankruptcy.html. See Voluntary Petition, Trump Entertainment Resorts, Inc., U.S. Bankruptcy Court, District of New Jersey, Case 09-13655-JHW, filed February 17, 2009, https://www.pacermonitor.com/view/UIAP7CQ/Trump_Entertainment_Resorts,_Inc._njbke-09-13655_0001.0.pdf (pdf of top of petition, accessed July 7, 2018).

120. Michael Hinman, "Former Trump Tower Tampa Buyers Sue Donald Trump," *Tampa Bay Business Journal*, November 13, 2009, https://www.bizjournals.com/tampabay/stories/2009/11/09/daily76.html.

120. "Deposition: Donald Trump Deposition-Trump Tampa-September 20, 2010." *Factbase*, https://factba.se/transcript/donald-trump-deposition-trump-tampa-september-20-2010.

120. "Steve Aaron, Et Al against The Trump Organization, Inc." United States District Court, Middle District of Florida, Tampa Division, www.washingtonpost.com/wp-stat/graphics/politics/trump-archive/docs/trump-depo-aaron-case-9-20-2010.pdf., page 70.

120. Ibid.

120. Steve Eder and Jennifer Medina, "Trump University Suit Settlement Approved by Judge," *New York Times*, March 31, 2017, https://www.nytimes.com/2017/03/31/us/trump-university-settlement.html.

121. Andrea Bernstein, et al, "How Ivanka Trump and Donald Trump, Jr., Avoided a Criminal Indictment," *New Yorker*, October 4, 2017, http://www.newyorker.com/news/news-desk/how-ivanka-trump-and-donald-trump-jr-avoided-a-criminal-indictment.

121. Ibid.

121. Ibid.

121. Andrea Bernstein, et al, "How Ivanka Trump and Donald Trump, Jr., Avoided a Criminal Indictment."

121. Mike McIntire, "Donald Trump Settled a Real Estate Lawsuit, and a Criminal Case Was Closed," *New York Times*, April 5, 2016, https://www.nytimes.com/2016/04/06/us/politics/donald-trump-soho-settlement.html.

122. Andrea Bernstein, et al, "How Ivanka Trump and Donald Trump, Jr., Avoided a Criminal Indictment."

122. Ibid.

122. Ibid.

122. Bagli, Charles V. "Real Estate Executive With Hand in Trump Projects Rose From Tangled Past." *The New York Times*. December 17, 2007. Accessed July 14, 2018. https://www.nytimes.com/2007/12/17/nyregion/17trump.html.

122. Richard Behar, "Donald Trump and the Felon: Inside His Business Dealings with a Mob-Connected Hustler," *Forbes*, October 3, 2016, http://www.forbes.com/sites/richardbehar/2016/10/03/donald-trump-and-the-felon-inside-his-business-dealings-with-a-mob-connected-hustler/.

122. *Kriss v. Bayrock Group LLC*, Case 1:10-cv-039590DCF, U.S. District Court, Southern District of New York, Verified Complaint, Filed June 20, 2016, para. 4 (available at www.documentcloud.org/documents/4173550-Kriss-Lawsuit-Bayrock-Verified-Complaint-6-20.html) (accessed July 7, 2018).

See also Timothy L. O'Brien, "Trump, Russia and a Shadowy Business Partner," *Bloomberg*, op-ed, June 21, 2017, https://www.bloomberg.com/view/articles/2017-06-21/trump-russia-and-those-shadowy-sater-deals-at-bayrock.

The case was settled for an undisclosed amount.

122. Hettena, Seth. "A Brief History of Michael Cohen's Criminal Ties." *Rolling Stone*. June 25, 2018. Accessed July 14, 2018. https://www.rollingstone.com/politics/politics-news/a-brief-history-of-michael-cohens-criminal-ties-628875/.

122. Brennan Weiss, "Inside the Close Relationship between Trump and His 'Pit Bull' Lawyer Michael Cohen, Who Paid Stormy Daniels, Says He'd 'Take a Bullet' for Trump, and Was Raided by the FBI," *Business Insider*, April 10, 2018, http://www.businessinsider.com/michael-cohen-history-with-trump-2018-3.

123. "Donald Trump Wants to See Obama's Birth Certificate," *YouTube* (3:10), published by politics2012bba, March 23, 2011, http://www.youtube.com/watch?v=LCKDTwu_g2M.

123. Jonathan Weisman and Scott Greenberg, "WSJ/NBC Poll: A Donald Trump Surprise," *Wall Street Journal*, April 6, 2011, https://blogs.wsj.com/washwire/2011/04/06/wsjnbc-poll-a-donald-trump-surprise/.

124. "Donald Trump on a Potential Presidential Run," *NBC Learn*, April 7, 2011, transcript available at archives.nbclearn.com/portal/site/k-12/flatview?cuecard=52817.

124. Michael Scherer, "Trump's Political Reality Show: Will the Donald Really Run for President?" *Time*, April 14, 2011, content.time.com/time/magazine/article/0,9171,2065235,00.html.

124. Roberts, Roxanne. "I Sat Next to Donald Trump at the Infamous 2011 White House Correspondents' Dinner." *The Washington Post*. April 28, 2016. Accessed July 14, 2018. https://www.washingtonpost.com/lifestyle/style/i-sat-next-to-donald-trump-at-the-infamous-2011-white-house-correspondents-dinner/2016/04/27/5cf46b74-0bea-11e6-8ab8-9ad050f76d7d_story.html?utm_term=.2a60ed944c43.

125. "Remarks by the President at the White House Correspondents Association Dinner." National Archives and Records Administration. Accessed July 14, 2018. https://obamawhitehouse.archives.gov/the-press-office/2011/05/01/remarks-president-white-house-correspondents-association-dinner.

125. "President Obama Roasts Donald Trump at White House Correspondents' Dinner!" YouTube, (5:33), published by SuchIsLifeVideos, April 30, 2011, https://www.youtube.com/watch?v=k8TwRmX6zs4.

126. Schwartzman, Paul, and Michael E. Miller. "Confident. Incorrigible. Bully: Little Donny Was a Lot like Candidate Donald Trump." *The Washington Post*. June 22, 2016. Accessed July 14, 2018. https://www.washingtonpost.com/lifestyle/style/young-donald-trump-military-school/2016/06/22/f0b3b164-317c-11e6-8758-d58e76e11b12_story.html.

126. Donald J. Trump, (@realDonaldTrump), 2011, "Made in America? @BarackObama called his 'birthplace' Hawaii 'here in Asia.' bit.ly/uKWii" Twitter, November 18, 2011, 7:54 a.m., https://twitter.com/realDonaldTrump/status/137559273394802690.

126. Donald J. Trump (@realDonaldTrump), 2012, "Let's take a closer look at that birth certificate. @BarackObama was described in 2003 as being 'born in Kenya.'" Twitter, May 18, 2012, 12:31 p.m., https://twitter.com/realDonaldTrump/status/203568571148800001.

126. Donald J. Trump (@realDonaldTrump), 2012,"An 'extremely credible source' has called my office and told me that @BarackObama's birth certificate is a fraud." Twitter, August 6, 2012, 1:23 p.m., https://twitter.com/realDonaldTrump/status/232572505238433794.

126. Donald J. Trump (@realDonaldTrump), 2012, "Why does Barack Obama's ring have an arabic inscription? bit.ly/VMN6Vn Who is this guy?" Twitter, October 11, 2012, 1:11 p.m., https://twitter.com/realdonaldtrump/status/256487311515209728.

126. Donald J. Trump (@realDonaldTrump), 2012, "How amazing, the State Health Director who verified copies of Obama's 'Birth Certificate' died in plane crash today. All others lived." Twitter, December 12, 2013, https://twitter.com/realdonaldtrump/status/411247268763676673.

127. Donald Trump deposition, December 19 2007. Page 32.

129. Donald J. Trump (@realDonaldTrump), Twitter, April 30, 2012, 11:03 a.m., https://twitter.com/realdonaldtrump/status/197023379344199681.

129. Haberman, Maggie, and Alexander Burns. "Donald Trump's Presidential Run Began in an Effort to Gain Stature." *The New York Times*. March 12, 2016. Accessed July 16, 2018. https://www.nytimes.com/2016/03/13/us/politics/donald-trump-campaign.html.

130. Mark Preston and Alan Silverleib, "Trump Endorses Romey," CNN, February 3, 2012, https://

www.cnn.com/2012/02/02/politics/campaign-wrap/index.html

Ashley Parker and Trip Gabriel, "Trump Endorses Romney in a 7-Minute Appearance," *New York Times*, The Caucus, February 2, 2012, https://thecaucus.blogs.nytimes.com/2012/02/02/confusion-over-trump-endorses-romney/.

130. See Trump Twitter Archive, www.trumptwitterarchive.com/ (accessed July 7, 2018).

130. See, for example, tweets from Donald J. Trump (@realDonaldTrump) on December 13, 2011, 9:16 a.m. ("Look, here's the deal: @BarackObama has been a total disaster. He has spent this country into the ground and destroyed jobs #TimeToGetTough"), https://twitter.com/realDonaldTrump/status/146639744363790337; and on January 9, 2012, 10:41 p.m. ("'Sadly, when it comes to using the energy industry to create American jobs, Obama has been a total disaster.' #TimeToGetTough"), https://twitter.com/realDonaldTrump/status/156445416257363968.

130. Donald J. Trump (@realDonaldTrump), 2012, "President @BarackObama's vacation is costing taxpayers millions of Dollars—Unbelievable!" Twitter, January 5, 2012, 11:56 a.m., https://twitter.com/realdonaldtrump/status/155014799909064704.

130. Donald J. Trump (@realDonaldTrump), 2012, "'The Wall Street Journal has reported that Obama's food stamp policies are ushering in a massive 'food stamp crime wave.'" #TimeToGet Tough." Twitter, January 3, 2012, 11:51 a.m., https://twitter.com/realdonaldtrump/status/154288899324260352.

130. Donald J. Trump (@realDonaldTrump), 2012, "9 million fewer people voted for Obama this election than last & yet the Republicans lost—do you think they might be doing something wrong!" Twitter, November 9, 2012, 11:07 a.m., https://twitter.com/realdonaldtrump/status/266980409995313153.

130. Donald J. Trump (@realDonaldTrump), Twitter, November 6, 2012, 8:39 p.m., https://twitter.com/realdonaldtrump/status/266037143628038144.

131. Karen Tumulty, "How Donald Trump Came up with 'Make America Great Again,'" *Washington Post*, January 18, 2017, https://www.washingtonpost.com/politics/how-donald-trump-came-up-with-make-america-great-again/2017/01/17/fb6acf5e-dbf7-11e6-ad42-f3375f271c9c_story.html?utm_term=.c198ae2079ce; see United States Patent and Trademark Office website, tsdr.uspto.gov/#caseNumber=85783371&caseSearchType=US_APPLICATION&caseType=DEFAULT&searchType=statusSearch (retrieved July 7, 2018).

131. Emma Margolin, "'Make America Great Again'—Who Said It First?" NBC News, September 9, 2016, https://www.nbcnews.com/politics/2016-election/make-america-great-again-who-said-it-first-n645716.

131. See Jason M. Breslow, "The FRONTLINE Interview: Roger Stone," PBS, Frontline, September 27, 2016, https://www.pbs.org/wgbh/frontline/article/the-frontline-interview-roger-stone/.

131. Ibid.

132. Ibid.

132. Donald J. Trump (@realDonaldTrump), Twitter, June 18, 2013, 8:00 p.m., https://twitter.com/realdonaldtrump/status/347187059653476352.

132. "Aras Agalarov." *Forbes.* Accessed July 16, 2018. https://www.forbes.com/profile/aras-agalarov/.

132. Michael Isikoff and David Corn, *Russian Roulette: The Inside Story of Putin's War on America and the Election of Donald Trump.* New York: Twelve/Hachette Book Group, 2018, 5.

133. *Russian Roulette,* 4

134. Donald J. Trump (@realDonaldTrump), 2013, "Do you think Putin will be going to The Miss Universe Pageant in November in Moscow-if so, will he become my new best friend?" Twitter, June 19, 2013, 8:17 p.m., https://twitter.com/realDonaldTrump/status/347191326112112640.

134. Eugene L. Meyer, "A Trump Makeover for Washington's Old Post Office," *New York Times*, May 27, 2014, https://www.nytimes.com/2014/05/28/realestate/commercial/finally-washingtons-old-post-office-gets-a-new-life.html.

134. NYS Attorney General, "A.G. Schneiderman Sues Donald Trump, Trump University & Michael Sexton for Defrauding Consumers Out of $40 Million with Sham 'University,'" Press Release, August 25, 2012, https://ag.ny.gov/press-release/ag-schneiderman-sues-donald-trump-trump-university-michael-sexton-defrauding-consumers

134. Donald J. Trump (@realDonaldTrump), 2013, "Lightweight NYS Attorney General Eric Schneiderman is trying to extort me with a civil law suit. See website 98percentapproval.com" Twitter, August 24, 2013, 3:41 p.m., https://twitter.com/realdonaldtrump/status/371401860344983552.

134. Max Fisher, "Vladimir Putin's *New York Times* Op-Ed, Annotated and Fact-Checked," *Washington Post*, September 12, 2013, https://www.washingtonpost.com/news/worldviews/wp/2013/09/12/vladimir-putins-new-york-times-op-ed-annotated-and-fact-checked/?utm_term=.91e64c996eef.

134. Donald J. Trump (@realDonaldTrump), 2013, "Putin is having such a good time. Our President is making him look like the genius of all geniuses. Do not fear, we are a NATION OF POTENTIAL[.]" Twitter, September 11, 2013, 6:11 a.m., https://twitter.com/realdonaldtrump/status/377781540698488832.

134. Van Susteren, Greta. "Trump: 'Embarrassing' How Putin Has Played' Obama." Fox News. Accessed July 16, 2018. http://www.foxnews.com/transcript/2013/09/13/trump-embarrassing-how-putin-has-played-obama.html.

134. Penzenstadler, Nick, and Susan Page. "Exclusive: Trump's 3,500 Lawsuits Unprecedented for a Presidential Nominee." *USA Today.* October 23, 2017. Accessed July 14, 2018. https://www.usatoday.com/story/news/politics/elections/2016/06/01/donald-trump-lawsuits-legal-battles/84995854/.

134. "Donald Trump: Three Decades, 4,095 Lawsuits," *USA Today* interactive, http://www.usatoday.com/pages/interactives/trump-lawsuits/ (accessed July 7, 2018).

134. *Abercrombie v. SB Hotel Associates, LLC*, Case 1:09-cv-21406-KMW, Broward County Circuit Court, Deposition of Donald J. Trump, November 5, 2013, transcript available at https://www.scribd.com/document/374847351/Trump-Florida-Deposition-2013 (accessed July 7, 2018).

135. Bagli, "Real Estate Executive with Hand in Trump Projects Rose from Tangled Past."

135. *Abercrombie v. SB Hotel Associates*, Deposition of Donald J. Trump, November 5, 2013, p. 157; Matthew Mosk and Brian Ross, "Memory Lapse? Trump Seeks Distance From 'Advisor' With Past Ties to Mafia." *ABC News*, ABC News Network, 10 December 2015, abcnews.go.com/Politics/memory-lapse-trump-seeks-distance-advisor-past-ties/story?id=34600826.

135. Donald J. Trump (@realDonaldTrump), 2013, "Success tip: Be ready for problems, and be patient—there are very few cases of instant gratification." Twitter, November 8, 2013, 9:32 a.m., https://twitter.com/realdonaldtrump/status/398865537020620800.

135. Silver, Vernon. "Flight Records Illuminate Mystery of Trump's Moscow Nights." Bloomberg.com. April 23, 2018. Accessed July 14, 2018. https://www.bloomberg.com/news/articles/2018-04-23/flight-records-illuminate-mystery-of-trump-s-moscow-nights.

135. Isikoff and Corn, *Russian Roulette*, 15.

136. Ibid.

136. Ken Dilanian and Jonathan Allen, "Trump Bodyguard Keith Schiller Testifies Russian Offered Trump Women, Was Turned Down," NBC News online, November 9, 2017, as updated, http://www.nbcnews.com/news/us-news/trump-bodyguard-testifies-russian-offered-trump-women-was-turned-down-n819386.

136. "there are very few cases of instant gratification." Twitter, November 8, 2013, 9:32 a.m., https://twitter.com/realdonaldtrump/status/398865537020620800.

Isikoff and Corn, *Russian Roulette*, 12.

136. Ibid., 12–13.

136. Ibid., 13

137. Jon Swaine and Shaun Walker, "Trump in Moscow: What Happened at Miss Universe in 2013," *The Guardian*, September 18, 2017, http://www.theguardian.com/us-news/2017/sep/18/trump-in-moscow-what-happened-at-miss-universe-in-2013.

137. Isikoff and Corn, *Russian Roulette*, 18.

137. Mollie Simon and Jim Zarroli, "Timeline of Events: The 2013 Miss Universe Pageant," NPR, July 17, 2017, www.npr.org/2017/07/17/536714404/timeline-of-events-the-2013-miss-universe-pageant.

137. Donald J. Trump (@realDonaldTrump), 2013, "@AgalarovAras I had a great weekend with you and your family. You have done a FANTASTIC Job. TRUMP TOWER-MOSCOW is next. EMIN was WOW!" Twitter, November 11, 2013, 8:39 a.m., https://twitter.com/realdonaldtrump/status/399939505924628480.

137. "Why Did Aras and Emin Agalarov Spend $20 Million on Miss Universe," Crocus Group website,

November 13, 2013, crocusgroup.com/press-center/news/749/.

137. Andrew Roth, "The Man Who Drives Trump's Russia Connection," *Washington Post*, July 22, 2017, http://www.washingtonpost.com/world/europe/the-man-who-drives-trumps-russia-connection/2017/07/21/43485a0e-6c98-11e7-abbc-a53480672286_story.html?utm_term=.ea674ec598f0.

138. "Q&A: The Magnitsky Affair." BBC News. July 11, 2013. Accessed July 14, 2018. https://www.bbc.com/news/world-europe-20626960.

138. Pub. L. 112–208, December 14, 2012, available at https://www.treasury.gov/resource-center/sanctions/Programs/Documents/pl112_208.pdf.

138. Alex Horton, "The Magnitsky Act, Explained," *Washington Post*, July 14, 2017, https://www.washingtonpost.com/news/the-fix/wp/2017/07/14/the-magnitsky-act-explained/?utm_term=.7b7688f60bed.

The Magnitsky Act was originally called the Russia and Moldova Jackson-Vanik Repeal and Sergei Magnitsky Rule of Law Accountability Act of 2012.

138. "Why Does the Kremlin Care So Much About the Magnitsky Act?" *The Atlantic.* July 27, 2017. Accessed July 14, 2018. https://www.theatlantic.com/international/archive/2017/07/magnitsky-act-kremlin/535044/.

138. Adam Taylor, "Ahead of Russian Elections, Putin Releases Official Details of Wealth and Income," *Washington Post*, February 7 2018, http://www.washingtonpost.com/news/worldviews/wp/2018/02/07/ahead-of-russian-elections-putin-releases-official-details-of-wealth-and-income/?utm_term=.177d80a87c6f.

138. "Russia to Ban US Adoptions in Retaliation to Magnitsky Act," *RT*, December 17, 2012, edited December 18, 2012, https://www.rt.com/politics/russia-ban-us-adoptions-183/.

138. Daniel Treisman, "Why Putin Took Crimea: The Gambler in the Kremlin," *Foreign Affairs*, May/June 2016, https://www.foreignaffairs.com/articles/ukraine/2016-04-18/why-putin-took-crimea.

138. "Ukraine and Russia Sanctions." U.S. Department of State. Accessed July 14, 2018. https://www.state.gov/e/eb/tfs/spi/ukrainerussia/.

138. Ibid.

138. Ioffe, Julia. "Why Does the Kremlin Care So Much About the Magnitsky Act?" *The Atlantic.* July 27, 2017. Accessed July 14, 2018. https://www.theatlantic.com/international/archive/2017/07/magnitsky-act-kremlin/535044/.

138. "U.S. Department of the Treasury." Ukraine-/Russia-related Designations and Identification Update; Syria Designations; Kingpin Act Designations; Issuance of Ukraine-/Russia-related General Licenses 12 and 13; Publication of New FAQs and Updated FAQ. Accessed July 14, 2018. https://www.treasury.gov/resource-center/sanctions/OFAC-Enforcement/Pages/20140912.aspx.

139. Ebola (Ebola Virus Disease), Centers for Disease Control and Prevention website, http://www.cdc.gov/

vhf/ebola/history/2014-2016-outbreak/index.html
(accessed July 7, 2018).

139. Ben Guarino, "Shaking Hands Is 'Barbaric':
Donald Trump, the Germaphobe in Chief,"
Washington Post, January 12, 2017, http://
www.washingtonpost.com/news/morning-mix/
wp/2017/01/12/shaking-hands-is-barbaric-
donald-trump-the-germaphobe-in-chief/?utm_
term=.01377d6845e3.

139. Brian Tashman, "Donald Trump: Ebola-Infected
Immigrants Will 'Just Walk Into the Country' Over
Mexican Border," Right Wing Watch, October 16,
2015, http://www.rightwingwatch.org/post/donald-
trump-ebola-infected-immigrants-will-just-walk-
into-the-country-over-mexican-border/ (audio clip
at Ebola-Infected Immigrants Can Walk Across the
Border, SoundCloud (1:30), https://soundcloud.com/
rightwingwatch/trump-ebola-infected-immigrants-
can-walk-across-the-border).

139. Donald J. Trump (@realDonaldTrump), 2013,
"If this doctor, who so recklessly flew into New York
from West Africa, has Ebola, then Obama should
apologize to the American people & resign!" Twitter,
October 23, 2014, 4:38 p.m., https://twitter.com/
realdonaldtrump/status/525431218910027776.

139. "Trump Twitter Archive." Trump Twitter
Archive. Accessed July 14, 2018. http://www.
trumptwitterarchive.com/.

139. Donald J. Trump (@realDonaldTrump), 2013, "If
Obama resigns from office now, thereby doing a great
service to the country—I will give him free lifetime
golf at any one of my courses!" Twitter, September
10, 2014, https://twitter.com/realdonaldtrump/
status/509814075787051008.

139. Donald Trump, "Donald Trump: Central Park
Five Settlement Is a 'Disgrace,'" *New York Daily News*,
June 21, 2014, http://www.nydailynews.com/new-york/
nyc-crime/donald-trump-central-park-settlement-
disgrace-article-1.1838467.

139. Ibid.

140. Images, DON EMMERT/AFP/Getty. "The
Celebrity Apprentice Ratings Haven't Been Great for a
Long, Long Time." *Vulture*, www.vulture.com/2017/01/
celebrity-apprentice-ratings-were-down-for-years.
html.

140. Al Weaver, "Donald Trump Slams Romney 2016:
'He Choked like a Dog' Last Time [VIDEO]," *The Daily
Caller*, January 19, 2015, video (2:13) and transcript at
http://www.dailycaller.com/2015/01/19/donald-trump-
slams-romney-2016-he-choked-like-a-dog-last-time-
video/.

140. Jeremy Diamond, "Donald Trump
Launches Presidential Exploratory
Committee," CNN online, March 18, 2015,
http://www.cnn.com/2015/03/18/politics/
donald-trump-2016-elections-exploratory-committee/.

140. Paul Feely, "Trump Won't Renew 'Apprentice'
so That He Might Focus on a Presidential Run,"
UL, February 27, 2015, http://www.unionleader.
com/apps/pbcs.dll/article?AID=%2F20150227%2
FNEWS0605%2F150229334%2F1010%2FArt.

141. Jose A. DelReal, "About That Donald Trump
Speech at CPAC . . ." *The Washington Post*, February
27, 2015, http://www.washingtonpost.com/news/post-
politics/wp/2015/02/27/about-that-donald-trump-
speech-at-cpac/?utm_term=.4ab603eb0f45.

141. Van Susteren, Greta. "Trump Forms Exploratory
Committee: 'I'm Very Serious . . . The Country Is in
Very Serious Trouble'." Fox News. Accessed July 14,
2018. http://www.foxnews.com/transcript/2015/03/19/
trump-forms-exploratory-committee-im-very-serious-
country-very-serious-trouble.html.

141. Donald J. Trump (@realDonaldTrump), 2015,
"Rodolfo Rosas Moya and his pals in Mexico owe
me a lot of money. Disgusting & Slow Mexico court
system. Mexico is not a U.S. friend." Twitter, April 16,
2015, 12:41 p.m., https://twitter.com/realdonaldtrump/
status/588789316836528128.

141. Donald J. Trump (@realDonaldTrump), 2015,
"Mexico's court system is a dishonest joke. I am owed
a lot of money & nothing happens." Twitter, April 16,
2015, 12:41 p.m., https://twitter.com/realdonaldtrump/
status/588789384209686528.

141. Trump, Donald J. "ISIS Is Operating a Training
Camp 8 Miles outside Our Southern Border Http://t.
co/P8arBncOOA We Need a Wall. Deduct Costs from
Mexico!" Twitter. April 17, 2015. Accessed July 14,
2018. https://mobile.twitter.com/realdonaldtrump/
status/589055094819258369.

141. "Is ISIS on the U.S.-Mexican Border?" *Snopes*,
April 20, 2015, http://www.snopes.com/fact-check/
tijuana-transfer/.

141. Donald J. Trump (@realDonaldTrump), 2015,
"For all of the haters and losers out there sorry, I
never went bankrupt—but I did build a world class
company and employ many people!" Twitter, April 18,
2015, 4:21 a.m., https://twitter.com/realDonaldTrump/
status/589388289456660480.

142. David Wright, "Trump Defends 'Brilliantly' Using
Bankruptcy Laws," CNN online, June 22, 2016, http://
www.cnn.com/2016/06/22/politics/donald-trump-
defends-bankruptcy-history/index.html.

142. Trump, Donald J. "Billions of Dollars Spent
on Baltimore and It's Still a Total Mess. Leadership
Is Needed, Not Dollars. Our Whole Country Is
Going to Hell!" Twitter. May 1, 2015. Accessed July
14, 2018. https://twitter.com/realdonaldtrump/
status/594144659032576001.

142. Trump, Donald J. "Oil Is Under $50/barrel.
Now Is the Time to Increase Sanctions against Iran,
Not Lift Them. No Deal Is Better than a Bad Deal.
#ArtOfTheDeal." Twitter. April 2, 2015. Accessed July
14, 2018. https://mobile.twitter.com/realdonaldtrump/
status/583734218162855938.

142. Donald J. Trump (@realDonaldTrump),
2015, "On this Memorial Day holiday, we honor
our fallen soldiers who have made the greatest
sacrifice for freedom. They are our country's finest."
Twitter, May 22, 2015, 8:58 a.m., https://twitter.com/
realdonaldtrump/status/601779145627033600.

142. Donald J. Trump (@realDonaldTrump), 2015,
"I would like to wish everyone, including all haters
and losers (of which, sadly, there are many) a truly
happy and enjoyable Memorial Day!" Twitter, May 24,

2015, 1:26 p.m., https://twitter.com/realdonaldtrump/
status/602571404861636608.

142. "Watch Donald Trump's Grand
Escalator Entrance to His Presidential
Announcement." ABC News. Accessed July 14,
2018. https://abcnews.go.com/Politics/video/
watch-donald-trumps-grand-escalator-entrance-

143. "Here's Donald Trump's Presidential
Announcement Speech," *Time*, June
16, 2015, http://www.time.com/3923128/
donald-trump-announcement-speech/.

143. See Federal Election Commission, First General
Counsel's Report, *American Democracy Legal Fund
v. Trump*, MUR 6961, complaint filed August 28, 2015;
report filed March 7, 2016, availble at http://eqs.fec.
gov/eqsdocsMUR/17044405316.pdf (accessed July 7,
2018).

Trump failed to pay the company that hired the
individuals for four months. It took an investigation of
the Federal Election Commission to get his campaign
to produce the $12,000 that was owed.

143. Neate, Rupert. "Donald Trump Announces
US Presidential Run with Eccentric Speech." *The
Guardian*. June 16, 2015. Accessed July 14, 2018.

143. "Donald Trump's Presidential
Announcement Speech." *Time*. June 16, 2015.
Accessed July 14, 2018. http://time.com/3923128/
donald-trump-announcement-speech/.

143. "Here's Donald Trump's Presidential
Announcement Speech," *Time*, June
16, 2015, http://www.time.com/3923128/
donald-trump-announcement-speech/.

143. Ibid.

144. Ibid.

144. "First Hour of Trump Campaign Coverage
Told Us Everything We Need to Know." CNNMoney.
Accessed July 15, 2018. https://money.cnn.
com/2016/06/16/media/trump-announcement-one-
year-later/index.html.

144 Burns, Alexander. "Choice Words from Donald
Trump, Presidential Candidate." *The New York Times*.
June 16, 2015. Accessed July 15, 2018. https://www.
nytimes.com/politics/first-draft/2015/06/16/choice-
words-from-donald-trump-presidential-candidate/.

147. Trump and Schwartz, 175.

148. Justin Wolfers, "If You're a Betting Man, It's Time
to Start Believing Donald Trump," *New York Times*,
June 9, 2015, http://www.nytimes.com/2015/06/10/
upshot/if-youre-a-betting-man-its-time-to-start-
believing-donald-trump.html.

148. Katie Glueck, "The Trump Show Hits
New Hampshire," *Politico*, June 17, 2015, as
updated, http://www.politico.com/story/2015/06/
the-trump-show-hits-nh-119137.

148. Niraj Chokshi, "The 100-Plus Times Donald
Trump Assured Us That America Is a Laughingstock,"
The Washington Post, January 27, 2016, http://www.
washingtonpost.com/news/the-fix/wp/2016/01/27/
the-100-plus-times-donald-trump-has-assured-us-

the-united-states-is-a-laughingstock/?utm_term=.
a236640c78a7.

149. "Trump in 1999: 'I Am Very Pro-Choice,'" NBC
News, Meet the Press (video), 1:22, October 24, 1999,
http://www.nbcnews.com/meet-the-press/video/
trump-in-1999-i-am-very-pro-choice-480297539914
(accessed July 7, 2018).

149. Glueck. "The Trump Show Hits New Hampshire."

149. Ibid.

150. See Memorandum for Sarah Sanders from Ronny
L. Jackson, MD, The President's Periodic Physical
Exam, January 16, 2018, https://www.whitehouse.gov/
wp-content/uploads/2018/01/Summary-of-Physical-
Exam-for-President-Trump-12-Jan-2018.pdf.

150. Lewandowski and Bossie, 17–18.

150. "Stormy Daniels' Explosive Full Interview
on Donald Trump Affair: 'I Can Describe His
Junk Perfectly' (EXCLUSIVE)," *In Touch*, March
25, 2018, http://www.intouchweekly.com/posts/
stormy-daniels-full-interview-151788.

150. Bruce Feirstein, "Trump's War on 'Losers': The
Early Years," *Vanity Fair*, August 12, 2015, www.
vanityfair.com/news/2015/08/spy-vs-trump.

150. Graydon Carter, "Steel Traps and Short Fingers,"
Vanity Fair, April 26, 2016, http://www.vanityfair.com/
culture/2015/10/graydon-carter-donald-trump.

151. Ibid.

151. Donald J. Trump (@realDonaldTrump), 2015,
"Sadly, I will no longer be doing @foxandfriends at
7:00 A.M. on Mondays. This is because I am running for
president and law prohibits. LOVE!" Twitter, June 22,
2015, 3:31 a.m., https://twitter.com/realdonaldtrump/
status/612930889920684032.

151. Lewandowski and Bossie. 17–18.

151. "Trump's Twitter Feed." Politico Magazine. April
26, 2016. Accessed July 15, 2018. https://www.politico.
com/magazine/gallery/2016/04/donald-trump-
twitter-account-history-social-media-campaign-
000631?slide=4.

151. Perkins, Lucy. "NBCUniversal Is Cutting
Ties With Donald Trump." NPR. June 29, 2015.
Accessed July 15, 2018. https://www.npr.org/
sections/thetwo-way/2015/06/29/418619850/
nbcuniversal-is-cutting-ties-with-donald-trump.

151. Killoran, Ellen. "Donald Trump's Miss USA
Pageant Won't Air On NBC: Maybe It's Time To
Retire The Crown." Forbes. October 21, 2015.
Accessed July 15, 2018. https://www.forbes.com/sites/
ellenkilloran/2015/06/30/donald-trumps-miss-usa-
pageant-wont-air-on-nbc-or-anywhere-maybe-its-
time-to-retire-the-crown/.

151. Littleton, Cynthia. "Donald Trump, Univision
Settle $500 Million Miss Universe Lawsuit." Variety.
February 11, 2016. Accessed July 15, 2018. https://
variety.com/2016/tv/news/donald-trump-univision-
settle-miss-universe-lawsuit-1201703508/.

152. Doug Ferguson, "Golf Groups Distance
Themselves from Trump after Immigration Remarks,"
PGA website, July 1, 2015, http://www.pga.com/news/

industry-news/golf-groups-distance-themselves-trump-after-immigration-remarks.

152. Andrew Anglin, "The Daily Stormer Endorses Donald Trump for President," *Daily Stormer*, June 28, 2015, http://www.dailystormer.name/the-daily-stormer-endorses-donald-trump-for-president/.

152. Wang, Amy B. "Donald Trump Plans to Immediately Deport 2 Million to 3 Million Undocumented Immigrants." *The Washington Post*. November 14, 2016. Accessed July 15, 2018. https://www.washingtonpost.com/news/the-fix/wp/2016/11/13/donald-trump-plans-to-immediately-deport-2-to-3-million-undocumented-immigrants/.

152. "Nancy Pelosi Claims 76% of Americans Support the DREAM Act." @politifact. September 20, 2017. Accessed July 15, 2018. http://www.politifact.com/california/statements/2017/sep/19/nancy-pelosi/nancy-pelosi-claims-three-quarters-americans-suppo/.

152. "Projections of the Size and Composition of the U.S. Population: 2014 to 2060." Census.gov. Census.gov/content/dam/Census/library/publications/2015/demo/p25-1143.pdf.

152. Kenneth Lim, "Michael Moore Prediction: Donald Trump Will Win," *The Inquisitr*, August 2, 2016, http://www.inquisitr.com/3375236/michael-moore-prediction-donald-trump-will-win/.

152. Evan Osnos, "Donald Trump and the White Nationalists," *New Yorker*, August 28, 2017, http://www.newyorker.com/magazine/2015/08/31/the-fearful-and-the-frustrated.

153. Ibid.

153. Lee, MJ. "Trump Draws Thousands to Phoenix Rally-CNNPolitics." CNN. July 12, 2015. Accessed July 15, 2018. https://www.cnn.com/2015/07/11/politics/donald-trump-phoenix-rally/index.html.

153. Ryan Lizza, "John McCain Has a Few Things to Say About Donald Trump," *New Yorker*, July 16, 2015, https://www.newyorker.com/news/news-desk/john-mccain-has-a-few-things-to-say-about-donald-trump?intcid=mod-latest.

153. Even as the population of immigrants has increased, crime in the nation has decreased. See Anna Flagg, "The Myth of the Criminal Immigrant," *New York Times*, March 30, 2018, http://www.nytimes.com/interactive/2018/03/30/upshot/crime-immigration-myth.html. Four studies by social scientists demonstrate that illegal immigration has neither increased violent crime nor increased the number of arrests for nonviolent crime including driving while intoxicated; nor has it increased drug or alcohol overdoses.

See John Burnett, "Illegal Immigration Does Not Increase Violent Crime, 4 Studies Show," NPR online, May 2, 2018, audio (3:53) and transcript at http://www.npr.org/2018/05/02/607652253/studies-say-illegal-immigration-does-not-increase-violent-crime.

What's more, immigration from Mexico has decreased. In 2015, there were fewer undocumented Mexican immigrants in the country than in 2009, and fewer still than in 2007, when undocumented immigrants made up 4 percent of the U.S. population. Since 2013, more immigrants have come to the United States from China and India than Mexico. See Jens Manuel Krogstad, Jeffrey S. Passel, and D'Vera Cohn, "5 Facts about Illegal Immigration in the U.S." Pew Research Center, April 27, 2017, http://www.pewresearch.org/fact-tank/2017/04/27/5-facts-about-illegal-immigration-in-the-u-s/.

153. Ryan Lizza, "John McCain Has a Few Things to Say About Donald Trump." *The New Yorker*. https://www.newyorker.com/news/news-desk/johnmccain-has-a-few-things-to-say-about-donald-trump.

153. Dylan Stableford, "Donald Trump Is 'a Wrecking Ball for the Future of the Republican Party,' Lindsey Graham Says," Yahoo! News, July 12, 2015, http://www.yahoo.com/news/donald-trump-is-a-wrecking-ball-for-the-future-of-123912263661.html.

153. Ibid.

154. See, for example, Michael Signer, "The Electoral College Was Created to Stop Demagogues Like Trump," *Time*, November 17, 2016, http://time.com/4575119/electoral-college-demagogues/.

154. Carroll, James. "The True Nature of John McCain's Heroism." *The New Yorker*. July 21, 2017. Accessed July 15, 2018. https://www.newyorker.com/news/news-desk/the-true-nature-of-john-mccains-heroism.

154. Amy Davidson Sorkin, "Trump and the Art of the War Hero," *New Yorker*, July 20, 2015, http://www.newyorker.com/news/amy-davidson/trump-and-the-art-of-the-war-hero.

154. "Trump and His Apologists." *Wall Street Journal*, op-ed, July 19, 2015, http://www.wsj.com/articles/trump-and-his-apologists-1437345060.

154. Ibid.

155. Todd Starnes, "Tone It down? No Way! Donald Trump Needs to Crank up the Volume." FOX online, July 9, 2015, http://www.foxnews.com/opinion/2015/07/09/donald-trump-was-taken-to-gop-woodshed-wednesday.html.

155. Jason Devaney, "Rush Limbaugh: 'Trump Has Changed the Entire Debate on Immigration,'" *Newsmax*, July 8, 2015, http://www.newsmax.com/Headline/rush-Limbaugh-Donald-Trump-changed-debate/2015/07/08/id/654107/.

155. Ibid.

156. Michael D'Antonio, "Trump Has a Long History of Seeking Political Favors. Here's How It Began." *Fortune*, September 13, 2016, http://www.fortune.com/2016/09/13/donald-trump-politicians-donations/.

156. "Donald Trump, Pam Bondi and $25K: Was It Pay to Play?" @politifact. Accessed July 15, 2018. http://www.politifact.com/florida/article/2016/sep/21/donald-trump-pam-bondi-and-25k-was-it-pay-play/.

157. "Editorial: Trump Should Pull the Plug on His Bloviating Side Show," *Des Moines Register*, op-ed, July 20, 2015, updated July 21, 2015, http://www.desmoinesregister.com/story/opinion/editorials/caucus/2015/07/20/donald-trump-end-campaign/30439253/.

157. Ibid.

157. Barbaro, Michael, and Megan Twohey. "Crossing the Line: How Donald Trump Behaved With Women in Private." *The New York Times*. May 14, 2016. Accessed July 15, 2018. https://www.nytimes.com/2016/05/15/us/politics/donald-trump-women.html?action=click.

157. Kranish and Fisher, *Trump Revealed*, 140–41.

157. Brandy Zadrozny and Tim Mak, "Ex-Wife: Donald Trump Made Me Feel 'Violated' During Sex," *The Daily Beast*, July 27, 2015, http://www.thedailybeast.com/ex-wife-donald-trump-made-me-feel-violated-during-sex.

157. Gass, Nick. "Trump Attacks Forbes for Saying His Net Worth Is Actually $4.5 Billion." *Politico*. September 29, 2015. Accessed July 15, 2018. https://www.politico.com/story/2015/09/donald-trump-net-worth-forbes-214204.

157. Donald J. Trump (@realDonaldTrump), 2015, "I wish good luck to all of the Republican candidates that traveled to California to beg for money etc. from the Koch Brothers. Puppets?" Twitter, August 2, 2015, 7 a.m., https://twitter.com/realdonaldtrump/status/627841345789558788.

158. "Donald Trump, Pam Bondi and $25K: Was It Pay to Play?"

158. Aaron Blake, "Here Are the Megyn Kelly Questions That Donald Trump Is Still Sore About," *Washington Post*, January 26, 2016, http://www.washingtonpost.com/news/the-fix/wp/2016/01/26/here-are-the-megyn-kelly-questions-that-donald-trump-is-still-sore-about/?utm_term=.9ea5b7279a65

"Transcript: Read the Full Text of the Primetime Republican Debate," *Time*, August 7, 2015, updated August 11, 2015, http://www.time.com/3988276/republican-debate-primetime-transcript-full-text/.

158. Ibid.

158. Ibid.

158. Ibid.

158. Philip Rucker, "Trump Says Fox's Megyn Kelly Had 'Blood Coming out of Her Wherever,'" *Washington Post*, August 8, 2015, http://www.washingtonpost.com/news/post-politics/wp/2015/08/07/trump-says-foxs-megyn-kelly-had-blood-coming-out-of-her-wherever/?utm_term=.127c031bcdbe.

159. David Lightman, "Trump's Latest Megyn Kelly Insult Gets Him Booted from Conservative Program," McClatchy, DC Bureau, August 8, 2015, as updated, http://www.mcclatchydc.com/news/politics-government/election/article30484860.html.

159. Donald J. Trump (@realDonaldTrump), 2015, "I just realized that if you listen to Carly Fiorina for more than ten minutes straight, you develop a massive headache. She has zero chance!" Twitter, August 9 2015, 12:06 p.m., https://twitter.com/realdonaldtrump/status/630455091091374080?lang=en.

159. See Halim Shebaya, "Trump 'Tells It Like It Is,'" *HuffPost*, The Blog, May 5, 2016, updated May 6, 2017, https://www.huffingtonpost.com/halim-shebaya/trump-tells-it-like-it-is_b_9836974.html.

159. Ben Jacobs, "Donald Trump Expands Lead in Iowa in First Poll Since Republican Debate," *Guardian*, August 12, 2015, https://www.theguardian.com/us-news/2015/aug/12/donald-trump-expands-lead-iowa-poll.

159. See "Immigration Reform that Will Make America Great Again," document, accessed July 8, 2018, https://assets.donaldjtrump.com/Immigration-Reform-Trump.pdf.

The Fourteenth Amendment to the U.S. Constitution was ratified in 1868, after the Civil War, and was meant to ensure formerly enslaved people were recognized as citizens. Birthright citizenship to all born on U.S. soil has been the law of the land since *United States v. Wong Kim Ark*, 169 U.S. 649 (1898), a case involving an American-born man of Chinese descent who was refused reentry to the country after visiting his parents overseas. Since that Supreme Court decision, being born in America is sufficient for citizenship.

159. Elise Foley, "Trump Would Deport Parents of U.S. Citizens But Keep Families Together," *HuffPost*, August 16, 2015, https://www.huffingtonpost.com/entry/donald-trump-immigration-plan_us_55d0b5cde4b07addcb433ecd.

160. Luke Harding, *Collusion: Secret Meetings, Dirty Money, and How Russia Helped Donald Trump Win*. New York: Vintage Books, 2017, 118, 123–25.

160. Lorenzo Ferrigno, "Donald Trump: Boston Beating Is 'Terrible,'" CNN online, August 21, 2015, as updated, http://www.cnn.com/2015/08/20/politics/donald-trump-immigration-boston-beating/index.html.

160. Justin Wm. Moyer, "Trump Says Fans Are 'Very Passionate' After Hearing One of Them Allegedly Assaulted Hispanic Man," *Washington Post*, August 21, 2015, https://www.washingtonpost.com/news/morning-mix/wp/2015/08/21/trump-says-fans-are-very-passionate-after-hearing-one-of-them-allegedly-assaulted-hispanic-man/?utm_term=.faff5d197aa9.

160. "Fox & Friends Hosts Have No Reaction To Donald Trump Saying Of Beaten Black Lives Matter Protester "Maybe He Should Have Been Roughed Up."" Media Matters for America. November 22, 2015. Accessed August 28, 2018. https://www.mediamatters.org/video/2015/11/22/fox-amp-friends-hosts-have-no-reaction-to-donal/207018.

160. "Trump Urges Crowd to 'knock the Crap out Of' Anyone with Tomatoes." Politico. February 1, 2016. Accessed August 28, 2018. https://www.politico.com/video/2016/02/trump-urges-crowd-to-knock-the-crap-out-of-anyone-with-tomatoes-041695..

160. "Donald Trump Town Hall Meeting in Rochester, New Hampshire." C-SPAN.org | National Politics | History | Nonfiction Books. Accessed July 15, 2018. 16:55-17:24. https://www.c-span.org/video/?328138-1%2Fdonald-trump-town-hall-meeting-rochester-hampshire.

161. Amy Davidson Sorkin, "Trump and the Man in the T-Shirt," *New Yorker*, September 18, 2015, http://www.newyorker.com/news/amy-davidson/trump-and-the-man-in-the-t-shirt.

161. Ibid.

161. Ibid.

161. Ibid.

161. Ibid.

161. Associated Press. "McCain Counters Obama 'Arab' Question." YouTube. October 11, 2008. Accessed July 15, 2018. https://m.youtube.com/watch?v=jrnRU3ocIH4.

161. Ibid.

161. Ibid.

162. Philip Bump, "Donald Trump and the 'Terrorist Training Camps' Conspiracy Theory, Explained," *Washington Post*, September 18, 2015, http://www.washingtonpost.com/news/the-fix/wp/2015/09/18/donald-trump-and-the-terrorist-training-camps-conspiracy-theory-explained/?utm_term=.eeff19abacaf.

162. The fear that terrorists are likely to kill Americans is an understandable one, given 9/11. But it's also overblown. According to the CATO Institute, between 1975 and 2015, terrorists murdered 3,432 Americans on U.S. soil, including the 2,983 killed on 9/11. Alex Nowrasteh, "Terrorism and Immigration: A Risk Analysis," Cato Institute, Policy Analysis No. 798, September 13, 2016, https://object.cato.org/sites/cato.org/files/pubs/pdf/pa798_1_1.pdf. This means, on average, eighty-four Americans a year have been killed by terrorists. The average sinks to eleven per year if you take 9/11 out of the equation.

Gun-related homicides in America, in contrast, were 12,979 for 2015—meaning an American is 154 times more likely to be shot to death than killed by a terrorist. See Centers for Disease Control and Prevention website, https://www.cdc.gov/nchs/fastats/homicide.htm (accessed July 8, 2018).

In 2017, the number of homicides had increased to 15,549. See "The First Estimate of 2017 Gun Deaths Is In," The Trace, January 9, 2018, updated April 25, 2018, https://www.thetrace.org/rounds/gun-deaths-increase-2017/.

What's more, domestic terrorism is rapidly becoming a concern: extremists in 2015 killed at least 52 people, more than the combined total for 2013 and 2014. See Murder and Extremism in the United States in 2015, an Anti-Defamation League Report, ADL website, https://www.adl.org/sites/default/files/documents/assets/pdf/combating-hate/Murder-and-Extremism-in-the-United-States-in-2015-web.pdf.

The likelihood of dying at the hands of a refugee in a terrorist attack is even smaller, according to the libertarian Cato Institute, which has conducted a risk analysis of terrorism and immigration and states the chance as "1 in 3.64 *billion* per year while the chance of being murdered in an attack committed by an illegal immigrant is . . . 1 in 10.9 *billion* per year. . . . the chance of being murdered by a tourist on a B visa . . . is 1 in 3.9 million per year." See Alex Nowrasteh, "Terrorism and Immigration: A Risk Analysis," Cato Institute, Policy Analysis, September 13, 2016, No. 798, https://object.cato.org/sites/cato.org/files/pubs/pdf/pa798_1_1.pdf.

You are more likely to win a Powerball jackpot than be killed by a refugee. See Aimee Picchi, "Powerball and Mega Millions: What Are the Odds of Winning?" CBS,

MoneyWatch, December 29, 2017, as updated, http://www.cbsnews.com/news/powerball-mega-millions-lottery-odds-of-winning/ (noting that odds are 1 in 292 million).

162. See Donald J. Trump (@realDonaldTrump), 2014, "NBC News just called it the great freeze—coldest weather in years. Is our country still spending money on the GLOBAL WARMING HOAX?", Twitter, January 25, 2014, 3:48 p.m., https://twitter.com/realDonaldTrump/status/427226424987385856; see generally Trump Twitter Archive, http://www.trumptwitterarchive.com/archive/hoax.

162. Donald J. Trump (@realDonaldTrump), 2012, Twitter, November 6, 2012, 11:15 a.m., https://twitter.com/realdonaldtrump/status/265895292191248385.

According to NASA, 97 percent of scientists who are actively publishing about climate science research agree: "Climate-warming trends over the past century are extremely likely due to human activities. In addition, most of the leading scientific organizations worldwide have issued public statements endorsing this position." NASA, "Scientific Consensus: Earth's Climate Is Warming," NASA website, 8 February 2018, climate.nasa.gov/scientific-consensus/.

163. Clinton, Josh, and Carrie Roush. "Poll: Persistent Partisan Divide Over 'Birther' Question." NBCNews.com. August 10, 2016. Accessed July 15, 2018. https://www.nbcnews.com/politics/2016-election/poll-persistent-partisan-divide-over-birther-question-n627446.

163. "Donald Trump's File." @politifact. Accessed July 15, 2018. http://www.politifact.com/personalities/donald-trump/.

163. Angie Drobnic Hilan and Linda Qiu, "2015 Lie of the Year: The Campaign Misstatements of Donald Trump," Politifact, December 21, 2015, http://www.politifact.com/truth-o-meter/article/2015/dec/21/2015-lie-year-donald-trump-campaign-misstatements/.

163. Spayd, Liz. "Not 'She Said, He Said.' Mockery, Plain and Simple," *The New York Times*, 10 Jan. 2017, www.nytimes.com/2017/01/10/public-editor/trump-streep-golden-globes.html.

163. "Lesley Stahl: Trump Admitted Mission to 'Discredit' Press," CBS News, May 23, 2018, as updated, http://www.cbsnews.com/news/lesley-stahl-donald-trump-said-attacking-press-to-discredit-negative-stories/.

163. Diamond, Jeremy. "Donald Trump: I Whine until I Win-CNNPolitics." CNN. August 11, 2015. Accessed July 15, 2018. https://www.cnn.com/2015/08/11/politics/donald-trump-refutes-third-party-run-report/index.html.

163. Scott Shane and Mark Mazzetti, "Inside a 3-Year Russian Campaign to Influence U.S. Voters." *New York Times*, February 16, 2018, http://www.nytimes.com/2018/02/16/us/politics/russia-mueller-election.html.

163. See Ryan C. Maness and Margarita Jaitner, "There's More to Russia's Cyber Interference than the Mueller Probe Suggests," *Washington Post*, March 12, 2018, https://www.washingtonpost.com/news/monkey-cage/wp/2018/03/12/

theres-more-to-russias-cyber-meddling-than-the-mueller-probe-suggests/?utm_term=.13e90fbbf2a6.

163. Ibid.

Jennifer Hansler, "Former US Ambassador to Russia: Putin 'Absolutely' Wanted Trump to Win," CNN politics, The Axe Files, May 24, 2018, http://www.cnn.com/2018/05/24/politics/michael-mcfaul-axe-files/index.html.

165. Donald J. Trump (@realDonaldTrump), 2016, Twitter, May 20, 2016, 9:09 a.m., https://twitter.com/realdonaldtrump/status/733691067829215232.

165. "Donald Trump on ISIS-'I Would Bomb the SHIT out of 'em!'" YouTube. November 12, 2015. Accessed July 15, 2018. https://m.youtube.com/watch?v=aWejiXvd-P8.

165. LoBianco, Tom. "Donald Trump on Terrorists: 'Take out Their Families,'" CNN. December 3, 2015. Accessed July 15, 2018. https://www.cnn.com/2015/12/02/politics/donald-trump-terrorists-families/index.html.

165. "Geneva Conventions Bar Donald Trump's Idea of Killing Terrorists' Families, as Rand Paul Says." @politifact. Accessed July 15, 2018. http://www.politifact.com/truth-o-meter/statements/2015/dec/17/rand-paul/rand-pauls-right-geneva-conventions-bar-donald-tru/.

165. In Campaigns, Elections & Parties, Journalistic Practice, Papers, Politics & Government, Research. "News Coverage of the 2016 General Election: How the Press Failed the Voters." Shorenstein Center. November 16, 2017. Accessed July 15, 2018. https://shorensteincenter.org/news-coverage-2016-general-election/?platform=hootsuite.

165. Agiesta, Jennifer. "Donald Trump Dominates GOP Field Heading into 2016." CNN. December 24, 2015. Accessed July 15, 2018. https://www.cnn.com/2015/12/23/politics/donald-trump-ted-cruz-cnn-orc-poll/index.html.

166. Jenna Johnson, "Donald Trump on Waterboarding: 'If It Doesn't Work, They Deserve It Anyway,'" *Washington Post*, November 23, 2015, video (1:29) and article at http://www.washingtonpost.com/news/post-politics/wp/2015/11/23/donald-trump-on-waterboarding-if-it-doesnt-work-they-deserve-it-anyway/?noredirect=on&utm_term=.4a73cdfe7bc8.

166. Ibid.

Radicalized Islamic terrorists have beheaded people, including Westerners. They also use cages as a form of public humiliation and torture. The *Daily Beast* reported that the Islamic State has a cage located in a public square where beheadings take place, and almost always there is someone inside as punishment for a variety of alleged offenses. The punishment might include being locked in the cage for a day or three days. The informant did not mention any cases of using the cage for drownings. Michael Weiss, "Inside ISIS's Torture Brigades," *The Daily Beast*, November 17, 2015, www.thedailybeast.com/inside-isiss-torture-brigades. There have been no reports of cages built for mass drownings.

166. Jenna Johnson, "Donald Trump on Waterboarding: 'If It Doesn't Work, They Deserve It Anyway.'"

167. Jean Maria Arrigo & Richard V. Wagner (2007) Psychologists and Military Interrogators Rethink the Psychology of Torture, Peace and Conflict: Journal of Peace Psychology, 13:4-393-309, DOI, https://doi.org/10.1080/1078190701665550

167. Raj Persaud, M.D. and Peter Bruggen, M.D., "Does Torture Work?" *Psychology Today*, Jauary 26, 2017, http://www.psychologytoday.com/us/blog/slightly-blighty/201701/does-torture-work.

167. The U.S. report on the subject to the United Nations in 1999 reads, "Torture is prohibited by law throughout the United States. It is categorically denounced as a matter of policy and as a tool of state authority. Every act constituting torture under the Convention constitutes a criminal offence under the law of the United States. No official of the Government, federal, state or local, civilian or military, is authorized to commit or to instruct anyone else to commit torture." United Nations, Convention against Torture and Other Cruel, Inhuman or Degrading Treatent or Punishment, Consideration of Reports Submitted by States Parties Under Article 19 of the Convention, United States of America, February 9, 2000, Introduction, para. 6, https://www.state.gov/documents/organization/100296.pdf. The United States is a party to the convention cited.

167. Louis Nelson, "Trump: 'I Am the Law and Order Candidate,'" *Politico*, July 11, 2016, http://www.politico.com/story/2016/07/trump-law-order-candidate-225372.

167. "Donald Trump's File." @politifact. Accessed July 15, 2018. http://www.politifact.com/personalities/donald-trump/.

167. Ibid.

168. "Here's the Preliminary Deal to Bring a Trump Tower to Moscow," CNN online, September 8, 2017, http://www.cnn.com/2017/09/08/politics/trump-moscow-document/index.html (includes pdf of agreement).

168. Ibid.

169. Drew Harwell and Anu Narayanswamy, "A Scramble to Assess the Dangers of President-Elect Donald Trump's Global Business Empire," *Washington Post*, November 20, 2016, http://www.washingtonpost.com/business/economy/a-scramble-to-assess-the-dangers-of-president-elects-global-business-empire/2016/11/20/1bbdc2a2-ad18-11e6-a31b4b6397e625d0_story.html.

169. Karen Tumulty, "How Donald Trump Came up with 'Make America Great Again,'" *Washington Post*, January 18, 2017, https://www.washingtonpost.com/politics/how-donald-trump-came-up-with-make-america-great-again/2017/01/17/fb6acf5e-dbf7-11e6-ad42-f3375f271c9c_story.html?utm_term=.c198ae2079ce.

169. Drew Harwell and Anu Narayanswamy, "A Scramble to Assess the Dangers of President-Elect Donald Trump's Global Business Empire."

170. Matt Apuzzo and Maggie Haberman, "Trump Associate Boasted that Moscow Business Deal 'Will Get Donald Elected,'" *New York Times*, August 28, 2017, http://www.nytimes.com/2017/08/28/politics/trump-tower-putin-felix-sater.html.

170. Ibid.

170. Eugene Kiely, "Timeline of Russia Investigation," FactCheck.org, June 7, 2017, http://www.factcheck.org/2017/06/timeline-russia-investigation/.

170. O'Key, Sean, and CNN. "Russia Hacking Report," DocumentCloud, www.documentcloud.org/documents/3254239-Russia-Hacking-report.html.

171. Chen, Adrian. "The Agency." *The New York Times*, 2 June 2015, www.nytimes.com/2015/06/07/magazine/the-agency.html.

171. "Background to 'Assessing Russian Activities and Intentions in Recent US Elections': The Analytic Process and Cyber Incident Attrribution, Office of the Director of National Intelligence, National Intelligence Council, January 6, 2017 (accessed July 8, 2018),. www.documentcloud.org/documents/3254239-Russia-Hacking-report.html.

171. Zachary Laub and James McBride, "Backgrounder" to "The Group of Seven (G7)," Council on Foreign Relations, May 30, 2017, http://www.cfr.org/backgrounder/group-seven-g7.

171. Robert Windrem, "Guess Who Came to Dinner with Flynn and Putin," NBC News, April 18, 2017, https://www.nbcnews.com/news/world/guess-who-came-dinner-flynn-putin-n742696.

In the United States, media are financially independent from the government. This is what makes it a "free" press. It is free from government control. In contrast, the state-owned RT, formerly known as Russia Today, is an instrumentality of the state.

171. Ibid.

171. Julia Ioffe, "What Is Russia Today?" *Columbia Journalism Review*, September/October 2010, http://archives.cjr.org/feature/what_is_russia_today.php.

172. "Transcript: Michael Flynn on ISIL." Israeli–Palestinian Conflict | *Al Jazeera*, 13 Jan. 2016, www.aljazeera.com/programmes/headtohead/2016/01/transcript-michael-flynn-160104174144334.html.

172. Stephen Braun and Robert Burns. "Flynn, Fired Once by a President, Now Removed by Another," AP, February 14, 2017, http://apnews.com/ce90066b4e20483da79adf21910da0c7.

172. Tim Hains, "FLASHBACK 2015: Mike Flynn's Much-Discussed Guest Appearances On 'Russia Today,'" RealClearPolitics, (videos, 17:55 and 44:51), http://www.realclearpolitics.com/video/2017/05/09/flashback_2015_mike_flynns_much-discussed_guest_appearances_on_russia_today.html.

172. Ibid.

172. Ken Dilanian, "Russians Paid Mike Flynn $45K for Moscow Speech, Documents Show." NBC News, March 16, 2017, http://www.nbcnews.com/news/us-news/russians-paid-mike-flynn-45k-moscow-speech-documents-show-n734506.

172. Luke Harding, *Collusion: Secret Meetings, Dirty Money, and How Russia Helped Donald Trump Win*, 124 (noting that if he earned money from a foreign power, he was supposed to declare it).

172. Jenna Johnson, "Trump Calls for 'Total and Complete Shutdown of Muslims Entering the United States,'" *Washington Post*, December 7, 2015, embedded video (0:26) and story at http://www.washingtonpost.com/news/post-politics/wp/2015/12/07/donald-trump-calls-for-total-and-complete-shutdown-of-muslims-entering-the-united-states/?utm_term=.1c5cee9832bb.

172. Ibid. In the Syria conflict, the United States government has sided with the rebels, while Russia and Iran support the Syrian president. Meanwhile, amidst the chaos, ISIS terrorists have moved in, giving the United States and Russia a shared enemy. Fighting on all sides has destroyed much of the Syrian economy and infrastructure, and millions have fled from violence, chaos, and starvation. "Life and Death in Syria," BBC News, March 15, 2016, www.bbc.co.uk/news/resources/idt-841ebc3a-1be9-493b-8800-2c04890e8fc9.

173. Johnson, "Trump Calls for 'Total and Complete Shutdown of Muslims Entering the United States.'"

173. Tom Barnes, "Trump Doctor's Letter in Full: Full Text of Harold Bornstein's Disputed Note Claiming President Had 'Astonishingly Excellent' Health," May 2, 2018, https://www.independent.co.uk/news/world/americas/trump-doctor-letter-healthiest-harold-bornstein-us-president-ever-full-text-fake-dictated-a8332066.html

Maggie Haberman and Lawrence K. Altman, "Donald Trump Releases Medical Report Calling His Health 'Extraordinary,'" *New York Times*, December 14, 2015, as updated, http://www.nytimes.com/politics/first-draft/2015/12/14/donald-trump-releases-medical-report-calling-his-health-extraordinary/.

173. Ibid.

173. Anna R. Schecter, Chris Francescani, and Tracy Connor, "Trump Doctor Wrote Health Letter in Just 5 Minutes as Limo Waited," NBC News, August 26, 2016, as updated, https://www.nbcnews.com/news/us-news/trump-doctor-wrote-health-letter-just-5-minutes-limo-waited-n638526.

Trump did not admit authoring the letter, but the letter disappeared from the DonaldJTrump.com campaign website after his doctor told reporters the letter had been dictated to him.

173. Theodore Schleifer, "Donald Trump: 'Schlonged' Is Not Vulgar," CNN politics, December 23, 2015, http://www.cnn.com/2015/12/22/politics/donald-trump-schlonged-is-not-vulgar/index.html.

174. *Merriam-Webster* defines *schlong* as "slang, usually vulgar"; "penis." *Merriam-Webster Collegiate Dictionary*, online, 11th ed.

174. Donald J. Trump (@realDonaldTrump), 2009, Twitter, December 23, 2015, 4:47 p.m., https://twitter.com/realdonaldtrump/status/679463426675097600.

174. Rosalind S. Helderman, Carol D. Leonnig, and Tom Hamburger, "Top Trump Organization Executive Asked Putin Aide for Help on Business Deal," *Washington Post*, August 28, 2017, http://www.washingtonpost.com/politics/top-trump-organization-executive-reached-out-to-putin-aide-for-help-on-business-deal/2017/08/28/095aebac-8c16-11e7-84c0-02cc069f2c37_story.html?utm_term=.f28d0468f74c.

174. Ginger Gibson, "Trump Draws Full House at Own Event as He Snubs Fox News Debate," Reuters, January 28, 2016, https://www.reuters.com/article/us-usa-election-trump-idUSKCNOV705T.

175. Lewandowski and Bossie, 92.

175. Ibid., 91. Dinner for Trump would be two Big Macs, two Filet-O-Fish, and a chocolate shake from McDonalds.

175. Ginger Gibson, "Trump Draws Full House at Own Event as He Snubs Fox News Debate."

175. Ibid.

175. "David A. Fahrenthold of *The Washington Post* Wins Pulitzer Prize." The Pulitzer Prizes, www.pulitzer.org/winners/david-fahrenthold.

175. Lewandowski and Bossie, 108.

175. Donald J. Trump (@realDonaldTrump), 2016, Twitter, February 3, 2016, 11:25 a.m., https://twitter.com/realdonaldtrump/status/694964856609439745.

176. Lewandowski and Bossie, 111.

176. Jeremy Carl, "Armageddon for the GOP Establishment," *National Review*, February 10, 2016, https://www.nationalreview.com/corner/trump-cruz-are-nh-winners-armageddon-gop-establishment/.

176. "New Hampshire Primary Exit Poll Analysis: How Trump And Sanders Won." ABC News, ABC News Network, 9 Feb. 2016, abcnews.go.com/PollingUnit/voted-live-hampshire-primary-exit-poll-analysis/story?id=36805930.

177. Graham, David A. "Which Republicans Oppose Donald Trump? A Cheat Sheet." *The Atlantic.* November 8, 2016. Accessed July 16, 2018. https://www.theatlantic.com/politics/archive/2016/11/where-republicans-stand-on-donald-trump-a-cheat-sheet/481449/.

177. Diamond, Jeremy. "Sen. Jeff Sessions Endorses Donald Trump." CNN. February 29, 2016. Accessed July 16, 2018. https://www.cnn.com/2016/02/28/politics/donald-trump-jeff-sessions-endorsement/index.html.

177. Herb, Jeremy, and Marshall Cohen. "Who Is George Papadopoulos?" CNN. October 30, 2017. Accessed July 16, 2018. https://www.cnn.com/2017/10/30/politics/who-is-george-papadopoulos/index.html.

177. Freedman, Dan. "N.Y. GOP's Cox Introduced Carter Page to Trump Campaign." *Times Union.* February 6, 2018. Accessed July 16, 2018. https://www.timesunion.com/7day-state/article/N-Y-GOP-s-Cox-introduced-Carter-Page-to-Trump-12553410.php.

177. "Carter Page Coordinated Russia Trip with Top Trump Campaign Officials." NBCNews.com. Accessed July 16, 2018. https://www.nbcnews.com/news/us-news/carter-page-coordinated-russia-trip-top-trump-campaign-officials-n818206.

177. Calabresi, Massimo, and Alana Abramson. "Carter Page Touted Russia Contacts in 2013 Letter." *Time.* February 4, 2018. Accessed July 16, 2018. http://time.com/5132126/carter-page-russia-2013-letter/.

177. Rosalind S. Helderman, "Memo Points to FBI's Sustained Interest in Carter Page, Ex-Adviser to Trump," *Washington Post*, February 2, 2018, http://www.washingtonpost.com/politics/memo-points-to-fbis-ongoing-interest-in-trump-adviser-carter-page/2018/02/02/89bfdee2-077c-11e8-8777-2a059f168dd2_story.html?utm_term=.b03d9e7ce105.

177. Harding, *Collusion*, 44.

177. Glenn Thrush, "To Charm Trump, Paul Manafort Sold Himself as an Affordable Outsider," *New York Times*, April 8, 2017, http://www.nytimes.com/2017/04/08/us/to-charm-trump-paul-manafort-sold-himself-as-an-affordable-outsider.html.

177. Ibid.

177. Helling, Dave. "Bob Dole Campaign Veterans Are Now Key Advisers to Donald Trump." Kansascity. Accessed July 16, 2018. https://www.kansascity.com/news/politics-government/article82021592.html.

178. Lewandowski and Bossie, 120.

178. Cam Wolf, "Paul Manafort Spent Over $1.3 Million at Clothing Stores," *GQ*, October 30, 2017, http://www.gq.com/story/paul-manafort-indictment-mens-clothing.

178. Stone, Peter. "Trump's New Right-hand Man Has History of Controversial Clients and Deals." *The Guardian.* April 27, 2016. Accessed July 16, 2018. https://www.theguardian.com/us-news/2016/apr/27/paul-manafort-donald-trump-campaign-past-clients.

178. Ibid.

178. Mike McIntire, "Manafort Was in Debt to Pro-Russia Interests, Cyprus Records Show," *New York Times*, July 19, 2017, http://www.nytimes.com/2017/07/19/us/politics/paul-manafort-russia-trump.html.

178. Dilanian, Ken, and Tom Winter. "Paul Manafort Has a New Legal Headache. A Russian Oligarch Is Suing Him." NBCNews.com. Accessed July 16, 2018. https://www.nbcnews.com/news/us-news/russian-oligarch-oleg-deripaska-sues-manafort-gates-ny-n836586.

178. See Jeremy Diamond, "Donald Trump's Bromance with Vladimir Putin," CNN politics, December 19, 2015, as updated, https://www.cnn.com/2015/12/18/politics/donald-trump-vladimir-putin-bromance/index.html.

179. Jeremy Diamond, "Timeline: Donald Trump's Praise for Vladimir Putin," CNN politics, July 29, 2016, http://www.cnn.com/2016/07/28/politics/donald-trump-vladimir-putin-quotes/.

179. Barrett, Brian. "DNC Lawsuit Reveals Key Details About Devastating 2016 Hack." *Wired.* April 21, 2018. Accessed July 16, 2018. https://www.wired.com/story/dnc-lawsuit-reveals-key-details-2016-hack/.

179. Sharon Lafraniere, Mark Mazzetti, and Matt Apuzzo, "How the Russia Inquiry Began: A Campaign Aide, Drinks and Talk of Political Dirt," *New York Times*, December 30, 2017, www.nytimes.com/2017/12/30/us/politics/how-fbi-russia-investigation-began-george-papadopoulos.html.

179. Meg Kelly, "All the Known Times the Trump Campaign Met with Russians," *Washington Post*, November 13, 2017, http://www.washingtonpost.com/news/fact-checker/wp/2017/11/13/all-of-the-known-times-the-trump-campaign-met-with-russians/?utm_term=.07594a2267d3.

179. Ibid.

180. David Sherfinski, "Donald Trump Questions NATO's Usefulness in Post-Cold War Era," *Washington Times*, March 28, 2016, https://www.washingtontimes.com/news/2016/mar/28/donald-trump-nato-very-obsolete/.

180. NATO website, Basic Points, https://www.nato.int/nato-welcome/ (accessed July 8, 2018).

180. Joel B. Pollak, "The Scrum: Video Shows Lewandowski Reaching in Michelle Field's Direction," Beitbart, March 11, 2016, "https://www.breitbart.com/big-government/2016/03/11/trump-presser-ben-terris-misidentified/.

180. Lewandowski and Bossie, 117.

180. In Lewandowski's book *Let Trump Be Trump*, he still maintains the reporter jumped a barricade, inviting readers to "watch the video." The video does not show the reporter jumping the barricade.

180. Ibid.

180. Ibid., 120.

180. Ibid.

180. Associated Press. "Has Trump's Campaign Hit a Wall after Loss in Wisconsin?" PBS. April 9, 2016. Accessed July 16, 2018. https://www.pbs.org/newshour/politics/has-trumps-campaign-hit-a-wall-after-loss-in-wisconsin.

181. Wise, Rhona. "How Paul Manafort Took Over the Trump Campaign." *New York* Magazine. Accessed July 16, 2018. http://nymag.com/daily/intelligencer/2016/04/how-paul-manafort-took-over-the-trump-campaign.html.

181. Harding. *Collusion*, 143–45.

181. Lewandowski and Bossie, 127.

181. Tom Hamburger, et al., "Manafort Offered to Give Russian Billionaire 'Private Briefings' on 2016 Campaign," *Washington Post*, September 20, 2017, http://www.washingtonpost.com/politics/manafort-offered-to-give-russian-billionaire-private-briefings-on-2016-campaign/2017/09/20/399bba1a-9d48-11e7-8ea1-ed975285475e_story.html?utm_term=.8313ca1123cf.

182. Ryan Teague Beckwith, "Donald Trump's 'America First' Foreign Policy Speech," April 27, 2016, as updated, http://time.com/4309786/read-donald-trumps-america-first-foreign-policy-speech/.

182. Calamur, Krishnadev. "A Short History of 'America First.'" *The Atlantic*. January 21, 2017. Accessed July 16, 2018. https://www.theatlantic.com/politics/archive/2017/01/trump-america-first/514037/.

182. "Peace Corps Mourns the Loss of Founder and Visionary Father, Sargent Shriver." Global Issues: Food Security. Accessed July 16, 2018. https://www.peacecorps.gov/news/library/

peace-corps-mourns-the-loss-of-founder-and-visionary-father-sargent-shriver/.

182. Susan Dunn, "Trump's 'America First' Has Ugly Echoes from U.S. History," CNN, op-ed, April 28, 2016, https://www.cnn.com/2016/04/27/opinions/trump-america-first-ugly-echoes-dunn/.

182. Peter Graff, "Trump's 'America First' Speech Alarms U.S. Allies," Reuters, April 29, 2016, http://www.reuters.com/article/us-usa-election-trump-idUSKCN0XO10R.

182. MacFarquhar, Neil, and Peter Baker. "Sergey Kislyak, Russian Envoy, Cultivated Powerful Network in U.S." *The New York Times*. March 3, 2017. Accessed July 16, 2018. https://www.nytimes.com/2017/03/02/world/europe/sergey-kislyak-russian-ambassador.html.

183. Entous, Adam, Ellen Nakashima, and Greg Miller. "Sessions Met with Russian Envoy Twice Last Year, Encounters He Later Did Not Disclose." *The Washington Post*. March 1, 2017. Accessed July 16, 2018. https://www.washingtonpost.com/world/national-security/sessions-spoke-twice-with-russian-ambassador-during-trumps-presidential-campaign-justice-officials-say/2017/03/01/77205eda-feac-11e6-99b4-9e613afeb09f_story.html?utm_term=.a6e6f1f0bff7.

183. Barrett, Devlin, Philip Rucker, and Karoun Demirjian. "Kushner Questioned by Senate Investigators on Russia." *The Washington Post*. July 24, 2017. Accessed July 16, 2018. https://www.washingtonpost.com/world/national-security/kushner-arrives-at-senate-for-closed-door-questioning-on-russia/2017/07/24/f5be2b26-7073-11e7-8f39-eeb7d3a2d304_story.html.

183. Barbaro, Michael, and Jonathan Mahler. "Quiet Fixer in Donald Trump's Campaign: His Son-in-Law, Jared Kushner." *The New York Times*. December 21, 2017. Accessed July 16, 2018. https://www.nytimes.com/2016/07/05/us/politics/jared-kushner-donald-trump.html.

183. Ibid.

183. Fox, Emily Jane. "'It's "Business as Usual' for Jared Kushner, Despite the F.B.I.'s Crosshairs." *Vanity Fair*. June 30, 2017. Accessed July 16, 2018. https://www.vanityfair.com/news/2017/05/jared-kushner-fbi-crosshairs.

183. Maya Salam and Matthew Haag, "5 Times David Pecker and The Enquirer Defended or Championed Trump," *New York Times*, March 30, 2018, http://www.nytimes.com/2018/03/29/us/politics/trump-national-enquirer-david-pecker.html.

183. "Donald Trump: Ted Cruz's Dad Was With JFK Assassin Lee Harvey Oswald." YouTube, 1:46, published by Inside Edition on May 3, 2016, http://www.youtube.com/watch?v=5SRLYWLirJI.

184. Ibid.

184. Ibid.

184. Owen, Paul. "George Papadopoulos Timeline: Trump Campaign Adviser Details Russia Links." *The Guardian*. October 30, 2017. Accessed July 16, 2018. https://www.theguardian.com/us-news/2017/oct/30/

george-papadopoulos-timeline-trump-campaign-adviser-russia-links.

184. Ibid.

184. U.S. v. Papadopoulos, 17 Cr. 182 (RDM), U.S. District Court, D.D.C., Statement of the Offense, filed October 5, 2017, available at http://www.justice.gov/file/1007346/download.

184. Tom Hamburger, Carol D. Leonnig, and Rosalind S. Helderman, "Trump Campaign Emails Show Aide's Repeated Efforts to Set up Russia Meetings," *Washington Post*, August 14, 2017, http://www.washingtonpost.com/politics/trump-campaign-emails-show-aides-repeated-efforts-to-set-up-russia-meetings/2017/08/14/54d08da6-7dc2-11e7-83c7-5bd5460f0d7e_story.html?utm_term=.bd219139be2c.

184. Jeremy Duda, "Michael Flynn Has Absolutely Nothing to Fear from the Logan Act," *Washington Post*, February 17, 2017, https://www.washingtonpost.com/posteverything/wp/2017/02/16/michael-flynn-has-absolutely-nothing-to-fear-from-the-logan-act/?utm_term=.cfdb28c7d53a.

184. U.S. v. Papadopoulos, Crim. No. 17-182 (RDM), U.S. District Court, D.D.C., Statement of the Offense, filed October 5, 2017, at 7, available at http://www.justice.gov/file/1007346/download.

184. http://winerooms.london/kensington/

184. Owen, Paul. "George Papadopoulos Timeline: Trump Campaign Adviser Details Russia Links."

185. Windrem, Robert. "Guess Who Came to Dinner with Flynn and Putin." NBCNews.com. Accessed July 16, 2018. https://www.nbcnews.com/news/world/guess-who-came-dinner-flynn-putin-n7426

185. Maza, Cristina. "These Russian Oligarchs on the U.S. Treasury List Have Ties to Trump." *Newsweek*. January 30, 2018. Accessed July 16, 2018. https://www.newsweek.com/these-russian-oligarchs-us-treasury-list-have-ties-trump-and-his-campaign-795051.

185. Interview of Donald J. Trump, Senate Judciary Committee of the U.S. Senate, September 7, 2017, Washngton, D.C., pp. 34–35, transcript available at https://www.documentcloud.org/documents/4464023-Trump-Jr-Transcript-Redacted.html.

185. Isikoff and Corn, *Russian Roulette*, 109.

185. Ibid.

185. Isikoff, Michael. "'Trump's Son Should Be Concerned': FBI Obtained Wiretaps of Putin Ally Who Met with Trump Jr." Yahoo! News. May 25, 2018. Accessed July 16, 2018. https://www.yahoo.com/news/trumps-son-concerned-wiretaps-show-trump-jr-met-putin-ally-231215529.html.

188. Bump, Philip. "Is Hillary Clinton the 'Most Experienced' Presidential Candidate in History?" *The Washington Post*. June 14, 2016. Accessed July 16, 2018. https://www.washingtonpost.com/news/the-fix/wp/2016/06/14/is-hillary-clinton-the-most-experienced-presidential-candidate-in-history/

191. Trump, Donald J. "It Is Impossible for the FBI Not to Recommend Criminal Charges against Hillary Clinton. What She Did Was Wrong! What Bill Did Was Stupid!" Twitter. July 2, 2016. Accessed

July 31, 2018. https://twitter.com/realdonaldtrump/status/749341789102960640.

191. Lee, Bruce Y. "Donald Trump's Sniffling Continues: Here Are The Possible Causes." *Forbes*. October 10, 2016. Accessed July 31, 2018. https://www.forbes.com/sites/brucelee/2016/10/09/donald-trumps-sniffling-continues-here-now-are-the-possible-causes/.

191. Silver, Nate. "Election Update: Early Polls Suggest A Post-Debate Bounce For Clinton." FiveThirtyEight. January 30, 2017. Accessed July 31, 2018. https://fivethirtyeight.com/features/election-update-early-polls-suggest-a-post-debate-bounce-for-clinton/.

Palmer, Anna, and Jake Sherman. "Poll: Hillary Clinton Won the Second Debate." *Politico*. October 11, 2016. Accessed July 31, 2018. https://www.politico.com/story/2016/10/clinton-trump-debate-poll-229581.

192. Trump, Donald J. "It Was Just Announced-by Sources-that No Charges Will Be Brought against Crooked Hillary Clinton. Like I Said, the System Is Totally Rigged!" Twitter. July 2, 2016. Accessed July 31, 2018. https://twitter.com/realdonaldtrump/status/749350193095667713.

192. Trump, Donald J. "The New Joke in Town Is That Russia Leaked the Disastrous DNC E-mails, Which Should Never Have Been Written (stupid), Because Putin Likes Me." Twitter. July 25, 2016. Accessed September 5, 2018. https://twitter.com/realdonaldtrump/status/757538729170964481.

192. Trump, Donald J. "The Polls Are Close so Crooked Hillary Is Getting out of Bed and Will Campaign Tomorrow. Why Did She Hammer 13 Devices and Acid-wash E-mails?" Twitter. September 4, 2016. Accessed July 31, 2018. https://twitter.com/realdonaldtrump/status/772574369633763329.

193. Trump, Donald J. "The Results Are in on the Final Debate and It Is Almost Unanimous, I WON! Thank You, These Are Very Exciting Times." Twitter. October 21, 2016. Accessed September 5, 2018. https://twitter.com/realdonaldtrump/status/789520268972601344.

193. Blake, Aaron. "The Final Trump-Clinton Debate Transcript, Annotated." *The Washington Post*. October 19, 2016. Accessed July 31, 2018. https://www.washingtonpost.com/news/the-fix/wp/2016/10/19/the-final-trump-clinton-debate-transcript-annotated/?utm_term=.18359d58d743.

193. Ibid.

193. Ibid.

193. Ibid.

193. Ibid.

194. Ibid.

196. https://www.documentcloud.org/documents/4464023-Trump-Jr-Transcript-Redacted.html page 22

196. Rhona Graff, Trump's executive assistant.

196. https://www.documentcloud.org/documents/4464023-Trump-Jr-Transcript-Redacted.html page 22

196. Jarrett, Gregg, and Fox News. "Fox News Host Wrong That No Law Bans Trump Collusion." @Politifact, 31 May 2017, www.politifact.com/punditfact/statements/2017/may/31/gregg-jarrett/fox-news-hosts-wrong-no-law-forbids-russia-trump-c/.

196. Kiely, Eugene. "A Timeline of Trump Tower Meeting Responses." FactCheck.org, 4 June 2018, www.factcheck.org/2018/06/a-timeline-of-trump-tower-meeting-responses/.

196. Donald Trump Jr. Senate testimony page 96, line 16, https://www.judiciary.senate.gov/imo/media/doc/Trump%20Jr%20Transcript_redacted.pdf

196. Canty, Jennifer. "Transcript-Speech: Donald Trump in Redondo Beach, CA-June 7, 2016." Factbase, CantyMedia, factba.se/transcript/donald-trump-speech-redondo-beach-ca-june-7-2016.

198. Kramer, Andrew E., and Sharon Lafraniere. "Lawyer Who Was Said to Have Dirt on Clinton Had Closer Ties to Kremlin Than She Let On." *The New York Times*, 27 Apr. 2018, www.nytimes.com/2018/04/27/us/natalya-veselnitskaya-trump-tower-russian-prosecutor-general.html.

198. Lafraniere, Sharon. "Lobbyist at Trump Campaign Meeting Has a Web of Russian Connections." *The New York Times*, 21 Aug. 2017, www.nytimes.com/2017/08/21/us/rinat-akhmetshin-russia-trump-meeting.html.

198. Ibid.

198. Kaveladze has set up thousands of Delaware-based corporations and bank accounts for Russians. A nine-month inquiry in 2000 found more than $1.4 billion moved through those accounts, a money-laundering flag. Kaveladze said he'd done nothing wrong and the Government Accountability Office investigation was a "witch hunt."

Bonner, Raymond. "Laundering Of Money Seen as 'Easy.'" *The New York Times*, 29 Nov. 2000, www.nytimes.com/2000/11/29/business/laundering-of-money-seen-as-easy.html.

199. Fandos, Nicholas, and Sharon Lafraniere. "Documents Show Promise, and Letdown, Around Trump Tower Meeting." *The New York Times*, 16 May 2018, www.nytimes.com/2018/05/16/us/trump-tower-meeting-interview-transcripts.html.

199. "Senate Judiciary Committee Interview of Rinat Akhmetshin." Senate Judiciary Committee, 14 Nov. 2017. 78, lines 13-15.

199. Goldstone testimony page 48, lines 16-21, https://www.judiciary.senate.gov/imo/media/doc/Goldstone%201%20Transcript_redacted.pdf

200. Trump Jr. said if he had received evidence of crimes committed by Clinton, he would have taken it to the authorities. "I think that kind of information would be relevant to the American public." https://www.documentcloud.org/documents/4464023-Trump-Jr-Transcript-Redacted.html p 109.

200. Akhmetshin transcript page 85, line 93.

200. Goldstone wrote again at the end of June with another offer: help for the campaign from Russia's equivalent to Facebook, VKontakte, which is owned by a Putin ally.

Scott, Mark. "Mail.ru Takes Full Ownership of VKontakte, Russia's Largest Social Network." *The New York Times*, 16 Sept. 2014, dealbook.nytimes.com/2014/09/16/mail-ru-takes-full-ownership-of-vkontakte-russias-largest-social-network/.

200. Goldstone testimony, page 54, lines 22-23.

200. Nakashima, Ellen. "Russian Government Hackers Penetrated DNC, Stole Opposition Research on Trump." *The Washington Post*, 14 June 2016, www.washingtonpost.com/world/national-security/russian-government-hackers-penetrated-dnc-stole-opposition-research-on-trump/2016/06/14/cf006cb4-316e-11e6-8ff7-7b6c1998b7a0_story.html?utm_term=.1da80db448b3.

200. Steele Report.

200. Ibid.

200. Bradner, Eric. "Trump: DNC Hacked Itself." CNN, 16 June 2016, www.cnn.com/2016/06/15/politics/dnc-hack-donald-trump/index.html.

201. Ackerman, Kevin Poulsen Spencer. "EXCLUSIVE: 'Lone DNC Hacker' Guccifer 2.0 Slipped Up and Revealed He Was a Russian Intelligence Officer." The Daily Beast, 22 Mar. 2018, www.thedailybeast.com/exclusive-lone-dnc-hacker-guccifer-20-slipped-up-and-revealed-he-was-a-russian-intelligence-officer.

201. Guccifer 2.0 once slipped up and failed to mask their IP address, revealing the link to Russian intelligence. https://www.thedailybeast.com/exclusive-lone-dnc-hacker-guccifer-20-slipped-up-and-revealed-he-was-a-russian-intelligence-officer

201. https://docs.google.com/document/d/1LLaaLzoTXn6E-teqkhJCdgFqbVsNWBZgEWPHsgZrA3A/edit

202. Glenn Simpson Senate testimony, August 22, 2017, 50.

202. Ibid., 77.

202. Ibid., 62.

202. Friedman, Robert I. "The Most Dangerous Mobster in the World." *Village Voice*. May 26, 1998. Accessed September 5, 2018. https://www.villagevoice.com/1998/05/26/the-most-dangerous-mobster-in-the-world/.

202. Glenn Simpson Senate testimony August 22, 2017, 70.

202. Ibid., 70.

204. Ibid., 79.

204. Ibid., 83.

204. Ibid., 82.

205. Ibid., 150.

205. Ibid., 158.

205. Ibid., 162.

205. Isikoff and Corn, 152.

205. Ibid., 83.

206. Ibid., 179.

206. Apuzzo, Matt, et al. "Code Name Crossfire Hurricane: The Secret Origins of the Trump Investigation." *The New York Times*, 16 May 2018, www.nytimes.com/2018/05/16/us/politics/crossfire-hurricane-trump-russia-fbi-mueller-investigation.html.

206. Menn, Joseph. "Exclusive: FBI Probes Hacking of Democratic Congressional Group." Reuters. July 29, 2016. Accessed September 5, 2018. https://www.reuters.com/article/us-usa-cyber-democrats-exclusive/exclusive-fbi-probes-hacking-of-democratic-congressional-group-sources-idUSKCN1082Y7.

207. Robertson, Lori, and Robert Farley. "Donald Trump Jr.'s Evolving Statements." FactCheck.org, 27 July 2017, www.factcheck.org/2017/07/donald-trump-jr-s-evolving-statements/.

207. Trump, Donald J. "For the Record, I Have ZERO Investments in Russia." Twitter, 26 July 2016, twitter.com/realdonaldtrump/status/758071952498159616.

207. *Inside Edition.* "Donald Trump Asks Russia To Share Hillary Clinton's Hacked Emails With FBI." YouTube, 27 July 2016, www.youtube.com/watch?v=-e-Vka_HkRU.

207. "netyksho_et_al_indictment.Pdf." The United States Department of Justice, www.justice.gov/file/1080281.

208. Allen, Cooper. "Was Melania Trump's Speech Plagiarized from Michelle Obama?" *USA Today*, 19 July 2016, www.usatoday.com/story/news/politics/onpolitics/2016/07/19/melania-trump-republican-convention-speech-plagiarism/87278088/.

208. Schwindt, Oriana. "Donald Trump Speech Ratings Fall Far Below GOP Record on Final Night of RNC." *Variety*, 22 July 2016, variety.com/2016/tv/news/2016-republican-national-convention-ratings-donald-trump-speech-romny-mccain-1201820515/.

208. Burns, Alexander, and Maggie Haberman. "How Donald Trump Finally Settled on Mike Pence." *The New York Times*. January 20, 2018. Accessed August 16, 2018. https://www.nytimes.com/2016/07/16/us/politics/mike-pence-donald-trump-vice-president.html.

208. Sanders, Linley. "Mike Pence Could Be the Next President and He Was Handpicked by Paul Manafort." *Newsweek*. October 30, 2017. Accessed August 16, 2018. https://www.newsweek.com/mike-pence-was-handpicked-paul-manafort-696412.

208. Schoofs, Mark. "Trump Intelligence Allegations." DocumentCloud. Accessed August 16, 2018. https://www.documentcloud.org/documents/3259984-Trump-Intelligence-Allegations.html. 7.

208. Ibid., 12.

209. Ibid., 7.

209. Kramer, Andrew E., et al. "Secret Ledger in Ukraine Lists Cash for Donald Trump's Campaign Chief." *The New York Times*, 15 Aug. 2016, www.nytimes.com/2016/08/15/us/politics/paul-manafort-ukraine-donald-trump.html.

Trump did not fire Manafort's associate Rick Gates, who served as deputy campaign chairman. A year later, Manafort and Gates would be charged with laundering $21 million through offshore accounts, among other crimes.

Mazzetti, Mark, and Maggie Haberman. "Rick Gates, Trump Campaign Aide, Pleads Guilty in Mueller Inquiry and Will Cooperate." *The New York Times*, 23 Feb. 2018, www.nytimes.com/2018/02/23/us/politics/rick-gates-guilty-plea-mueller-investigation.html.

"Manafort-gates_edva_indictment.Pdf." The United States Department of Justice, www.justice.gov/file/1038391.

212. Lichtblau, Eric, and Steven Lee Myers. "Investigating Donald Trump, F.B.I. Sees No Clear Link to Russia." *The New York Times*, 1 Nov. 2016, www.nytimes.com/2016/11/01/us/politics/fbi-russia-election-donald-trump.html.

213. Apuzzo, Matt, et al. "Code Name Crossfire Hurricane: The Secret Origins of the Trump Investigation." *The New York Times*, 16 May 2018, www.nytimes.com/2018/05/16/us/politics/crossfire-hurricane-trump-russia-fbi-mueller-investigation.html.

213. The FBI stopped talking with Steele in October of 2016 after he discussed his findings with the news media. The bureau had instructed him to speak only with law enforcement. Nonetheless, the FBI maintained they still considered Steele a reliable source.

Savage, Charlie. "Carter Page FISA Documents Are Released by Justice Department." *The New York Times*. July 21, 2018. Accessed July 22, 2018. https://www.nytimes.com/2018/07/21/us/politics/carter-page-fisa.html?hp.

213. Silver, Nate. "The Comey Letter Probably Cost Clinton The Election." FiveThirtyEight, 3 May 2017, fivethirtyeight.com/features/the-comey-letter-probably-cost-clinton-the-election/.

213. Trump, Donald J. "This Will Prove to Be a Great Time in the Lives of ALL Americans. We Will Unite and We Will Win, Win, Win!" Twitter, Twitter, 12 Nov. 2016, twitter.com/realdonaldtrump/status/797455295928791040.

214. The deal will keep the president-elect from having to testify in a trial in San Diego that was set to begin November 28. "Donald Trump Settles Trump University Lawsuits." CNNMoney, money.cnn.com/2016/11/18/news/trump-university-settlement/index.html.

214. Bender, Michael C., and Carol E. Lee. "RNC Chair Reince Priebus Is Named Donald Trump's Chief of Staff." *The Wall Street Journal*, 14 Nov. 2016, www.wsj.com/articles/leading-contender-for-donald-trump-s-chief-of-staff-is-rnc-chairman-reince-priebus-1479069597.

215. Trump, Donald J. "Very Organized Process Taking Place as I Decide on Cabinet and Many Other Positions. I Am the Only One Who Knows Who the Finalists Are!" Twitter, 16 Nov. 2016, mobile.twitter.com/realDonaldTrump/status/798721142525665280.

215. Wolff, Michael. "Ringside With Steve Bannon at Trump Tower as the President-Elect's Strategist Plots 'An Entirely New Political Movement.'" *The Hollywood Reporter*, 19 Dec. 2016, www.hollywoodreporter.com/

news/steve-bannon-trump-tower-interview-trumps-strategist-plots-new-political-movement-948747.

215. Peters, Jeremy W. "Stephen Bannon Reassures Conservatives Uneasy About Trump." *The New York Times*, 24 Feb. 2017, www.nytimes.com/2017/02/23/us/politics/cpac-stephen-bannon-reince-priebus.html.

217. Goldstein, Dana. "Betsy DeVos, Pick for Secretary of Education, Is the Most Jeered." *The New York Times*, 3 Feb. 2017, www.nytimes.com/2017/02/03/us/politics/betsy-devos-nominee-education-secretary.html.

217. Mooney, Chris, et al. "Trump Names Scott Pruitt, Oklahoma Attorney General Suing EPA on Climate Change, to Head the EPA." *The Washington Post*, 8 Dec. 2016, www.washingtonpost.com/news/energy-environment/wp/2016/12/07/trump-names-scott-pruitt-oklahoma-attorney-general-suing-epa-on-climate-change-to-head-the-epa/?utm_term=.83fd6cb1f9c6.

217. Cillizza, Chris. "Trump's Former Event Planner Could Soon Be in Charge of Federal Housing Programs in New York." CNN, 16 June 2017, www.cnn.com/2017/06/16/politics/lynne-patton-wedding-trump/index.html.

217. Shear, Michael D. "Obama Warned Trump About Hiring Flynn, Officials Say." *The New York Times*, 8 May 2017, www.nytimes.com/2017/05/08/us/politics/obama-flynn-trump.html.

217. Trump, Donald J. "I Settled the Trump University Lawsuit for a Small Fraction of the Potential Award Because as President I Have to Focus on Our Country." Twitter, 19 Nov. 2016, twitter.com/realdonaldtrump/status/799969130237542400.

218. Mele, Christopher, and Patrick Healy. "'Hamilton' Had Some Unscripted Lines for Pence. Trump Wasn't Happy." *The New York Times*, 19 Nov. 2016, www.nytimes.com/2016/11/19/us/mike-pence-hamilton.htm

218. Trump, Donald J. "Our Wonderful Future V.P. Mike Pence Was Harassed Last Night at the Theater by the Cast of Hamilton, Cameras Blazing.This Should Not Happen!" Twitter. November 19, 2016. Accessed August 16, 2018. https://twitter.com/realdonaldtrump/status/799972624713420804?lang=en.

218. Trump, Donald J. "If the Election Were Based on Total Popular Vote I Would Have Campaigned in N.Y. Florida and California and Won Even Bigger and More Easily." Twitter, 15 Nov. 2016, twitter.com/realdonaldtrump/status/798519600413601792.

218. Bump, Philip. "Analysis | Trump Declares That His Voter-fraud Conspiracy Theory Is 'Not a Conspiracy Theory.'" *The Washington Post*. April 5, 2018. Accessed August 16, 2018. https://www.washingtonpost.com/news/politics/wp/2018/04/05/trump-declares-that-his-voter-fraud-conspiracy-theory-is-not-a-conspiracy-theory/?utm_term=.3837ae98ddba.

218. "Donald Trump: TIME Person of the Year Interview Transcript." *Time*, 7 Dec. 2016, time.com/4591183/time-person-of-the-year-2016-donald-trump-interview/.

219. https://www.washingtonpost.com/world/national-security/

russian-ambassador-told-moscow-that-kushner-wanted-secret-communications-channel-with-kremlin/2017/05/26/520a14b4-422d-11e7-9869-bac8b446820a_story.html?utm_term=.b0b1ebb87ce7

219. Nakashima, Ellen, et al. "Russian Ambassador Told Moscow That Kushner Wanted Secret Communications Channel with Kremlin." *The Washington Post*, 26 May 2017, www.washingtonpost.com/world/national-security/russian-ambassador-told-moscow-that-kushner-wanted-secret-communications-channel-with-kremlin/2017/05/26/520a14b4-422d-11e7-9869-bac8b446820a_story.html?utm_term=.c8330008a6dd.

219. Filipov, David, Amy Brittain, Rosalind S. Helderman, and Tom Hamburger. "Explanations for Kushner's Meeting with Head of Kremlin-linked Bank Don't Match up." *The Washington Post*. June 1, 2017. Accessed August 16, 2018. https://www.washingtonpost.com/politics/explanations-for-kushners-meeting-with-head-of-kremlin-linked-bank-dont-match-up/2017/06/01/dd1bdbb0-460a-11e7-bcde-624ad94170ab_story.html?utm_term=.aa607309be6d.

219. Entous, Adam, Ellen Nakashima, and Greg Miller. "Secret CIA Assessment Says Russia Was Trying to Help Trump Win White House." *The Washington Post*. December 9, 2016. Accessed August 16, 2018. https://www.washingtonpost.com/world/national-security/obama-orders-review-of-russian-hacking-during-presidential-campaign/2016/12/09/31d6b300-be2a-11e6-94ac-3d324840106c_story.html?utm_term=.53c51ce4b8d9.

219. This is not true. Trump's electoral college margin is one of the smallest in history. Only thirteen presidents in 58 elections have had closer results.

219. Toosi, Nahal. "Trump Team Rejects Intel Agencies' Claims of Russian Meddling." *Politico*. December 10, 2016. Accessed August 16, 2018. https://www.politico.com/story/2016/12/trump-team-russia-cia-intel-election-232460.

220. Sanger, David E. "Obama Strikes Back at Russia for Election Hacking." *The New York Times*. December 29, 2016. Accessed August 16, 2018. https://www.nytimes.com/2016/12/29/us/politics/russia-election-hacking-sanctions.html.

220. "Flynn_statement_of_offense.pdf." The United States Department of Justice. Accessed August 16, 2018. https://www.justice.gov/file/1015126/.

220. Trump, Donald J. "Great Move on Delay (by V. Putin)-I Always Knew He Was Very Smart!" Twitter, 30 Dec. 2016, twitter.com/realdonaldtrump/status/814919370711461890.

220. *Assessing Russian Activities and Intentions in Recent US Elections*. PDF. Washington DC: Director of National Intelligence, January 6, 2017.

221. Comey, James B. *A Higher Loyalty: Truth, Lies, and Leadership*. New York: Flatiron Press, 2018. 214.

221. Steele dossier, page 2, from the June 20 memo.

221. Hodge, Nathan, and Thomas Grove. "Trump Dossier Spotlights Russian History of 'Kompromat.'" *The Wall Street Journal*. January 11, 2017. Accessed August 16, 2018. https://www.wsj.com/articles/

trump-dossier-spotlights-russian-history-of-kompromat-1484171169.

221. Comey. *A Higher Loyalty*, 216.

221. Ibid.

222. Ibid., 217–218.

222. Sanger, David E., and Matthew Rosenberg. "From the Start, Trump Has Muddied a Clear Message: Putin Interfered." *The New York Times*. July 19, 2018. Accessed July 20, 2018. https://www.nytimes.com/2018/07/18/world/europe/trump-intelligence-russian-election-meddling-.html.

222. Comey, James B. *A Higher Loyalty*, 220.

222. Ibid.

222. Ibid., 223.

223. Ibid., 224–225.

223. Sanger, David E., and Matthew Rosenberg. "From the Start, Trump Has Muddied a Clear Message: Putin Interfered."

223. "Donald Trump's Statement After Intelligence Briefing on Hacking." *The New York Times*, 22 Dec. 2017, www.nytimes.com/2017/01/06/us/politics/donald-trump-statement-hack-intelligence-briefing.html.

224. Hilton, Perez. "EXCLUSIVE! The Rockettes Are Performing At Donald Trump's Inauguration-And The Dancers Could Get SUED If They Refuse!" FitPerez RSS, perezhilton.com/2016-12-22-donald-trump-the-rockettes-inauguration/?from=post#.Wyql7S2ZOCR.

224. Trump, Donald J. "The So-Called 'A' List Celebrities Are All Wanting Tixs to the Inauguration, but Look What They Did for Hillary, NOTHING. I Want the PEOPLE!" Twitter, 23 Dec. 2016, twitter.com/realdonaldtrump/status/812115501791006720.

224. Bensinger, Ken, Miriam Elder, and Mark Schoofs. "These Reports Allege Trump Has Deep Ties To Russia." BuzzFeed. January 10, 2017. Accessed June 22, 2018. https://www.buzzfeed.com/kenbensinger/these-reports-allege-trump-has-deep-ties-to-russia?utm_term=.tpnNdXO79#.jj15bglLo.

225. Ibid.

225. Trump, Donald J. "Russia Just Said the Unverified Report Paid for by Political Opponents Is 'A COMPLETE AND TOTAL FABRICATION, UTTER NONSENSE.' Very Unfair!" Twitter. January 11, 2017. Accessed June 22, 2018. https://twitter.com/realdonaldtrump/status/819155311793700865.

225. Trump, Donald J. "I Win an Election Easily, a Great 'Movement' Is Verified, and Crooked Opponents Try to Belittle Our Victory with FAKE NEWS. A Sorry State!" Twitter. January 11, 2017. Accessed June 22, 2018. https://twitter.com/realdonaldtrump/status/819162968592183298.

225. Trump, Donald J. "Intelligence Agencies Should Never Have Allowed This Fake News to 'Leak' into the Public. One Last Shot at Me.Are We Living in Nazi Germany?" Twitter, 11 Jan. 2017, twitter.com/realdonaldtrump/status/819164172781060096.

225. Comey, 226.

226. Ibid., 227.

226. Kiely, Eugene, Robert Farley, and Lori Robertson. "False Statements on Russia." FactCheck.org. November 20, 2017. Accessed August 16, 2018. https://www.factcheck.org/2017/10/false-statements-russia/.

226. Miller, Greg, Adam Entous, and Ellen Nakashima. "National Security Adviser Flynn Discussed Sanctions with Russian Ambassador, despite Denials, Officials Say." *The Washington Post*. February 9, 2017. Accessed August 16, 2018. https://www.washingtonpost.com/world/national-security/national-security-adviser-flynn-discussed-sanctions-with-russian-ambassador-despite-denials-officials-say/2017/02/09/f85b29d6-ee11-11e6-b4ff-ac2cf509efe5_story.html.

229. Trump, Donald J. "The Forgotten Men and Women of Our Country Will Be Forgotten No Longer. From This Moment On, It's Going to Be #AmericaFirst 🇺🇸." Twitter. January 20, 2017. Accessed July 2, 2018. https://twitter.com/realdonaldtrump/status/822502450007515137.

229. Wolff, Michael. *Fire and Fury: Inside the Trump White House*. New York: Henry Holt and Company, 2018. 43.

229. Ruiz, Michelle. "Are We Really Surprised That President Trump Doesn't Hold the Door for Melania?" *Vogue*. May 26, 2017. Accessed July 3, 2018. https://www.vogue.com/article/donald-trump-melania-inauguration-drama.

230. Sanders, Linley. "Trump's Inauguration Money Is Still Missing One Year after His Administration Took Control of the White House." *Newsweek*. January 18, 2018. Accessed August 16, 2018. https://www.newsweek.com/trump-inauguration-money-still-missing-783934.

232. "The Inaugural Address." The White House. Accessed August 16, 2018. https://www.whitehouse.gov/briefings-statements/the-inaugural-address/.

232. Ibid.

232. Ibid.

232. Wolff, 44.

232. Ibid.

233. Pressman, Jeremy, and Erica Chenoweth. "Crowd Estimates, 1.21.2017." Google Slides. Accessed July 2, 2018. https://docs.google.com/spreadsheets/d/1xa0iLqYKz8x9Yc_rfhtmSOJQ2EGgeUVjvV4A8LsIaxY/edit

233. Broomfield, Matt. "2 Charts Which Show Just How Huge the Women's Marches against Trump Were." *The Independent*. January 23, 2017. Accessed July 2, 2018. https://www.independent.co.uk/news/world/americas/womens-march-anti-donald-trump-womens-rights-largest-protest-demonstration-us-history-political-a7541081.html.

234. "Remarks by President Trump and Vice President Pence at CIA Headquarters." The White House. Accessed July 4, 2018. https://www.whitehouse.gov/briefings-statements/remarks-president-trump-vice-president-pence-cia-headquarters/.

234. Wolff, 48.

234. "Remarks by President Trump and Vice President Pence at CIA Headquarters." The White House. Accessed July 4, 2018. https://www.whitehouse.gov/briefings-statements/remarks-president-trump-vice-president-pence-cia-headquarters/.

234. Ibid.

235. Mitchell, Andrea, and Ken Dilanian. "Ex-CIA Boss Brennan, Others Rip Trump Speech in Front of Memorial Wall." NBCNews.com. Accessed July 2, 2018. https://www.nbcnews.com/news/us-news/ex-cia-boss-brennan-others-rip-trump-speech-front-memorial-n710366.

235. LoBianco, Tom. "Ex-CIA Chief: Russians Contacted Trump Camp." CNN. May 23, 2017. Accessed July 9, 2018. https://www.cnn.com/2017/05/23/politics/john-brennan-house-intelligence-committee/index.html.

235. Trump, Donald J. "Had a Great Meeting at CIA Headquarters Yesterday, Packed House, Paid Great Respect to Wall, Long Standing Ovations, Amazing People. WIN!" Twitter. January 22, 2017. Accessed July 2, 2018. https://twitter.com/realdonaldtrump/status/823146987117772800.

236. Trump, Donald J. "Watched Protests Yesterday but Was Under the Impression That We Just Had an Election! Why Didn't These People Vote? Celebs Hurt Cause Badly." Twitter. January 22, 2017. Accessed July 2, 2018. https://twitter.com/realdonaldtrump/status/823150055418920960.

237. "White House Briefing by Sean Spicer-Full Transcript, Jan. 23, 2017." CBS News. January 24, 2017. Accessed July 3, 2018. https://www.cbsnews.com/news/sean-spicer-press-conference-transcript-jan-23-2017/.

237. Coble, Christopher. "What Are the Consequences of Lying to the FBI?" Law and Daily Life. Accessed July 4, 2018. https://blogs.findlaw.com/blotter/2017/02/what-are-the-consequences-of-lying-to-the-fbi.html.

237. Rosenberg, Matthew. "6 Takeaways From Monday's Senate Hearing on Russia." The New York Times. May 8, 2017. Accessed July 3, 2018. https://www.nytimes.com/2017/05/08/us/politics/sally-yates-james-clapper-russia-hearing.html.

237. Cillizza, Chris. "Sally Yates Told White House Aides Flynn Was a Russian Blackmail Risk. 18 Days Later, He Was Fired." CNN. May 9, 2017. Accessed July 3, 2018. https://www.cnn.com/2017/05/08/politics/sally-yates-flynn-russia/index.html.

238. "Executive Order Protecting the Nation from Foreign Terrorist Entry into the United States." The White House. Accessed August 16, 2018. https://www.whitehouse.gov/presidential-actions/executive-order-protecting-nation-foreign-terrorist-entry-united-states/.

238. Ibid.

238. Wolff, 65.

239. "Green Room." Resolute Desk-White House Museum. Accessed July 4, 2018. http://www.whitehousemuseum.org/floor1/green-room.htm.

240. "White House Statement on Acting Attorney General." CNN. January 31, 2017. Accessed July 3, 2018. https://www.cnn.com/2017/01/30/politics/white-house-statement-attorney-general/index.html.

240. Rogers, Katie. "All the President's Handshakes." The New York Times. July 14, 2017. Accessed July 5, 2018. https://www.nytimes.com/2017/07/14/us/politics/president-donald-trump-handshakes.html.

240. Wolff, 85–87.

241. Miller, Greg, Adam Entous, and Ellen Nakashima. "National Security Adviser Flynn Discussed Sanctions with Russian Ambassador, Despite Denials, Officials Say." The Washington Post. February 9, 2017. Accessed July 3, 2018. https://www.washingtonpost.com/world/national-security/national-security-adviser-flynn-discussed-sanctions-with-russian-ambassador-despite-denials-officials-say/2017/02/09/f85b29d6-ee11-11e6-b4ff-ac2cf509efe5_story.html?utm_term=.7532a67a07d9.

241. Rosenberg, Matthew, and Glenn Thrush. "Trump Will 'Look Into' Reports That Flynn Discussed Sanctions With Russia." The New York Times. February 11, 2017. Accessed July 5, 2018. https://www.nytimes.com/2017/02/10/us/politics/donald-trump-michael-flynn-russia-sanctions.html.

242. Borger, Julian. "Missile Crisis by Candlelight: Donald Trump's Use of Mar-a-Lago Raises Security Questions." The Guardian. February 14, 2017. Accessed August 17, 2018. https://www.theguardian.com/us-news/2017/feb/13/mar-a-lago-north-korea-missile-crisis-trump-national-security.

242. Ibid.

242. CNBC. "Trump's Use of Private Cellphone Raises Security Concerns." CNBC. May 31, 2017. Accessed July 9, 2018. https://www.cnbc.com/2017/05/30/trump-to-world-leaders-call-me-maybe—on-my-cellphone.html.

242. Beckwith, Ryan Teague. "Michael Flynn Resignation: Read Transcript of His Letter." Time. February 14, 2017. Accessed July 5, 2018. http://time.com/4670178/michael-flynn-resignation-transcript-letter/.editmore horizontal

243. Day, Chad, and Associated Press. "Ex-FBI Director James Comey's Memos." DocumentCloud. Accessed August 17, 2018. https://www.documentcloud.org/documents/4442900-Ex-FBI-Director-James-Comey-s-memos.html. 10.

243. Ibid.

243. Shield laws in the United States specifically protect journalists from having to reveal their sources.

243. Day, Chad, and Associated Press, 11.

243. Ibid.

243. Schmidt, Michael S., and Matt Apuzzo. "Comey Told Sessions: Don't Leave Me Alone With Trump." The New York Times. June 6, 2017. Accessed August 17, 2018. https://www.nytimes.com/2017/06/06/us/politics/comey-sessions-trump.html.

244. Kim, Tae. "Here's What Happens to Shares of Companies That Trump Attacks." CNBC. April 5, 2018. Accessed August 17, 2018. https://www.cnbc.com/2018/04/05/

heres-what-happens-to-shares-of-companies-that-trump-attacks.html.

244. Wolff, 145–149.

244. Cillizza, Chris. "This Is Trump at His Absolute Best So Far. VERY Nice Grace Note about Our Shared Humanity to Start Speech." Twitter. March 1, 2017. Accessed July 5, 2018. https://twitter.com/CillizzaCNN/status/836760917048197120?ref_src=twsrc%5Etfw%7Ctwcamp%5Etweet embed%7Ctwterm%5E836760917048197120.edit

244. Chris Wallace: "I Feel like Tonight @realDonaldTrump Became the President of the United States." #TrumpAddress Https://t.co/dAlG7h8ytD Pic. twitter.com/PF6ERD8HCO. Twitter. March 1, 2017. Accessed July 5, 2018. https://twitter.com/FoxNews/status/836780523221471232?ref_src=twsrc%5Etfw%7Ctwcamp%5Etweetembed%7Ctwterm%5E836780523221471232.edit

244. Bump, Philip. "Analysis | What Jeff Sessions Said about Russia, and When." *The Washington Post.* March 2, 2017. Accessed July 5, 2018. https://www.washingtonpost.com/news/politics/wp/2017/03/02/what-jeff-sessions-said-about-russia-and-when/.

245. Ibid.

245. Farley, Robert. "Did Sessions 'Lie'?" FactCheck.org. March 3, 2017. Accessed August 17, 2018. https://www.factcheck.org/2017/03/did-sessions-lie/.

245. Keneally, Meghan. "Timeline Leading up to Jeff Sessions' Recusal and the Fallout." ABC News. July 26, 2017. Accessed July 4, 2018. https://abcnews.go.com/Politics/timeline-leading-jeff-sessions-recusal-fallout/story?id=45855918.

245. Trump, Donald J. "Jeff Sessions Is an Honest Man. He Did Not Say Anything Wrong. He Could Have Stated His Response More Accurately, but It Was Clearly Not . . ." Twitter. March 3, 2017. Accessed August 17, 2018. https://twitter.com/realdonaldtrump/status/837488402438176769?lang=en.

245. Trump, Donald J. ". . . intentional. This Whole Narrative Is a Way of Saving Face for Democrats Losing an Election That Everyone Thought They Were Supposed . . ." Twitter. March 3, 2017. Accessed July 4, 2018. https://twitter.com/realdonaldtrump/status/837489578193846278.

245. Trump, Donald J. ". . . to Win. The Democrats Are Overplaying Their Hand. They Lost the Election, and Now They Have Lost Their Grip on Reality. The Real Story . . ." Twitter. March 3, 2017. Accessed July 4, 2018. https://twitter.com/realdonaldtrump/status/837491607171629057.

245. Trump, Donald J. ". . . is All of the Illegal Leaks of Classified and Other Information. It Is a Total 'Witch Hunt!'" Twitter. March 3, 2017. Accessed July 4, 2018. https://twitter.com/realdonaldtrump/status/837492425283219458.

246. Trump, Donald J. "Terrible! Just Found out That Obama Had My 'Wires Tapped' in Trump Tower Just before the Victory. Nothing Found. This Is McCarthyism!" Twitter. March 4, 2017. Accessed July 4, 2018. https://twitter.com/realDonaldTrump/status/837989835818287106.

246. Trump, Donald J. "How Low Has President Obama Gone to Tapp My Phones during the Very Sacred Election Process. This Is Nixon/Watergate. Bad (or Sick) Guy!" Twitter. March 4, 2017. Accessed July 4, 2018. https://twitter.com/realdonaldtrump/status/837996746236182529.

246. Obama's director of national intelligence, James Clapper, said on NBC's *Meet the Press* that he would have known about a "FISA court order on something like this. Absolutely, I can deny it." FBI Director James Comey testified to Congress that neither his agency nor the Justice Department had evidence to support the president's allegations. Trump's Justice Department and the FBI said in a September 2017 court filing that they did not have evidence to support Trump's claims.

246. Wolff, 97.

247. "Excerpts From The Times's Interview With Trump." *The New York Times.* July 20, 2017. Accessed July 4, 2018. https://www.nytimes.com/2017/07/19/us/politics/trump-interview-transcript.html.

247. Zurcher, Anthony. "Could FBI Investigation into Russia Links Ensnare Trump?" BBC News. March 20, 2017. Accessed July 4, 2018. https://www.bbc.com/news/world-us-canada-39331555.

247. Entous, Adam, and Ellen Nakashima. "Trump Asked Intelligence Chiefs to Push Back against FBI Collusion Probe after Comey Revealed Its Existence." *The Washington Post.* May 22, 2017. Accessed July 5, 2018. https://www.washingtonpost.com/world/national-security/trump-asked-intelligence-chiefs-to-push-back-against-fbi-collusion-probe-after-comey-revealed-its-existence/2017/05/22/394933bc-3f10-11e7-9869-bac8b446820a_story.html?utm_term=.061b83a2f7c5.

248. Wolff, 70.

248. "5 U.S. Code § 3110-Employment of Relatives; Restrictions." LII / Legal Information Institute. Accessed August 17, 2018. https://www.law.cornell.edu/uscode/text/5/3110.

248. Becker, Jo, and Matthew Rosenberg. "Kushner Omitted Meeting With Russians on Security Clearance Forms." *The New York Times.* April 7, 2017. Accessed July 4, 2018. https://www.nytimes.com/2017/04/06/us/politics/jared-kushner-russians-security-clearance.html?_r=0.

248. Le Miere, Jason. "Jared Kushner's Security Clearance Forms Had More Mistakes than One Leading Official Has Ever Seen." *Newsweek.* October 13, 2017. Accessed July 4, 2018. http://www.newsweek.com/jared-kushner-security-clearance-form-684590.

248. Brittain, Amy, Ashley Parker, and Anu Narayanswamy. "Jared Kushner and Ivanka Trump Made at Least $82 Million in Outside Income Last Year While Serving in the White House, Filings Show." *The Washington Post.* June 11, 2018. Accessed July 5, 2018. https://www.washingtonpost.com/news/politics/wp/2018/06/11/jared-kushner-and-ivanka-trump-made-at-least-82-million-in-outside-income-last-year-while-serving-in-the-white-house-filings-show/?utm_term=.c9a5ffcc1027.

249. Day, Chad, and Associated Press. "Ex–FBI Director James Comey's Memos," 13.

249. Ibid.

249. Trump, Donald J. "Mike Flynn Should Ask for Immunity in That This Is a Witch Hunt (Excuse for Big Election Loss), by Media & Dems, of Historic Proportion!" Twitter. March 31, 2017. Accessed July 4, 2018. https://twitter.com/realdonaldtrump/status/847766558520856578.

250. Thompson, Alex. "Trump Gets a Folder Full of Positive News about Himself Twice a Day." VICE News. August 9, 2017. Accessed July 5, 2018. https://news.vice.com/en_ca/article/zmygpe/trump-folder-positive-news-white-house.

250. Ibid.

250. Hensch, Mark. "CNN Host: 'Donald Trump Became President' Last Night." The Hill. April 7, 2017. Accessed July 6, 2018. http://thehill.com/homenews/administration/327779-cnn-host-donald-trump-became-president-last-night.

250. Day, Chad, and Associated Press. "Ex–FBI Director James Comey's Memos." 15.

250. Ibid.

251. "Read the Full Testimony of FBI Director James Comey in Which He Discusses Clinton Email Investigation." The Washington Post. May 3, 2017. Accessed July 5, 2018. https://www.washingtonpost.com/news/post-politics/wp/2017/05/03/read-the-full-testimony-of-fbi-director-james-comey-in-which-he-discusses-clinton-email-investigation/?utm_term=.21322b43433f.

251. Baker, Peter, and Michael D. Shear. "Trump Shifts Rationale for Firing Comey, Calling Him a 'Showboat.'" The New York Times. May 11, 2017. Accessed August 17, 2018. https://www.nytimes.com/2017/05/11/us/politics/trump-comey-showboat-fbi.html.

251. "Top-Secret NSA Report Details Russian Hacking Effort Days Before 2016 Election." The Intercept. June 5, 2017. Accessed July 5, 2018. https://theintercept.com/2017/06/05/top-secret-nsa-report-details-russian-hacking-effort-days-before-2016-election/.

252. "Full Transcript: Sally Yates and James Clapper Testify on Russian Election Interference." The Washington Post. May 8, 2017. Accessed August 17, 2018. https://www.washingtonpost.com/news/post-politics/wp/2017/05/08/full-transcript-sally-yates-and-james-clapper-testify-on-russian-election-interference/?utm_term=.09a70e4d813f.

252. Ibid.

252. Wolff, 214.

253. Wilkinson, Tracy, W.J. Hennigan, and Kurtis Lee. "Read President Trump's Letter to FBI Director Comey." Los Angeles Times. May 9, 2017. Accessed August 17, 2018. http://www.latimes.com/politics/washington/la-na-essential-washington-updates-read-president-trump-s-letter-to-fbi-1494367417-htmlstory.html.

253. Hannity, Sean. "Comey Fired!!! Finally." Twitter. May 9, 2017. Accessed July 6, 2018. https://twitter.com/seanhannity/status/862063190343024640.

253. Cohen, Michael. "#ComeyFired #Hallelujah! Need Anyone Say More?" Twitter. May 9, 2017. Accessed July 6, 2018. https://twitter.com/MichaelCohen212/status/862066225064660993?

253. Krieg, Gregory. "Tick-tock: How Comey's Firing Played out in Real Time." CNN. May 9, 2018. Accessed July 5, 2018. https://www.cnn.com/2018/05/09/politics/inside-trump-comey-firing-as-it-happened/index.html.

253. Apuzzo, Matt, Maggie Haberman, and Matthew Rosenberg. "Trump Told Russians That Firing 'Nut Job' Comey Eased Pressure From Investigation." The New York Times. May 19, 2017. Accessed July 5, 2018. https://www.nytimes.com/2017/05/19/us/politics/trump-russia-comey.html.

254. Blum, Howard. "Exclusive: What Trump Really Told Kislyak After Comey Was Canned." Vanity Fair. December 21, 2017. Accessed July 5, 2018. https://www.vanityfair.com/news/2017/11/trump-intel-slip.

254. Trump, Donald J. "James Comey Better Hope That There Are No 'Tapes' of Our Conversations before He Starts Leaking to the Press!" Twitter. May 12, 2017. Accessed July 5, 2018. https://twitter.com/realdonaldtrump/status/863007411132649473.

254. Trump, Donald J. "As President I Wanted to Share with Russia (at an Openly Scheduled W.H. Meeting) Which I Have the Absolute Right to Do, Facts Pertaining. . . ." Twitter. May 16, 2017. Accessed July 5, 2018. https://twitter.com/realdonaldtrump/status/864436162567471104.

254. "Donald Trump's The New York Times Interview: Full Transcript." The New York Times. January 20, 2018. Accessed July 5, 2018. https://www.nytimes.com/2016/11/23/us/politics/trump-new-york-times-interview-transcript.html?hp.

The law provides an exemption for the president and vice president, assuming they will do the right thing and not put their personal profit over the interests of the nation. The founding fathers were greatly concerned with conflicts of interest, especially when foreign governments were involved.

Kessler, Glenn, and Michelle Ye Hee Lee. "Trump's Claim That 'the President Can't Have a Conflict of Interest.'" The Washington Post. November 23, 2016. Accessed July 5, 2018. https://www.washingtonpost.com/news/fact-checker/wp/2016/11/23/trumps-claim-that-the-president-cant-have-a-conflict-of-interest/?utm_term=.2a776f7e1d7b.

255. Ruiz, Rebecca R., and Mark Landler. "Robert Mueller, Former F.B.I. Director, Is Named Special Counsel for Russia Investigation." The New York Times. May 17, 2017. Accessed August 17, 2018. https://www.nytimes.com/2017/05/17/us/politics/robert-mueller-special-counsel-russia-investigation.html.

255. Ibid.

257. Trump, Donald J. "The Big Story Is the 'Unmasking and Surveillance' of People That Took Place during the Obama Administration." Twitter. June 1, 2017. Accessed July 25, 2018. https://mobile.twitter.com/realdonaldtrump/status/870234811616677889.

258. Graff, Garrett M. "The Untold Story of Robert Mueller's Time in Combat." *Wired.* June 7, 2018. Accessed July 20, 2018. https://www.wired.com/story/robert-mueller-vietnam.

258. Mueller, Robert. "Bob Mueller '66—Lacrosse." Princeton Varsity Club. Accessed July 20, 2018. http://princetonvarsityclub.org/2008/09/bob-mueller-66-lacrosse/.

258. Mueller had his first physical in the middle of 1966. He sat in the waiting room with a lineman for the Philadelphia Eagles who was ruled medically unfit. Mueller's knee had to heal before he was allowed to serve.

He earned a master's degree in International Relations from New York University and got married as his knee healed.

Graff, Garrett M. "The Untold Story of Robert Mueller's Time in Combat."

259. Ibid.

259. Ibid.

259. Folkenflik, David. "Final Words: Cronkite's Vietnam Commentary." NPR. July 18, 2009. Accessed July 21, 2018. https://www.npr.org/templates/story/story.php?storyId=106775685.

259. Sisk, Richard. "Robert Mueller: A 'Magnificent Bastard.'" *Military.com*, CodyUnderwood, www.military.com/daily-news/2017/05/21/magnificent-bastard-is-investigating-russian-meddling-in-us.html.

259. Graff, Garrett M. "The Untold Story of Robert Mueller's Time in Combat."

259. Ibid.

259. Goldman, Russell. "Donald Trump's Own Secret: Vietnam Draft Records." ABC News. April 29, 2011. Accessed July 25, 2018. https://abcnews.go.com/Politics/donald-trumps-vietnam-draft-records-secret-documents-deferments/story?id=13492639.

260. "Trump Boasted of Avoiding STDs: Vaginas 'Are Landmines . . . It Is My Personal Vietnam.'" PEOPLE.com. Accessed July 25, 2018. https://people.com/politics/trump-boasted-of-avoiding-stds-while-dating-vaginas-are-landmines-it-was-my-personal-vietnam/.

260. Ibid.

260. Vitkovskaya, Julie, and *Washington Post.* "Read Mueller's Military Documents." DocumentCloud. Accessed July 20, 2018. https://www.documentcloud.org/documents/4386090-Read-Mueller-s-military-documents.html.editmore

260. Ibid.

260. National Archives and Records Administration. Accessed July 21, 2018. https://georgewbush-whitehouse.archives.gov/news/releases/2001/07/20010705-2.html.

260. Lawrence K. Altman With David Johnston. "View After Cancer Surgery Is Good for F.B.I. Director." *The New York Times.* August 15, 2001. Accessed July 21, 2018. https://www.nytimes.com/2001/08/15/us/view-after-cancer-surgery-is-good-for-fbi-director.html.

261. "September 11th Warning Signs Fast Facts." CNN Library. September 2, 2017. Accessed July 23, 2018. https://www.cnn.com/2013/07/27/us/september-11th-warning-signs-fast-facts/index.html.

261. Ibid.

261. Ibid.

261. Ibid.

261. Graff, Garrett M. *The Threat Matrix: The FBI at War.* New York: Back Bay Books, 2012.

261. Ballesteros, Carlos. "Robert Mueller Is a Hothead Who Can't Own up to His Mistakes, Former Aides Say." *Newsweek.* November 27, 2017. Accessed July 25, 2018. https://www.newsweek.com/robert-mueller-special-counsel-russia-aides-criticize-722670.

261. Ibid.

261. "Former Director of the FBI Robert Mueller III Joins WilmerHale." WilmerHale. March 24, 2014. Accessed July 25, 2018. https://www.wilmerhale.com/en/insights/news/former-director-of-the-fbi-robert-mueller-iii-joins-wilmerhale.

261. Chaffetz, Jason. "Mueller Is a Great Selection. Impeccable Credentials. Should Be Widely Accepted." Twitter. May 17, 2017. Accessed July 20, 2018. https://twitter.com/jasoninthehouse/status/864964765608624130?lang=en.

Gingrich, Newt. "Robert Mueller Is Superb Choice to Be Special Counsel. His Reputation Is Impeccable for Honesty and Integrity. Media Should Now Calm Down." Twitter. May 18, 2017. Accessed July 20, 2018. https://twitter.com/newtgingrich/status/864998445244743684?lang=en.

261. Rupar, Terri. "Democratic Leaders Respond to Mueller's Appointment." *The Washington Post.* Accessed August 17, 2018. https://www.washingtonpost.com/politics/2017/live-updates/trump-white-house/trump-comey-and-russia-how-key-washington-players-are-reacting/pelosi-calls-muellers-appointment-a-first-step/?utm_term=.7e3ea8271806.

261. "Read Donald Trump's Speech at U.S. Coast Guard Graduation." *Time.* May 17, 2017. Accessed July 20, 2018. http://time.com/4782382/donald-trump-coast-guard-commencement-graduation-speech/.

261. Trump, Donald J. "This Is the Single Greatest Witch Hunt of a Politician in American History!" Twitter. May 18, 2017. Accessed July 20, 2018. https://twitter.com/realDonaldTrump/status/865173176854204416.

261. Schmidt, Michael S., and Maggie Haberman. "Trump Ordered Mueller Fired, but Backed Off When White House Counsel Threatened to Quit." *The New York Times.* January 26, 2018. Accessed July 20, 2018. https://www.nytimes.com/2018/01/25/us/politics/trump-mueller-special-counsel-russia.html.

261. Ibid.

264. Cohen, Marshall, Tal Yelling, Caroline Kelly, and Liz Stark. "Meet the Mueller Team." CNN. Accessed July 20, 2018. https://edition.cnn.com/interactive/2018/politics/meet-the-mueller-team/index.html.

264. Trump, Donald J. "We Need to Be Smart, Vigilant and Tough. We Need the Courts to Give Us Back Our Rights. We Need the Travel Ban as an Extra Level of Safety!" Twitter. June 3, 2017. Accessed July 21, 2018. https://twitter.com/realdonaldtrump/status/871143765473406976.

Trump, Donald J. "People, the Lawyers and the Courts Can Call It Whatever They Want, but I Am Calling It What We Need and What It Is, a TRAVEL BAN!" Twitter. June 5, 2017. Accessed July 21, 2018. https://twitter.com/realdonaldtrump/status/871674214356484096.

Trump, Donald J. "That's Right, We Need a TRAVEL BAN for Certain DANGEROUS Countries, Not Some Politically Correct Term That Won't Help Us Protect Our People!" Twitter. June 6, 2017. Accessed July 21, 2018. https://twitter.com/realdonaldtrump/status/871899511525961728.

264. https://www.apnews.com/2c7a5afc13824161a25d8574e10ff4e7

264. Farley, Robert. "Trump's Bogus Voter Fraud Claims." *FactCheck.org*, 19 Oct. 2016, www.factcheck.org/2016/10/trumps-bogus-voter-fraud-claims/.

264. Berman, Mark, and David Weigel. "Trump's Voting Commission Asked States to Hand over Election Data. Some Are Pushing Back." *The Washington Post*, 1 July 2017, www.washingtonpost.com/national/trumps-voting-commission-asked-states-to-hand-over-election-data-theyre-pushing-back/2017/06/30/cd8f812a-5dce-11e7-9b7d-14576dc0f39d_story.html?utm_term=.a0d12ec218d4.

265. Wolff, 257.

265. Parker, Ashley, Carol D. Leonnig, Philip Rucker, and Tom Hamburger. "Trump Dictated Son's Misleading Statement on Meeting with Russian Lawyer." *The Washington Post*. July 31, 2017. Accessed July 21, 2018. https://www.washingtonpost.com/politics/trump-dictated-sons-misleading-statement-on-meeting-with-russian-lawyer/2017/07/31/04c94f96-73ae-11e7-8f39-eeb7d3a2d304_story.html?utm_term=.c758d1d46206.

265. "Was Trump Tower Meeting Statement Accurate?" @politifact. June 7, 2018. Accessed July 21, 2018. http://www.politifact.com/truth-o-meter/statements/2018/jun/07/president-trumps-lawyers/was-initial-trump-statement-ny-times-accurate-lawy/.

265. Davis, Julie Hirschfeld. "Trump and Putin Held a Second, Undisclosed, Private Conversation." *The New York Times*. July 18, 2017. Accessed July 21, 2018. https://www.nytimes.com/2017/07/18/world/europe/trump-putin-undisclosed-meeting.html.

266. Ibid.

266. Ibid

266. Ibid.

266. Ibid.

266. "Excerpts From The Times's Interview With Trump." *The New York Times*. July 20, 2017. Accessed July 22, 2018. https://www.nytimes.com/2017/07/19/us/politics/trump-interview-transcript.html.

267. Ibid.

267. Disis, Jill. "All the Things Donald Trump and His Team Have Said about Releasing His Tax Returns." CNN Money. Accessed July 23, 2018. https://money.cnn.com/2017/04/17/news/donald-trump-tax-returns/index.html.

267. Begley, Sarah. "Donald Trump: Americans Don't Care About My Tax Returns." Time. January 11, 2017. Accessed July 23, 2018. http://time.com/4631541/donald-trump-tax-returns-press-conference/.

267. Leonnig, Carol D., Ashley Parker, Rosalind S. Helderman, and Tom Hamburger. "Trump Team Seeks to Control, Block Mueller's Russia Investigation." *The Washington Post*. July 21, 2017. Accessed July 22, 2018. https://www.washingtonpost.com/politics/trumps-lawyers-seek-to-undercut-muellers-russia-investigation/2017/07/20/232ebf2c-6d71-11e7-b9e2-2056e768a7e5_story.html?utm_term=.2bce54544c5e.

267. Ibid.

267. Ibid.

267. Ibid.

268. Baker, Peter, and Maggie Haberman. "Reince Priebus Is Ousted Amid Stormy Days for White House." *The New York Times*. July 28, 2017. Accessed July 21, 2018. https://www.nytimes.com/2017/07/28/us/politics/reince-priebus-white-house-trump.html.

268. Tenpas, Kathryn Dunn, Elaine Kamarck, and Nicholas W. Zeppos. "Tracking Turnover in the Trump Administration." Brookings. July 20, 2018. Accessed July 21, 2018. https://www.brookings.edu/research/tracking-turnover-in-the-trump-administration/. editmore horizontal

268. Benjamin Freed. "Paul Manafort's Washington." *Washingtonian*. October 30, 2017. Accessed July 22, 2018. https://www.washingtonian.com/2017/10/30/paul-manaforts-washington/.

269. Trump, Donald J. "After Consultation with My Generals and Military Experts, Please Be Advised That the United States Government Will Not Accept or Allow. . . ." Twitter. July 26, 2017. Accessed July 22, 2018. https://twitter.com/realDonaldTrump/status/890193981585444864.

269. Trump, Donald J. ". . . Transgender Individuals to Serve in Any Capacity in the U.S. Military. Our Military Must Be Focused on Decisive and Overwhelming . . ." Twitter. July 26, 2017. Accessed August 17, 2018. https://twitter.com/realdonaldtrump/status/890196164313833472.

269. Trump, Donald J. ". . .victory and Cannot Be Burdened with the Tremendous Medical Costs and Disruption That Transgender in the Military Would Entail. Thank You." Twitter. July 26, 2017. Accessed September 5, 2018. https://twitter.com/realdonaldtrump/status/890197095515546369.

269. Davis, Julie Hirschfeld, and Helene Cooper. "Trump Says Transgender People Will Not Be Allowed in the Military." *The New York Times*. July 26, 2017. Accessed July 22, 2018. https://www.nytimes.com/2017/07/26/us/politics/trump-transgender-military.html.

269. Gates, Gary J., and Jody L. Herman. *Transgender Military Service in the United States*. Los Angeles: The Williams Institute-UCLA School of Law, May 2014.

270. Lizza, Ryan. "Anthony Scaramucci Called Me to Unload About White House Leakers, Reince Priebus, and Steve Bannon." *The New Yorker*. December 1, 2017. Accessed July 21, 2018. https://www.newyorker.com/news/ryan-lizza/anthony-scaramucci-called-me-to-unload-about-white-house-leakers-reince-priebus-and-steve-bannon.

270. Ibid.

270. Ibid.

270. Bykowicz, Julie, and Jonathan Lemire. "Scaramucci, with Vulgar Language, Signals Internal White House Fight." PBS. July 27, 2017. Accessed July 22, 2018. https://www.pbs.org/newshour/politics/scaramucci-colorful-language-signals-internal-white-house-fight.editmore

270. Ibid.

270. "Statement_of_the_offense.filed_.pdf." The United States Department of Justice. Accessed July 21, 2018. https://www.justice.gov/file/1007346.

271. Ibid.

271. Ibid.

271. "Mueller Is Moving Quickly Compared To Past Special Counsel Investigations." FiveThirtyEight. December 4, 2017. Accessed July 22, 2018. https://fivethirtyeight.com/features/mueller-is-moving-quickly-compared-to-past-special-counsel-investigations/.

273. Litman, Harry. "Why George Papadopoulos Is More Dangerous Than Paul Manafort." *The New York Times*. October 30, 2017. Accessed July 21, 2018. https://www.nytimes.com/2017/10/30/opinion/george-papadopoulos-manafort-indictment.html.

273. Trump, Donald J. "In Other Words, Russia Was against Trump in the 2016 Election-and Why Not, I Want Strong Military & Low Oil Prices. Witch Hunt! Https://t.co/mMSxj4Su5z." Twitter. July 29, 2017. Accessed July 25, 2018. https://mobile.twitter.com/realdonaldtrump/status/891253798500487168.

274. "Press Briefing by Press Secretary Sarah Sanders." The White House. Accessed July 21, 2018. https://www.whitehouse.gov/briefings-statements/press-briefing-press-secretary-sarah-sanders-080117/.

274. Ibid.

274. Hans M. Kristensen & Robert S. Norris. (2018) "North Korean nuclear capabilities," 2018, *Bulletin of the Atomic Scientists*, 74:1, 41-51, DOI: 10.1080/00963402.2017.1413062

274. "Fact Sheets & Briefs." Arms Control Association. Accessed July 23, 2018. https://www.armscontrol.org/factsheets/Nuclearweaponswhohaswhat.

274. Warrick, Joby, Ellen Nakashima, and Anna Fifield. "North Korea Now Making Missile-ready Nuclear Weapons, U.S. Analysts Say." *The Washington Post*. August 8, 2017. Accessed July 22, 2018. https://www.washingtonpost.com/world/national-security/north-korea-now-making-missile-ready-nuclear-weapons-us-analysts-say/2017/08/08/e14b882a-7b6b-11e7-9d08-b79f191668ed_story.html?utm_term=.2dff21ecc9a6.

Thrush, Glenn, and Peter Baker. "Trump's Threat to North Korea Was Improvised." *The New York Times*. August 9, 2017. Accessed July 22, 2018. https://www.nytimes.com/2017/08/09/us/politics/trump-north-korea.html.

275. Ibid.

275. Cohen, Zachary, and Euan McKirdy. "North Korea Threatens Strike on Guam." CNN. August 9, 2017. Accessed July 22, 2018. https://www.cnn.com/2017/08/08/politics/north-korea-considering-guam-strike-trump/index.html.

275. Hamedy, Saba. "All the Times Trump Has Insulted North Korea." CNN. March 9, 2018. Accessed July 22, 2018. https://www.cnn.com/2017/09/22/politics/donald-trump-north-korea-insults-timeline/index.html.

275. Trump, Donald J. "I Spoke with President Moon of South Korea Last Night. Asked Him How Rocket Man Is Doing. Long Gas Lines Forming in North Korea. Too Bad!" Twitter. September 17, 2017. Accessed July 22, 2018. https://twitter.com/realdonaldtrump/status/909384837018112000.

275. "Full Text of Kim Jong-un's Response to President Trump." *The New York Times*. September 22, 2017. Accessed July 22, 2018. https://www.nytimes.com/2017/09/22/world/asia/kim-jong-un-trump.html.

275. "Statement by President Donald J. Trump on the Signing of H.R. 3364." The White House, www.whitehouse.gov/briefings-statements/statement-president-donald-j-trump-signing-h-r-3364/.

275. Trump, Donald J. "Our Relationship with Russia Is at an All-time & Very Dangerous Low. You Can Thank Congress, the Same People That Can't Even Give Us HCare!" Twitter. August 3, 2017. Accessed August 21, 2018. https://twitter.com/realdonaldtrump/status/893083735633129472

275. White separatists and white nationalists believe that Western nations should be white, according to the Southern Poverty Law Center, which monitors hate groups such as the Ku Klux Klan, as well as neo-confederates, neo-Nazis, and racist skinheads.

These groups oppose immigration of non-whites and believe the Civil Rights Act of 1964 amounts to "white genocide."

They want to form a white nation, claiming this comes from a love of whiteness as opposed to a hatred of people of color.

The SPLC reports these groups have two strategies for bringing about their vision of a white nation: infiltrating existing political institutions (sometimes by disguising their politics), and fomenting a revolution through public demonstrations and anonymous online activism as a means of polarizing and collapsing America.

276. Heaphy, Timothy. *Final Report: Independent Review of the 2017 Protest Events in Charlottesville, Virginia*. Charlottesville: Hunton & Williams, 2017.

276. Manchester, Julia. "David Duke: Charlottesville Protests about 'Fulfilling Promises of Donald Trump.'" The Hill. August 13, 2017. Accessed July 22, 2018. http://thehill.com/blogs/blog-briefing-room/news/346326-david-duke-charlottesville-protests-about-fulfilling-promises

276. Heim, Joe. "How a Rally of White Nationalists and Supremacists at the University of Virginia Turned into a 'Tragic, Tragic Weekend.'" The Washington Post. Accessed July 22, 2018. https://www.washingtonpost.com/graphics/2017/local/charlottesville-timeline/?utm_term=.e14286d41550.

276. Ibid.

276. Ibid.

276. "History and Gardens of Market Street Park." A Green City | City of Charlottesville. Accessed July 22, 2018. http://www.charlottesville.org/departments-and-services/departments-h-z/parks-recreation/parks-trails/city-parks/emancipation-park-formerly-known-as-lee-park/history-and-gardens-of-emancipation-park.

276. Ibid.

277. Heaphy, Timothy. Final Report: Independent Review of the 2017 Protest Events in Charlottesville, Virginia.

277. Ibid., 71.

277. Ibid., 86.

277. Ibid.

278. Holan, Angie Drobnic. "In Context: Trump's 'Many Sides' Remarks on Charlottesville." @politifact. Accessed August 21, 2018. https://www.politifact.com/truth-o-meter/article/2017/aug/14/context-president-donald-trumps-saturday-statement/.

278. Trump, Donald J. "We ALL Must Be United & Condemn All That Hate Stands For. There Is No Place for This Kind of Violence in America. Lets Come Together as One!" Twitter. August 12, 2017. Accessed July 22, 2018. https://twitter.com/realDonaldTrump/status/896420822780444672?ref_src=twsrc%5Etfw%7Ctwcamp%5Etweetembed%7Ctwterm%5E896420822780444672.edit

278. Duke, David. "I Would Recommend You Take a Good Look in the Mirror & Remember It Was White Americans Who Put You in the Presidency, Not Radical Leftists. Https://t.co/Rkfs7O2Ykr." Twitter. August 12, 2017. Accessed July 22, 2018. https://twitter.com/drdavidduke/status/896431991821926401?lang=en.

278. Robertson, Lori. "The DACA Population Numbers." FactCheck.org. August 10, 2018. Accessed August 17, 2018. https://www.factcheck.org/2018/01/daca-population-numbers/.

278. "Ending DACA Was an Act of Pure Cruelty by Trump." Los Angeles Times. September 5, 2017. Accessed July 23, 2018. http://www.latimes.com/opinion/editorials/la-ed-trump-daca-sessions-congress-20170905-story.html.

278. Michael Shear and Julie Hirschfeld Davis. "Trump Moves to End DACA and Calls on Congress to Act." The New York Times. September 5, 2017. Accessed July 22, 2018. https://www.nytimes.

com/2017/09/05/us/politics/trump-daca-dreamers-immigration.html.

279. Jarrett, Laura. "Lying to Congress Can Put You in Jail, Even If You're Not under Oath." CNN. July 24, 2017. Accessed July 23, 2018. https://www.cnn.com/2017/07/24/politics/penalty-for-lying-to-congress/index.html.

279. Testimony of Donald Trump, Jr. Washington DC: United States Senate Judiciary Committee, September 7, 2017.

279. Ibid.

279. "The Trump Lawyers' Confidential Memo to Mueller, Explained." The New York Times. June 2, 2018. Accessed July 22, 2018. https://www.nytimes.com/interactive/2018/06/02/us/politics/trump-legal-documents.html.

279. Ibid.

279. "Costliest U.S. Tropical Cyclones Tables Updated." National Oceanic and Atmospheric Administration. January 26, 2018. Accessed July 22, 2018. https://www.nhc.noaa.gov/news/UpdatedCostliest.pdf.

280. U.S. Department of Commerce, and NOAA. "Major Hurricane Maria-September 20, 2017." National Weather Service. May 6, 2018. Accessed July 22, 2018. https://www.weather.gov/sju/maria2017

280. Nixon, Ron, and Matt Stevens. "Harvey, Irma, Maria: Trump Administration's Response Compared." The New York Times. September 27, 2017. Accessed July 22, 2018. https://www.nytimes.com/2017/09/27/us/politics/trump-puerto-rico-aid.html.

280. Jerome, Sara. "Thousands Of Puerto Ricans Still Waiting On Clean Water." www.wateronline.com. Accessed July 22, 2018. https://www.wateronline.com/doc/thousands-puerto-ricans-waiting-clean-water-0001.

280. Sullivan, Emily. "Nearly A Year After Maria, Puerto Rico Officials Claim Power Is Totally Restored." NPR. August 15, 2018. Accessed August 17, 2018. https://www.npr.org/2018/08/15/638739819/nearly-a-year-after-maria-puerto-rico-officials-claim-power-totally-restored.

280. Kessler, Glenn. "Analysis | Did 4,645 People Die in Hurricane Maria? Nope." The Washington Post. June 1, 2018. Accessed July 22, 2018. https://www.washingtonpost.com/news/fact-checker/wp/2018/06/02/did-4645-people-die-in-hurricane-maria-nope/?utm_term=.4b38b13d9a1b.

281. USATODAY. "Trump: 'Get That Son-of-a-b****' off the Field.'" YouTube. September 23, 2017. Accessed July 23, 2018. https://m.youtube.com/watch?v=GhPWVFHqm7s.

281. Trump, Donald J. ". . . our Great American Flag (or Country) and Should Stand for the National Anthem. If Not, YOU'RE FIRED. Find Something Else to Do!" Twitter. September 23, 2017. Accessed July 23, 2018. https://mobile.twitter.com/realdonaldtrump/status/911655987857281024.

282. Brown, Lauretta. "Sen. Cory Booker on NFL Anthem Protests: 'Protest Is Patriotism.'" Townhall. September 27, 2017. Accessed July 23, 2018. https://

townhall.com/tipsheet/laurettabrown/2017/09/27/
sen-cory-booker-on-nfl-anthem-protests-protest-is-
patriotism-n2387285.

282. According to published reports, Mueller's team
interviewed Rinat Akhmetshin, who attended the
Trump tower meeting; Paul Manafort's spokesman
Jason Maloni; National Security Director Mike
Rogers; Director of National Intelligence Dan Coats;
Deputy Attorney General Rod Rosenstein; British
former spy Christopher Steele; Reince Priebus; Sean
Spicer; former campaign official Sam Clovis; a Dutch
lawyer named Alex van der Zwaan; Jared Kushner;
Irakly Kaveladze; White House counsel Don McGahn;
communications director Hope Hicks; former FBI
Director James Comey; CIA Director Mike Pompeo;
Manafort's associate Rick Gates; former FBI deputy
director Andrew McCabe; former Trump legal team
spokesman Mark Corallo; and Attorney General Jeff
Sessions.

"A List of People Special Counsel Robert Mueller's
Investigators Have Interviewed." CBS News. March 29,
2018. Accessed July 25, 2018. https://www.cbsnews.
com/news/a-list-of-people-special-counsel-robert-
muellers-investigators-have-interviewed/.

282. Trump, Donald J. "All of This 'Russia' Talk Right
When the Republicans Are Making Their Big Push
for Historic Tax Cuts & Reform. Is This Coincidental?
NOT!" Twitter. October 29, 2017. Accessed August
21, 2018. https://twitter.com/realdonaldtrump/
status/924649059520073730.

282. "Special Counsel's Office." The United States
Department of Justice. July 13, 2018. Accessed July 25,
2018. https://www.justice.gov/sco.

282. Haberman, Maggie, and Kenneth P. Vogel.
"Trump's Inaugural Committee Paid $26 Million to
Firm of First Lady's Adviser." *The New York Times.*
February 15, 2018. Accessed July 25, 2018. https://www.
nytimes.com/2018/02/15/us/politics/trumps-inaugural-
committee-paid-26-million-to-first-ladys-friend.html.

283. "Read the Charges Against Paul Manafort and
Rick Gates." *The New York Times,* 30 Oct. 2017, www.
nytimes.com/interactive/2017/10/30/us/politics/
document-paul-manafort-rick-gates-indictment.html.

283. "Trump on Papadopoulos: 'He's an Excellent
Guy.'" *The Washington Post.* Accessed July 21,
2018. https://www.washingtonpost.com/video/
politics/trump-on-papadopoulos-hes-an-excellent-
guy/2017/10/30/225c584c-bd8b-11e7-9294-
705f80164f6e_video.html?utm_term=.1237774267a2.

283. Vazquez, Maegan. "Ex-Trump Campaign Adviser:
Papadopoulos Just a 'Coffee Boy.'" CNN. October
31, 2017. Accessed July 23, 2018. https://www.cnn.
com/2017/10/31/politics/caputo-papadopoulos-coffee-
boy-cnntv/index.html.

284. Trump, Donald J. "Sorry, but This Is
Years Ago, before Paul Manafort Was Part of
the Trump Campaign. But Why Aren't Crooked
Hillary & the Dems the Focus?????" Twitter, 30
Oct. 2017, mobile.twitter.com/realdonaldtrump/
status/925005659569041409.

284. Trump, Donald J. ". . . Also, There Is NO
COLLUSION!" Twitter, 30 Oct. 2017, mobile.twitter.
com/realdonaldtrump/status/925006418989715456.

284. "CNN Transcript: Wolf Blitzer and Donald
Trump." CNN. Accessed July 24, 2018. http://
transcripts.cnn.com/TRANSCRIPTS/1605/09/wolf.01.
html.

284. "Flynn_statement_of_offense.pdf." The United
States Department of Justice. Accessed July 24, 2018.
https://www.justice.gov/file/1015126.

285. Ibid.

285. Seitzinger, Michael V. *Conducting Foreign
Relations Without Authority: The Logan Act.*
Washington, D.C.: Congressional Research Service,
March 11, 2015.

285. Trump, Donald J. "I Had to Fire General Flynn
Because He Lied to the Vice President and the FBI. He
Has Pled Guilty to Those Lies. It Is a Shame Because
His Actions during the Transition Were Lawful.
There Was Nothing to Hide!" Twitter. December 2,
2017. Accessed July 24, 2018. https://twitter.com/
realdonaldtrump/status/937007006526959618.

285. Haberman, Maggie, and Jonathan Martin.
"Trump Once Said the 'Access Hollywood' Tape
Was Real. Now He's Not Sure." *The New York Times.*
November 29, 2017. Accessed July 25, 2018. https://
www.nytimes.com/2017/11/28/us/politics/trump-
access-hollywood-tape.html.

285. Ibid.

286. Bush, Billy. "Billy Bush: Yes, Donald Trump,
You Said That." *The New York Times.* December 4,
2017. Accessed July 25, 2018. https://www.nytimes.
com/2017/12/03/opinion/billy-bush-trump-access-
hollywood-tape.html.

286. Leonhardt, David, and Stuart A. Thompson.
"President Trump's Lies, the Definitive List." *The New
York Times.* June 23, 2017. Accessed July 25, 2018.
https://www.nytimes.com/interactive/2017/06/23/
opinion/trumps-lies.html.

286. A variety of publications, including the *Wall
Street Journal,* carried the report of the subpoena,
which Mueller's office denied doing.

Strasburg, Jenny. "Mueller Subpoenas Deutsche Bank
Records Related to Trump." *The Wall Street Journal.*
December 6, 2017. Accessed July 24, 2018. https://
www.wsj.com/articles/trumps-deutsche-bank-records-
subpoenaed-by-mueller-1512480154.

286. Haberman, Maggie, and Michael S. Schmidt.
"Trump Sought to Fire Mueller in December." *The New
York Times.* April 10, 2018. Accessed July 24, 2018.
https://www.nytimes.com/2018/04/10/us/politics/
trump-sought-to-fire-mueller-in-december.html.

286. Trump, Donald J. "Republicans Senators Are
Working Hard to Pass the Biggest Tax Cuts in the
History of Our Country. The Bill Is Getting Better
and Better. This Is a Once in a Generation Chance.
Obstructionist Dems Trying to Block Because They
Think It Is Too Good and Will Not Be Given the
Credit!" Twitter. December 1, 2017. Accessed July
24, 2018. https://twitter.com/realdonaldtrump/
status/936555753946705920.

287. Trump, Donald J. "Democrats Refusal to Give
Even One Vote for Massive Tax Cuts Is Why We Need
Republican Roy Moore to Win in Alabama. We Need

His Vote on Stopping Crime, Illegal Immigration, Border Wall, Military, Pro Life, V.A., Judges 2nd Amendment and More. No to Jones, a Pelosi/Schumer Puppet!" Twitter. December 4, 2017. Accessed July 24, 2018. https://twitter.com/realDonaldTrump/status/937641904338063361?ref_src=twsrc%5Etfw%7Ctwcamp%5Etweetembed%7Ctwterm%5E937641904338063361.

287. Robertson, Campbell. "Roy Moore, Alabama Chief Justice, Suspended Over Gay Marriage Order." *The New York Times*. September 30, 2016. Accessed July 24, 2018. https://www.nytimes.com/2016/10/01/us/roy-moore-alabama-chief-justice.html.

287. McCaskill, Nolan D. "The 7 Most Inflammatory Things Roy Moore Has Said." *Politico*. September 27, 2017. Accessed July 24, 2018. https://www.politico.com/story/2017/09/27/roy-moore-outrageous-things-he-said-243207.

287. Rosenberg, Eli. "'How Is My Daughter a Pervert?': Alabama Dad's Plain-spoken Rebuke of Roy Moore Strikes a Nerve." *The Washington Post*. December 11, 2017. Accessed July 24, 2018. https://www.washingtonpost.com/news/politics/wp/2017/12/11/how-is-my-daughter-a-pervert-alabama-dads-plain-spoken-rebuke-of-roy-moore-strikes-a-nerve/?utm_term=.501cbe321404.

287. Sullivan, Justin. "Who the Heck Is Doug Jones, Anyway? Five Things to Know about Alabama's New Senator." *Boston Globe*. December 12, 2017. Accessed July 25, 2018. https://www.bostonglobe.com/news/politics/2017/12/12/who-heck-doug-jones-anyway-five-things-know-about-guy-running-against-roy-moore/p1XAdxtpNS3LzNrrrhOvLI/story.html.

288. Tankersley, Jim, and Alan Rappeport. "How Republicans Rallied Together to Deliver a Tax Plan." *The New York Times*. December 20, 2017. Accessed July 24, 2018. https://www.nytimes.com/2017/12/19/us/politics/republican-tax-bill.htm

288. Amadeo, Kimberly. "How Much Did Obama Add to the Nation's Debt?" The Balance. June 26, 2018. Accessed July 24, 2018. https://www.thebalance.com/national-debt-under-obama-3306293.

288. Stewart, Emily. "Historians on the Tax Fight: 'This Was Manufactured Urgency.'" Vox. December 18, 2017. Accessed July 24, 2018. https://www.vox.com/policy-and-politics/2017/12/18/16773376/republican-tax-bill-history.

289. Long, Heather. "Analysis | The Final GOP Tax Bill Is Complete. Here's What Is in It." *The Washington Post*. December 15, 2017. Accessed July 24, 2018. https://www.washingtonpost.com/news/wonk/wp/2017/12/15/the-final-gop-tax-bill-is-complete-heres-what-is-in-it/?utm_term=.5919a14e5b19.

289. "The GOP Tax Cuts Are Even More Unpopular Than Past Tax Hikes." FiveThirtyEight. November 29, 2017. Accessed July 24, 2018. https://fivethirtyeight.com/features/the-gop-tax-cuts-are-even-more-unpopular-than-past-tax-hikes/.

289. Reuters. "Trump Signs Tax Bill: 'I Didn't Want You Folks to Say That I Wasn't Keeping My Promise'—Video." *The Guardian*. December 22, 2017. Accessed July 24, 2018. https://www.theguardian.com/us-news/video/2017/dec/22/trump-signs-tax-bill-i-didnt-want-you-folks-to-say-that-i-wasnt-keeping-my-promise-video.

289. "Remarks by President Trump at Signing of H.R. 1, Tax Cuts and Jobs Bill Act, and H.R. 1370." The White House. Accessed July 24, 2018. https://www.whitehouse.gov/briefings-statements/remarks-president-trump-signing-h-r-1-tax-cuts-jobs-bill-act-h-r-1370/.

289. Ibid.

289. Ibid.

289. Jacobson, Louis. "Has Donald Trump Signed More Bills than Anyone? No." @politifact. December 29, 2017. Accessed July 24, 2018. https://www.politifact.com/truth-o-meter/statements/2017/dec/29/donald-trump/has-donald-trump-signed-more-bills-anyone-no/.

290. Diamond, Jeremy, Sara Murray, and Manu Raju. "Trump Predicts Exoneration in Russia Investigation as Allies Fear a 'Meltdown.'" CNN. December 19, 2017. Accessed July 24, 2018. https://www.cnn.com/2017/12/18/politics/trump-russia-investigation/index.html.

290. Lee, Michelle Ye Hee. "Trump Settles into the 'Winter White House' for the Holidays." *The Washington Post*. December 22, 2017. Accessed July 24, 2018. https://www.washingtonpost.com/politics/president-trump-arrives-at-mar-a-lago—the-winter-white-house—for-the-holidays/2017/12/22/cae2d17e-e673-11e7-833f-155031558ff4_story.html?utm_term=.597eb60b6be9.

290. "The Trump Lawyers' Confidential Memo to Mueller, Explained." *The New York Times*. June 2, 2018. Accessed July 22, 2018. https://www.nytimes.com/interactive/2018/06/02/us/politics/trump-legal-documents.html.

290. Trump, Donald J. "As Has Been Stated by Numerous Legal Scholars, I Have the Absolute Right to PARDON Myself, but Why Would I Do That When I Have Done Nothing Wrong? In the Meantime, the Never Ending Witch Hunt, Led by 13 Very Angry and Conflicted Democrats (& Others) Continues into the Mid-terms!" Twitter. June 4, 2018. Accessed July 6, 2018. https://twitter.com/realDonaldTrump/status/1003616210922147841.

293. Ibid.

293. Trump doubled the membership fee at Mar-a-Lago from $100,000 to $200,000 after he became president. The club doesn't keep visitor logs, so it is not possible to track who meets Trump at the club. Typically, presidential meetings are part of the public record.

Dangremond, Sam. "The Secret Service Says Mar-a-Lago Visitor Logs Don't Exist." *Town & Country*. April 11, 2018. Accessed August 6, 2018. https://www.townandcountrymag.com/society/money-and-power/a9606/mar-a-lago-facts/.

294. Yourish, Karen, and Troy Griggs. "Tracking the President's Visits to Trump Properties." *The New York Times*. April 5, 2017. Accessed July 31, 2018. https://www.nytimes.com/interactive/2017/04/05/us/politics/tracking-trumps-visits-to-his-branded-properties.html.

294. Ballhaus, Rebecca. "President Trump Spent Nearly One-Third of First Year in Office at Trump-Owned Properties." *The Wall Street Journal.* December 25, 2017. Accessed August 1, 2018. https://www.wsj.com/articles/president-trump-spent-nearly-one-third-of-first-year-in-office-at-trump-owned-properties-1514206800.

The cost of Trump's travel to Mar-a-Lago alone is more than the cost of the Mueller investigation as of June 2018.

Bump, Philip. "Analysis | Trump's Spent Far More Going to Mar-a-Lago Alone than the Mueller Probe Has Cost." *The Washington Post.* June 1, 2018. Accessed August 6, 2018. https://www.washingtonpost.com/news/politics/wp/2018/06/01/trumps-spent-far-more-going-to-mar-a-lago-alone-than-the-mueller-probe-has-cost/.

294. "Judicial Watch Sues for Secret Service Trump Travel-Expense Records." Judicial Watch. Accessed August 1, 2018. https://www.judicialwatch.org/press-room/press-releases/judicial-watch-sues-secret-service-trump-travel-expense-records/.

294. Kwong, Jessica. "Trump's Golf Trips Have Cost Nearly $150,000 in Cart Rentals for the Secret Service." *Newsweek.* November 30, 2017. Accessed August 1, 2018. https://www.newsweek.com/trump-golf-trips-have-cost-nearly-150000-cart-rentals-secret-service-727933.

295. Lafraniere, Sharon. "In Ruling Against Trump, Judge Defines Anticorruption Clauses in Constitution for First Time." *The New York Times.* July 25, 2018. Accessed July 31, 2018. https://www.nytimes.com/2018/07/25/us/politics/trump-emoluments-lawsuit.html.

295. Marimow, Ann E., Jonathan O'Connell, and David A. Fahrenthold. "Federal Judge Allows Emoluments Case against Trump to Proceed." *The Washington Post.* July 25, 2018. Accessed August 3, 2018. https://www.washingtonpost.com/politics/federal-judge-allows-emoluments-case-against-trump-to-proceed/2018/07/25/c8070206-8fa4-11e8-8322-b5482bf5e0f5_story.html.

295. Eichenwald, Kurt. "How Donald Trump's Business Ties Are Already Jeopardizing U.S. Interests." *Newsweek.* February 15, 2017. Accessed July 31, 2018. https://www.newsweek.com/2016/12/23/donald-trump-foreign-business-deals-jeopardize-us-531140.html.

295. Kessler, Glenn, and Michelle Ye Hee Lee. "Trump's Claim That 'the President Can't Have a Conflict of Interest.'" *The Washington Post.* November 23, 2016. Accessed July 31, 2018. https://www.washingtonpost.com/news/fact-checker/wp/2016/11/23/trumps-claim-that-the-president-cant-have-a-conflict-of-interest/?utm_term=.567789000801.

295. Congressional Research Service. *Conflicts of Interest and the Presidency.* Washington, DC: CRS Reports and Analysis, October 14, 2016.

295. Ibid.

296. Kessler and Lee. "Trump's Claim That 'the President Can't Have a Conflict of Interest.'"

296. "Donald Trump's Tangled Web." *The New York Times.* November 16, 2016. Accessed August 1, 2018.

https://www.nytimes.com/2016/11/17/opinion/what-trump-can-do-to-eliminate-his-conflicts-of-interest.html.

296. Trump, Donald J. "North Korean Leader Kim Jong Un Just Stated That the 'Nuclear Button Is on His Desk at All Times.' Will Someone from His Depleted and Food Starved Regime Please Inform Him That I Too Have a Nuclear Button, but It Is a Much Bigger & More Powerful One than His, and My Button Works!" Twitter. January 3, 2018. Accessed July 26, 2018. https://mobile.twitter.com/realDonaldTrump/status/948355557022420992.

296. Trump, Donald J. "Crooked Hillary Clinton's Top Aid, Huma Abedin, Has Been Accused of Disregarding Basic Security Protocols. She Put Classified Passwords into the Hands of Foreign Agents. Remember Sailors Pictures on Submarine? Jail! Deep State Justice Dept Must Finally Act? Also on Comey & Others." Twitter. January 2, 2018. Accessed August 3, 2018. https://twitter.com/realDonaldTrump/status/948174033882927104?ref_src=twsrc%5Etfw%7Ctwcamp%5Etweetembed%7Ctwterm%5E948174033882927104.edit

296. Trump, Donald J. "I Will Be Announcing THE MOST DISHONEST & CORRUPT MEDIA AWARDS OF THE YEAR on Monday at 5:00 O'clock. Subjects Will Cover Dishonesty & Bad Reporting in Various Categories from the Fake News Media. Stay Tuned!" Twitter. January 3, 2018. Accessed August 3, 2018. https://twitter.com/realDonaldTrump/status/948359545767841792?ref_src=twsrc%5Etfw%7Ctwcamp%5Etweetembed%7Ctwterm%5E948359545767841792.

296. Walt, Stephen M. "10 Ways to Tell If Your President Is a Dictator." Foreign Policy. July 26, 2017. Accessed July 26, 2018. https://foreignpolicy.com/2016/11/23/ten-ways-to-tell-if-your-president-is-a-dictator/.

297. Ibid.

297. Trump routinely uses his personal, unsecured cell phone for state business, even giving out his phone number to foreign leaders, in breach of protocol.

Brown, Pamela, and Sarah Westwood. "Trump Ramps up Personal Cell Phone Use." CNN. April 24, 2018. Accessed July 26, 2018. https://www.cnn.com/2018/04/23/politics/donald-trump-cell-phone/index.html.

297. Trump, Donald J. "It Just Shows Everyone How Broken and Unfair Our Court System Is When the Opposing Side in a Case (such as DACA) Always Runs to the 9th Circuit and Almost Always Wins before Being Reversed by Higher Courts." Twitter. January 10, 2018. Accessed July 26, 2018. https://mobile.twitter.com/realdonaldtrump/status/951094078661414912.

297. Trump, Donald J. "Why Is A.G. Jeff Sessions Asking the Inspector General to Investigate Potentially Massive FISA Abuse. Will Take Forever, Has No Prosecutorial Power and Already Late with Reports on Comey Etc. Isn't the I.G. an Obama Guy? Why Not Use Justice Department Lawyers? DISGRACEFUL!" Twitter. February 28, 2018. Accessed July 26, 2018. https://mobile.twitter.com/realDonaldTrump/status/968856971075051521?ref_src=twsrc%

5Etfw%7Ctwcamp%5Etweetembed%7Ctw
term%5E968856971075051521.editmore horizontal

297. "Excerpts From Trump's Interview With The Times." *The New York Times*, 29 Dec. 2017, www.nytimes.com/2017/12/28/us/politics/trump-interview-excerpts.html.

297. Wemple, Erik. "Donald Trump Wielded an Authoritarian Press Ban against Various Media Outlets for More than a Year." *The Washington Post.* September 7, 2016. Accessed August 4, 2018. https://www.washingtonpost.com/blogs/erik-wemple/wp/2016/09/07/donald-trump-wielded-an-authoritarian-press-ban-against-various-media-outlets-for-more-than-a-year/?utm_term=.0e608ce28114.

297. "Trump's War on Journalism." *Los Angeles Times.* Accessed August 4, 2018. http://www.latimes.com/projects/la-ed-trumps-war-on-journalism/.

297. "Query: 'Fake News.'" Trump Twitter Archive. Accessed July 26, 2018. http://www.trumptwitterarchive.com/archive.

297. Trump, Donald J. "The failing @nytimes Has Disgraced the Media World. Gotten Me Wrong for Two Solid Years. Change Libel Laws? Https://t.co/QIqLgvYLLi." Twitter. March 30, 2017. Accessed July 26, 2018. https://mobile.twitter.com/realdonaldtrump/status/847455180912181249.

297. Wemple, Erik. "Opinion | President Trump's Cultural Assault on the First Amendment." *The Washington Post.* March 12, 2018. Accessed August 4, 2018. https://www.washingtonpost.com/blogs/erik-wemple/wp/2018/03/12/president-trumps-cultural-assault-on-the-first-amendment/?utm_term=.283bdb731afa.

298. Brenner, Marie. "After the Gold Rush."

298. "Introduction to the Holocaust." United States Holocaust Memorial Museum. Accessed August 6, 2018. https://www.ushmm.org/wlc/en/article.php?ModuleId=10005143.

298. Noack, Rick. "The Ugly History of 'Lügenpresse,' a Nazi Slur Shouted at a Trump Rally." *The Washington Post.* October 24, 2016. Accessed August 6, 2018. https://www.washingtonpost.com/news/worldviews/wp/2016/10/24/the-ugly-history-of-luegenpresse-a-nazi-slur-shouted-at-a-trump-rally/?utm_term=.86d00044f94c.

298. Trump, Donald J. "The FAKE NEWS Media (failing @nytimes, @NBCNews, @ABC, @CBS, @CNN) Is Not My Enemy, It Is the Enemy of the American People!" Twitter. February 17, 2017. Accessed August 1, 2018. https://twitter.com/realDonaldTrump/status/832708293516632065.

298. Englund, Will. "Why Trump's 'Enemy of the People' Bluster Can't Be Compared to Stalin's Savage Rule." *The Washington Post.* January 17, 2018. Accessed August 1, 2018. https://www.washingtonpost.com/news/retropolis/wp/2018/01/16/why-trumps-enemy-of-the-people-bluster-cant-be-compared-to-stalins-rule/?utm_term=.087c25a0d442.

299. "READ: President Trump's Full Exchange with Reporters." CNN. January 25, 2018. Accessed August 4, 2018. https://www.cnn.com/2018/01/24/politics/trump-white-house-interview-reporters/index.html.

299. The Associated Press. "Trump Calls Media 'Horrendous People.'" *The New York Times.* August 3, 2018. Accessed August 4, 2018. https://www.nytimes.com/video/us/politics/100000006038904/donald-trump-rally.html.

299. Johnson, Ted. "Trump Criticizes CNN, NBC for Coverage of North Korea Summit: 'Fake News' Is America's 'Biggest Enemy.'" *Variety.* June 13, 2018. Accessed August 4, 2018. https://variety.com/2018/politics/news/trump-north-korea-media-1202844311/.

299. Victor, Daniel. "Trump, Calling Journalists 'Sick People,' Puts Media on Edge." *The New York Times*, 23 Aug. 2017, www.nytimes.com/2017/08/23/business/media/trump-rally-media-attack.html.

299. "100 Days of Trump Claims." *The Washington Post.* Accessed July 26, 2018. https://www.washingtonpost.com/graphics/politics/trump-claims/?tid=a_inl.

299. Glasser, Susan B. "It's True: Trump Is Lying More, and He's Doing It on Purpose." *The New Yorker.* August 3, 2018. Accessed August 4, 2018. https://www.newyorker.com/news/letter-from-trumps-washington/trumps-escalating-war-on-the-truth-is-on-purpose?mbid=nl_Daily%2B080318.

299. Leonhardt, David, Ian Prasad Philbrick, and Stuart A. Thompson. "Trump's Lies vs. Obama's." *The New York Times.* December 14, 2017. Accessed July 26, 2018. https://www.nytimes.com/interactive/2017/12/14/opinion/sunday/trump-lies-obama-who-is-worse.html.

299. Kessler, Glenn, Salvador Rizzo, and Meg Kelly. "Analysis | President Trump Has Made 3,001 False or Misleading Claims so Far." *The Washington Post.* May 1, 2018. Accessed July 26, 2018. https://www.washingtonpost.com/news/fact-checker/wp/2018/05/01/president-trump-has-made-3001-false-or-misleading-claims-so-far/?utm_term=.098b84012d55.

300. The *Washington Post's* fact checker, Glenn Kessler, tallied 4,229 false statements by Trump in the first 558 days of his presidency.

Obama was president for 2,922 days.

Eighteen lies spread across 2,922 days is a rate of .006 lies per day.

Trump's 4,229 lies in 558 days give him a 7.57 lie-per-day rate.

This is 1,230 times as high as Obama's rate.

Kessler, Glenn, et al. "Analysis | President Trump Has Made 4,229 False or Misleading Claims in 558 Days." *The Washington Post*, 1 Aug. 2018, www.washingtonpost.com/news/fact-checker/wp/2018/08/01/president-trump-has-made-4229-false-or-misleading-claims-in-558-days/?noredirect=on.

300. Glum, Julia. "Poll Shows 57 Percent of Trump Voters Still Think Obama Was Born in Kenya." *Newsweek.* December 15, 2017. Accessed August 3, 2018. https://www.newsweek.com/trump-birther-obama-poll-republicans-kenya-744195.

300. Sanger, David E., and Matthew Rosenberg. "From the Start, Trump Has Muddied a Clear Message: Putin Interfered." *The New York Times.* July 19, 2018. Accessed August 4, 2018. https://www.nytimes.com/2018/07/18/world/europe/trump-intelligence-russian-election-meddling-.html.

300. Silver, Nate. "Is Rasmussen Reports Biased?" FiveThirtyEight. January 3, 2010. Accessed July 26, 2018. https://fivethirtyeight.com/features/is-rasmussen-reports-biased/.

300. "Voters More Likely Now to See Mueller Probe As Partisan Witch Hunt." Rasmussen Reports. Accessed July 26, 2018. http://www.rasmussenreports.com/public_content/politics/trump_administration/april_2018/voters_more_likely_now_to_see_mueller_probe_as_partisan_witch_hunt.

301. Gambino, Lauren, David Smith, Edward Helmore, and Sabrina Siddiqui. "Fire and Fury Released Early in Defiance of Attempt to Ban Tell-all Trump Book." *The Guardian.* January 5, 2018. Accessed August 1, 2018. https://www.theguardian.com/us-news/2018/jan/04/trump-lawyers-book-steve-bannon-white-house.

301. Sinclair, Harriet. "Author of 'Fire and Fury' Says Things in Trump's White House Are so Bad, the 25th Amendment Is Mentioned Daily." *Newsweek.* January 7, 2018. Accessed August 1, 2018. https://www.newsweek.com/michael-wolff-says-trumps-white-house-bad-25th-amendment-mentioned-every-day-773340.

301. Trump's twitter account isn't exclusively his own. Sometimes his aides tweet on his behalf, even mimicking his unusual use of capital letters for emphasis.

Loeb, Saul. "Does Donald Trump Write His Own Tweets? Sometimes." *The Boston Globe*, 22 May 2018, www.bostonglobe.com/news/nation/2018/05/21/trump-tweets-include-grammatical-errors-and-some-them-are-purpose/JeL7AtKLPevJDIIOMG7TrN/story.html.

301. Trump, Donald J. "Now That Russian Collusion, after One Year of Intense Study, Has Proven to Be a Total Hoax on the American Public, the Democrats and Their Lapdogs, the Fake News Mainstream Media, Are Taking out the Old Ronald Reagan Playbook and Screaming Mental Stability and Intelligence. . . ." Twitter. January 6, 2018. Accessed August 4, 2018. https://twitter.com/realdonaldtrump/status/949616329463615489?lang=en

302. Trump, Donald J. ". . . Actually, throughout My Life, My Two Greatest Assets Have Been Mental Stability and Being, Like, Really Smart. Crooked Hillary Clinton Also Played These Cards Very Hard And, as Everyone Knows, Went down in Flames. I Went from VERY Successful Businessman, to Top T.V. Star . . ." Twitter. January 6, 2018. Accessed August 04, 2018. https://twitter.com/realDonaldTrump/status/949618475877765120?ref_src=twsrc%5Etfw%7Ctwcamp%5Etweetembed%7Ctwterm%5E949618475877765120.

302. Trump, Donald J. ". . . to President of the United States (on My First Try). I Think That Would Qualify as Not Smart, but Genius. . . . and a Very Stable Genius at That!" Twitter. January 6, 2018. Accessed

July 26, 2018. https://twitter.com/realDonaldTrump/status/949619270631256064.

302. Trump, Donald J. "Russian Collusion with the Trump Campaign, One of the Most Successful in History, Is a TOTAL HOAX. The Democrats Paid for the Phony and Discredited Dossier Which Was, along with Comey, McCabe, Strzok and His Lover, the Lovely Lisa Page, Used to Begin the Witch Hunt. Disgraceful!" Twitter. August 1, 2018. Accessed August 4, 2018. https://twitter.com/realDonaldTrump/status/1024656465158721536.

302. Trump, Donald J. "Look How Things Have Turned around on the Criminal Deep State. They Go after Phony Collusion with Russia, a Made up Scam, and End up Getting Caught in a Major SPY Scandal the Likes of Which This Country May Never Have Seen Before! What Goes Around, Comes Around!" Twitter. May 23, 2018. Accessed August 6, 2018. https://twitter.com/realdonaldtrump/status/999242039723163648.

302. Trump, Donald J. "It Just Shows Everyone How Broken and Unfair Our Court System Is When the Opposing Side in a Case (such as DACA) Always Runs to the 9th Circuit and Almost Always Wins before Being Reversed by Higher Courts." Twitter. January 10, 2018. Accessed August 6, 2018. https://twitter.com/realdonaldtrump/status/951094078661414912.

302. Robertson, Lori. "The DACA Population Numbers." FactCheck.org. January 12, 2018. Accessed August 6, 2018. https://www.factcheck.org/2018/01/daca-population-numbers/.

302. Dawsey, Josh. "Trump Derides Protections for Immigrants from 'Shithole' Countries." *The Washington Post.* January 12, 2018. Accessed August 1, 2018. https://www.washingtonpost.com/politics/trump-attacks-protections-for-immigrants-from-shithole-countries-in-oval-office-meeting/2018/01/11/bfc0725c-f711-11e7-91af-31ac729add94_story.html?utm_term=.fceb1c584d6a.

Africa is not a country. It is a continent.

303. Gearan, Anne. "Trump Says 'I'm Not a Racist' and Denies 'Shithole Countries' Remark." *The Washington Post.* January 14, 2018. Accessed August 1, 2018. https://www.washingtonpost.com/news/post-politics/wp/2018/01/14/trump-says-im-not-a-racist-and-denies-shithole-countries-remark/?utm_term=.b455952bc628.

303. Cotton, Tom and David Perdue. "Senator Cotton & Senator Perdue Comment on Yesterday's White House Meeting." January 12, 2018. Accessed August 6, 2018. https://www.cotton.senate.gov/?p=press_release&id=866

303. Kiely, Eugene. "What Did Trump Say at Immigration Meeting?" FactCheck.org. February 1, 2018. Accessed August 1, 2018. https://www.factcheck.org/2018/01/trump-say-immigration-meeting/.

303. Ibid.

304. Wire, Sarah D. "California Rep. Devin Nunes Named to Trump's Transition Team." *Los Angeles Times.* November 11, 2016. Accessed August 1, 2018. http://www.latimes.com/politics/essential/la-pol-ca-essential-politics-updates-rep-devin-nunes-named-to-trump-s-1478893307-htmlstory.html.

304. Landay, Jonathan. "FBI Expresses 'Grave Concerns' over Republican Memo's Accuracy." Reuters. February 1, 2018. Accessed August 1, 2018. https://www.reuters.com/article/us-usa-trump-russia-memo/fbi-expresses-grave-concerns-over-republican-memos-accuracy-idUSKBN1FK25P.

304. McKew, Molly K. "How Twitter Bots and Trump Fans Made #ReleaseTheMemo Go Viral." *Politico.* February 4, 2018. Accessed August 1, 2018. https://www.politico.com/magazine/story/2018/02/04/trump-twitter-russians-release-the-memo-216935.editmore

Sit, Ryan. "Russian Bots Might Be behind Controversial #ReleaseTheMemo Campaign, Democrats Say." *Newsweek.* January 24, 2018. Accessed August 1, 2018. https://www.newsweek.com/release-memo-russian-bots-campaign-democrats-789317.

304. Trump, Donald J. "This Memo Totally Vindicates 'Trump' in Probe. But the Russian Witch Hunt Goes on and On. Their Was No Collusion and There Was No Obstruction (the Word Now Used Because, after One Year of Looking Endlessly and Finding NOTHING, Collusion Is Dead). This Is an American Disgrace!" Twitter. February 3, 2018. Accessed August 1, 2018. https://mobile.twitter.com/realDonaldTrump/status/959798743842349056?ref_src=twsrc%5Etfw%7Ctwcamp%5Etweet embed%7Ctwterm%5E959798743842349056.edit

305. "FISA Surveillance Court Orders and Applications." FBI. July 21, 2018. Accessed August 1, 2018. https://vault.fbi.gov/d1-release/d1-release/view.

305. Fandos, Nicholas. "2 Weeks After Trump Blocked It, Democrats' Rebuttal of G.O.P. Memo Is Released." *The New York Times.* February 24, 2018. Accessed August 1, 2018. https://www.nytimes.com/2018/02/24/us/politics/democratic-memo-released-fbi-surveillance-carter-page.html.

"FISA Surveillance Court Orders and Applications." FBI. July 21, 2018. Accessed August 1, 2018. https://vault.fbi.gov/d1-release/d1-release/view.

305. Illing, Sean. "'Post-truth Is Pre-fascism': A Holocaust Historian on the Trump Era." Vox. March 9, 2017. Accessed August 1, 2018. https://www.vox.com/conversations/2017/3/9/14838088/donald-trump-fascism-europe-history-totalitarianism-post-truth.

305. Snyder, Timothy. "10: Believe in Truth." In *On Tyranny: Twenty Lessons from the Twentieth Century.* London: Bodley Head, 2017, 65.

306. Guardianwires. "Donald Trump Says Lack of Applause from Democrats Is Treasonous." YouTube. February 5, 2018. Accessed August 1, 2018. https://m.youtube.com/watch?v=zjwPiE1wCUO.

306. "18 U.S. Code § 2381-Treason." LII / Legal Information Institute. Accessed August 1, 2018. https://www.law.cornell.edu/uscode/text/18/2381.editmore horizontal

306. MacFarquhar, Neil. "Yevgeny Prigozhin, Russian Oligarch Indicted by U.S., Is Known as 'Putin's Cook.'" *The New York Times.* February 16, 2018. Accessed August 1, 2018. https://www.nytimes.com/2018/02/16/world/europe/prigozhin-russia-indictment-mueller.html.

306. "Internet Research Agency Indictment." The United States Department of Justice. February 16, 2018. Accessed August 1, 2018. https://www.justice.gov/file/1035477.

306. Ibid., 4.

306. Ibid., 14–15.

307. Jacobs, Ben. "Lawyer Alex Van Der Zwaan Jailed for 30 Days in Mueller's First Conviction." *The Guardian.* April 3, 2018. Accessed August 6, 2018. https://www.theguardian.com/us-news/2018/apr/03/alex-van-der-zwaan-jail-sentence-mueller-trump-russia-investigation.

307. Trump, Donald J. "WITCH HUNT!" Twitter. February 27, 2018. Accessed August 1, 2018. https://mobile.twitter.com/realdonaldtrump/status/968468176639004672.

307. Liptak, Kevin. "Trump on China's Xi Consolidating Power: 'Maybe We'll Give That a Shot Some Day.'" CNN. March 4, 2018. Accessed August 1, 2018. https://www.cnn.com/2018/03/03/politics/trump-maralago-remarks/index.html.

307. Ibid.

308. He tweeted "crooked Hillary" 269 times by July 2018.

"Trump Twitter Archive: 'Crooked Hillary' Query String." Trump Twitter Archive. Accessed August 6, 2018. http://www.trumptwitterarchive.com/archive.

308. Lewandowski and Bossie, *Let Trump Be Trump,* p. 126.

308. Dawsey, Josh, and Nick Miroff. "The Hostile Border between Trump and the Head of DHS." *The Washington Post.* May 25, 2018. Accessed August 6, 2018. https://www.washingtonpost.com/politics/were-closed-trump-directs-his-anger-over-immigration-at-homeland-security-secretary/2018/05/24/4bd686ec-5abc-11e8-8b92-45fdd7aaef3c_story.html?utm_term=.23f7fc56a7d5.

Schmidt, Michael S., and Maggie Haberman. "Trump Humiliated Jeff Sessions After Mueller Appointment." *The New York Times.* September 14, 2017. Accessed August 6, 2018. https://www.nytimes.com/2017/09/14/us/politics/jeff-sessions-trump.html.

308. Cummings, William. "Watch a Teeth-Gritting Trump Rip a Page from His Notes at Debate's Close." *USA Today,* Gannett Satellite Information Network, 21 Oct. 2016, www.usatoday.com/story/news/politics/onpolitics/2016/10/20/watch-teeth-gritting-trump-rip-page-his-notes-debates-close/92487878/.

308. "Presidential Records Act (PRA) of 1978." National Archives and Records Administration, www.archives.gov/presidential-libraries/laws/1978-act.html.

308. Karni, Annie. "Meet the Guys Who Tape Trump's Papers Back Together." *Politico.* June 10, 2018. Accessed August 6, 2018. https://www.politico.com/story/2018/06/10/trump-papers-filing-system-635164.

308. Ibid.

308. Ibid.

309. Gaouette, Nicole, and Kevin Liptak. "After 'Moron' Report, Tillerson Reaffirms Commitment to

Trump." CNN, 5 Oct. 2017, www.cnn.com/2017/10/04/politics/tillerson-trump-commitment-moron/index.html.

309. Trump, Donald J. "I Told Rex Tillerson, Our Wonderful Secretary of State, That He Is Wasting His Time Trying to Negotiate with Little Rocket Man . . ." Twitter. October 1, 2017. Accessed August 1, 2018. https://mobile.twitter.com/realdonaldtrump/status/914497877543735296.

309. Apuzzo, Matt, and Adam Goldman. "Andrew McCabe, a Target of Trump's F.B.I. Scorn, Is Fired Over Candor Questions." The New York Times. March 17, 2018. Accessed August 1, 2018. https://www.nytimes.com/2018/03/16/us/politics/andrew-mccabe-fbi-fired.html.

309. Phillips, Amber. "Analysis | So Why Exactly Did Andrew McCabe Get Fired?" The Washington Post. March 19, 2018. Accessed August 17, 2018. https://www.washingtonpost.com/news/the-fix/wp/2018/03/19/wait-why-exactly-did-andrew-mccabe-get-fired/?utm_term=.6ec02fb58faa.

309. Ibid.

309. Erickson, Amanda. "'My Strength Is Growing Daily': Yulia Skripal Speaks out for the First Time since Poisoning." The Washington Post. April 5, 2018. Accessed August 2, 2018. https://www.washingtonpost.com/news/worldviews/wp/2018/04/05/my-strength-is-growing-daily-yulia-skripal-speaks-out-for-the-first-time-since-poisoning/.

309. Baynes, Chris. "Nerve Agent Which Poisoned Ex-spy Sergei Skripal and His Daughter Was Delivered 'in a Liquid Form.'" The Independent. April 17, 2018. Accessed August 2, 2018. https://www.independent.co.uk/news/uk/home-news/nerve-agent-sergei-skripal-liquid-how-poison-yulia-salisbury-defra-a8308411.html.

309. "Vladimir Putin: 'Nonsense' to Think Russia Would Poison Spy in UK." The Guardian. March 18, 2018. Accessed August 2, 2018. https://www.theguardian.com/uk-news/2018/mar/18/vladimir-putin-nonsense-to-think-russia-would-poison-spy-in-uk.

309. Filipov, David. "Here Are 10 Critics of Vladimir Putin Who Died Violently or in Suspicious Ways." The Washington Post. March 23, 2017. Accessed August 2, 2018. https://www.washingtonpost.com/news/worldviews/wp/2017/03/23/here-are-ten-critics-of-vladimir-putin-who-died-violently-or-in-suspicious-ways/?utm_term=.8d5cb7b3542d.

310. Baker, Peter. "White House Penalizes Russians Over Election Meddling and Cyberattacks." The New York Times. March 15, 2018. Accessed August 2, 2018. https://www.nytimes.com/2018/03/15/us/politics/trump-russia-sanctions.html.

310. Ibid.

310. "Alert (TA18-074A)." Virus Basics | US-CERT. Accessed August 2, 2018. https://www.us-cert.gov/ncas/alerts/TA18-074A.

310. Mak, Aaron. "What Does It Mean to Hack an Electrical Grid?" Slate. March 15, 2018. Accessed August 6, 2018. https://slate.com/technology/2018/03/electrical-grid-hack-russia-explanation.html.

310. Troianovski, Anton. "Putin Cruises to Victory in Russia, Tells Supporters: 'Success Awaits Us!'" The Washington Post. March 18, 2018. Accessed August 1, 2018. https://www.washingtonpost.com/world/europe/russia-scrambles-to-get-voters-to-polls-to-legitimize-election-ahead-of-expected-putin-landslide/2018/03/18/f8d31426-2963-11e8-a227-fd2b009466bc_story.html?utm_term=.1f5f599c1e2e.

310. Arkhipov, Ilya, and Jennifer Epstein. "Trump Congratulated Putin on Election 'Victory,' Kremlin Says." Bloomberg.com. March 20, 2018. Accessed August 1, 2018. https://www.bloomberg.com/news/articles/2018-03-20/trump-hasn-t-called-putin-and-that-s-fine-kremlin-says-really.

311. Miller, Jonathan Lemire and Zeke. "Briefing Papers Warned Trump: 'DO NOT CONGRATULATE' Putin." PBS. March 21, 2018. Accessed August 1, 2018. https://www.pbs.org/newshour/politics/briefing-papers-warned-trump-do-not-congratulate-putin.

311. Landler, Mark. "Trump Congratulates Putin, but Doesn't Mention Meddling in U.S." The New York Times. March 20, 2018. Accessed August 2, 2018. https://www.nytimes.com/2018/03/20/us/politics/trump-putin-russia.html.

311. McCain, John. "An American President Does Not Lead the Free World by Congratulating Dictators on Winning Sham Elections. And by Doing so with Vladimir Putin, President Trump Insulted Every Russian Citizen Who Was Denied the Right to Vote in a Free and Fair Election. Https://T.co/lcQTBi7CA1." Twitter, Twitter, 20 Mar. 2018, twitter.com/senjohnmccain/status/976147002244378625.

311. Ewing, Philip. "Trump National Security Adviser H.R. McMaster To Resign, Be Replaced By John Bolton." NPR, 22 Mar. 2018, www.npr.org/2018/03/22/593283104/trump-national-security-adviser-h-r-mcmaster-to-resign-be-replaced-by-john-bolton.

312. "Statement from the Press Secretary Regarding Russia's Expulsion of American Diplomats." The White House. Accessed August 1, 2018. https://www.whitehouse.gov/briefings-statements/statement-press-secretary-regarding-russias-expulsion-american-diplomats/.

312. "Attorney General Announces Zero-Tolerance Policy for Criminal Illegal Entry." The United States Department of Justice. April 6, 2018. Accessed August 2, 2018. https://www.justice.gov/opa/pr/attorney-general-announces-zero-tolerance-policy-criminal-illegal-entry.editmore horizontal

312. Poolreports. "Subject: Pool Report #2-Immigration Comments." Public Pool. June 18, 2018. Accessed August 2, 2018. https://publicpool.kinja.com/subject-pool-report-2-immigration-comments-1826920847.

312. Flagg, Anna. "The Myth of the Criminal Immigrant." The New York Times. March 30, 2018. Accessed August 2, 2018. https://www.nytimes.com/interactive/2018/03/30/upshot/crime-immigration-myth.html.

312. "Who's Really Crossing the U.S. Border, and Why They're Coming." Lawfare. June 27, 2018. Accessed

August 2, 2018. https://www.lawfareblog.com/whos-really-crossing-us-border-and-why-theyre-coming.

312. Qiu, Linda. "Border Crossings Have Been Declining for Years, Despite Claims of a 'Crisis of Illegal Immigration.'" *The New York Times*. June 21, 2018. Accessed August 2, 2018. https://www.nytimes.com/2018/06/20/us/politics/fact-check-trump-border-crossings-declining-.html.

312. "Who's Really Crossing the U.S. Border, and Why They're Coming." Lawfare. June 27, 2018. Accessed August 2, 2018. https://www.lawfareblog.com/whos-really-crossing-us-border-and-why-theyre-coming.

312. Ibid.

312. Mancheno, Luis. "Analysis: How the Asylum Process Works, and How It Needs to Change." CBS News. June 8, 2018. Accessed August 2, 2018. https://www.cbsnews.com/news/asylum-seekers-in-us-how-process-works-needs-to-change-analysis/.

312. "Asylum & the Rights of Refugees." International Justice Resource Center, 28 Mar. 2018, ijrcenter.org/refugee-law/.editmore horizontal

313. Harris, Lindsay M. "Perspective | Seeking Asylum Isn't a Crime. Why Do Trump and Sessions Act like It Is?" *The Washington Post*, WP Company, 29 June 2018, www.washingtonpost.com/outlook/seeking-asylum-isnt-a-crime-why-do-trump-and-sessions-act-like-it-is/2018/06/29/dc4cf136-7a7c-11e8-93cc-6d3beccdd7a3_story.html?utm_term=.d083a5d19137.

313. Diaz, Daniella. "Kelly: DHS Is considering Separating Undocumented Children from Their Parents at the Border." CNN. March 7, 2017. Accessed August 2, 2018. https://www.cnn.com/2017/03/06/politics/john-kelly-separating-children-from-parents-immigration-border/.

313. Wingman, Brooke. "Kelly Says Full-scale Border Wall 'Unlikely,' Clarifies Position on Family Detentions." Fox News. April 5, 2017. Accessed August 2, 2018. http://www.foxnews.com/politics/2017/04/05/kelly-says-full-scale-border-wall-unlikely-clarifies-position-on-family-detentions.html.

313. Dickerson, Caitlin. "Hundreds of Immigrant Children Have Been Taken From Parents at U.S. Border." *The New York Times*. April 21, 2018. Accessed August 2, 2018. https://www.nytimes.com/2018/04/20/us/immigrant-children-separation-ice.html.

313. *The Separation of Family Members Apprehended by or Found Inadmissible While in U.S. Customs and Border Protection (CBP) Custody at the U.S.-Mexico Border*. PDF. New York: Women's Refugee Commission, December 11, 2017.

313. "U.S. Centers Force Migrant Children to Take Drugs: Lawsuit." Reuters, 21 June 2018, www.reuters.com/article/us-usa-immigration-medication/u-s-centers-force-migrant-children-to-take-drugs-lawsuit-idUSKBN1JH076.

313. "Who's Really Crossing the U.S. Border, and Why They're Coming." Lawfare. June 27, 2018. Accessed August 2, 2018. https://www.lawfareblog.com/whos-really-crossing-us-border-and-why-theyre-coming.

313. Long, Colleen. "DHS Reports about 2,000 Minors Separated from Families." AP News. June 16, 2018. Accessed August 2, 2018. https://apnews.com/3361a7d5fa714ea4b028f0a29db1cabc.

314. Bacon, John. "Amid Outrage, Homeland Security Chief Kirstjen Nielsen 'Will Not Apologize' for Separating Families." *USA Today*. June 18, 2018. Accessed August 2, 2018. https://www.usatoday.com/story/news/nation/2018/06/18/homeland-security-chief-denies-policy-separates-families-border/709378002/.

314. "Judge: Trump Administration Reunification Efforts Are 'Unacceptable.'" NBCNews.com. Accessed August 6, 2018. https://www.nbcnews.com/politics/immigration/judge-calls-trump-administration-family-reunification-efforts-unacceptable-n897531.

314. Allen, Jonathan. "Trump Form Discloses Debt Payment to Cohen, Lawyer Who Paid Stormy Daniels." NBCNews.com. Accessed August 2, 2018. https://www.nbcnews.com/politics/white-house/trump-discloses-stormy-daniels-payment-debt-financial-disclosure-form-n874331.

Turak, Natasha, and Dan Mangan. "Trump Paid off 'Three Additional Women' after Affairs, Michael Avenatti Says." CNBC. July 27, 2018. Accessed August 6, 2018. https://www.cnbc.com/2018/07/27/stormy-daniels-lawyer-alleges-trump-paid-off-three-additional-women.html.

314. Liptak, Kevin. "Trump Says He Didn't Know about Stormy Daniels Payment." CNN. April 6, 2018. Accessed August 2, 2018. https://www.cnn.com/2018/04/05/politics/donald-trump-stormy-daniels/index.html.

314. Allen, Jonathan. "Trump Form Discloses Debt Payment to Cohen, Lawyer Who Paid Stormy Daniels." NBCNews.com. Accessed August 2, 2018. https://www.nbcnews.com/politics/white-house/trump-discloses-stormy-daniels-payment-debt-financial-disclosure-form-n874331.

314. Gordon, Greg. "Mueller Probe Tracking down Trump Business Partners, with Cohen a Focus of Queries." Mcclatchydc. Accessed August 2, 2018. https://www.mcclatchydc.com/news/nation-world/national/article208090764.html.

315. Trump, Donald J. "Attorney–client Privilege Is Dead!" Twitter. April 10, 2018. Accessed August 2, 2018. https://twitter.com/realdonaldtrump/status/983662868540346371.

315. Trump, Donald J. "Much of the Bad Blood with Russia Is Caused by the Fake & Corrupt Russia Investigation, Headed up by the All Democrat Loyalists, or People That Worked for Obama. Mueller Is Most Conflicted of All (except Rosenstein Who Signed FISA & Comey Letter). No Collusion, so They Go Crazy!" Twitter. April 11, 2018. Accessed August 2, 2018. https://twitter.com/realdonaldtrump/status/984053549742067712.

315. Trump, Donald J. "Our Relationship with Russia Is Worse Now than It Has Ever Been, and That Includes the Cold War. There Is No Reason for This. Russia Needs Us to Help with Their Economy, Something That Would Be Very Easy to Do, and We Need All Nations to Work Together. Stop the Arms Race?" Twitter. April

11, 2018. Accessed August 2, 2018. https://twitter.com/
realdonaldtrump/status/984032798821568513.

315. Hille, Kathrin. "Russia's Economy: Challenges
Facing Vladimir Putin." *Financial Times.* February 28,
2018. Accessed August 2, 2018. https://www.ft.com/
content/3aac3faa-1bb6-11e8-aaca-4574d7dabfb6.

316. *Senate Select Committee on Intelligence.*
Washington DC: United States Senate, July 3, 2018.

316. "In His Own Words: The President's Attacks on
the Courts | Brennan Center for Justice." America's
Faulty Perception of Crime Rates | Brennan
Center for Justice. June 5, 2017. Accessed August
6, 2018. https://www.brennancenter.org/analysis/
his-own-words-presidents-attacks-courts.

317. Macron, Emmanuel. "The American President
May Not Mind Being Isolated, but Neither Do We
Mind Signing a 6 Country Agreement If Need
Be. Because These 6 Countries Represent Values,
They Represent an Economic Market Which
Has the Weight of History behind It and Which
Is Now a True International Force Https://t.co/
UA86fcjozs." Twitter. June 7, 2018. Accessed August
6, 2018. https://twitter.com/emmanuelmacron/
status/1004812693348511751?lang=en.

317. Sang-hun, Choe. "Kim Jong-un's Image Shift:
From Nuclear Madman to Skillful Leader." *The New
York Times.* June 6, 2018. Accessed August 6, 2018.
https://www.nytimes.com/2018/06/06/world/asia/kim-
korea-image.html.

317. Fisher, Max. "What Happened in the Trump-Kim
Meeting and Why It Matters." *The New York Times.*
June 12, 2018. Accessed August 6, 2018. https://www.
nytimes.com/2018/06/12/world/asia/trump-kim-
meeting-interpreter.html.

318. Lafraniere, Sharon. "Judge Orders Paul Manafort
Jailed Before Trial, Citing New Obstruction Charges."
The New York Times. June 15, 2018. Accessed August 6,
2018. https://www.nytimes.com/2018/06/15/us/politics/
manafort-bail-revoked-jail.html.

318. Trump, Donald J. "Wow, What a Tough Sentence
for Paul Manafort, Who Has Represented Ronald
Reagan, Bob Dole and Many Other Top Political People
and Campaigns. Didn't Know Manafort Was the Head
of the Mob. What about Comey and Crooked Hillary
and All of the Others? Very Unfair!" Twitter. June 15,
2018. Accessed August 6, 2018. https://twitter.com/
realdonaldtrump/status/1007679422865006593.

318. Kevin Russell. "Kavanaugh on Presidential
Power: Law-review Article on Investigations of Sitting
Presidents (UPDATED)." SCOTUSblog. July 16, 2018.
Accessed August 6, 2018. http://www.scotusblog.
com/2018/07/kavanaugh-on-presidential-power-law-
review-article-on-investigations-of-sitting-presidents/.

318. "VIKTOR BORISOVICH NETYKSHO, Et Al
Indictment." The United States Department of Justice.
Accessed August 6, 2018. https://www.justice.gov/
file/1080281.

318. Cuomo, Christopher C. "Roger Stone: I
Probably Am the Person in the Indictment. Https://t.
co/zOWDTXBFFy." Twitter. July 14, 2018. Accessed
August 6, 2018. https://twitter.com/ChrisCuomo/
status/1017939029143113729?ref_src=twsrc%5Et-

fw%7Ctwcamp%5Etweetembed%7Ctwter-
m%5E1017939029143113729.edit

319. "Transcript: Dan Coats Warns The Lights Are
'Blinking Red' On Russian Cyberattacks." NPR. July
18, 2018. Accessed August 6, 2018. https://www.npr.
org/2018/07/18/630164914/transcript-dan-coats-
warns-of-continuing-russian-cyberattacks.

319. *United States of America v Mariia Butina
A.k.a. Maria Butina, Defendant.* Washington, D.C.:
U.S. District Court for the District of Columbia, July
18, 2018.

319. Helderman, Rosalind S., Tom Jackman, and
Devlin Barrett. "Maria Butina, Russian Gun-rights
Advocate Who Sought to Build Ties with NRA,
Charged with Acting as a Covert Russian Agent."
The Washington Post. July 16, 2018. Accessed
August 6, 2018. https://www.washingtonpost.
com/local/public-safety/maria-butina-russian-
gun-rights-advocate-charged-in-us-with-
acting-as-russian-federation-agent/2018/07/16/
d1d4832a-8929-11e8-85ae-511bc1146b0b_story.
html?utm_term=.8034b4a5eaa8.

319. https://www.washingtonpost.com/politics/
she-was-like-a-novelty-how-alleged-russian-agent-
maria-butina-gained-access-to-elite-conservative-
circles/2018/07/17/1bb62bbc-89d2-11e8-a345-a1bf-
7847b375_story.html?utm_term=.b33733541001

319. The NRA gave Trump's campaign about
$30 million during his election—the highest the
organization has ever spent on a presidential
candidate, and it is likely Mueller has access to the
organization's tax filings, which would enable him
to determine whether any of that money came from
Russia. It is illegal for foreign nationals to make
political donations in the United States.

Smith, Chris. "The N.R.A. Spent $30 Million to Elect
Trump. Was It Russian Money?" *Vanity Fair.* June 22,
2018. Accessed August 6, 2018. https://www.vanityfair.
com/news/2018/06/the-nra-spent-dollar30-million-to-
elect-trump-was-it-russian-money.

Leblanc, Paul. "Robert Mueller's Russia Investigators
Likely Has the NRA's Tax Returns, According to
Legal Experts." *Newsweek.* July 19, 2018. Accessed
August 6, 2018. https://www.newsweek.com/
robert-mueller-nra-russia-tax-returns-1004008.

"Foreign Nationals." FEC.gov. June 23, 2017. Accessed
August 6, 2018. https://www.fec.gov/updates/
foreign-nationals/.

320. Meyer, David. "President Trump
Reportedly Threatened to Pull the U.S.
Out of NATO." *Fortune.* Accessed August
6, 2018. http://fortune.com/2018/07/12/
trump-nato-pull-out-withdraw-threat/.

320. The KGB functioned both as an intelligence
agency and secret police during the Cold War and
until the collapse of the Soviet Union.

320. Foley, James B. "Don't Let Vladimir Putin Destroy
NATO." *Time,* Time, 31 Mar. 2016, time.com/4276525/
vladimir-putin-nato/.

320. Associated Press. "Democrats Call
on Trump to Cancel Putin Summit." PBS.
July 13, 2018. Accessed August 6, 2018.

https://www.pbs.org/newshour/politics/
democrats-call-on-trump-to-cancel-putin-summit.

321. Diaz, Daniella. "McCain: Trump's Meeting
with Putin 'Should Not Move Forward.'" CNN. July
13, 2018. Accessed August 6, 2018. https://www.cnn.
com/2018/07/13/politics/john-mccain-donald-trump-
russia-putin/index.html.

321. Trump, Donald J. "Our Relationship with Russia
Has NEVER Been Worse Thanks to Many Years of
U.S. Foolishness and Stupidity and Now, the Rigged
Witch Hunt!" Twitter. July 16, 2018. Accessed August
21, 2018. https://twitter.com/realdonaldtrump/
status/1018738368753078273?lang=en.

321. Sharkov, Damien. "Who Else Is in the Room
with Trump and Putin?" *Newsweek.* July 16, 2018.
Accessed August 6, 2018. https://www.newsweek.com/
trump-putin-meet-helsinki-who-else-room-1025963.

322. Ibid.

323. "Statement on Russia." Speaker.gov. July 16,
2018. Accessed August 6, 2018. https://www.speaker.
gov/press-release/statement-russia.

323. Flake, Jeff. "I Never Thought I Would See the
Day When Our American President Would Stand
on the Stage with the Russian President and Place
Blame on the United States for Russian Aggression.
This Is Shameful." Twitter. July 16, 2018. Accessed
August 6, 2018. https://twitter.com/JeffFlake/
status/1018891518654976000.

323. Ibid.

323. Brennan, John O. "Donald Trump's Press
Conference Performance in Helsinki Rises to
& Exceeds the Threshold of 'High Crimes &
Misdemeanors.' It Was Nothing Short of Treasonous.
Not Only Were Trump's Comments Imbecilic, He Is
Wholly in the Pocket of Putin. Republican Patriots:
Where Are You???" Twitter. July 16, 2018. Accessed
August 6, 2018. https://twitter.com/JohnBrennan/
status/1018885971104985093.

323. Trump, Donald J. "So President Obama Knew
about Russia before the Election. Why Didn't He
Do Something about It? Why Didn't He Tell Our
Campaign? Because It Is All a Big Hoax, That's
Why, and He Thought Crooked Hillary Was Going
to Win!!!" Twitter. July 22, 2018. Accessed August
6, 2018. https://twitter.com/realdonaldtrump/
status/1021158915206152193.

323. Trump, Donald J. "Looking More & More like
the Trump Campaign for President Was Illegally
Being Spied upon (surveillance) for the Political
Gain of Crooked Hillary Clinton and the DNC. Ask
Her How That Worked out-She Did Better with
Crazy Bernie. Republicans Must Get Tough Now.
An Illegal Scam!" Twitter. July 22, 2018. Accessed
August 6, 2018. https://twitter.com/realdonaldtrump/
status/1020984152357777408.

324. Trump, Donald J. "To Iranian President Rouhani:
NEVER, EVER THREATEN THE UNITED STATES
AGAIN OR YOU WILL SUFFER CONSEQUENCES THE
LIKES OF WHICH FEW THROUGHOUT HISTORY
HAVE EVER SUFFERED BEFORE. WE ARE NO
LONGER A COUNTRY THAT WILL STAND FOR
YOUR DEMENTED WORDS OF VIOLENCE & DEATH.
BE CAUTIOUS!" Twitter. July 23, 2018. Accessed

August 6, 2018. https://twitter.com/realdonaldtrump/
status/1021234525626609666.

328. https://www.nytimes.com/2017/01/21/upshot/
what-does-the-order-against-the-health-law-
actually-do.html.

328. https://www.cnn.com/2017/01/25/politics/donald-
trump-build-wall-immigration-executive-orders/index.
html; https://www.nytimes.com/2017/01/25/us/politics/
refugees-immigrants-wall-trump.html.

328. https://www.nytimes.com/2017/01/26/us/trump-
immigration-deportation.html.

328. https://www.nytimes.com/2017/01/27/us/politics/
trump-syrian-refugees.html.

328. https://www.cnn.com/2017/01/30/politics/donald-
trump-immigration-order-department-of-justice/
index.html.

328. https://www.nytimes.com/2017/01/31/us/politics/
supreme-court-nominee-trump.html.

328. https://www.brookings.edu/research/tracking-
turnover-in-the-trump-administration/; http://
thewashingtonstandard.com/former-nsc-official-
everything-president-wants-mcmaster-opposes/

328. https://www.nytimes.com/2017/03/06/us/
politics/travel-ban-muslim-trump.html; https://
abcnews.go.com/Politics/timeline-president-trumps-
immigration-executive-order-legal-challenges/
story?id=45332741

328. https://www.nytimes.com/2017/03/06/us/politics/
affordable-care-act-obamacare-health.html.

329. https://www.politico.com/story/2017/03/
trump-deputy-chief-of-staff-katie-walsh-moving-
to-outside-political-groups-236706; https://www.
cosmopolitan.com/politics/a8618269/katie-walsh-
trump-deputy-chief-staff/; http://www.foxnews.
com/politics/2017/07/29/kelly-bringing-dhs-
deputy-to-white-house.html; https://www.nytimes.
com/2017/07/21/us/politics/sean-spicer-resigns-as-
white-house-press-secretary.html.

329. https://www.nytimes.com/2017/04/06/us/politics/
neil-gorsuch-supreme-court-senate.html.

329. https://www.nbcnews.com/politics/congress/neil-
gorsuch-confirmed-supreme-court-after-senate-uses-
nuclear-option-n743766

329. https://www.nytimes.com/2017/04/26/us/politics/
trump-tax-cut-plan.html.

329. https://www.nytimes.com/2017/05/04/us/politics/
health-care-bill-vote.html.

329. https://www.nytimes.com/2017/05/09/us/politics/
james-comey-fired-fbi.html.

329. https://www.nytimes.com/2017/05/17/us/politics/
robert-mueller-special-counsel-russia-investigation.
html.

329. https://www.nytimes.com/2017/05/30/us/
politics/trump-dubke-white-house-staff-changes.html;
https://www.washingtonpost.com/news/post-politics/
wp/2017/05/30/dubke-resigns-as-white-house-
communications-director/?utm_term=.17759461e253

329. https://www.washingtonpost.com/news/the-fix/wp/2017/06/08/6-takeaways-from-james-comeys-extraordinary-testimony-about-trump/?utm_term=.c73dd7902c08

329. https://www.washingtonpost.com/world/national-security/special-counsel-is-investigating-trump-for-possible-obstruction-of-justice/2017/06/14/9ce02506-5131-11e7-b064-828ba60fbb98_story.html?utm_term=.bf1e639078dc

329. https://www.washingtontimes.com/news/2017/dec/2/peter-strzok-mueller-investigator-removed-case/

329. https://docs.google.com/spreadsheets/d/1utamO_EzX9VMyTKqWGF4x2upqohYCRYIdzyrx6YEyyk/edit#gid=12

329. https://www.nytimes.com/2018/01/25/us/politics/trump-mueller-special-counsel-russia.html; https://www.businessinsider.com/trump-ordered-mueller-fired-last-year-2018-1/

329. https://www.cnn.com/2017/06/16/politics/trump-transition-campaign-officials-told-to-keep-russia-related-documents/index.html; https://www.nytimes.com/2017/06/16/us/politics/trump-transition-team-russia-inquiry.html.

329. https://www.bloomberg.com/news/articles/2017-07-20/mueller-is-said-to-expand-probe-to-trump-business-transactions

329. https://www.nytimes.com/2017/07/21/us/politics/sean-spicer-resigns-as-white-house-press-secretary.html; https://www.thesun.co.uk/news/6611918/who-sarah-huckabee-sanders-ejected-red-hen-restaurant-lexington-work-donald-trump/

329. https://www.wsj.com/articles/trump-wont-say-if-he-will-fire-attorney-general-sessions-1501010025

330. https://www.bostonglobe.com/news/politics/2017/08/09/fbi-raided-home-former-trump-campaign-chair-july/oYGJpfwcC42453Pte1b6yL/story.html.

330. https://www.nytimes.com/2017/07/27/us/politics/obamacare-partial-repeal-senate-republicans-revolt.html.

330. https://www.washingtonexaminer.com/longtime-aide-and-chief-of-staff-to-mike-pence-resigns/article/2627450

330. https://www.nytimes.com/2017/07/28/us/politics/reince-priebus-white-house-trump.html.

330. https://www.nytimes.com/2017/08/18/us/politics/steve-bannon-trump-white-house.html; https://www.theatlantic.com/politics/archive/2016/08/the-radical-anti-conservatism-of-stephen-bannon/496796/

330. https://www.cnn.com/2017/09/01/politics/keith-schiller-donald-trump/index.html; https://people.com/politics/president-trump-bodyguard-keith-schiller-leaving-white-house/; https://www.washingtonpost.com/politics/white-house-communications-director-hope-hicks-to-resign/2018/02/28/13760a8c-1ccf-11e8-b2d9-08e748f892c0_story.html?utm_term=.e3a6e747a752;

330. https://www.bloomberg.com/news/articles/2017-09-16/facebook-is-said-to-tell-mueller-more-on-russia-ad-spending; https://www.wsj.com/articles/facebook-gave-special-counsel-robert-mueller-more-details-on-russian-ad-buys-than-congress-1505514552

330. https://www.businessinsider.com/who-is-george-papadopoulos-pleaded-guilty-fbi-russia-contacts-2017-10; https://www.washingtonexaminer.com/news/george-papadopoulos-agrees-with-robert-mueller-to-move-to-sentencing-phase

330. https://www.cbsnews.com/news/who-is-richard-gates/; https://assets.documentcloud.org/documents/4163372/Paul-Manafort-Rick-Gates-Indictment.pdf

330. https://www.nytimes.com/2017/11/16/us/politics/tax-bill-house-vote.html.

330. https://www.brookings.edu/research/tracking-turnover-in-the-trump-administration/

330. https://www.nytimes.com/2017/12/01/us/politics/michael-flynn-guilty-russia-investigation.html.

330. https://www.nytimes.com/2017/12/01/us/politics/senate-tax-bill.html.

330. https://www.washingtonpost.com/politics/dina-powell-deputy-national-security-adviser-to-depart-trump-white-house/2017/12/08/85d8c9ea-dc31-11e7-a841-2066faf731ef_story.html?utm_term=.5b684f879fa8; https://www.businessinsider.com/dina-powell-joins-goldman-sachs-powerful-investment-banking-division-2018-5

330. https://www.usatoday.com/story/news/politics/2017/12/13/omarosa-manigault-newman-trumps-apprentice-televisreality-star-turned-trump-presidential-aide-resign/947822001/

331. https://www.washingtonexaminer.com/trump-announces-white-house-policy-team/article/2611014; https://www.newyorker.com/news/news-desk/a-year-into-the-trump-era-white-house-staff-turnover-is-off-the-charts

331. https://www.nytimes.com/2017/12/20/us/politics/tax-bill-republicans.html.

331. https://www.nytimes.com/2017/12/22/us/politics/trump-tax-bill.html; https://hbr.org/ideacast/2017/12/breaking-down-the-new-u-s-corporate-tax-law

331. http://www.foxnews.com/politics/2017/12/21/trump-deputy-chief-staff-rick-dearborn-resigns.html; https://www.businessinsider.com/white-house-deputy-chief-of-staff-rick-dearborn-is-resigning-2017-12

331. https://www.aljazeera.com/news/2018/04/mueller-probe-george-nader-convicted-paedophile-180404110222649.html; https://www.cnn.com/2018/03/06/politics/george-nader-robert-mueller/index.html.

331. https://www.nytimes.com/interactive/2018/06/02/us/politics/trump-legal-documents.html

331. https://www.nytimes.com/interactive/2018/06/02/us/politics/trump-legal-documents.html

331. https://www.nytimes.com/2018/02/07/us/politics/rob-porter-resigns-abuse-white-house-staff-secretary.html.

331. https://www.newsweek.com/who-richard-pinedo-mueller-defendant-guilty-809783

331. https://www.nytimes.com/2018/02/16/us/politics/russians-indicted-mueller-election-interference.html.

331. https://www.nytimes.com/2018/02/20/us/politics/alex-van-der-zwaan-gates-russia-mueller.html.

331. https://www.nbcnews.com/politics/politics-news/new-indictment-hits-manafort-gates-tax-bank-fraud-charges-n850411

https://docs.google.com/spreadsheets/d/1utamO_EzX9VMyTKqWGF4x2upqohYCRYIdzyrx6YEyyk/edit#gid=13

331. https://www.cbsnews.com/news/rick-gates-expected-to-plead-live-updates/

331. https://www.nytimes.com/2018/06/15/us/politics/manafort-bail-revoked-jail.html.

332. https://www.washingtonpost.com/news/the-fix/wp/2018/03/01/why-did-hope-hicks-resign-even-the-good-option-looks-bad/; http://thehill.com/homenews/administration/376108-hope-hicks-resigns-from-white-house

332. https://www.brookings.edu/research/tracking-turnover-in-the-trump-administration/

332. https://www.thedailybeast.com/trumps-lawyer-its-time-to-fire-robert-mueller

332. https://www.cnn.com/2018/03/22/politics/john-dowd-white-house/index.html.

332. https://www.cnbc.com/2018/03/23/trump-threatens-to-veto-omnibus-spending-bill-over-daca-and-the-border-wall.html.

332. https://www.usatoday.com/story/news/politics/2018/03/28/justice-inspector-general-probe-surveillance-abuses-russia-election-case/467105002/

332. https://www.cbsnews.com/news/fbi-raids-michael-cohen-office-trump-personal-lawyer-today-2018-04-09/; https://www.nbcnews.com/politics/politics-news/fbi-raids-office-trump-lawyer-michael-cohen-n86412; https://www.wsj.com/articles/fbi-raids-trump-lawyers-office-1523306297?mod=searchresults&page=1&pos=1; https://www.washingtonexaminer.com/news/michael-cohen-under-investigation-for-possible-bank-fraud-campaign-finance-violations-report

332. https://www.cnn.com/2018/04/10/politics/tom-bossert-homeland-security-adviser/index.html; https://www.nbcnews.com/politics/politics-news/tom-bossert-trump-s-homeland-security-adviser-resign-n864321

332. https://docs.google.com/spreadsheets/d/1utamO_EzX9VMyTKqWGF4x2upqohYCRYIdzyrx6YEyyk/edit#gid=13

332. www.nydailynews.com/news/politics/white-house-lawyer-ty-cobb-exiting-emmet-flood-replace-article-1.3967672

332. https://www.nytimes.com/interactive/2018/05/07/world/middleeast/iran-deal-before-after.html.

332. https://www.politico.com/story/2018/05/15/white-house-eliminates-cyber-adviser-post-542916;

https://www.securityweek.com/white-house-cuts-cybersecurity-coordinator-role

332. https://www.cnn.com/2018/05/17/politics/paul-manafort-son-in-law-plea/index.html.

332. https://www.cbsnews.com/news/trump-hereby-demands-doj-look-into-whether-fbi-infiltrated-campaign/

333. https://twitter.com/realdonaldtrump/status/1003616210922147841?lang=en

333. https://www.nytimes.com/2018/06/08/us/politics/manafort-obstruction-kilimnik-charges.html.

333. https://twitter.com/realdonaldtrump/status/1007679422865006593; | https://twitter.com/politifact/status/1007687181266243585?lang=en

333. https://www.cnbc.com/2018/06/15/white-house-legislative-affairs-director-marc-short-told-staff-he-will-leave-administration.html.

333. https://www.nytimes.com/2018/06/26/us/politics/supreme-court-trump-travel-ban.html.

333. https://www.wsj.com/articles/key-trade-adviser-leaves-trump-administration-1530056219; https://www.msn.com/en-us/news/politics/top-trump-trade-adviser-everett-eissenstat-to-leave-white-house/ar-AAzdeuo; https://www.marketwatch.com/story/top-trade-adviser-everett-eissenstat-is-leaving-trump-administration-2018-06-26; https://www.whitehouse.gov/presidential-actions/white-house-national-security-advisor-director-national-economic-council-announce-senior-staff-appointment/

333. https://www.cbsnews.com/news/senate-intel-agrees-with-assessment-that-russia-meddled-to-help-trump/;

https://www.cbsnews.com/news/report-on-russian-hacking-released-by-intelligence-community/

333. https://www.cnn.com/2018/07/05/politics/scott-pruitt-epa-resigns/index.html

333. https://www.cnbc.com/2018/07/05/trump-picks-brett-kavanaugh-for-supreme-court.html.

333. https://www.washingtonpost.com/world/national-security/rod-rosenstein-expected-to-announce-new-indictment-by-mueller/2018/07/13/bc565582-86a9-11e8-8553-a3ce89036c78_story.html?utm_term=.e6e7028573f0; https://www.nbcnews.com/news/us-news/mueller-charges-russian-intelligence-officers-hacking-dnc-clinton-n891236

334. Pramuk, Jacob. "Trump Spent Less than Half of What Clinton Did per Electoral Vote." CNBC. December 9, 2016. Accessed July 30, 2018. https://www.cnbc.com/2016/12/09/trump-spent-less-than-half-of-what-clinton-did-per-electoral-vote.html.

334. Abramson, Alana. "The White House Said Paul Manafort Had a 'Limited' Role in Trump's Campaign. Here's a Timeline of the Facts." *Fortune*. March 22, 2017. Accessed July 30, 2018. http://fortune.com/2017/03/22/paul-manafort-donald-trump-vladimir-putin/.

334. Megerian, Chris and Joseph Tanfani. "Mueller More than Doubles Criminal Charges against Manafort and Gates." *Los Angeles Times*. February 22, 2018.

Accessed July 30, 2018. http://www.latimes.com/ politics/la-na-pol-essential-washington-updates-mueller-files-new-charges-in-manafort-1519335654-htmlstory.html.

334. Hsu, Spencer S., Ellen Nakashima, and Devlin Barrett. "Manafort Ordered to Jail after Witness-Tampering Charges." *Washington Post.* June 15, 2018. Accessed July 30, 2018. https://www.washingtonpost. com/local/public-safety/manafort-ordered-to-jail-after-witness-tampering-charges/2018/06/15/ ccc526cc-6e68-11e8-afd5-778aca903bbe_story. html?utm_term=.8ef9ea602e78.

335. Choma, Russ. "Who Is Rick Gates?" *Mother Jones.* October 30, 2017. Accessed July 30, 2018. https://www.motherjones.com/politics/2017/10/ who-is-rick-gates/.

335. Ibid.

336. Barrett, Devlin, and Spencer S. Hsu. "Former Trump Campaign Official Rick Gates Pleads Guilty to 2 Charges." *Washington Post.* February 23, 2018. Accessed July 30, 2018. https://www. washingtonpost.com/politics/former-trump-campaign-official-rick-gates-expected-to-plead-guilty-and-cooperate-with-special-counsel-in-probe-of-russian-election-interference/2018/02/23/ ceaaeac8-16b4-11e8-b681-2d4d462a1921_story. html?utm_term=.f1b4efa58dca.

336. Martin, Jonathan, Jim Rutenberg, and Maggie Haberman. "Donald Trump Appoints Media Firebrand to Run Campaign." *New York Times.* August 17, 2016. Accessed July 30, 2018. https://www.nytimes. com/2016/08/18/us/politics/donald-trump-stephen-bannon-paul-manafort.html.

Sullivan, Sean. "Trump Hires Ex-Cruz Super PAC Strategist Kellyanne Conway." *Washington Post.* July 1, 2016. Accessed July 30, 2018. https://www.washingtonpost.com/news/ post-politics/wp/2016/07/01/trump-hires-ex-cruz-super-pac-strategist-kellyanne-conway/?utm_ term=.2a4546d7df78.

336. Jacobs, Sarah. "Kellyanne Conway Gets a High White House Salary, but She Made a Ton of Money before Joining Trump—Here's How She Made and Spends Her $39 Million Fortune." *Business Insider.* October 19, 2017. Accessed July 30, 2018. https://www.businessinsider.com/ how-kellyanne-conway-became-rich-2017-7.

336. Sebastian, Michael. "Who Is Kellyanne Conway? 21 Things to Know About Donald Trump's Presidential Counselor." *Cosmopolitan.* March 6, 2018. Accessed July 30, 2018. https:// www.cosmopolitan.com/politics/news/a62994/ kellyanne-conway-trump-new-campaign-manager/.

336. McCarthy, Tom. "Hope Hicks: The Political Novice Who Rose to Be Trump's Closest Aide." *The Guardian.* February 28, 2018. Accessed July 30, 2018. https://www.theguardian.com/us-news/2018/feb/28/ hope-hicks-who-is-she-resigns-trump-white-house.

337. Phillips, Amber. "Meet the Man Behind Donald Trump's Presidential Campaign." *Washington Post.* July 23, 2015. Accessed July 30, 2018. https://www. washingtonpost.com/news/the-fix/wp/2015/07/23/

meet-the-man-behind-donald-trumps-presidential-campaign/?utm_term=.56a63a1ce238.

Sanders, Kerry, and John Schuppe. "Trump's Campaign Manager Won't Be Prosecuted." NBCNews. com. Accessed July 30, 2018. https://www.nbcnews. com/news/us-news/authorities-drop-battery-charges-against-trump-campaign-manager-corey-lewandowski-n556051.

337. Evon, Dan. "Does Roger Stone Have a Tattoo of Richard Nixon on His Back?" Snopes.com. Accessed July 30, 2018. https://www.snopes.com/fact-check/ roger-stone-nixon-tattoo/.

"About Roger Stone." Roger Stone | Stone Cold Truth. Accessed July 30, 2018. https://stonecoldtruth.com/ about-roger-stone/.

337. "GOP Trickster Roger Stone Defects to Libertarian Party." *Washington Post.* February 16, 2012. Accessed July 30, 2018. https://www. washingtonpost.com/blogs/reliable-source/post/ gop-trickster-roger-stone-defects-to-libertarian-party/2012/02/16/gIQASIvUIR_blog.html?utm_term=. d3b752c76590.

337. "Trump Adviser Roger Stone Reveals New Meeting with Russian Operative." CNBC. June 18, 2018. Accessed July 30, 2018. https://www.cnbc. com/2018/06/18/trump-adviser-roger-stone-reveals-new-meeting-with-russian.html.

337. Walker, Hunter. "Sam Nunberg Has a History of Provocative and Racial Facebook Posts." *Business Insider.* July 31, 2015. Accessed July 30, 2018. https://www.businessinsider.com/ trump-advisers-racist-facebook-posts-2015-7.

337. Kranish, Michael. "Trump's Campaign: Big Macs, Screaming Fits and Constant Rivalries." *Washington Post.* December 2, 2017. Accessed July 30, 2018. https://www.washingtonpost.com/ politics/trumps-campaign-big-macs-screaming-fits-and-constant-rivalries/2017/12/02/18bcfa30-d6bd-11e7-b62d-d9345ced896d_story. html?utm_term=.3aa816dfe4be.

337. Stracqualursi, Veronica and Paola Chavez. "7 Team Trump Members You Need to Know." ABC News. April 22, 2016. Accessed August 3, 2018. https:// abcnews.go.com/Politics/team-trump-members/ story?id=38511098.

337. Vogel, Kenneth P. and Alex Isenstadt. "Trump Tasks Aide Michael Glassner with Convention Planning." *Politico.* May 6, 2016. Accessed July 30, 2018. https://www.politico.com/story/2016/05/ donald-trump-michael-glassner-convention-222878.

337. Gstalter, Morgan. "Trump Reelection Campaign Denies Reports 'Keep America Great' Flags are Being Made in China." The Hill. July 28, 2018. Accessed August 3, 2018. http://thehill.com/homenews/ campaign/399370-trump-2020-reelection-campaign-denies-reports-keep-america-great-flags-are.

338. Haberman, Maggie and Ashley Parker. "Roger Ailes Is Advising Donald Trump Ahead of Presidential Debates." *New York Times.* August 16, 2016. Accessed August 4, 2018. www.nytimes.com/2016/08/17/us/ politics/donald-trump-roger-ailes.html.

338. "Who We Are: David N. Bossie," Citizens United website. Accessed August 4, 2018. www.citizensunited. org/about-david-bossie.aspx.

338. Kaczynski, Andrew, Chris Massie, and Paul LeBlanc. "Trump Pick Sam Clovis Stoked Birther Conspiracy, Called Eric Holder a 'Racist Black.'" CNN Politics. August 11, 2017. www.cnn.com/2017/08/10/ politics/kfile-sam-clovis-on-the-radio/index.html.

338. Sanders, Linley. "George Papadopoulos Lied on His Resume to Get Trump Campaign Foreign Policy Job, Former Employer Says." *Newsweek.* November 1, 2017. www.newsweek.com/ george-papadopoulos-lied-his-resume-698409.

338. Ducharme, Jamie. "Donald Trump: What to Know About Brad Parscale, Donald Trump's 2020 Campaign Manager." *Time.* February 27, 2018. Accessed August 4, 2018. http://time.com/5177627/ brad-parscale-donald-trump-campaign-manager/.

339. Costa, Robert, Philip Rucker, and Elise Viebeck. "Pence Replaces Christie as Leader of Trump Transition Effort." *Washington Post.* November 11, 2016. www.washingtonpost.com/news/powerpost/ wp/2016/11/11/pence-to-lead-trump-transition-effort/.

339. Farand, Chloe. "Donald Trump Did Not Write His Inauguration Speech, White House Admits." *Independent.* January 22, 2017. Accessed August 4, 2017. www.independent.co.uk/news/world/ politics/white-house-admitted-donald-trump- inauguration-speech-stephen-miller-steve-bannon- batman-a7540046.html.

339. Merica, Dan. "Travel Ban Architect Writing Trump's Speech on Islam." CNN Politics. May 20, 2017. Accessed August 4, 2018. www.cnn.com/2017/05/19/ politics/stephen-miller-islam-travel-ban-speech- writing/index.html

339. Davis, Julie Hirschfeld and Michael D. Shear. "How Trump Came to Enforce a Practice of Separating Migrant Families." *New York Times.* June 16, 2018. www.nytimes.com/2018/06/16/us/politics/family- separation-trump.html.

339. Edwards, Haley Sweetland. "Russia Investigation: The Short, Happy Political Career of George Papadopoulos." *Time.* October 31, 2017. Accessed August 4, 2018. time.com/5002832/ george-papadopoulos-guilty-plea-indictment/.

339. *United States v. Papadopoulos, Crim. No. 17-182 (RDM), U.S. Dist. Court, D.C.,* filed October 5, 2017, Statement of the Offense. Accessed August 4, 2018. www.justice.gov/file/1007346/.

339. Savage, Charlie. "Carter Page FISA Documents Are Released by Justice Department." *New York Times.* July 21, 2018. Accessed July 30, 2018. https://www. nytimes.com/2018/07/21/us/politics/carter-page-fisa. html.

340. Bertoni, Steven. "Exclusive Interview: How Jared Kushner Won Trump the White House." *Forbes.* December 20, 2016. Accessed August 4, 2018. https:// www.forbes.com/sites/stevenbertoni/2016/11/22/ exclusive-interview-how-jared-kushner-won-trump- the-white-house/.

340. Brittain, Amy, Ashley Parker, and Anu Narayanswamy. "Jared Kushner and Ivanka Trump Made at Least $82 Million in Outside Income Last Year While Serving in the White House, Filings Show." *Washington Post.* June 11, 2018. Accessed July 30, 2018. https://www.washingtonpost.com/ politics/jared-kushner-and-ivanka-trump-made-at- least-82-million-in-outside-income-last-year-while- serving-in-the-white-house-filings-show/2018/06/11/ a41d0720-6dab-11e8-bd50-b80389a4e569_story. html?utm_term=.e8f81c8973c8.

340. "Read the Emails on Donald Trump Jr.'s Russia Meeting." *New York Times.* July 11, 2017. Accessed July 30, 2018. https://www.nytimes.com/ interactive/2017/07/11/us/politics/donald-trump-jr- email-text.html.

341. https://www.vanityfair.com/news/2017/06/ donald-trump-roy-cohn-relationship

341. Brenner, Marie. "How Donald Trump and Roy Cohn's Ruthless Symbiosis Changed America." *Vanity Fair.* June 30, 2017. Accessed August 11, 2018. https://www.vanityfair.com/news/2017/06/ donald-trump-roy-cohn-relationship.

341. Hornblower, Margot, and *Washington Post.* "Roy Cohn Is Disbarred By New York Court." *The Washington Post.* June 24, 1986. Accessed August 11, 2018. https://www. washingtonpost.com/archive/politics/1986/06/24/ roy-cohn-is-disbarred-by-new-york-court/ c5ca9112-3245-48f0-ab01-c2c0f3c3fc2e/.

341. Mark, Mary Ellen. "LIFE MAGAZINE - THE SNARLING DEATH OF ROY M. COHN." Accessed August 11, 2018. http://www.maryellenmark.com/text/ magazines/life/905W-000-035.html.

341. Schwirtz, Michael, William K. Rashbaum, and Danny Hakim. "Trump Foot Soldier Sidelined Under Glare of Russia Inquiry." *The New York Times.* July 2, 2017. Accessed August 11, 2018. https://www.nytimes. com/2017/07/02/us/politics/michael-cohen-donald- trump.html.

341. Helderman, Rosalind S. "Michael Cohen Will Stay Trump's Personal Attorney - Even in the White House." *The Washington Post.* January 19, 2017. Accessed August 11, 2018. https://www.washingtonpost.com/ news/post-politics/wp/2017/01/19/michael-cohen- special-counsel-to-donald-trump-will-follow-him-to- washington/?utm_term=.d43feedc537f.

341. Ibid.

341. Megerian, Chris, David Willman, and Michael Finnegan. "Michael Cohen Turned His Access to Trump into Big Money - and Now Big Trouble." *Los Angeles Times.* May 10, 2018. Accessed August 11, 2018. http://www.latimes.com/politics/la-na-pol-cohen- trump-swamp-20180510-story.html.

341. Apuzzo, Matt. "F.B.I. Raids Office of Trump's Longtime Lawyer Michael Cohen; Trump Calls It 'Disgraceful.'" *The New York Times.* April 9, 2018. Accessed August 11, 2018. https://www.nytimes. com/2018/04/09/us/politics/fbi-raids-office-of-trumps- longtime-lawyer-michael-cohen.html.

341. CBS/AP. "Trump Retains Longtime Attorney Marc Kasowitz to Aid in Russia Probe." CBS News. May 24, 2017. Accessed August 11, 2018. https://www. cbsnews.com/news/trump-retains-longtime-attorney- marc-kasowitz-to-aid-in-russia-probe/.

CBS News. "Marc Kasowitz and Mark Corallo Depart Trump's Legal Team." CBS News. July 21, 2017. Accessed August 11, 2018. https://www.cbsnews.com/news/corallo-kasowitz-depart-trump-legal-team/.

341. https://www.washingtonpost.com/news/politics/wp/2017/06/08/team-trumps-official-response-to-the-comey-testimony-now-with-context/?utm_term=.6ce70eefa20a

341. https://www.cbsnews.com/news/report-trump-attorney-sends-threatening-emails-to-stranger/

http://thehill.com/homenews/news/343069-trumps-personal-lawyer-resigns-from-top-post-amid-legal-team-shakeup

342. Schmidt, Michael S., and Maggie Haberman. "Trump's Lawyer Resigns as President Adopts Aggressive Approach in Russia Inquiry." *The New York Times*. March 22, 2018. Accessed August 11, 2018. https://www.nytimes.com/2018/03/22/us/politics/john-dowd-resigns-trump-lawyer.html.

342. https://www.theguardian.com/world/2008/jan/30/usa.rudygiuliani

342. Walshe, Shushannah. "Rudy Giuliani for President 2012: Will He Run Again?" The Daily Beast. March 17, 2011. Accessed August 11, 2018. https://www.thedailybeast.com/rudy-giuliani-for-president-2012-will-he-run-again.

342. "Jay Sekulow." American Center for Law and Justice. Accessed August 11, 2018. https://aclj.org/jay-sekulow.

343. Kranish, Michael. "Trump Needed New Lawyers for Russia Probe. He Found Them at a Tiny Florida Firm." *The Washington Post*. April 25, 2018. Accessed August 11, 2018. https://www.washingtonpost.com/politics/trump-needed-new-lawyers-for-russia-probe-he-found-them-at-a-tiny-florida-firm/2018/04/25/7288a4f2-47cd-11e8-9072-f6d4bc32f223_story.html?utm_term=.4ba4a1fe72ed.

343. Zeleny, Jeff, Kaitlan Collins, Eli Watkins, and Jim Acosta. "Ty Cobb out as White House Lawyer." CNN. May 3, 2018. Accessed August 11, 2018. https://www.cnn.com/2018/05/02/politics/trump-ty-cobb/index.html.

343. Apuzzo, Matt, and Michael S. Schmidt. "Trump Adds Clinton Impeachment Lawyer, Bracing for a Fight on Multiple Fronts." *The New York Times*. May 2, 2018. Accessed August 11, 2018. https://www.nytimes.com/2018/05/02/us/politics/emmet-flood-ty-cobb-white-house-lawyer-special-counsel.html.

343. "Thoughts on the Proper Role of the White House Counsel." Lawfare. February 23, 2017. Accessed August 11, 2018. https://www.lawfareblog.com/thoughts-proper-role-white-house-counsel.

343. Terris, Ben. "Trump's Own Beltway Establishment Guy: The Curious Journey of Don McGahn." *The Washington Post*. April 11, 2016. Accessed August 11, 2018. https://www.washingtonpost.com/lifestyle/style/trumps-own-beltway-establishment-guy-the-curious-journey-of-don-mcgahn/2016/04/11/856229a8-fb9a-11e5-80e4-c381214de1a3_story.html.

343. Wilson, Reid. "Former FEC Chairman Donald McGahn Resigns from Panel." *The Washington Post*. September 17, 2013. Accessed August 11, 2018. https://www.washingtonpost.com/politics/former-fec-chairman-donald-mcgahn-resigns-from-panel/2013/09/17/84ff1a88-1fca-11e3-94a2-6c66b668ea55_story.html.

344. Galeotti, Mark. "Gangster's Paradise: How Organised Crime Took over Russia." *The Guardian*. March 23, 2018. Accessed July 31, 2018. https://www.theguardian.com/news/2018/mar/23/how-organised-crime-took-over-russia-vory-super-mafia.

344. http://nymag.com/daily/intelligencer/2017/08/felix-sater-donald-trump-russia-investigation.html.

344. https://www.bloomberg.com/view/articles/2017-08-29/felix-sater-is-a-lean-mean-trump-russia-machine

344. O'Brien, Timothy L. "Trump, Russia and a Shadowy Business Partnership." Bloomberg Opinion. Bloomberg.com. June 21, 2017. Accessed July 31, 2018. https://www.bloomberg.com/view/articles/2017-06-21/trump-russia-and-those-shadowy-sater-deals-at-bayrock.

345. Pagliery, Jose. "Trump's Casino Was a Money Laundering Concern Shortly after It Opened." CNN. May 22, 2017. Accessed July 31, 2018. https://www.cnn.com/2017/05/22/politics/trump-taj-mahal/index.html.

346. *United States v. Manafort, Jr., Crim. No. 17-201*, Superseding Indictment, U.S. District Court, D.C., filed June 8, 2018. Accessed July 31, 2018. https://www.justice.gov/file/1070306/download.

347. Nakashima, Ellen, et al. "Russian Ambassador Told Moscow That Kushner Wanted Secret Communications Channel with Kremlin." *Washington Post*. May 26, 2017. www.washingtonpost.com/world/national-security/russian-ambassador-told-moscow-that-kushner-wanted-secret-communications-channel-with-kremlin/2017/05/26/520a14b4-422d-11e7-9869-bac8b446820a_story.html?utm_term=.c8330008a6dd.

BIBLIOGRAPHY

Barrett, Wayne. *Trump: The Greatest Show on Earth: The Deals, the Downfall, the Reinvention*. New York: Regan Arts, 2016. Originally published as *Trump: The Deals and the Downfall*. New York: HarperCollins, 1992.

Blair, Gwenda. *The Trumps: Three Generations of Builders and a Presidential Candidate*. New York: Simon & Schuster, 2015.

Comey, James. *A Higher Loyalty: Truth, Lies, and Leadership*. New York: Flatiron Books, 2018.

Frum, David. *Trumpocracy: The Corruption of the American Republic*. New York: HarperCollins, 2018.

Gibbs, Nancy, and Michael Duffy. *The Presidents Club: Inside the World's Most Exclusive Fraternity*. New York: Simon & Schuster, 2013.

Graff, Garrett. *The Threat Matrix: The FBI at War*. New York: Back Bay Books. 2012.

Harding, Luke. *Collusion: Secret Meetings, Dirty Money, and How Russia Helped Donald Trump Win*. New York: Vintage Books, 2017.

Hurt, Harry, III. *Lost Tycoon: The Many Lives of Donald J. Trump*. London: Orion, 1993.

Isikoff, Michael, and David Corn. *Russian Roulette: The Inside Story of Putin's War on America and the Election of Donald Trump*. New York: Twelve, 2018.

Johnston, David Cay. *It's Even Worse Than You Think: What the Trump Administration Is Doing to America*. New York: Simon & Schuster, 2018.

Johnston, David Cay. *The Making of Donald Trump*. Paperback ed. New York: Melville House, 2017.

Kasparov, Garry, and Mig Greengard. *Winter Is Coming: Why Vladimir Putin and the Enemies of the Free World Must Be Stopped*. New York: PublicAffairs, 2015.

Kranish, Michael, and Marc Fisher. *Trump Revealed: An American Journey of Ambition, Ego, Money, and Power*. New York: Scribner, 2016.

Lewandowski, Corey R., and David N. Bossie. *Let Trump Be Trump: The Inside Story of His Rise to the Presidency*. New York: Center Street, 2017.

O'Brien, Timothy L. *TrumpNation: The Art of Being The Donald*. New York: Grand Central, 2016.

Putin, Vladimir, with ed. Nataliya Gevorkyan, Natalya Timakova, and Andrei Kolesnikov. *First Person: An Astonishingly Frank Self-Portrait by Russia's President Vladimir Putin*. Translated by Catherina A. Fitzpatrick. New York: PublicAffairs, 2000.

Siskind, Amy. The *List: A Week-by-Week Reckoning of Trump's First Year*. New York: Bloomsbury, 2018.

Snyder, Timothy. *On Tyranny: Twenty Lessons from the Twentieth Century*. New York: Crown, 2017.

Sunstein, Cass R. *Impeachment: A Citizen's Guide*. Cambridge: Harvard University Press, 2017.

Trump, Donald with Bill Zanker. *Think Big: Make It Happen in Business and Life*. Rev. paperback ed. New York: HarperBusiness, 2008. Originally published in hardcover as *Think Big and Kick Ass in Business and Life*. New York: HarperCollins, 2007.

Trump, Ivana. *Raising Trump*. New York: Gallery Books, 2017.

Trump, Ivanka. *The Trump Card: Playing to Win in Work and Life*. New York: Simon & Schuster, 2010.

Wolff, Michael. *Fire and Fury: Inside the Trump White House*. New York: Henry Holt, 2018.

INDEX